The Joan Palevsky  Imprint in Classical Literature

In honor of beloved Virgil—

"O degli altri poeti onore e lume . . ."

—Dante, *Inferno*

The publisher gratefully acknowledges the generous contributions to this book provided by the Classical Literature Endowment Fund of the University of California Press Foundation, which is supported by a major gift from Joan Palevsky, and by the Indiana University Department of History.

City and School in Late
Antique Athens and Alexandria

THE TRANSFORMATION OF THE CLASSICAL HERITAGE

Peter Brown, General Editor

City and School in Late Antique Athens and Alexandria

Edward J. Watts

UNIVERSITY OF CALIFORNIA PRESS

Berkeley   Los Angeles   London

University of California Press, one of the most distinguished
university presses in the United States, enriches lives around the
world by advancing scholarship in the humanities, social sciences,
and natural sciences. Its activities are supported by the UC Press
Foundation and by philanthropic contributions from individuals
and institutions. For more information, visit www.ucpress.edu.

University of California Press
Berkeley and Los Angeles, California

University of California Press, Ltd.
London, England

© 2006 by The Regents of the University of California

Library of Congress Cataloging-in-Publication Data

Watts, Edward, 1975–.
    City and school in late antique Athens and Alexandria /
Edward Watts.
        p.   cm. — (The transformation of the classical heritage)
    Includes bibliographical references and index.
    ISBN 0-520-24421-4 (cloth : alk. paper)
        1. Education—Greece—Athens—History—To 1500.
    2. Education—Egypt—Alexandria—History—To 1500.
    3. Athens (Greece)—Intellectual life.   4. Alexandria (Egypt)—
    Intellectual life.   5. Rome—History—Empire, 30 B.C.–476 A.D.
    I. Title.   II. Series.
    LA75.W38   2006
    370'.0938—dc22   2005005830

Manufactured in Canada.
13 12 11 10 09 08 07 06 05
10 9 8 7 6 5 4 3 2 1

This book is printed on New Leaf EcoBook 60, containing 60%
post-consumer waste, processed chlorine free; 30% de-inked
recycled fiber, elemental chlorine free; and 10% FSC-certified
virgin fiber, totally chlorine free. EcoBook 60 is acid-free and
meets the minimum requirements of ANSI/ASTM D5634-01
(Permanence of Paper).

To Manasi . . .

Ἀφέντες τὰ ἐφήμερα, τὸν αἰώνιον φιλῶμεν.
JOHN CHRYSOSTOM, *Expositiones in Psalmos* 55.164.55–57

CONTENTS

ACKNOWLEDGEMENTS

This project began life as a question about a passage in the *Life of Proclus* that John Matthews asked of me in the fall of 1997. Over the next four years, it became a dissertation under his supervision, and now, over the past three, it has undergone its final transformation into a book. In this study, I have moved far beyond topics found in the *Life of Proclus* and for that I owe debts of gratitude to many different individuals. At the initial stages of research, I benefited from the advice and assistance of Joseph Pucci, Garth Fowden, Susan Harvey, Bentley Layton, Neil McLynn, Dominic O'Meara, Polymnia Athanassiadi, Dale Martin, David Konstan, Harry Attridge, Veronika Grimm, Dimitri Gutas, and Peter Heather. These individuals were extremely generous with their wisdom and their contributions are evident throughout this book.

In preparing this manuscript, I have benefited greatly from conversations with David Frankfurter, Istvan Perczel, Fritz Graf, Walter Kaegi, and my many new colleagues in the departments of History, Classical Studies, and Religious Studies at Indiana University. During the process of revision, an earlier version of a part of chapter 5 appeared as "Justinian, Malalas, and the Closing of the Athenian Neoplatonic School in A.D. 529," *Journal of Roman Studies* 94 (2004): 168–82. The feedback I received to that article has been of great help. Thanks are also owed to Richard Sorabji, Bert van den Berg, Richard Layton, and David Brakke for their ideas and willingness to share forthcoming material with me. The comments of Susanna Elm, the useful suggestions of Ann Hanson, and the timely advice of John Dillon have helped transform (and significantly improve) the manuscript itself. They are owed a special gratitude.

Particular thanks must be given to Peter Brown, whose personal and scholarly generosity is well known and is greatly reflected in this project. His suggestions (both editorial and otherwise) helped to refine my thinking throughout the process of revision and to broaden my general conceptions of late antique intellectual life.

This project began at the side of John Matthews and it has never strayed far from its source. His fresh insights and probing questions opened up numerous productive avenues of research and quickly turned me away from many fruitless searches. I cannot thank him sufficiently for the time and energy he put into me and my work. One could not hope for a better advisor or a better friend. After so many contributions from all of the above people, the shortcomings that remain in this work are exclusively the fault of its author.

A final word of thanks must be reserved for my wife Manasi. Though this project has occupied a large part of her life from the time of our engagement in Athens, she has remained unflagging in her support of it. Without her love and encouragement this work would never have taken shape. Without her keen editing skills, it would certainly not have taken the shape it now has. For both, I dedicate this book to her.

Chapter 1

Academic Life in the Roman Empire

. . . Now that I have gained two governors as my friends through your agency, I return your gift with one person crammed full of learning. For this man is Harpocration, a good poet and a better teacher: he is clever enough to instill the works of ancient authors into young men, and clever enough to make himself an equal to those authors . . . He shared a common upbringing and education with Eudaemon, in times past as a pupil and now as a teacher, and though almost of one flesh and blood with his friend, he has been torn away by your irresistible attraction . . . I will comfort Eudaemon but you, become [a friend] to Harpocration just as I am to Eudaemon.

LIBANIUS TO ARISTAENETUS[1]

This letter of 358 A.D. from Libanius to his Nicomedian friend Aristaenetus is not an exceptional document. It contains the simple request that Aristaenetus provide hospitality to Harpocration, a young rhetorician on his way from Antioch to a more prestigious teaching position in Constantinople.[2] Harpocration was relatively unknown outside of Antioch and, when he decided to make the trip to the capital, he turned to Libanius to provide him with letters of introduction to men who could help him along the way. The letters Libanius wrote on his behalf were like countless others in antiquity.[3] They were carried to their addressee and served both as a letter of introduction and as a recommendation of the character of the bearer. Though typical of the genre, Libanius's recommendation reveals something crucial about late antique society. Libanius's introduction emphasizes Harpocration's education as the foremost indication of his good character. To clarify the point, Libanius spells out that Harpocration is well read, skilled at composition, and

---

1. Libanius, *Ep.* 364 (Foerster).

2. A similar letter on his behalf (*Ep.* 368) serves to introduce the rhetor to the Constantinopolitan philosopher Themistius. It seems that Themistius was able to oblige Libanius's request, because a later letter from Libanius (*Ep.* 818) speaks of Harpocration as if he was an established teacher.

3. On this convention, see C. H. Kim, *Form and Structure of the Familiar Greek Letter of Recommendation,* Society of Biblical Literature Dissertation Series 4 (Missoula, Mont., 1972).

effective in his communication with his students. All of these were products of his education.

By virtue of their training, Harpocration, Aristaenetus, and Libanius were all initiates into the common culture of the educated man *(paideia)*. Paideia was the unique possession of those who had separated themselves from the average man by their knowledge of and appreciation for the words, ideas, and texts of classical antiquity.[4] *Paideia* was acquired through an expensive and time-consuming process of education that not only taught literature but also allowed men of culture to master a code of socially acceptable behavior.[5] Consequently, when Aristaenetus met Harpocration and read Libanius's letter, he would recognize the visitor as a gentleman with similar intellectual interests. Above all, he would recognize the stranger as a fellow man of culture.

Although something of a typical document, this letter illustrates the premium men of high status placed upon literary and philosophical education in the late Roman world. By the late Roman period, the training of young men in rhetoric and philosophy was well established as the basic form of elite education.[6] The influence of *paideia* did not rest solely upon its function as a tool to acquire basic literacy. The system of education in the Roman world was essentially two-tiered and, at its most accessible level, not geared towards the literary training of *paideia*.[7] For the average man, education consisted of study at a school of letters.[8] These schools taught basic, functional literacy, and their students left with an education unencumbered by classical reminiscences or arcane rules of grammar and composition. The average student

4. For this idea, see most notably J. Matthews, *The Roman Empire of Ammianus* (London, 1989), 78; and P. Brown, *Power and Persuasion in Late Antiquity: Towards a Christian Empire* (Madison, 1992), 35–36. For an earlier period, note as well S. Goldhill, *Being Greek under Rome: Cultural Identity, the Second Sophistic, and the Development of Empire* (Cambridge, 2001), 13–14.

5. For education as a process of socialization, see particularly M. Bloomer, "Schooling in Persona: Imagination and Subordination in Roman Education," *Classical Antiquity* 16.1 (1997): 57–78.

6. Hence the remarkable cohesion of the Hellenic, Hellenistic, and Roman sections of H. I. Marrou's *Histoire de l'Éducation dans l'Antiquité* (Paris, 1956). This cohesion is, of course, also a product of Marrou's methodological interests and emphasis upon educational continuity. For a critique of these methods, see Y. L. Too, "Introduction: Writing the History of Ancient Education," in *Education in Greek and Roman Antiquity*, ed. Y. L. Too, 1–21 (Leiden, 2001).

7. Marrou's *Histoire de l'Éducation dans l'Antiquité* remains the standard work on ancient education. For more specific recent treatments see R. Cribiore, *Gymnastics of the Mind: Greek Education in Hellenistic and Roman Egypt* (Princeton, 2001); and T. Morgan, *Literate Education in the Hellenistic and Roman Worlds* (Cambridge, 1998). As Cribiore has recently shown, the division between basic and literate education was quite fluid. On this point, see as well R. A. Kaster, *Guardians of Language: The Grammarian and Society in Late Antiquity* (Berkeley and Los Angeles, 1988), 45–47; and A. D. Booth, "Elementary and Secondary Education in the Roman Empire," *Florilegium* 1 (1979): 1–14.

8. The γραμματοδιδασκαλεον.

who had attended these schools could presumably read and write enough to get by on a daily basis, but he would certainly never recite poetry with correct inflection or compose orations. These skills were not taught in the schools of letters.[9]

Those who had the means received a more specialized education.[10] This emphasized such things as correct grammatical rules, eloquence in composition, and the knowledge of a canon of authors. Students who followed this track would first pass through the school of the grammarian. In his classroom they would learn such aspects of grammar as correct pronunciation and the behavior of each part of a sentence. The grammarian would also read texts with his students, stopping at each mention of a significant figure or event in order to explain its moral and historical significance.[11] This was the initial phase of grammatical training. At its more advanced stage, the grammarian's training centered upon a series of exercises called the *progymnasmata*, compositional exercises in which students were taught how to elaborate upon stories or themes using the linguistic skills they had acquired in the previous years.[12]

The school of rhetoric was the next level in classical literary education.

9. The availability of this basic educational track did not, by any means, lead to widespread literacy in the Roman world. For some estimates of the levels of literacy, see W. V. Harris, *Ancient Literacy* (Cambridge, Mass., 1989), 256–83. Note, as well, the more optimistic picture provided by the various essays collected by M. Beard et al., *Literacy in the Roman World* (Ann Arbor, 1991). Note also the important work of H. C. Youtie, "*ΑΓΡΑΜΜΑΤΟΣ*: An Aspect of Greek Society in Egypt," *Harvard Studies in Classical Philology* 75 (1971): 161–76 and "βραδέως γράφων: Between Literacy and Illiteracy," *Greek, Roman, and Byzantine Studies* 12 (1971): 239–61.

10. What follows is a description of the ideal path a student followed. The realities of late antique education were often more complicated, however. Some students, for example, did their grammatical training with rhetoricians like Libanius. On this, see Libanius, *Ep.* 625 and 678, as well as R. Cribiore's *Gymnastics of the Mind*, 37–43; and P. Wolf, *Vom Schulwesen der Spätantike: Studien zu Libanius* (Baden, 1952), 69–70. Grammar schools that taught elementary letters as well as rhetoric are attested. For these, see A. C. Dionisotti, "From Ausonius' Schooldays? A Schoolbook and its Relatives," *Journal of Roman Studies* 72 (1982): 83–125.

11. For the function of the grammarian see R. A. Kaster, *Guardians of Language*, 12–14; S. F. Bonner, *Education in Ancient Rome* (Berkeley and Los Angeles, 1977); and H. I. Marrou, *Histoire de l'Éducation dans l'Antiquité*, 243 ff.

12. For an especially thorough discussion of the *progymnasmata* see R. Cribiore, *Gymnastics of the Mind*, 221–30. For the exercises as a sort of primer for the lifestyle of the cultivated, see R. Webb, "The Progymnasmata as Practice," in *Education in Greek and Roman Antiquity*, ed. Y. L. Too, 289–316. A number of *progymnasmata* have come down to us. Most important among them are probably the works of Theon and Hermogenes. The former has recently been edited and translated into French by M. Patillon in *Aelius Theon: Progymnasmata* (Paris, 1997). The latter was translated by C. Baldwin in *Medieval Rhetoric and Poetic (to 1400) Interpreted from Representative Works* (Gloucester, Mass., 1959), 23–38. These continued to play a role in rhetorical education through the Middle Ages and, in some parts, even into the twentieth century. See now also G. Kennedy trans., *Progymnasmata: Greek textbooks of prose composition and rhetoric* (Leiden, 2003).

When a student arrived there he initially continued with the *progymnasmata,* usually under the tutelage of one of the rhetorician's assistants.[13] The student would also be taught rhetorical technique by the rhetorician himself (usually by listening to the man give declamations). When he had finished with the basic rhetorical exercises, the student would then move to more advanced study with the rhetorician in which the literary allusions mentioned by the grammarian were expanded and their moral and historical significance was re-emphasized. At this stage in the training, students were expected to know these anecdotes and write expositions about their meaning. When they left school, it was assumed that students would be perfectly able to apply the morals of these short stories to their daily conduct.[14] As the student progressed in the rhetorician's school, he was expected to produce his own full-length compositions of increasing difficulty. Each of these was done according to the specifics of each rhetorical genre.[15]

In late antiquity, many of those who wished to continue with their schooling would go on to the school of the philosopher. Here they would listen to what amounted to line-by-line discussions of philosophical texts and their meaning.[16] These discussions often worked to place the ideas of the text within the larger doctrinal system of the philosopher or the school. If he followed the course through to completion, a student was expected to understand the philosophical system taught by the school and the place of each text within it.[17] The philosophical curriculum too had an important moral element. Though the study of appropriate behavior was only one of its pursuits, philosophy discussed what the ideals of conduct were and why they were so. In the second century, the Platonist Alcinous centered his discussion of these virtues upon teaching about "the care of morals, the administration

---

13. This seems to be the role played by Eusebius and Thalassius in Libanius's school. For a description of their role see *Ep.* 905–9 and 922–26. For a discussion see A. F. Norman, *Libanius: Autobiography and Selected Letters,* vol. 2 (Cambridge, Mass., 1990), Appendix, 454–61.

14. To make these messages even clearer, professors of rhetoric such as Libanius and Himerius gave their students lectures about how to behave. Himerius's lecture is preserved as *Or.* 12. Libanius, *Ep.* 407, mentions his version of this lecture.

15. Rhetorical education taught students the correct way to compose many different types of orations. For a discussion of these various genres and how they were taught, see H. I. Marrou, *Histoire de l'Éducation dans l'Antiquité,* 277–81.

16. This was the basic pattern. For the probable variations of approach from school to school, see R. Lamberton, "The Schools of Platonic Philosophy of the Roman Empire: The Evidence of the Biographies," in *Education in Greek and Roman Antiquity,* ed. Y. L. Too, 442–45, 455.

17. The various prolegomena to philosophy written in late antiquity played a crucial part in making this possible. They introduced each philosopher's system of thought before a student studied the texts. By starting with a complete picture of the system, it was easier for students to understand where each individual text fit. For these discussions see J. Mansfeld, *Prolegomena: Questions to Be Settled before the Study of an Author or Text* (Leiden, 1994) and, less directly, J. Mansfeld, *Prolegomena Mathematica: From Apollonius of Perga to Late Neoplatonism* (Leiden, 1998).

of a household, and the state and its preservation."[18] In the fifth century, these teachings about behavior were given equal weight, but they were grouped under a new heading, that of moral and political virtue. The first part of the philosophical curriculum was devoted to explaining them.[19] Aristotle's *Ethics* was used for moral virtues and his *Politics* (along with Plato's *Laws* and the *Republic*) was used to teach political virtues.[20] Indeed, these virtues were so important to teachers of philosophy that some even turned away students whose moral failings were without remedy.[21]

The course of study pursued under teachers of rhetoric and philosophy was long, detailed, and expensive.[22] Because of this, it is likely that few who began the course with the grammarian were able even to finish the course of study with the rhetor. Indeed, of the fifty-seven students of Libanius whose term of study is known, fully thirty-five dropped out by the end of their second year.[23] Not surprisingly, the reason a student abandoned his education was often family financial trouble.[24] The cost meant that only wealthy, fortunate, or doggedly determined families could provide their children with a thorough classical education. But this education was a sound investment. This crucial tool had become a way of distinguishing the elite of Roman society from the average man. At the same time, it also bound the men who possessed it closer together.[25]

The value of *paideia* was widely recognized in ancient society. Indeed, there was a belief, common to men throughout the ancient world, that the edu-

18. Alcinous, *Didaskalikos* 3.3.

19. *Prolégomènes à la philosophie de Platon*, ed. and trans. L. G. Westerink (Paris, 1990), 26.30–33.

20. For Aristotle and ethical philosophy see Marinus, *Vit. Proc.* 12–13. For Aristotle and Plato as texts for political virtues see *Vit. Proc.* 14. In the sixth century, Plato's *Gorgias* had come to replace the *Laws* and *Republic* (*Anon. Prol.* 26.33).

21. As Proclus did with the Antiochene Hilarius. Damascius, *Vit. Is.*, fragment 91B in *Damascius: The Philosophical History*, ed. and trans. P. Athanassiadi (Athens, 1999), and *Epit.* 266 in *Vitae Isidori Reliquiae*, ed. C. Zintzen (Hildesheim, 1967). Because the Athanassiadi edition of this text has not yet become the recognized standard, all citations to the *Life of Isidore* will contain references to both her edition (Ath.) and that of Zintzen (Z.).

22. Part of the expense came in the salaries of professors. There are a number of pieces of evidence for the relative salaries. The most important of these is Diocletian's Maximum Price Edict (*Pret. Ed.* 7.70–71), which sets the salary of the teacher of letters at 50 *denarii* per pupil per month. Grammarians were to get 200 *denarii* per pupil per month and rhetoricians 250. In addition, rhetoricians customarily received a *solidus* whenever a student completed a composition.

23. R. Kaster, *Guardians of Language*, 26–27, based upon P. Petit, *Les Étudiants de Libanius* (Paris, 1957), 62–65. See Libanius, *Ep.* 379, for a case of a student who left his care before completing his course.

24. This was sometimes alleviated by funds given to poor students by city governors. This was the case with Letoius, the *principalis* of Antioch (Libanius, *Ep.* 552), and Procopius (*Ep.* 319, 550).

25. R. Kaster, *Guardians of Language*, 29.

cated man was one whose soul progressed "towards excellence and the condition proper to humanity" while his uneducated contemporaries were less rational, less refined, and less humane.[26] The inherent civilizing value of education was so great that some men advertised their cultivation in their epitaphs[27] and others in monumental inscriptions.[28] Cultural attainment was also frequently celebrated in letters.[29]

This indicates a belief, held by many in the Roman world, that education and excellence went together.[30] The excellence that ancient men associated with education did not arise from, say, a thorough knowledge of the works of Demosthenes. Instead, it was derived from the understanding that an educated man had learned a code of proper behavior. Thus, classical learning also defined one as a gentleman.[31] With *paideia* came an understanding of essential virtues like "what is honorable and what is shameful, what is just and what is unjust . . . how a man must bear himself in his interactions with the gods, with his parents, with his elders, with the laws, with strangers, with those in authority, with friends, with women, with children, and with servants."[32] These are the words of Plutarch of Chaeronea and, though they were penned in the early second century, his description of education's importance remained accurate throughout antiquity.

Education provided a young gentleman with an outline of how one was to act, how he was to treat other men, what role he was to play in his community, and the manner in which he ought to approach the divine. In his

---

26. *IPriene* 112.73; see also H. Marrou, *ΜΟΥΣΙΚΟΣ ΑΝΗΡ*: Étude sur les scènes de la vie intellectuelle figurant sur les monuments funéraires romains (Grenoble, 1937), 209–10; and R. Kaster, *Guardians of Language*, 15–16.

27. See the example of Didius Taxiarches, *CIL* VI.16843.

28. For example, the Epicurean inscription erected by Diogenes in his hometown of Oinoanda, published in English by M. F. Smith, *The Philosophical Inscription of Diogenes of Oinoanda* (Vienna, 1996); and in French by A. Etienne and D. O'Meara, *La philosophie épicurienne sur pierre: Les fragments de Diogène d'Oenoanda* (Paris, 1996). See as well the supplemental publication of M. F. Smith, *Supplement to Diogenes of Oinoanda, The Epicurean Inscription* (Naples, 2003).

29. One of the best expressions of this idea is Libanius, *Ep.* 1036.

30. This remained essentially true despite the increasingly Christian and military identity of the upper echelons of the Roman state in late antiquity. It becomes clear from authors as diverse as Paulinus of Nola (*Carm.* 24.481–82) and the emperor Constantine. Constantine's oration on Easter is one of the more interesting examples that prove this point. In this speech, Constantine shows an awareness of the works of Virgil (ch. 19–20) and Cicero (ch. 19) to illustrate his grasp of literature and, by implication, the cultural values that accompanied this knowledge.

31. For this line of thought see P. Brown, *Power and Persuasion in Late Antiquity*, 122. M. Bloomer, "Schooling in Persona," 59–63, has described the particular role that *fictio personae* played in developing a student's conception of gentlemanly behaviors.

32. Plutarch, *Moralia* 7E. Here Plutarch is speaking about the benefits that came from studying philosophy. In his mind, this was the pinnacle of a man's education.

personal comportment, an educated gentleman was trained to demonstrate his status by maintaining his composure at all times.[33] The educational system also emphasized that one was supposed to treat a similarly cultivated man with respectfulness appropriate to his cultural achievements.[34] Libanius's letter to Aristaenetus has already shown how this worked on a social level. On the legal level, a man who was a city councilor was exempt from disfiguring penalties like torture or lashings.[35] In addition, traditional education also taught those in power to pay the utmost attention to the requests made of them by cultured men simply because they were eloquently presented.[36] For this reason, men of culture were often called upon to act as emissaries to the emperor and to plead cases on behalf of their cities. Common to both emissary and official, the set of values taught in the schools enabled these educated men to command respect. [37]

Late Roman schools did more than provide a blueprint for the appropriate activities of a gentleman. Liberal education also assisted in the development and maintenance of interpersonal relationships. The Roman world was a vast collection of cities and towns scattered like islands throughout a sea of countryside. Within these cities were cultivated men, but the connections of these men to their cultural compatriots were rarely sustained by face-to-face contact.[38] Nevertheless, the administration of the empire rested upon these men, and anyone who hoped to have his interests protected needed to develop a network of connections among the cultured class. The common cultural and educational background that they all shared lay at the heart of these networks.

33. Plutarch, *Moralia* 10C: "Being without anger is the mark of a wise man." For additional elements of this ideal, see Plutarch, *Moralia* 10F, 37C; and Philostratus, *Vit. Soph.* 561. For the evolving view of anger and the necessity of its restraint in antiquity see W. V. Harris, *Restraining Rage: The Ideology of Anger Control in Classical Antiquity* (Cambridge, Mass., 2001), 88–127 (esp. 112–27). P. Brown, *Power and Persuasion in Late Antiquity,* 48–58, discusses these ideas in the late antique environment.

34. P. Brown, *Power and Persuasion in Late Antiquity,* 52–57.

35. P. Brown, *Power and Persuasion in Late Antiquity,* 54. Libanius, *Ep.* 994, describes a complaint filed against a governor who violated this code. For the specific case Libanius complains about in Antioch, see J. H. W. G. Liebeschuetz, *Antioch: City and Imperial Administration in the Later Roman Empire* (Oxford, 1972), 166.

36. P. Brown, *Power and Persuasion in Late Antiquity,* 44–45.

37. Without these shared values, such embassies were doomed to fail. When Eustathius, a highly educated philosopher of moderate social status, was sent on an embassy to Persia, the Persians, who did not share in the values of *paideia*, did not recognize Eustathius's education as a mark of distinction. Instead, they were insulted that he, a man of such middling status, was sent to them and they dismissed the embassy with an unfavorable response. Eunapius's story (*Vit. Soph.* 465–66) of this event acknowledges the cultural differences at the heart of this incident. Ammianus (17.5.14) merely reports on the embassy and its failure.

38. See, for example, the amusing stories Philostratus tells of sophists who know each other by the rhythms of their speech but not by their personal appearance (as was the case in *Vit. Soph.* 529 when Marcus of Byzantium visited Polemo).

These cultural links were established early in life. For many youths the first strands in a social network were formed when they left home to go to the schools of grammarians or rhetoricians. This was often their first time away from home and, in many cases, brought their first real encounters with youths from other cities. Often, the bonds they made with their peers at school lasted a lifetime. The scholastic interactions of Basil, the future bishop of Caesarea, and Gregory, the future bishop of Constantinople, show how one such friendship developed.

Gregory and Basil were both students of the same teacher in Athens. When Basil first arrived, Gregory had already been studying in Athens for a year. After a short time in Athens, Basil was miserable. Gregory says "I tried to relieve his unhappiness, both by discussing these things logically and enchanting him with reasoning . . . In this way I restored his happiness, and through this exchange of ideas he was the more closely united to me."[39] He continues, "As time went on, we pledged our affection for one another . . . we were everything to each other, housemates, table companions, intimates, who looked towards one goal—making our affection for one another grow warmer and more secure."[40] Though Gregory has perhaps exaggerated the depth of their attachment here, the friendship that developed between the two men seems to have been a strong one and, despite some disagreements, it lasted for decades.[41]

It was by no means exceptional that friendships of this sort developed at school. The schools provided a comfortable social environment in which youths could meet, interact, and make friends. At the same time, teachers taught these young men the responsibilities that accompanied friendship and how to sustain these relationships in both formal and informal ways. A student came to know that one man could expect a friend to "join him on a trip, another to help him in defending a lawsuit, another to sit with him as judge, another to help in managing his commerce, another to help him

---

39. Gregory Nazianzen, *Panegyric on St. Basil,* 18.

40. Ibid., 19.

41. On this friendship, see now the excellent discussion of R. Van Dam, *Families and Friends in Late Roman Cappadocia* (Philadelphia, 2003), 129–30 and 155–84. This friendship is notable both for the amount of surviving documentation it produced and for the eventual tensions that developed between the two men. These documents reveal a fundamental tension between the "presupposed consistency in values, character, beliefs and devotion" inculcated by teachers and the inevitable changes a person undergoes in a lifetime. On this, see Van Dam, *Families and Friends,* 130. For a discussion of Gregory's oration as a somewhat idealized representation of this friendship, see D. Konstan, "How to Praise a Friend: Gregory Nazianzus's Funeral Oration for St. Basil the Great," in *Greek Biography and Panegyric in Late Antiquity,* ed. T. Hägg and P. Rousseau, 160–79 (Berkeley and Los Angeles, 2000). Among the many other friendships that were begun at school were the one between Apuleius and Pontianus, that of Prohaeresius and Hephaestion, and the bond between Zacharias Scholasticus and Severus of Antioch.

celebrate a wedding."[42] He would also learn that he was expected to return his friend's favor whenever he was asked.[43]

Over the course of one's life, friendships formed at school and sustained in this way could prove quite useful, especially when they were between boys from the same region. When Gregory and Basil returned to Cappadocia, they dealt with the same regional administration and the same governors for most of their lives. They also faced some of the same problems. Their friendship allowed them to turn to one another for help when these problems arose. Consequently, when the emperor Valens split the province of Cappadocia in two in order to curb Basil's influence in the churches of the region, Basil could call upon Gregory to help him counter the move.[44]

One development that helped form bonds such as these was the tendency for certain regions to send many of their students to one teacher or one intellectual center. The Roman world provides many examples of this phenomenon. In the first century B.C., Athens became the place to which the young men of Italy went to finish their education.[45] It later played the same role for North Africans like Apuleius and his roommate-cum-son-in-law Pontianus.[46] Athens was also full of Cappadocians in the mid-fourth century and Alexandrians in the mid-fifth.[47] Alexandria itself became the site to which three generations of Gazan students traveled for schooling beginning in the 470s.[48]

This sort of travel was common, but it was still probably atypical of the av-

42. Plutarch, *On Having Many Friends* 95C; an example of the teaching of friendship is found in Iamblichus, *On the Pythagorean Life* 33.

43. Plutarch, *On Having Many Friends* 95F.

44. Basil's decision to make Gregory the bishop of Sasima in response to Valens's actions proved a severe test of their friendship. Instead of taking up the position, Gregory went into seclusion. On this conflict and its aftermath, see R. Van Dam, *Families and Friends*, 163–65.

45. Cicero and his son were among the many Italians who studied in Athens in this period. The academic career of Cicero's son shows both how many Italians were in Athens in the first century and how their parents often competed with one another to show their wealth through their children. Consistent with his character, Cicero ensured that his son had the largest allowance of all the Roman students in the city (*ad Atticum* xii.32.2; xv.15.4; xv.17.4).

46. For Apuleius's account of his time in Athens see his *Apologia* 72 ff.

47. Athens's attraction to these Alexandrian students will be explored in chapter 4.

48. This began with the generation of Aeneas of Gaza in the 470s. The rhetorician Procopius of Gaza and the bishop Zacharias were the next generation. When Procopius returned, he began teaching in Gaza. The writings of Zacharias and Procopius, however, continued to be geared towards an Alexandrian audience. On this, see E. Watts, "An Alexandrian Christian Response to Neoplatonic Influence," in *The Philosopher and Society in Late Antiquity*, ed. A. Smith, 215–30 (Swansea, 2005). It is not until Choricius that a truly independent Gazan literary culture develops. It is not difficult to understand how ties of this sort developed. As is the case today, a prestigious center of teaching like Athens or Alexandria attracted a population of students as long as it was able to maintain a reputation for excellence. For more on this process see E. Watts, "Student travel to intellectual centers: What was the attraction?" in *Travel, Communication, and Geography in Late Antiquity*, ed. L. Ellis and F. Kidner, 11–21 (Aldershot, 2004)

erage student in late antiquity. One needs only to recall the struggles that the family of Augustine had to endure to send him away to school. Despite the fact that Augustine came from a curial family in the North African town of Thagaste, his education was interrupted for a year while the family scraped together enough money to pay for him to study in Carthage.[49] In this, the efforts of Augustine's father were exceptional. As Augustine said, "No one had anything but praise for my father who, despite his slender resources, was ready to provide his son with all that was needed to enable him to travel so far for the purpose of study. Many of our townsmen, who were far richer than my father, went to no such trouble for their children's sake."[50] It is hard to believe that Thagaste was unique in this regard. Though they would not know as broad a range of people as their peers who had traveled to study, even those students who were educated near to their own town began building their social network while in school.

Scholastic friendships were important even when students came from different regions. As these friendships were secured by the common experiences of student life, a young man could expect them to last long after he left school. Hence Synesius wrote to his schoolmate Herculian in 398, "a holy law demands that we who are joined in mind, which is the best part of us, honor each other's qualities."[51] Their bond as students was kept strong by the regular exchange of letters. It remained so strong that Synesius remarked, years later, "whatever Synesius says to himself, he says also to your honored soul, to you, his only friend, or at least, his best friend."[52]

Besides showing the intensity of the bond that existed between former classmates, Synesius's letters also reveal how useful these bonds could prove to be. Synesius relied upon his classmates for advice,[53] philosophical discussions,[54] lodging, help in recapturing a lost slave,[55] and even bows and arrows when his city was under siege.[56] Like Libanius, he also relied upon his school friends to provide hospitality and assistance to other companions of his who were traveling.[57] Even later in his life, Synesius did not hesitate to depend upon his school friends. This was, after all, what he had been taught to expect of them.

49. *Confessions* 2.3. His break was during the 369–70 school year.
50. Ibid.
51. Synesius, *Ep.* 137. On the dating of Synesius's correspondence with Herculian, see D. Roques, *Études sur la Correspondance de Synésios de Cyrène* (Brussels, 1989), 87–103.
52. *Ep.* 145. On Synesius's interactions with Herculian, see Alan Cameron and J. Long, *Barbarians and Politics at the Court of Arcadius* (Berkeley and Los Angeles, 1993), 86–89.
53. See, for example, *Ep.* 96, where Synesius asks Olympius for advice about the priesthood.
54. This is apparent from *Ep.* 137, 138 to Herculian.
55. *Ep.* 145.
56. *Ep.* 133.
57. *Ep.* 99.

Though the friendships a student made with his peers were both emotionally rewarding and potentially useful later in life, the most important friendship a student could develop at school was with his professor. This was especially true when the professor was a well-known rhetorician or philosopher. In many cases, such a professor would have been one of the most important and influential people a student met outside of his family, and such professors were sometimes rather difficult to get to know.[58] Nevertheless, it was expected that even the most renowned teachers would take an interest in their students by looking in on their charges when they were sick, inviting them to dine at their house, and allowing the more insecure youngsters to accompany them to religious services.[59] In fact, it was not uncommon for teachers and students alike to see their relationship in familial terms. Hence Libanius styles himself a father to his students and Synesius describes his teacher, the philosopher Hypatia, as his mother.[60]

The close relationship between a teacher and his student had more concrete importance as well. A student could call upon his teacher to support him if he got into trouble with the law.[61] He could also ask the professor to use his influence to convince government officials to give the student's family special treatment.[62] Finally, and perhaps most important in a student's eyes, a young man could sometimes convince his teacher to ask for a raise in his allowance (ostensibly to buy books).[63] Professors also looked out for the general welfare of their students. Libanius prevailed upon a number of government officials to set aside funds to enable poor students to study.[64] Nearly a century later, the Athenian philosopher Proclus made appearances before the town council to argue for the interests of his students.[65]

When a student finished his schooling, the ties to his professor did not dissolve. Indeed, it was often just at the completion of his studies that a student most depended upon his professor's friendship. Then, as now, many students leaving school were looking for jobs and, when the imperial administration looked to fill bureaucratic vacancies, it asked teachers to rec-

---

58. One suspects that the philosopher Isidore was a bit like this. Though friendly and concerned about his students (Damascius, *Vit. Is.* Ath. 30D; Z. Ep. 307), he also was difficult to understand (*Vit. Is.* Ath. 37D; Z. Ep. 246). For an example from an earlier period, Philostratus leaves no doubt that the sophist Polemo was a difficult man to know and like.

59. Eunapius, *Vit. Soph.* 486; Marinus, *Vit. Proc.* 8; Zacharias, *Life of Severus* 15.

60. Libanius, *Ep.* 931, 1009, 1070, 1257; Synesius, *Ep.* 16. For a discussion of this type of language see P. Petit, *Les Étudiants de Libanius*, 35–36.

61. Eunapius, *Vit. Soph.* 483. This especially applied when a student was brought into court for something he did on his teacher's behalf.

62. Libanius, *Ep.* 359.

63. Ibid., *Ep.* 428.

64. Ibid., *Ep.* 552.

65. *Vit. Proc.* 16.

ommend qualified candidates.[66] As one might expect, Libanius was especially energetic in putting forth the names of his students. In 363, for example, his former student Hyperechius traveled to Constantinople in search of a position in the administration. Libanius gave his student a series of letters to carry to the teacher's well-placed friends.[67] In these letters, Libanius introduced Hyperechius to each man and, in the subtlest terms, appealed to his friends to help the young man.[68]

While a professor could help his students get a government job, his assistance was especially useful for those who sought a teaching position. As contemporary scholars can understand, good teaching jobs were especially difficult to find. Many a promising student of rhetoric or philosophy found himself entirely shut out of the teaching profession.[69] However, when a chair did open, the recommendation of a famous teacher was often the only way for a student to get the position. Sometimes the committee assigned to choose a new holder of the chair might even ask an especially well-regarded teacher to appoint one of his own students to fill the opening. This was the case when the city of Rome asked the sophist Prohaeresius to appoint one of his students to fill a chair of Greek rhetoric.[70]

After students left school, many continued to rely upon the friendships they developed with their teachers for help and enjoyment. Synesius's correspondence with Hypatia shows how close a student could remain with his teacher. Because his family was wealthy, Synesius had no need of his teacher's assistance in finding employment for himself.[71] Not long after he left school, however, he asked her to use her influence to help two of his friends with a legal matter.[72] He also relied upon her to maintain his ties to the larger cultural world. Synesius wrote to her asking that she secure a hydroscope for him.[73] He also sent Hypatia two manuscripts and requested that she review them.[74] In the last case, the letter described why the works

66. H. I. Marrou, *Histoire de l'Éducation dans l'Antiquité*, 310–12.

67. Libanius, *Ep.* 805, 810. For parallel cases see *Ep.* 832, 1119.

68. This was despite Libanius's personal distaste for such jobs. He seems to have found them a waste of the talent that men trained in liberal arts had developed (see *Ep.* 331.3–5 for this sentiment).

69. Libanius, *Or.* 1.27: "If I had heard about the sale [of the family property] when I was in Athens, I would still be there now, making no use at all of the learning I possessed, a fate which falls upon many students who, unable to get one of the endowed chairs there, approach old age without showing their eloquence."

70. Eunapius, *Vit. Soph.* 493.

71. On Synesius's family estates, see D. Roques, *Synésios de Cyrène et la Cyrénaïque du Bas-Empire*, Études d'antiquités africaines (Paris, 1987), 136–38.

72. Synesius, *Ep.* 81.

73. *Ep.* 15. The hydroscope was an astrological instrument.

74. *Ep.* 154.

were composed and asked that Hypatia advise him about whether he ought to publish them.[75] It seems that if she found them acceptable, Synesius would then pass along a finished version of each text for her to circulate in Alexandria. Hypatia served as both Synesius's link to the mainstream cultural world of Alexandria and the conduit through which his writings passed into this environment.

Literary culture not only dominated the long-distance interactions between men (and women) of *paideia,* it also played a significant role in the face-to-face gatherings of the well-placed in the late Roman world. Gatherings in which the educated came together and discussed ideas existed in many cities. In a letter to his friend Pylaemenes, Synesius speaks of such a circle of intellectuals in Constantinople; he calls it the "Panhellenion."[76] In the letter, Synesius notes that his manner of expression has been quite careful because "there is no small danger that the letter would be read aloud in the Panhellenion."[77] Synesius describes it as "a place in which many a time I have thought deep thoughts, where the well-known from all parts of the world meet, in which one hears the sacred voice of the old gentlemen whose research comprehends tales both past and present."[78] In essence, the Panhellenion was a literary circle made up of the most cultivated men of Constantinople and their counterparts who were visiting the city at the time. When they assembled, these men read original compositions and discussed literary culture.[79]

The sort of literary discussion that made the Panhellenion a significant part of upper-class life in fourth-century Constantinople was not unique to the capital. Indeed, even in Synesius's home city of Cyrene, intellectual life was vibrant enough to generate disputatious exchanges of texts on subjects like the possible synthesis of oratory and philosophy.[80] While far from the only social outlets available to the cultivated men of the empire, interactions of this sort cemented the ties that bound men of education together in cities like Cyrene. The further exchange of written work that grew out of local discussions bound

75. The "publication" of works in antiquity was difficult, especially when an author desired to publish the works in a city where he did not live. On the difficulty an author faced when trying to preserve his ideas while also insuring the authenticity of his publications, see A. Hanson, "Galen: Author and Critic," in *Editing Texts,* ed. G. Most, 22–53 (Göttingen, 1998).

76. The name is used in *Ep.* 101. This name probably refers to a regular gathering of intellectuals and not an actual building devoted to literary discussion. For discussion of the informal nature of this gathering, see Alan Cameron and J. Long, *Barbarians and Politics,* 72–84.

77. Synesius, *Ep.* 101.

78. Ibid.

79. This perhaps explains Libanius's complaint in *Ep.* 476 that Themistius was publicizing his letters too quickly. It is possible that Themistius was reading aloud letters that contained material Libanius did not yet want made public.

80. Synesius, *Ep.* 154.

these smaller, regional circles into the larger cultural sphere of the late Roman world. Hence, the books that Synesius wrote in response to criticism from men in Cyrene were sent to Alexandria for Hypatia to review and circulate. These exchanges ensured that the literature upon which *paideia* was founded continued to have vibrancy and immediate relevance long after one left school. They also made it possible for men of culture from the smaller and more remote cities of the empire to get their work known in the larger cultural centers of the Roman world. Most importantly, they provided a framework around which men from diverse parts of the Roman world could continue to interact in a familiar setting.

To this point the relevance of traditional education to late antique society has been discussed in purely practical terms. Education marked a man as someone who possessed excellence of character. It taught him how to comport himself, how to treat his fellow men of culture, and what his public responsibilities were to be. The schools of late antiquity allowed young men to meet their cultural equals and establish friendships with them. The teachers taught these men how to conduct friendships and showed them the appropriate ways to keep in touch with one another. Their classes also were the matrix in which important intellectual questions were formulated, questions that would continue to occupy these men for the rest of their lives. All of this was essential in a society where the strength of one's friendships and personal connections determined whether one would be an effective advocate for his own rights and the rights of his associates.

There was another, less practical draw to *paideia*—the literature one studied was beautiful and pleasurable to read. Then, as now, men of learning developed a taste for certain authors, compiled lists of their favorite quotations, and relished the powerful imagery of classical language.[81] *Paideia* gave men the background to appreciate this literature and the skills to produce similarly elegant compositions of their own. It ultimately engendered a love of classical language and literature among educated men, and men who loved this literature seldom objected to living by the rules it laid out.

In this way, the teachers of the late Roman world fostered a self-sustaining intellectual culture that, while inherently concerned with the beauty of language, played a large and fundamental role in developing, sustaining, and governing social interactions on the highest levels of ancient society. The educational system of late antiquity was entrusted with the task of passing along the skills that were necessary to function in the social world of the cultivated. Hence, the growth of Christianity and the development of Christian

---

81. See, for example, Libanius's love of his copy of Thucydides' *History* (*Or.* 1. 148–49). The sayings of Greeks and Romans in Plutarch's *Moralia* are one of the biggest collections of quotations preserved from antiquity.

culture did little to change the influence of *paideia* over late antique social relationships. Despite the protests of certain Christians like Augustine and Jerome, the social world that developed around literary culture was as important for upper-class Christians as it was for anyone else.[82] Though bishops sometimes denounced the influence of this culture, it must be remembered that they themselves were usually highly educated men. This is, indeed, true of Jerome and Augustine. Despite their memorable denunciations of the influence of classical authors, their works are still stylistically influenced by the techniques of the rhetorical schools. Augustine's *On Christian Doctrine*, for example, is essentially a work of Christian rhetorical training. It even uses the rhetoric of Cicero to teach Christian students to speak persuasively.[83] And for every Jerome there was a Sidonius Apollinaris who eagerly embraced both Christianity and classical culture.

In the East, educated Christians were usually less shy about showing their affection for and reliance upon classical education. To Basil of Caesarea, the set of virtues taught in the schools of rhetoric and philosophy played an undeniably important role in a youth's upbringing. In his mind, a Christian was to aspire to the same set of virtues that poets, historians, and philosophers spoke about. Basil urged Christians "to apply themselves especially to such literature" and advised his readers to take the "deeds of good men to heart" and from this "trace out a kind of rough sketch of what virtue is."[84] Christian gentlemen were still expected keep their emotions in check and not display them publicly. As both the emperor Valens and his praetorian prefect Modestus learned, observers equated the display of passions in one's public conduct with a boorish and unrefined character, regardless of one's creed.[85] Upper-class Christians were also expected to treat their cultural compatriots as equals. Furthermore, educated Christians were often selected to serve their cities by go-

82. For this criticism see especially Jerome, *Ep.* 22, 30. For Augustine see H. I. Marrou, *Saint Augustin et la Fin de la Culture Antique* (Paris, 1938), 339–56.

83. This is in the final section of *On Christian Doctrine*.

84. Basil, *Letter to Young Men on How to Derive Benefit from Pagan Literature* 5.1, 4.1, 10.1. Though they were not to be disregarded, it is clear that Basil also thought that these virtues were fully realized only in a Christian context. On the text in general, see N. G. Wilson, *Saint Basil on the Value of Greek Literature* (London, 1975); and R. Van Dam, *Kingdom of Snow: Roman Rule and Greek Culture in Cappadocia* (Philadelphia, 2002), 181–85. For the broader context, see as well Averil Cameron, *Christianity and the Rhetoric of Empire: The Development of Christian Discourse* (Berkeley and Los Angeles, 1991), 138–39.

85. Ammianus describes Valens as "something of a boor" who was "unjust and passionate." He continues, "This is a shameful failing, to be feared even in private and everyday affairs" (Ammianus, 31.14). Modestus was classified as a man with an artificial exterior who was "by nature a simpleton unrefined by the study of classical literature" (Ammianus, 30.4.1). Ammianus passes a similar judgment on the emperor Valentinian in 29.2.3. For discussion of these attitudes in late antiquity, see P. Brown, *Power and Persuasion in Late Antiquity*, 55, 60.

ing on embassies; not even bishops were exempt from this duty.[86] The common cultural values of *paideia* remained as relevant as ever to these men. The schools of late antiquity also provided Christians with ways to establish and maintain social relationships of their own. As the examples cited above have shown, Gregory, Basil, and Synesius developed friendships with their fellow students. Like their non-Christian contemporaries, the bishops of late antiquity built and sustained relationships by exchanging letters with educated Christian and non-Christian correspondents. Education also continued to create personal relationships among the upper-class Christian laity. This is clear from the examples of the Gazan authors Procopius, Zacharias, and Aeneas, all of whom followed the same code of friendship outlined by Plutarch. Their friendships were sustained by literary letters that, in some cases, were tinged with mythological references and allusions to classical authors.[87] Despite the steady Christianization of the empire's upper classes and the objections of some of its religious leaders, the code of conduct emphasized in the rhetorical and philosophical schools of late antiquity continued to have a great significance for well-heeled Christians.

Christian affection for the ideas and forms of classical literature also extended beyond their mere utility. Christians appreciated the literary culture in which they were educated and took pleasure in cultural participation. Among bishops, the works of Basil and Gregory in the fourth century and those of Theodoret in the fifth are conspicuous for the influence of classical thought on their composition.[88] In addition, a string of philosophically influenced texts from the pens of bishops and future bishops survive from this period. They include Basil's *Hexameron* in the fourth century, Theodoret of Cyrrhus's *Cure of Hellenic Maladies* in the fifth, and the *Ammonius* of Zacharias (the future bishop of Mytilene) in the sixth century. While all of these texts approached philosophy from a Christian perspective and disproved those parts of philosophical teaching that conflicted with Christian doctrine, the argumentation that each author uses is primarily philosophical.[89] Each of these texts represents an engagement of the classical tradition

---

86. Synesius's *De Regno* was a result of such an embassy on behalf of Cyrene. Procopius's *Panegyric of Anastasius* is a later work in this vein. Bishop Flavian of Antioch famously went to Constantinople in the aftermath of the Riot of the Statues in 387. For his role, see John Chrysostom, *Homily 17: On the Statues.*

87. For Aeneas's letters see *Enea di Gaza, Epistole,* ed. and trans. L. Positano (Naples, 1962). For the letters of Procopius of Gaza, see *Epistolae et declamationes,* ed. A. Garzya and R. J. Loenertz (Ettal, 1963).

88. The often complicated "marriage of Hellenism and Christianity" is treated particularly well in S. Elm, "Hellenism and Historiography: Gregory of Nazianzus and Julian in Dialog," *Journal of Medieval and Early Modern Studies* 33.3 (2003): 493–515. Note as well the important earlier study of G. Bowersock, *Hellenism in Late Antiquity* (Ann Arbor, 1990), esp. 1–13.

89. This had been a part of Christian intellectual life from at least the time of Justin Martyr.

by an author who still valued its tenets and methods. Even bishops felt the aesthetic appeal of classical language and literature.

This was equally true among lay Christians. Before his selection as bishop, Synesius wrote poetry, treatises, and speeches.[90] All of these were grounded solidly in the literary world that traditional education sustained. Indeed, the most amusing of his works, the *Eulogy of Baldness,* was a satire composed by the bald Synesius in response to the second-century rhetorician Dio Chrysostom's *Eulogy on Hair.* It surely delighted the Panhellenion. Synesius's eagerness to embrace classical culture was normal among Christians even into the sixth century. During the reign of Justinian, Procopius of Gaza and his younger contemporary Choricius show the same interest in creating witty and eloquent rhetorical compositions based upon classical models. Indeed, the encomiums of paintings that Procopius penned worked from the same model as the pagan Philostratus's *Eikones* in the third century.[91]

In the same way that certain ancient sources raise questions about Christian comfort with the educational system, some ancient authors appear to question the degree to which dogmatic pagans adhered to the values of *paideia.* This debate has centered primarily upon Neoplatonic philosophers, a group of people whom both ancient and contemporary observers have portrayed as socially disengaged. Indeed, the fourth-century philosopher Themistius chastised them for leading an overly contemplative life in which they did "not deign to emerge from their couches and secluded spots."[92]

Themistius's criticism is unrepresentative of the historical reality. Even those pagan philosophers most dedicated to a life of contemplation acted in accordance with the norms of conduct expected of men in their social position. For these men, the code of *paideia* represented nothing less than an outline of ideal and virtuous living. In fact, in their view, a truly virtuous life depended upon the possession and exercise of a set of personal, social, and religious excellences.[93] Marinus's biography of the philosopher Proclus

---

90. His hymns are the poetic compositions of Synesius that have come down to us.

91. For these texts by Procopius, see *Spätantiker Gemäldezyklus in Gaza: Des Prokopios von Gaza Ekphrasis eikonos,* ed. P. Friedländer (Vatican City, 1939). For Philostratus, see *Imagines,* trans. A. Fairbanks (New York, 1931).

92. Themistius *Or.* 28. 341d. Themistius's attack is part of an ongoing argument he had with a group of less politically active philosophers. A more charitable modern view is that of G. Fowden ("The Pagan Holy Man in Late Antique Society," *Journal of Hellenic Studies* 102 [1982]: 54–57), who feels that Neoplatonic philosophers took on less of a public role both because they preferred a life of contemplation and because their "lack of rapport with the common man" doomed whatever attempts they made.

93. *Vit. Proc.* 2. In support of this view, Damascius states, "Men tend to bestow the name of virtue on a life of inactivity, but I do not agree with this view. For the virtue which engages in the midst of public life through political activity and discourse fortifies the soul and strengthens what is healthy and perfect" (*Vit. Is.* Ath. 124; Z. fr. 324). As P. Athanassiadi (*Damascius,*

makes this connection especially clear. The text described Proclus as a man who followed the teachings of philosophy in every aspect of his life. This also meant that he followed the code of conduct that philosophy emphasized. Proclus was liberal in his giving and restrained in expressing his emotions. More importantly, "he checked his anger as much as is possible."[94] Proclus's conduct towards his friends and associates was equally in keeping with that expected of an educated man. "Proclus revealed a liberality with his possessions and a generosity in his giving to both friends and relatives, strangers and fellow townspeople, and showed himself altogether above the possession of money."[95]

Proclus was also active on behalf of his city, a role that Marinus presents as an integral part of the virtuous life. He is careful to note that Proclus "effectively demonstrated his political disposition in another way when he wrote to governors and in this way benefited all cities."[96] Proclus was not alone. Indeed, the emperor Julian's teacher, Maximus of Ephesus, willingly served as a patron for those men of his region who needed help from the court.[97] At a later date, Damascius states that Ammonius, Proclus's student, used his influence with government officials to his advantage in clashes with the praetorian prefect of the East.[98] It seems hard to deny that even the most religiously inclined Neoplatonists still thought it appropriate to continue acting as public advocates for friends and communities.

Despite seeing a vital religious significance in traditional education, even the most dogmatic Neoplatonists appreciated the utility of the social system traditional education sustained. Like their Christian contemporaries, pagans valued the code of conduct and the rules of communication that were taught in the schools. Pagans too developed friendships in school and sustained them with letters written according to the rules of scholastic culture. The letters of Libanius have shown this well enough, but even the least conciliatory pagans observed the code of the educated class. The letters of Julian, written in appropriately allusive language, make requests of friends and share classical reminiscences with pagans like Libanius and Christians like Basil of Caesarea.[99] As a man of culture who was communicating with

---

287 n. 335) has perceptively observed, Damascius's statement appears to be an answer to Themistius's criticism of Neoplatonists.

94. *Vit. Proc.* 21. For a parallel see *Vit. Is.* Ath. 15A; Z. Ep. 18.

95. *Vit. Proc.* 13.

96. Ibid., 16.

97. Eunapius, *Vit. Soph.* 477.

98. *Vit. Is.* Ath. 78E; Z. fr. 178.

99. Those addressed to Basil are letters 26 and 81. *Ep.* 26 contains an allusion to Astydamas that Basil was expected to know. Julian treated other Christian correspondents in the same way.

other educated men, Julian wrote according to the conventions of *paideia*. In so doing, he acknowledged that his correspondents were men of culture. Not to do so would both insult the recipient of the letter and make Julian himself look uncultured. The common culture of the schools bound even the emperor.[100]

While most upper-class men appreciated the beauty of classical language and the utility of the values taught in the classrooms of late antiquity, there remained a very real component of classical pagan mythology and theology in the teaching curriculum.[101] This was by design. The Roman system of education was supposed to teach a boy not only how to behave but also "how a man must bear himself in his relationships with the gods."[102] This last element was unquestionably pagan and, although the Christianization of the ruling class meant it was less forcefully expressed in late antiquity, its presence in the curriculum disconcerted Christians. On occasion it could even lead to the pagan conversion of Christian youth.[103] Although this frightened some Christians, most do not seem to have been especially concerned. Nevertheless, even when the rhetoric of men like Augustine, Jerome, and their more extreme Western contemporaries is disregarded,[104] Christians did not agree about how to deal with this awkward component of classical education. Most Christians saw the utility of the personal and social skills taught in the schools, but they were divided about the significance of the pagan elements. On one side were men like Zacharias Scholasticus[105] who were concerned with the religious implications of some parts of teaching. They actively sought to reform teaching by neutralizing pagan elements. Arrayed against them

---

100. The friendships of the pagan *iatrosophist* Gessius with Aeneas and Procopius of Gaza show that *paideia* still sustained pagan-Christian friendships into the sixth century. Ironically, Gessius was also well known by Damascius, the uncompromisingly pagan final scholarch of the Academy. For Aeneas's correspondence with Gessius, see *Ep.* 19, 20. For Procopius's, see *Ep.* 16, 102, 122, 125, 164. Damascius mentions him in *Vit. Is.* Ath. 128; Z. fr. 334–35.

101. This was especially true of the philosophy classrooms of the time. For mythology and its role in teaching, see Hermogenes, *Progymnasmata* (23–24 in Baldwin's translation).

102. Plutarch, *Moralia* 7E. The particular religious importance of the training can be seen in the colloquia of *hermeneumata*, a collection of exercises in which a student works through the narrative of an ideal day. They begin with a prayer to the gods for a good outcome. On these exercises and their role in defining student social behaviors, see M. Bloomer, "Schooling in Persona," 71–74.

103. E. Watts, "The Late Antique Student's Perspective on Education Life," *New England Classical Journal*, 27.2 (2000): 73–78.

104. Among the more creatively extreme is Caesarius of Arles who once fell asleep over a classical book and, as he dreamt, saw it change into a coiled serpent (*Vit. Caes.* 1.8–9). For more on this see R. Kaster, *Guardians of Language*, 70–71.

105. Zacharias will be discussed in chapter 8.

was a group of Christians who focused upon the utility of the system and laughed off the pagan elements as irrelevant triflings. These were men like Choricius of Gaza, a Christian who saw that one could "cull from poetry whatever was useful while smiling at the myths."[106] He saw no need to eliminate the pagan elements of the educational system.

While Christian opinion was divided, many pagans understood the deep religious meaning in the myths and writing of the ancients to be an essential part of the educational system. This was especially true of the later Neoplatonists, for whom philosophy was a part of one's cultural patrimony that taught one how approach the divine. To purists, this element of philosophical training could never be sacrificed but, given the constraints Christian society placed upon pagans, religious teaching had to be done with great care.

Much teaching in late antiquity was done by pagan teachers and, when Christian attention was directed elsewhere, those professors tended to make the religious elements of their teaching more pronounced.[107] This increased religious focus usually did little to alter the utility of *paideia* for both Christians and pagans. It did have the potential to do so, however. The emperor Julian's edict that prohibited Christians from teaching was merely a natural extension of the idea that pagan religion needed to be appropriately emphasized in teaching.[108] Standing behind this edict was the frighteningly logical notion that one could not effectively teach the classics, which were in truth religious works, if one did not accept their religiosity. If one saw Homer as a work of religion, as Julian did, then a Christian who taught it in an allegorical or non-religious way was intentionally not teaching the work correctly.[109] While logical, the exclusion of Christians from teaching endangered the cultural unity that *paideia* encouraged. For Julian, this was a side effect of an otherwise beneficial law. For more moderate pagans, however, the threat it posed to established custom was uncomfortable. Their reactions ranged from the strange silence of Eunapius[110] to Ammianus's criticism of "the harsh decree forbidding Christians to teach rhetoric or grammar."[111] At the heart of their discomfort was the unexpressed fear that this edict would eventually lead to a fragmentation of elite culture. In the end, pagans were of two minds about the purpose of education. On the one hand, pagans appreciated the practical utility of the common cultural values of *paideia*. On

106. Choricius, *Laud. Marc.* 1.4. See also R. Kaster, *Guardians of Language*, 80–81. This is actually a passage taken from a description of the bishop of Gaza.

107. This tendency is fully explored in chapter 8.

108. Julian's law is described in chapter 3.

109. For Homer's religious importance, see R. Lamberton, *Homer the Theologian: Neoplatonist Allegorical Reading and the Growth of the Epic Tradition* (Berkeley and Los Angeles, 1986).

110. Eunapius's silence is especially notable given his normally positive reaction to all that Julian did. This law, however, negatively affected Eunapius's teacher, Prohaeresius.

111. Ammianus, 22.10.7; 25.4.20.

the other, their paganism demanded that the religious aspects of the training be acknowledged.

The story of education in late antiquity chronicles the conflict between its religious aspects and its vital purpose as a source of upper-class cultural unity. As we have seen, upper-class pagans and Christians of all religious attitudes loved classical literature, accepted the tenets of behavior it laid out, and remained joyously engaged in literary pursuits. Education provided a set of values common to people of all religions and, in a time of religious tension, it allowed men of all faiths to bridge religious gaps while interacting as equals. At the same time, Christians and pagans had dramatically different views of the religious significance of classical education. For Christians, the pagan religious elements present in the schools conflicted with their own beliefs. Their emphasis in the classrooms presented a real danger that Christian students would prefer pagan ideas to their own. Pagans experienced a different sort of frustration. Many wanted to express freely the religious teachings that, while inherent in the educational system, were prudently downplayed under Christian emperors. Just as pagans and Christians agreed upon the utility of *paideia* as a common culture, they disagreed about how its religious elements were to be perceived. Men of all faiths privileged the utility of classical education as a unifying force, but there were times when religious conflicts about education allowed individuals more concerned with religion to dominate the discussion. At times like these, when events caused moderate people to abandon their natural conservatism, *paideia* was susceptible to change. The eventual shape of education at the dawn of the Middle Ages, then, was determined by how often and in what places religious divisions disrupted this common culture and endangered its utility.

This situation reveals an important truth. The evolution of classical education in late antiquity was not propelled by a steady empire-wide intellectual and political movement against pagan teaching. Instead, it occurred within a cultural environment typified not by Christian opposition to pagan teaching but by almost constant mainstream Christian support for traditional education. This support wavered only occasionally and, on such occasions, the cause was not imperial or ecclesiastical policy but local events and concerns. Consequently, the ultimate fate of pagan education can only be understood properly by exploring the historical interaction between local power structures and pagan teachers.

To this point, my discussion has focused upon the general significance of education in late antiquity and the trends that affected its development. The rest of this work will focus upon two cities, Athens and Alexandria, and the determinative effect that their specific local settings had upon the shape of teaching in each place. The study will tell the story of education in these two cities from the second until the sixth centuries.

By emphasizing the cultural similarities between each city while illustrating their religious and political distinctions, it will show that local, historically defined attitudes towards education created unique Athenian and Alexandrian ideas about the position of pagan religious content in classical education. It will also reveal that these ideas and the patterns of interaction that helped to form them ensured that Athenian and Alexandrian schools would not share the same final fate.

In late antiquity, these two cities were as different as can be. Athens was a poor, sleepy city, which possessed few industries besides its schools. It also had a relatively influential pagan population well into the sixth century. This meant that education was always a major part of life in the city and pagan teachers had a degree of freedom to teach as they pleased. Alexandria, by contrast, was a major city with a diverse and vibrant economy in which education played but a small part. Socially, Alexandria was equally vibrant and diverse. The various Christian communities in the city engaged in vigorous and occasionally violent debate with one another and with the city's declining yet still potent pagan minority. While a part of public life, education only occasionally represented a major concern in Alexandria.

The distinctions between these two cities and the role education played in each one are mirrored by the differences in their educational institutions. In Athens, the institutions and their leaders were influential, well connected, and, in many cases, adept at working together with the city council to protect their interests. Consequently, the schools, and their pagan teachers, enjoyed a high level of autonomy that enabled Athenian professors to preserve many religious elements of their teaching. In the end, however, the teaching done in Athenian schools proved unable to adapt to changing political and religious circumstances. The most prominent teachers in the city fell out of favor with those controlling political life and the government closed the city's most famous school in 529.

In Alexandria the situation was more complicated. The major schools in the city had long interacted with the city's Christian community. From the second century forward, Alexandrian pagan teachers had taught Christian students and had become accustomed to their particular needs. In the second, third, and fourth centuries, the Alexandrian Christian community had deep intellectual ties to Alexandrian pagan teachers. Consequently, it developed mechanisms to control the impact of pagan intellectual culture upon Christian students. As the Alexandrian church grew into a major local power, this relationship changed. The informal contacts between church and school were supplemented by the distant but intense scrutiny and meddling of the city's clergy. Over time, this official pressure combined with Alexandria's historically inclusive intellectual culture to create an environment in which the religious aspects of classical education were controlled, but pagan teaching was never officially destroyed.

The ultimate fates of pagan teaching in Athens and Alexandria differed despite the close relationship between the doctrines and methods used in each place. The religious and social differences between the cities did much to determine the fate of teaching, but they are not the sole reason teaching continued in Alexandria and was stopped in Athens. At the center of the story were the teachers, students, and men of education in the two cities. These men, and their responses to the religious and systemic tensions surrounding the schools of late antiquity, determined the fates of the Athenian and Alexandrian schools.

Chapter 2

Athenian Education in the Second through Fourth Centuries

After Thessaly there is the province of Achaea, the land of Greece and Laconia, which abounds in learning, but in other respects is not self-sufficient, for it is a small and mountainous province and cannot produce as much grain as Thessaly. But it yields a small amount of oil and Attic honey, and it is to be praised for the renown of its philosophy and rhetoric; in other respects not so much.[1]

This description encapsulates the economic and cultural condition of Athens in the mid-fourth century. In its schools, Athens possessed a set of cultural institutions almost unmatched in the Mediterranean world. The schools were sources of economic prosperity and prestige for the city and its teachers. There was a certain air to the men who had studied in the city, an attitude that almost demanded one to do "reverence to the learning of those who come back from Athens."[2] Men of *paideia* also revered the schools themselves. Indeed, the high reputation of Athenian schools so pervaded late Roman culture that, as young boys growing up in Syria, Libanius and his friends were enchanted by tales of the schools and teachers of Athens.[3] In stories and conversations, adults and young men alike celebrated the words of Athenian teachers and the deeds of their students. If *paideia* bestowed a certain status on a man, Athenian *paideia* placed one on yet a higher pedestal. For ambitious fourth-century youths, the opportunity to spend time studying in Athens under its famous teachers seemed almost impossibly fortuitous. Many echoed the sentiments of Libanius when he wrote, "Like Odysseus, I think that I would have looked past even marriage with a goddess for a glimpse of the smoke of Athens."[4]

The ethereal smoke that Libanius thought emanated from the Athenian schools obscured a grim reality. Those not directly connected to teaching

---

1. *Expositio Totius Mundi et Gentium*, ed. J. Rougé, *Sources Chrétiennes* 124 (Paris, 1966), 52.4–10.
2. These are the words of a sarcastic Synesius (*Ep.* 54). Synesius was an Alexandrian student who felt a bit put out by the pretension of Athenian scholars.
3. Libanius, *Or.* 1. 11.
4. *Or.* 1.12. This is an allusion to Philostratus, *Imagines* 1.15.

lived in an economically depressed city. Athens had stopped serving as the commercial *entrepôt* for the Eastern Mediterranean more than six hundred years before. Throughout the Roman period, the economic fortunes of the city underwent a slow and steady decline. This situation created a peculiar dynamic within the city of perhaps twenty thousand inhabitants.[5] Athens was home to one world-class industry, which brought great fame by attracting wealthy teachers and students to the city. Education was, however, an industry that directly employed few people and, since many of the teachers were not native Athenians, it involved even fewer natives of the city. Students helped the city's fortunes by spending their allowances but, for most Athenians, the students and their habitual rioting probably inspired more hate than love.

This created a peculiar dynamic within the city. Education, the most lucrative Athenian industry, was the source of some of the most intractable local problems. As a result, the regulation and control of education became one of the most important Athenian concerns. In an effort to explain the challenges this presented to the local Athenian governing structure in late antiquity, this chapter will explore the dynamic between Athenian schools and the institutions that governed them in the second through fourth centuries. As one would expect, Athenian life changed a great deal in this two-hundred-year period. The local economy evolved in such a way that the number of independent farmers and the quantity of industrial exports declined precipitously. Politically, the city changed almost as dramatically. By the third century, the members of only a few families were wealthy enough to hold the most important local offices. While the ranks of large Athenian landholders were contracting, the schools continued to support a population of wealthy teachers. The importance of these teachers in local affairs was magnified by the contraction of the Athenian landed class. Hence, as the fourth century dawned, teachers increasingly made their concerns and disputes a major part of the local governing agenda. In truth, however, the particulars of the relationship between Athens and its teachers at the turn of the fourth century were determined by the social and economic developments of the preceding centuries. In order to understand the state of education at that time, it is necessary to explain these trends and what determinative effect they had on education's position in early-fourth-century Athens.

5. The figure of approximately twenty thousand is based upon the calculations of J. Day, *An Economic History of Athens under Roman Domination* (New York, 1942), 279. Literary evidence presents two possible indications of its size. The first, found in a fragment of Dexippus's *History*, mentions the marshaling of two thousand soldiers from the population to help fight off an invading force (fr. 28). This number of able-bodied men is not inconsistent with Day's estimate. The second comes from a passage of Porphyry (*In Cate.* 109.17–21, ed. Busse) that speaks of there being three thousand Athenian males. The passage is, however, a metaphor and cannot be seen as an estimate of the city's population.

ATHENS: CITY AND SCHOOL IN THE SECOND AND THIRD CENTURIES

In Athens, as in much of the Roman world, social roles and local political power were determined by an individual's wealth and status.[6] Consequently, any study of Athenian political dynamics should begin by analyzing the economic foundations of local influence. Among those Athenians who were not teachers, the wealth that allowed one to participate in public life was usually generated by productive agricultural land.[7] The estates of wealthy Athenians, which were often located in Athens and the surrounding lands of Attica, were almost entirely devoted to the large-scale cultivation of cash crops (primarily honey and olive oil). In spite of the high regard in which honey was held,[8] the olive was the king of the Attic agricultural economy. Not only was Attica's climate ideal for olive production, but, historically, the olive had been the most prominent crop in the region. In the imperial period, Attica remained a productive olive-growing region.[9] However, not all producers profited equally. Smaller-scale producers were dependent on wholesalers to get their product to the export market. These merchants purchased quantities of oil at the current rate in Attica and resold it abroad for a substantial profit. Many larger producers, however, were probably able to sell their oil without involving a middleman. Consequently, they kept a larger portion of the eventual sale price of the product.[10] This increased profit margin made them better able to absorb declines in prices. At the same time, it made it more difficult for smallholders to remain in the market profitably.[11]

6. For the general economic foundations of local influence, see P. Garnsey and R. Saller, *The Roman Empire: Economy, Society, and Culture* (Berkeley and Los Angeles, 1987), 43–63.

7. The Roman economy also included wealth derived from money lending, rental properties, and other commercial ventures. Much of this wealth likely remained under the control of the same people who owned agricultural land. On this question, see R. S. Bagnall, "Landholding in Late Roman Egypt: The Distribution of Wealth," *Journal of Roman Studies* 82 (1992): 128; and, more extensively, H. W. Pleket, "Urban Elites and the Economy of the Greek Cities of the Roman Empire," *Münsterische Beiträge z. antiken Handelsgeschichte* 3 (1984): 3–36.

8. An interesting mosaic found in Rome shows the prestige attached to Attic honey. This mosaic (described in M. Blake, *Memoirs of the American Academy in Rome* 13 [1936]: 166) depicts two boxers fighting next to an inscription that reads A.MEL/AT.TI/CV. This seems to show that a pot of Attic honey was the prize awarded the victor. Petronius give further confirmation of this when he describes Trimalchio bringing bees from Attica to his estate so that he could enjoy true Attic honey (*Sat.* 38). For other references to Attic honey see Pliny, *Natural History* 11.13, 32; Strabo, 9.399–400.

9. Pausanias, 10.32.19.

10. For a larger discussion of the olive-based economy in the Roman world, see D. J. Mattingly, "First Fruit? The Olive in the Roman World," in *Human Landscapes in Classical Antiquity: Environment and Culture,* ed. G. Shipley and J. Salmon, 213–53 (London, 1996).

11. The emperor Hadrian's law requisitioning Attic oil (*IG* II/III² 1100) demonstrates the disparity in profitability between large and small producers. In general terms, the law mandates that cultivators of olive oil sell one third of their crop to the state at the market price in

As time passed, this created a situation in which the largest and most profitable producers came to acquire much of the land that had formerly belonged to smaller farmers.

The best evidence for this process comes from an early-second-century A.D. inscription that lists parcels of land and assigns them monetary values.[12] The inscription lists a number of large landholders whose estates consisted of many pieces of land scattered around Attica. Although these properties were not contiguous, the aggregate size of these familial estates was substantial and their value greatly exceeded that of the large Attic estates of the past.[13] Even the wealthiest Athenian landholding families followed this pattern of acquisition and, as this process was repeated, much of Attica's agricultural wealth became controlled by a few families.[14]

Athens. This had the effect of limiting the profits of the wholesalers who bought oil in Athens for export and resale. This happened because the price the state paid for oil in Athens was clearly below that paid on the international export market (if it had not been, there would have been no need to require producers to sell to the state). However, so as not to shortchange the producers, government agents paid the standard rate in Attica at the time. The result was that middlemen, who could only sell oil to the state at cost, could not profit. Larger producers too saw their profitability reduced because, instead of getting full export price for their oil, they were now forced to sell one third of their crop at a lower rate. For more discussion of this law see P. Graindor, *Athènes sous Hadrien* (Cairo, 1934), 74–79; and J. Day, *Economic History of Athens*, 189–92. On this law as a part of Hadrian's larger Athenian reforms, note E. Kapetanopoulos, "The Reform of the Athenian Constitution under Hadrian," *Horos* 10–12 (1992/98): 215–37. For a later discussion that presents the law as an effort to encourage the wider cultivation of land see F. Quass, "Zum Problem der Kultivierung brachliegenden Gemeindelandes kaiserzeitlicher Städte Griechenlands," *Tekmeria* 2 (1996): 82–117.

12. *IG* II² 2776. See S. Miller, "A Roman Monument in the Athenian Agora," *Hesperia* 41 (1972): 66–93 and J. Day, *Economic History of Athens*, 221–30. This document seems to be a record of mortgage payments on the landholdings of the people mentioned. On the dating of this law, note S. Follet, *Athènes au IIe et au IIIe Siècle* (Paris, 1976), 123 n. 12, 185–87.

13. By comparing the value of the estates listed in this inscription with evidence from the fourth century B.C. (a time when estates in Attica were considered particularly large), J. Day (*Economic History of Athens*, 230) concluded that the values and sizes of these estates far exceeded those of estates in that earlier period. It is worth noting the existence of a similar (though somewhat distinct) inequality in land distribution in Roman Egypt. Note A. K. Bowman, "Landholding in the Hermopolite Nome in the 4th century AD," *Journal of Roman Studies* 75 (1985): 137–63; and the more equitable distribution described by R. S. Bagnall, "Landholding in Late Roman Egypt: The Distribution of Wealth," *Journal of Roman Studies* 82 (1992): 128–49.

14. The best documented large estate is that of Herodes Atticus. Philostratus (*Vit. Soph.* 558–59) mentions that he erected statues of his foster sons around the perimeter of his properties. A number of herms bearing the names of Herodes' sons have been found at sites around Attica. These are *IG* II/III² 3970, 3971, 13188, 13189, 13192, 13194, 13197. From their placement, it is possible to construct a partial list of Herodes' lands in the region, as P. Graindor has done (*Un Milliardaire antique, Hérode Attique et sa famille* [Cairo, 1930], 115). By this reckoning, Herodes had substantial estates in Kifisia and Marathon along with properties in Ninoi, Masi, Varnava, and at Loukou. On this, see the detailed study of J. Tobin, *Herodes Attikos and the City of*

The list of magistrates, and particularly the list of archons, shows how this development affected the public life of the city. In local Athenian politics, officeholding entailed a substantial public monetary contribution, oftentimes in the form of a payment to each citizen.[15] This had the practical effect of limiting officeholding to only the very wealthy. Hence, as these land-acquisition patterns put a few families in control of much of the productive land in Attica, their members came to dominate the important civic offices in Athens. The most prestigious local office, the archonship, became an honor open to only a few outside of these clans.[16]

The increasing frequency of years of anarchy (years when no archon was selected) illustrates how few families were able to shoulder the financial burden the office demanded. Anarchic years were unknown before the time of Augustus[17] but, since the office of archon was a one-year position that a man could hold only once in his life, they became common as its cost grew beyond the reach of most Athenians in the second and third centuries.[18] Eventually this problem was acknowledged and, in the third century, a change was made to allow individuals to hold the office multiple times. This reform reduced the number of years of anarchy, but it did so only by letting members of the wealthy elite serve multiple terms.[19]

While much of the agricultural wealth in second- and third-century Attica was concentrated among this group of leading families, the Athenian schools also provided a lucrative alternative source of income for those involved in teaching.[20] In contrast to the agricultural economy, the income from teaching was widely distributed among the teachers in the city. Philostratus,

---

Athens: Patronage and Conflict under the Antonines, Αρχαια Ελλας 4 (Amsterdam, 1997), 211–84, 333–72; and D. Geagan, "Roman Athens: Some Aspects of Life and Culture I, 86 B.C.–A.D. 267," in Aufstieg und Niedergang der Römischen Welt 2.7.1 (1979): 404. The holdings of Herodes' father were smaller but still included lands across Attica as well as elsewhere in Greece. On this see, W. Ameling, Herodes Atticus, vol. 1 (Hildseheim, 1983), 34.

15. For example, IG II/III² 3546 records one archon who made a gift of two denarii to each citizen.

16. P. Graindor (Chronologie des archontes athéniens sous l'empire [Brussels, 1922]) provides a detailed discussion of these families and, in many cases, stemmata listing the archons that came from each family. The genealogies are impressive, with supposed links to Pericles, Themistocles, and even Alexander the Great found within them. On this, note as well S. Follet, Athènes au IIe et au IIIe Siècle, 296–99, 513–18.

17. P. Graindor, Chronologie des archontes, 291–98.

18. There were also occasions when emperors and other foreign notables held the title (e.g., Domitian in 84/5, the future emperor Hadrian in 111/2, Gallienus in 264/5). Such occasions, of course, obscure the possible lack of an eligible Athenian.

19. D. Geagan, The Athenian Constitution After Sulla, Hesperia Supplement 12 (Princeton, 1967), 3.

20. P. A. Brunt, "The Bubble of the Second Sophistic," Bulletin of the Institute of Classical Studies 39 (1994): 25–52, has questioned the social and economic impact of sophistic teaching in

in his description of Lollianus of Ephesus, makes clear how much money a renowned Athenian teacher could take in. Besides serving as a teacher of rhetoric, Lollianus was appointed hoplite general, a civic office that, in the imperial period, made him the food controller for the city. "When a cargo of grain came by sea from Thessaly and there was no public money to pay for it, Lollianus asked his inner circle of pupils[21] to contribute, and a large sum was collected . . . by forgiving the fee for his lectures he repaid this money to those who had paid it."[22] The yearly fees paid by a segment of Lollianus's student body, then, were equal to the cost of a shipload of grain. This was an immense sum, but one that seems to be indicative of the wealth a successful teacher could generate.[23]

The organization of educational institutions in the second and third centuries enabled teaching to become such a lucrative occupation. In his account of the career of Proclus of Naucratis,[24] Philostratus describes the fee structure one could expect to find in Athenian schools. "The following rules were laid down by Proclus. When one paid one hundred *drachmae*, it was possible for a student to listen to lectures at any time they were given. In addition, he had a library in his house which he shared with his pupils in order to complement his lectures."[25]

The set of fees and privileges that Proclus established applied to the majority of his students. These students, for whom Philostratus uses the term *akroatai* (or listeners), paid for the privilege of hearing a teacher speak in school. This was not a very personalized instruction, but it (and the payment of the fee) did establish something of a personal relationship between teacher

---

the period, largely through a thorough examination of the evidence provided by Philostratus. His points about the atypical achievements of Philostratus's subjects are well taken, but the impact of sophistic activity certainly extends farther than he suggests. J. Geiger, "Notes on the Second Sophistic in Palestine," *Illinois Classical Studies* 19 (1994): 221–30, has pointed to a group of Palestinian sophists. More significant is the work of S. Swain ("The Reliability of Philostratus' *Lives of the Sophists*," *Classical Antiquity* 10.1 [1991]: 148–63). This has demonstrated how well information presented by Philostratus is confirmed by other sources. In at least one case (that of Soterus in *Vit. Soph.* 605), Philostratus seems to have deliberately understated his economic and political significance. While not all teachers of rhetoric were wealthy and important, it is quite reasonable to suppose that Philostratus's subjects are representative of a wider group of teachers.

21. The word used is *gnōrimoi* (γνώριμοι).

22. *Vit. Soph.* 526–27.

23. See S. Swain, "Reliability of Philostratus' *Lives*," 158, for Philostratus's likely source of information about Lollianus and its basic reliability.

24. Proclus lived in the late second and third century. Philostratus states that he attended lectures of the sophist Hadrian (who died sometime near the end of the reign of Commodus). Because Proclus lived to the age of ninety, he probably thrived well into the third century.

25. *Vit. Soph.* 604. It is not clear whether the fees entitled one to a lifetime of lectures or only those that occurred over the course of a year. The latter idea is, of course, more probable.

and student. In some cases this relationship, regardless of how ephemeral and superficial, was a great source of pride to the *akroatēs*. Herodes Atticus, for example, was fond of styling himself an *akroatēs* of the sophist Polemo. Although he had only heard the sophist speak on three occasions, the combination of these experiences (and the 250,000 *drachmae* he paid) allowed Herodes to claim a connection to the man.[26] Because of the nature of this relationship, it may not have been uncommon for a student to pay to become an *akroatēs* at the schools of a number of different teachers.[27] In the case of Herodes, he sat in on the classes of Polemo as well as those of Polemo's rivals, Favorinus and Scopelian.[28]

There was another class of students made up of those men with whom the instructor shared a more intimate teacher-student relationship. These students were given a specific sort of direct instruction by professors of rhetoric and philosophy. If the experience of Herodes is any guide, one normally had this sort of relationship with only one teacher.[29] Described by Philo-

26. For the use of the term *akroatēs* (ἀκροατής) to describe Herodes' relationship with Polemo, see *Vit. Soph.* 538. On the dating of their interaction, see S. Swain, "Reliability of Philostratus' *Lives*," 154–55.

27. *P. Oxy.* 2190 demonstrates how this arrangement may have worked for some less wealthy students. In it, a student named Neilus writes to his father about his difficulties finding a teacher of rhetoric. He has decided that, instead of enrolling formally under a teacher of rhetoric and paying the full fees required of those joining his circle, he will pay a small supervision fee to the man (lines 23–34). Neilus would work on rhetorical exercises on his own and supplement this basic supervision with regular attendance at public lectures given by other sophists (lines 33–35; he mentions a Posidonios as one of the sophists whose public lectures he would regularly attend). Although his arrangement differed from that of Herodes, Neilus would likely have been an *akroatēs* of the sophists to whom he listened. On this arrangement from the student's perspective, see B. Winter, *Philo and Paul among the Sophists: Alexandrian and Corinthian Responses to a Julio-Claudian Movement,* 2nd ed. (Cambridge, 2002), 24–34. As R. Cribiore suggests (*Gymnastics of the Mind: Greek Education in Hellenistic and Roman Egypt* [Princeton, 2001], 239), such arrangements evidently also helped to provide good publicity for sophists.

28. Polemo lectured in Smyrna and Herodes visited his school on a trip to the region. He presumably listened to the other two teachers while both were teaching in Athens (W. Ameling, *Herodes Atticus,* vol. 1, 46, suggests that Herodes and Favorinus may have had prior interactions as well). These would have been in addition to the regular lessons he attended at the school of Secundus. For Herodes' own classification of his relationships with various teachers, see Philostratus, *Vit. Soph.* 564. On Herodes' education and the nature of his interaction with these teachers, see as well W. Ameling, *Herodes Atticus,* vol. 1, 39–46.

29. Philostratus seems to use both the verb φοιτῶ to describe this sort of study and the noun γνώριμος to describe a member of the group. In the case of Herodes, it seems he studied (ἐφοίτησεν) under Secundus before the two men began to argue (*Vit. Soph.* 564). It is likely that students of this type formed the *choroi* of a teacher. For a general discussion of other terms associated with a student's relationship to a teacher, see J. W. H. Walden, *The Universities of Ancient Greece* (New York, 1909), 296 n. 1.

stratus as the *gnōrimoi* of a teacher,[30] these students were selected based upon their personal merit. Once chosen, they came to form a sort of inner circle at the philosophical or rhetorical school. Our best description of how such a group worked in the Athenian rhetorical schools again comes from Philostratus. When Herodes Atticus began teaching, he established a regular meeting of his inner circle called the Klepsydrion.[31] This was, in essence, a lunchtime group dedicated to high-level discussion of intellectual culture. Within Herodes' school, participation in the Klepsydrion not only indicated a high degree of scholastic achievement but also testified to a man's scholarly potential. In general, an invitation to join such a group showed that a professor felt the student would benefit from more personal attention. It also indicated that the professor liked the student enough to establish a close personal relationship with him.

We are ill informed about the teaching of philosophy in second- and third-century Athens, but it seems that this gradation of students also existed in philosophical schools of the time. In describing Plotinus's school in Rome, Porphyry indicates that the philosopher's lectures were open to all who were interested in coming.[32] Nevertheless, Porphyry also states, "[O]n the one hand, Plotinus had many *akroatai* but, on the other, he had those who were eager to model their life *(zēlotai)* upon philosophy."[33] The names of the members of this second group are then listed with a brief description of each person. The same situation appears to have been the case in the fifth-century Athenian school of the philosopher Proclus (to be distinguished from Proclus of Naucratis). Marinus, in his biography of this Proclus, describes the divisions of his school thus: "students came either simply for listening *(akroasei)*, or to be disciples *(zēlotai)* and companions in philosophy with him."[34] In the philosophical schools, the bonds between the teacher and the members of his intimate circle were particularly strong. Instead of merely sharing a knowledge and appreciation of the techniques of rhetoric, these men pursued a more elevated lifestyle together. At the same time, there was also a much larger group of students who had more interest in learning basic phi-

---

30. For the use of the term see *Vit. Soph.* 578. In this case, a rival of Herodes picks a fight with one of Herodes' γνώριμοι. He is met with the wrath of the teacher.

31. *Vit. Soph.* 585–86. The passage describes the future sophist Hadrian's initiation into this circle and emphasizes the speed with which he ascended to the same rank as Herodes' older pupil, Amphicles. Elsewhere (*Vit. Soph.* 578) Philostratus refers to Amphicles as one of Herodes' γνώριμοι.

32. We know this from the story of the painter who secretly attended the lectures of Plotinus in order to make sketches of the master's face. He then used these sketches to prepare a portrait of the philosopher (*Vit. Plot.* 11–19).

33. *Vit. Plot.* 7.1–3.

34. *Vit. Proc.* 38.

losophy than they had in establishing a relationship with a circle of philo-sophical intimates. These could have been students of rhetoric looking to fill out their education or merely casual students interested in learning about philosophy, but they had no desire to change their lives in order to become a part of an intimate circle.[35]

The crowd of Athenian students and their tendency to study under one teacher while paying to attend the lectures of others provided many oppor-tunities for teachers in the city to earn money. Indeed, the custom of pay-ing to hear the lectures of multiple teachers meant that the arrival of each student in Athens could lead to a direct financial gain for a number of in-dividual teachers. A prominent sophist could teach as many as one hundred paying pupils[36] and collect the considerable fees that would come along with this. Some of these students would have been *akroatai* who paid to attend the occasional morning lecture before they went off to the schools of other teachers in the afternoon.[37] A substantial number, however, would have been his own students. They had tacit financial obligations to their teacher that went beyond the mere payment of fees. It was assumed, for example, that a student would provide substantial gifts for his instructor when he completed his studies. Indeed, Apuleius claims to have spent a great deal of his two mil-lion *sesterces* inheritance showing "substantial gratitude to many of [his] in-structors, on more than one occasion going so far as to provide dowries for their daughters."[38]

The wealth generated by teaching enabled professors to play important public roles in Athens. Philostratus records a number of teachers who held either major priesthoods or local office. As has already been noted, Lollianus

35. Specific examples of students of rhetoric who were looking to round out their training are not known in third- or fourth-century Athens (though men such as Gregory Nazianzen and Basil are possible candidates). The type is well known from the fifth-century Alexandrian schools (see the cases of Zacharias and Damascius, discussed in chapter 8).

36. Philostratus (*Vit. Soph.* 591) says casually that Chrestus of Byzantium had over one hun-dred paying pupils in Byzantium. With the student population in Athens much higher than that of Byzantium, it may be assumed that a prominent teacher in Athens would have at least that many.

37. For a non-Athenian example of this phenomenon see the case of Majorinus. Even though he was officially enrolled under another professor, Majorinus periodically listened to the lec-tures of Libanius. Libanius, however, describes him as a *phoitētēs* (φοιτητής). In his vocabulary, this term indicated a student of lesser status than an *homilētēs* (ὁμιλητής). See Libanius, *Ep.* 533, and P. Petit, *Les Étudiants de Libanius* (Paris, 1957), 19; P. Wolf's objection that Majorinus was a former student who had completed his studies (*Vom Schulwesen der Spätantike: Studien zu Liba-nius* [Baden, 1952], 57–58) is implausible. Libanius indicates that students like Majorinus were common in Athens during the time he studied there in the mid-fourth century. In *Oration* 1.16 he says that he attended the lessons of Diophantus and "those of the other two according to the custom of public declamation."

38. Apuleius, *Apologia* 23.

of Ephesus was food controller and oversaw the Athenian grain treasury. Theodotus was an archon *basileus*.[39] Apollonius of Athens was food controller, eponymous archon, and also a hierophant in Eleusis.[40] Finally, Herodes Atticus served the city in a broad range of administrative and religious capacities.[41] These renowned teachers had to be quite prosperous in order to meet the financial obligations of these offices. However, as the case of Herodes illustrates, many professors probably only used their fees to supplement revenues derived from substantial agricultural estates. These lands could have been either inherited or purchased with money collected from students. In any event, teachers too were large landholders, but the locations of their estates differentiated their properties from the lands owned by other wealthy Athenians. Because teachers came from many different regions, they had estates all over the Roman world.[42] Other wealthy Athenians, by contrast, apparently owned estates mostly comprised of land in Attica.

While teachers were active in city life, the city and provincial governments also played an active part in the Athenian schools. Their most notable activity concerned the selection of teachers to hold the chairs of rhetoric and philosophy. At the turn of the third century, the imperial government funded chairs in Athens—one each in rhetoric, Epicurean philosophy, Platonic philosophy, Aristotelian philosophy, and Stoicism.[43] In addition, there existed another chair in rhetoric that predated the foundation of these five and was probably funded by the city of Athens.[44] These chairs were lucrative. The imperial chair of rhetoric paid a salary of ten thousand *drachmae*[45] and the

39. *Vit. Soph.* 566; Theodotus thrived in the mid-second century.

40. Ibid., 600–601.

41. On his benefactions, see J. Tobin, *Herodes Attikos*, 161–210.

42. In some cases, these estates proved more lucrative than their teaching positions. Hippodromus of Thessaly, for example, resigned his teaching post at the insistence of his wife so that he could return to his estate (*Vit. Soph.* 618). Subsequent generations of his family continued the practice of teaching in Athens while maintaining estates abroad. On this see, J. Pouilloux, "Une famille de sophistes thessaliens à Delphes au deuxième siècle ap. J.C.," *Revue des Études Grecques* 80 (1967): 379–84.

43. For this see H. I. Marrou, *Histoire de l'Éducation dans l'Antiquité* (Paris, 1956), 405.

44. The indication that there was an Athenian civic chair distinct from the imperial chairs is found in Philostratus's account of the career of Lollianus of Ephesus. He was said to be the first appointed to *tou Athēnēsi thronou* (τοῦ Ἀθήνῃσι θρόνου) (*Vit. Soph.* 521). The chair held by Lollianus must predate the endowment of the other five chairs because he was a contemporary of Hadrian and was likely not still teaching when the other chairs were established. On the Athenian chairs, see I. Avotins, "The Holders of the Chairs of Rhetoric at Athens," *Harvard Studies in Classical Philology* 79 (1975): 313–24. Avotins suggests a date in the reign of Antoninus Pius for the establishment of the civic chair (319) on the basis of *Historia Augusta, Vita Pii* 113.

45. *Vit. Soph.* 591. When Chrestus was offered the imperial chair at this salary he was reputed to have said, "Ten thousand drachmae do not make a man." If we assume he charged the same fees as Proclus of Naucratis, he was already making as much from the tuition of his one hundred students in Byzantium. This says nothing of the gifts he would collect from them.

municipal chair brought a salary of one talent.[46] While these were substantial amounts, the appeal of these chairs derived from the status attached to the position and not from the salaries they paid.[47] The prestige of holding a publicly funded chair in Athens ensured that the name of the teacher would be known throughout the intellectual circles of the empire. This recognition enabled him to draw students from a wide range of places and helped him to attract *akroatai* from the schools of other Athenian teachers.[48]

Although references to the civic chair are rare, we are uncommonly well informed about the imperial chairs and the selection process used to choose their occupants. The emperor Marcus Aurelius personally selected the initial occupant of the rhetoric position, Theodotus. Marcus, however, delegated the choice of the teachers of philosophy to Herodes Atticus.[49]

After the death of Herodes, the choice of men to hold the chairs of rhetoric and philosophy was left to a committee of Athenian notables. They followed a standard procedure. The process began with an initial review of applications in which the committee narrowed the pool of candidates. Next, the panel interviewed the top candidates who emerged from this group and invited them to give a public lecture in the city.[50] The committee then selected the new appointee based upon his public performance. In the case

---

46. *Vit. Soph.* 600. One talent equaled six thousand *drachmae.*

47. Philostratus indicates that Hippodromus of Thessaly resigned his endowed chair at Athens because it was actually costing his family money (*Vit. Soph.* 618). Even those forced to resign their position saw their earnings increase, as was the case with Heracleides of Lycia. When he was turned out of his chair in Athens, he started teaching in Smyrna and earned enough money to become one of the city's primary public benefactors (*Vit. Soph.* 613). To illustrate how the situation had changed in the fourth century, it is worth consulting R. A. Kaster, "The Salaries of Libanius," *Chiron* 13 (1983): 37–59.

48. It remained a great honor to be named to a municipal or imperial chair in Athens. Philostratus mentions a number of men who were so honored (among them were Philiscus, Philostratus of Lemnos, Heracleides, Hadrian of Tyre, Pausanias, Apollonius of Athens, Pausanias, Theodotus, and Lollianus of Ephesus). For each man, the chair is a highlight of his career. Nevertheless, Philostratus is careful to emphasize that holding the chair alone did not make one a truly exceptional figure (see *Vit. Soph.* 567).

49. *Vit. Soph.* 567. The personal appointment of Theodotus by the emperor was a sign of his great respect. It also surely took into account a personal quarrel between Theodotus and Herodes that would have prevented Herodes from choosing Theodotus. Indeed, G. Anderson (*The Second Sophistic: A Cultural Phenomenon in the Roman Empire* [London, 1993], 35–39) sees Theodotus's involvement in a court case against Herodes as something connected to his desire to secure the chair.

50. This was the process set out in Lucian's satirical *Eunuch.* Personal qualities played as large a role in this process as professional abilities. The text conveys the absurdity of this. Though Lucian is certainly alluding to the quarrel between Favorinus (a reputed eunuch) and Polemo, he cannot be describing an actual conflict involving them. Favorinus was dead long before chairs in Platonic philosophy were funded in Athens. On the conflict between Favorinus and Polemo, see the intriguing study of M. Gleason (*Making Men: Sophists and Self-Presentation in Ancient Rome* [Princeton, 1995]).

of the imperially funded chairs, the governor apparently confirmed the choice. At times, the process was not so transparent. Sometimes a committee would select a candidate without opening the position to other people and, at least once, the provincial governor selected his own candidates without even assembling a committee.[51] Nevertheless, these would have been exceptional circumstances. For the most part, the selection process ensured that rhetoricians and philosophers competed for the chairs in a relatively open way that allowed distinguished members of the city to judge their efforts and their worthiness.

The provincial government was also forced to adjudicate disputes between teachers. Though the system of casual *akroatai* and committed *gnōrimoi* was generally beneficial to all instructors, it did not encourage teachers to work together. Their rivalries were as intense as those of modern academics; whatever goodwill came from the mutual benefits they enjoyed was easily destroyed by jealousies. These rivalries often got out of control and, when they did, imperial authorities were left to resolve the problem.

One of the most colorful examples of government intervention in the Athenian schools involved Herodes Atticus. As one might expect, Herodes' wealth and political connections brought him into conflict with some of his colleagues in the city. The longest-lasting of these involved an Athenian teacher named Demostratus and his relatives Praxagoras and Theodotus.[52] These men had nursed a grievance against Herodes that was related to the holding of hereditary priesthoods.[53] This dispute had simmered for some time, but, although Demostratus and his associates were prominent and held places in the city government,[54] Herodes was too potent an adversary to attack directly.[55] A former consul, Herodes had established friendships with

51. Libanius mentions both cases. In *Or.* 1.25 he mentions a governor selecting replacements for three teachers he dismissed. Later in the same text he mentions a case in Constantinople when the candidate was selected without an open competition (*Or.* 1.35). Eunapius seems to indicate that this happened in Rome as well (*Vit. Soph.* 493). It would not be surprising to learn that Athens occasionally followed the example of both capitals.

52. For this dispute see *Vit. Soph.* 559–62. The sequence of these events is far from clear in Philostratus's text. This reconstruction is based upon that of G. Bowersock, *Greek Sophists in the Roman Empire* (Oxford, 1969), 93–100; and W. Ameling, *Herodes Atticus*, vol. 1, 137–51.

53. On the roots of this dispute, see W. Ameling, *Herodes Atticus*, vol. 1, 68–76 and 137–38.

54. Demostratus served as an archon in Athens around this time. His father had previously played a prominent role in the celebration of the Eleusinian Mysteries (*IG* II/III² 2342; 4071). Praxagoras himself had served as archon (*IG* II/III² 2067) and Theodotus was a prominent sophist in the city. For the careers of these men see G. Bowersock, *Greek Sophists*, 97. J. H. Oliver (*Marcus Aurelius: Aspects of Civic and Cultural Policy in the East,* Hesperia Supplement 13 [1970], 559–60) has shown other Athenian notables to have been involved in the suit as well.

55. Herodes had served as consul in 143 and was not immediately susceptible to attack. His friends, however, were more susceptible and suffered from the attention of Demostratus and his family. On this, see W. Ameling, *Herodes Atticus*, vol. 1, 140–41.

many high-ranking government officials, including Marcus Aurelius. Only a foolhardy proconsul would have chosen to punish Herodes and invite the retaliation of his friends at court. In 171, however, two brothers, Sextus Quintilius Condianus and Sextus Quintilius Valerius Maximus, were chosen to serve as the *corrector* and *comes* of Achaea, positions that held more authority than that of an ordinary proconsul.[56] They had previously been hostile to Herodes and, consequently, their arrival threatened to make Herodes more susceptible to the charges of his opponents.[57] As was customary, the Quintilii were invited to attend a meeting of the Athenian assembly shortly after taking office. At this meeting, a number of speeches urging that the brothers release the city from the "tyranny" of Herodes were given to great applause. The broad popular and aristocratic support for these complaints gave the brothers the opportunity to take action against Herodes while appearing to placate an enraged and victimized populace. Under these circumstances, even a former consul was susceptible to the complaints of an entire aggrieved city.

While the Quintilii enabled his efforts to bear fruit, Demostratus and his relatives had been trying to stir up aristocratic feeling against Herodes long before the brothers arrived in the city.[58] Sometime between 151 and 161, Herodes became sufficiently irked to file a lawsuit charging Demostratus with inciting the people against him.[59] Then, soon after the demonstration in the assembly hall in 171, Demostratus and his relatives filed suit against Herodes. With the backing of the influential Quintilii, this suit quickly reached the court of Marcus Aurelius and, in the end, the decision came out against Herodes.[60]

The key to Demostratus's eventual (albeit partial) success was his ability to build upon the resentment against Herodes in Athens[61] to establish a relatively large contingent of people who would speak against Herodes. Like

---

56. A brief description of these men and their careers is found in Cassius Dio, 73.5.3–6.5.

57. On their prior history, see W. Ameling, *Herodes Atticus,* vol. 1, 108–9.

58. *Vit. Soph.* 559.

59. Ibid., 560. In this matter, Fronto, a teacher of the future emperor Marcus Aurelius, successfully defended Demostratus.

60. Though it was rumored that Marcus had ordered Herodes to be exiled from Athens, Philostratus (*Vit. Soph.* 562) says that Marcus actually handed down a gentle judgment against him out of respect for their friendship. Even so, after this incident, it seems that Herodes lived the rest of his days beyond the walls of Athens (though he still taught students in the city). J. H. Oliver (*Marcus Aurelius,* 3–9) has independently confirmed Philostratus's statement. See as well C. P. Jones, "The Reliability of Philostratus," in *Approaches to the Second Sophistic,* ed. G. Bowersock (University Park, 1974), 14–15.

61. Philostratus (*Vit. Soph.* 549) indicates that this popular dislike arose from Herodes' actions following the death of his father. His father's will called for each Athenian citizen to receive a *mina* annually. Herodes convinced the assembly to sanction a provision whereby each citizen would get a onetime award of five *minae.* On the day of the distribution of this award,

Demostratus, other Athenian teachers who wanted to use the provincial government to punish a rival needed to have a unified group of teachers and councilors echoing their claims. When these forces came together to oppose a teacher, the teacher did not survive for long. The fate of Heracleides of Lycia illustrates this. A man of great rhetorical skill and creativity, Heracleides was also a rather hard-luck character. He often found himself in the midst of disputes and usually emerged from them much worse off. With his skill, he was able to gain appointment to the imperial chair of rhetoric in Athens. Fortune, however, contrived that he run afoul of the friends and associates of a rival teacher. Though it is not clear how, the combined influence of these men (and, especially, that of their leader Marcianus) got Heracleides deposed from his chair.[62] Heracleides left Athens and began teaching in Smyrna. Unlike Herodes, Heracleides had no connection with the imperial court (save for the time when he so negatively impressed the emperor that he had his immunity from civic duty revoked) and he enjoyed no substantial support among local aristocrats.[63] If the proconsul was approached by Marcianus and his associates, it would have been easy for him to sanction the removal of Heracleides. To punish the already embattled teacher would have no negative political consequences for the proconsul. In fact, acceding to the will of a broad segment of the aristocracy made governing the province easier because those who benefited from the exile of Heracleides would be more willing to co-operate with the proconsul in the future.[64] Under these circumstances, it was only natural for him agree to their request.

In both the case of Herodes and that of Heracleides, the economic power, political influence, and cultural prestige of the Athenian schools enabled teachers to draw much of the political firepower in their region into their professorial squabbles. The attention the government paid to these disputes testifies to the importance of teaching in Athens. The involvement of the highest government officials in academic spitting contests represented a practical policy on the part of those governing Achaea. Since teachers played an integral part in the region, any situation that threatened the proper functioning of the schools needed to be addressed as a measure of effective regional government.

At the end of the third century, the strength of education contrasted with

---

Herodes ordered that the debts each Athenian owed to his father be deducted from the money being distributed. For good reason, this upset the Athenians.

62. *Vit. Soph.* 613. See also I. Avotins, "The Chairs of Rhetoric at Athens," 321–24.

63. *Vit. Soph.* 601. While the loss of civic immunity was a disgrace, it did not cost Heracleides his chair. On this, see I. Avotins, "The Chairs of Rhetoric at Athens," 323.

64. For this attitude, in a different context, see P. Brown, *Power and Persuasion in Late Antiquity: Towards a Christian Empire* (Madison, Wisc., 1992), 22.

the relative weakness of agriculture, the other main element of the Athenian economy. While the reputation of the Athenian schools ensured that a constant flow of students would provide income to the city's teachers, the consolidation of farms typical of Attic agriculture in the period meant that there were fewer and fewer wealthy non-intellectual families. Hence, while the number of wealthy teachers must have remained relatively constant throughout the imperial period, their economic and political influence within the city continued to grow due to the decline in landed Attic families. By the middle of the third century, education was more important to the proper functioning of Athenian civic and religious institutions than it had ever been before.

THE HERULS IN ATHENS AND THEIR AFTERMATH

The social and political prominence of Athenian teachers created by the economic developments of the second and third centuries was enhanced by the Herulian invasion of 267.[65] The Heruls were a barbarian tribe who lived along the coast of the Black Sea. They had some skill in seafaring[66] and, along with a collection of other tribes, the Heruls organized a daring naval attack on the cities of the Aegean. They constructed six thousand vessels, manned them, and forced their way through the Propontis and into the Aegean. After their arrival in Greece, the Heruls ravaged all the major cities of Achaea, both coastal and inland, including Corinth, Sparta, and Argos.[67] The Heruls abandoned their boats at some point during their attack on the Peloponnese and, on their march back to the north, they sacked Athens. Following this, the Heruls seem to have stayed in Attica for a short period of time and plundered its land.[68]

Archaeological evidence shows that the destruction in Athens was quite substantial. Nearly all of the buildings of the Agora, the central public space of the city, were destroyed. From what excavations have revealed, it is apparent that the destroyed structures there and elsewhere in the city were not rebuilt. Furthermore, many of the public buildings that were damaged in the raid were torn down. The materials from them were used to build an in-

---

65. The main texts that discuss the Heruls are Zosimus, 1.39 and 42–43; Zonaras, 12.23; George Syncellus, 466.1–6; and a passing reference in Ammianus, 31.5.17. A more detailed account was found in the *Scythica* of Dexippus, a text that unfortunately is preserved in only a few fragments. For more on Dexippus, see F. Millar, "P. Herennius Dexippus: The Greek World and the Third Century Invasions," *Journal of Roman Studies* 59 (1969): 12–29.

66. Zosimus 1.42–44.

67. Syncellus 715–17.

68. During this time, the Athenians organized a force of resistance fighters and ambushed the Heruls during their retreat. Dexippus led this force, and the supposed speech he gave to the force before it went to battle is among the preserved fragments of his history (fr. 28).

ner wall of defense for the city.[69] Substantial destruction also occurred in the other areas of the city. The industrial and residential quarter lying in the district southwest of the Agora suffered nearly complete devastation.[70] In the district to the southeast of the Agora, an area filled with private homes and pock-marked with their wells, the effect of the Herulian sack is shown by a universal cessation of well usage in the later 260s.[71] Many of the ornate houses of pre-Herulian Athens were utterly destroyed and show no signs of being rebuilt.[72]

The Attic countryside suffered from this assault as well.[73] The Heruls advanced into Attica from the south, quickly captured Athens (which the indefensibly vast expanse of walls surrounding the small city would have made relatively easy), and then retreated through the district by land. Their army had then marched through and devastated much of the territory of Attica (except perhaps the peninsula tipped by Sounion). Furthermore, a Herulian occupation of Athens, even though it lasted for a very short time, would have forced the invaders to forage from the produce of Attica. This series of events greatly disrupted the agricultural life of Attica.

Athens experienced an uneven recovery from the Herulian sack. The small-scale craftsmen and potters rebuilt their shops and began production again relatively soon after the invasion.[74] In particular, the lamp industry of the city recovered almost immediately. The quality and originality of its designs were minimally impacted by the chaos.[75] In addition, many of the residential areas south of the Areopagus were reoccupied soon after the invasion. The rebuilt homes, however, lacked the ornate furnishings and expansive layouts of their predecessors.[76]

Other aspects of Athenian life did not rebound with such ease.[77] The physical damage to the city was repaired very slowly. The only major public construction projects in the aftermath of the invasion were defensive structures.[78]

69. See A. Frantz, *The Athenian Agora XXIV: Late Antiquity; 267–700* (Princeton, 1988), 3–5, for a brief summary of what is known to have been destroyed.

70. A. Frantz, *Athenian Agora XXIV*, 14.

71. Ibid.,13.

72. A telling description of the fate of one such house is found in H. Thompson, "Athenian Twilight: A.D. 267–600," *Journal of Roman Studies* 49 (1959): 62–63.

73. Zosimus (1.43) describes the Heruls attacking the countryside and "carrying off everyone they found in the country outside the cities."

74. P. Castrén, "General Aspects of Life in Post-Herulian Athens," in *Post Herulian Athens: Aspects of Life and Culture in Athens, A.D. 267–529*, ed. P. Castrén (Helsinki, 1994), 1.

75. Thompson, "Athenian Twilight," 70.

76. Frantz, *Athenian Agora XXIV*, 14.

77. Evidence for some small Athenian industries (like portrait sculpture and sarcophagus manufacture) disappears after the Heruls. For this, see F. Millar, "P. Herennius Dexippus," 27.

78. These were the post-Herulian wall, which was filled with the pieces of the destroyed and despoiled buildings of the Agora, and the rebuilt Themistoclean wall (newly renamed as the Valerian wall).

Indeed, far from rebuilding any of the impressive public buildings that had stood in the Agora, the residents of the city allowed their foundations to become a garbage dump.[79] It seems that there was little interest in immediately reconstructing the space and even less money available with which to do so.

Like the rest of the city, the economic revival of aristocratic families also proceeded at a varied pace. As we have seen, a large portion of the Athenian aristocracy depended primarily upon agriculture for their income. Most of their estates were made up of agricultural lands in Attica, and the Herulian devastation of the countryside eliminated most of the immediate value of their lands. It also would have affected their productivity for many years afterward. Since new olive trees take between fifteen and twenty years to reach full productivity, the burning and destruction of farms had especially severe consequences for olive growers.[80]

The losses sustained by these landholding families greatly retarded the aristocratic recovery. Archaeological evidence testifies to the post-Herulian poverty of the Athenian upper class. As previously stated, there is no evidence for non-defensive public construction in the late third and early fourth centuries. The fact that none of the great Athenian families were able to pay for the rehabilitation of the Agora indicates the state of their finances. More telling, though, is the absence of evidence for elaborate house construction in the aftermath of the raid. Though there was ample space for and need of new housing, most private construction in the century following the sack was done in a simple style and served merely to replace damaged buildings.[81]

The Athenian epigraphic evidence dating from the immediate aftermath of the Herulian sack also points to aristocratic decline. Most of the major families that had held strings of offices and made frequent appearances in the epigraphy of the second and third centuries disappear from the epigraphic record after 267.[82]

---

79. See A. Frantz, *Athenian Agora XXIV*, 13, for the Agora as a dumping ground.

80. On the time it takes an olive tree to reach productive maturity, see D. J. Mattingly, "First Fruit," 219. In some modern contexts, a tree grown from a cutting can begin producing in as little as eight years.

81. In the areas of the city for which there is archaeological evidence of post-Herulian construction, the pattern of building suggests that owners rebuilt on the sites of houses demolished in the raid. These new dwellings were simpler in structure and less elaborately furnished than their predecessors. A house on the west slope of the Areopagus is an example of this. The original house, built in the Hellenistic period, covered an area of approximately 300 square meters and was destroyed in 267. It was partially rebuilt on a smaller scale with uncomplicated interior decorations and a hard earth floor (A. Frantz, *Athenian Agora XXIV*, 33–35).

82. The family of the historian Dexippus is a prime example of this trend. Members of his clan figure prominently in inscriptions of the pre-Herulian period. F. Millar ("P. Herennius Dexippus," 19) gives a stemma listing genealogy, careers of family members, and all of the epigraphy that refers to them. Dexippus himself held a hereditary priesthood and the offices of

TEACHING IN POST-HERULIAN ATHENS

People involved in teaching proved much more resilient than the landed aristocracy. The Herulian invasion does seem to have resulted in a temporary decline in the number of students going to Athens and a consequent reduction in the number of professors the educational community there was able to sustain.[83] It is also likely that, as in Alaric's attack on the city in 395, some professors were caught and killed by the invaders.[84] The fortunes of those who survived, however, seem to have rebounded soon after the sack.[85] One reason for this was the fact that many teachers owned land outside of Attica. These holdings were unaffected by the Herulian attack and suffered no loss of productivity. In addition, students seem to have returned to Athens soon after the Herulian attack. Though there is no ancient author who fully describes Athenian intellectual life in the years immediately following the raid, there are selective references to teachers who were active in the city in the later third century. Eunapius mentions Paulus and Andromachus as prominent Athenian rhetoricians of the 260s and 270s.[86] In addition, the *Suda* mentions that an Onasimus continued to teach in Athens through the post-Herulian period.[87] Later, in the 290s, the sophist Julianus of Cappadocia came to Athens to teach and became such a draw that "he had numerous pupils who came, so to speak, from all parts of the world."[88] The size of his student body (and the fees they paid him) allowed him to build a house that contained a small theater of marble and was decorated with statues of his pupils.[89]

The best indication that the wealth-generating potential of teaching remained relatively unaffected by the Herulian assault was the continued prominence of local families with teaching backgrounds. While the major landholding families disappeared from the epigraphic and historical record in the later third century, families that had a long history of involvement in teaching remained at the forefront of Athenian political life. In 326,

---

eponymous archon, archon *basileus,* herald of the Areopagus, *agonothetes* of the Panathenaea, and *panegyriarch* (see *IG* II/III² 3669). This impressive string of offices suggests that his family possessed considerable wealth and great political influence.

83. Day, *Economic History of Athens,* 260.

84. Eunapius (*Vit. Soph.* 482) tells of Hilarion, who was captured by the Goths and beheaded outside the city walls. A number of scholars shared this fate.

85. It is worth comparing the late-third-century situation with that following the Sullan sack of the city in 86 B.C. Despite the devastation of much of the city, students continued to come to study. On this, see T. L. Shear, "Athens: From City-State to Provincial Town," *Hesperia* 50 (1981): 356–77 (esp. 357).

86. *Vit. Soph.* 457.

87. *Suda* A 4736, O 327.

88. *Vit. Soph.* 483.

89. Ibid.

Nicagoras, a teacher of rhetoric whose father, grandfather, and great-grand-father had held the same position, was selected by the emperor Constantine to go on a mission to Egypt.[90] Without a doubt, this selection was due to his local prominence.[91] It was Nicagoras's family background in teaching, which extended back into the pre-Herulian period, that made this possible.[92] His father, Minucianus, taught in Athens immediately following the Herulian sack.[93] Minucianus's wealth and importance are shown by a dedication he set up to a proconsul of Achaea in the late 270s.[94] Minucianus continued to attract students and collect fees while his peers in the agricultural nobility faced financial ruin. Consequently, unlike many prominent third-century Athenian families, Minucianus and his descendants weathered the Herulian storm and remained a respected family well into the 340s.[95]

The increasing wealth and power of Athenian teachers relative to the rest of the city brought about dramatic changes in teaching and learning in Athens in the early fourth century. For one thing, student riots became more common. These "riots" were physical disputes between the most committed students of one particular teacher and those of another. They were also proxy battles that reflected the petty jealousies that existed between the schools and demonstrated the amount of loyalty students felt for each teacher. Nevertheless, before the fourth century, it seems that they were relatively uncommon in Athens. Philostratus mentioned student violence once in his account of Athenian education, treating it as an exceptionally scandalous aspect of a teacher's career.[96] By contrast, student violence is a

90. Nicagoras is best known to us from graffiti found in Thebes, Egypt. The most recent discussion of them is that of G. Fowden, "Nicagoras of Athens and the Lateran Obelisk," *Journal of Hellenic Studies* 107 (1987): 51–57. The contention by O. Schissel ("Die Familie des Minukianos," *Klio* 21 [1926/7]: 361–73) that Minucianus, the rival of Hermogenes, was a member of this family seems incorrect. On this, see M. Heath, "The Family of Minucianus?" *Zeitschrift für Papyrologie und Epigraphik* 113 (1996): 66–70.

91. Besides this mission, Nicagoras also distinguished himself by serving as the torchbearer at Eleusis.

92. The sophist Nicagoras is mentioned by Philostratus (*Vit. Soph.* 628). Like the younger Nicagoras, this ancestor was a herald of the Eleusinian Mysteries (see *IG* II² 3814).

93. The *Suda* (M 1086) attributes a series of rhetorical works to him. He is probably also the teacher of the otherwise obscure sophist, Genethlius (G 132). On this, see M. Heath, "The Family of Minucianus?" 67.

94. *IG* II/III² 3689, 3690.

95. The wealth and position of Nicagoras's family led to a marriage in which the breeding, wealth, and reputation of Nicagoras's daughter was joined to the talent and potential of the young Bithynian rhetor Himerius in the early part of the fourth century. This is known from Himerius, *Or.* 33.21 (ed. Colonna). For another arranged marriage between a prominent family of teachers and an up-and-coming young rhetorician, see Philostratus, *Vit Soph.* 610.

96. Philostratus seems to be mentioning student rioting when he recounts the scandal surrounding Hadrian of Tyre (*Vit. Soph.* 587–88).

common and almost celebrated motif in the portraits of student life in Athens painted by Libanius and Eunapius.[97] Libanius mentions skirmishes as if they were routine occurrences and notes something called "the Great Riot," which involved nearly all Athenian students.[98] For his part, Eunapius celebrates the speech his teacher gave to defend violent activity as a career highlight.[99]

Some of this riotous behavior was typical of the time. By the end of the fourth century, student violence had become a major problem in educational centers throughout the empire.[100] Nevertheless, it seems that the degree to which violence played a role in Athenian student life was a unique feature of the city's schools. Indeed, this riotous behavior had gotten so out of control by the turn of the fourth century that Athenian teachers apparently no longer taught in public. Even those who held publicly funded chairs taught in their homes to avoid being cornered by the students of a rival.[101] Such a grave situation is unattested in the rest of the empire at this time. Despite the scope of the problem, the ritualized character suggested by the Athenian sources indicates that student violence had become an expected, if not entirely accepted, part of the student experience.[102]

Teachers too became involved in antics of questionable legality. These incidents usually involved the recruitment of students and included acts like encouraging their *gnōrimoi* to kidnap arriving students at the port. In these cases, the new arrivals were freed only when they agreed to study with the kidnapping teacher.[103] Often, this agreement was sealed by the swearing of an oath to study under that instructor alone. In some cases, the promise not to be the casual *akroatēs* of another professor was also co-

97. Libanius, *Or.* 1.19–22, 25; Eunapius, *Vit. Soph.* 483; Himerius, *Or.* 48.37. By contrast, Himerius *Or.* 19 is addressed to students so that they do not devote so much time to fighting that they neglect their studies.

98. *Or.* 1.21.

99. This will be discussed at greater length in chapter 3.

100. Augustine's peers, the *eversores* of Carthage, are among the more colorful examples. Though student violence is not explicitly condemned, the *Theodosian Code* (14.9.1) contains legislation that attempts to regulate the conduct of students in the schools of Rome and dissuade them from rioting, among other things. While much of it was conventional, some of the student violence may have been due to a loosening of discipline in the schools. Libanius and other teachers apparently suffered student transfers if they punished students too severely. On this situation, see P. Wolf, *Schulwesen der Spätantike*, 55.

101. Eunapius (*Vit. Soph.* 483) says that the teacher Julianus, like all his contemporaries, taught out of his private home because of the "conflict *(stasis)* at that time of men and youths." This happened despite the fact that Julianus held a publicly funded teaching position. It is worth noting a similar story told by Aelian about an elderly Plato being forced to teach from his house because of the aggressive verbal attacks of Aristotle. On the incident, see J. Dillon, *The Heirs of Plato: A Study of the Old Academy* (Oxford, 2003), 3–4.

102. Libanius, *Or.* 1.17–21.

103. This happened most famously to Libanius (*Or.* 1.16, 20).

erced.[104] By mutual agreement of the teachers, once a student had been enrolled in such a way, he was not normally permitted to transfer.[105]

This system ensured that, almost regardless of ability, teachers would always be able to gather a group of students for whom they would serve as a primary instructor (and from whom they would receive both fees and gifts). Despite their rivalries and quarrels, teachers were complicit in this scheme because it prevented the students they had from defecting. It was, in effect, a cartel system that benefited all established professors in the city. It is perhaps not surprising that all the city's teachers seem to have abided by this informal system. Despite their individual differences, they never complained about the forced enrollment of arriving students. For their part, the students themselves also viewed this system with an almost ritualized respect. Just as both Libanius and Eunapius show that student violence was an accepted part of the Athenian scholastic experience, they also indicate that participation in these kidnappings was something a youth expected to do while a student in the city.[106]

The growing wildness of the Athenian schools at the turn of the fourth century came at a time when the imperial government was becoming increasingly interested in the activities of teachers. The imperial authorities first began to register both public and private teachers for tax purposes at the beginning of the fourth century.[107] In addition to this basic organization of the profession on an imperial level, the early fourth century saw more specific attempts to control what was happening in the Athenian schools.

104. For this sort of oath see Libanius *Or.* 18.14. He says of Julian: "His amazing teacher bound him with great oaths never to be a casual student of Libanius or to be enrolled in his circle of students."

105. Eunapius, *Vit. Soph.* 488. Libanius's contention that students could not transfer under any circumstances may well be an exaggeration intended to demonstrate a precedent for his efforts to prevent student transfers in Antioch. On Libanius's Antiochene efforts against transfers, see P. Wolf, *Schulwesen der Spätantike,* 59–60.

106. Libanius was not keen on this custom. Nevertheless, when he details the activities typical of Athenian students at the time, trips to the port to snatch new arrivals is mentioned alongside brawling (*Or.* 1. 17–21).

107. As early as 321, Constantine granted taxation exemptions to professors of grammar, medicine, and rhetoric (*C. Th.* 13.3.1). This law, which also commands that they be paid their municipal salaries and their fees, clearly was intended to apply to both those who taught privately and those who held public chairs. It was complemented by a further law of 333 giving professors freedom from all types of compulsory public service (*C. Th.* 13.3.3). This stands in contrast to the limited exemptions in the second century described by V. Nutton ("Two Notes on Immunities: Digest 27.1.6.10 and 11," *Journal of Roman Studies* 61 (1971): 52–63). A similar blanket exemption from the hated *chrysarguron* tax was extended to all teachers. The law establishing this (*Leg. Saec.* 116) is unfortunately without a date. It is clear, however, that it dates before the late fifth century. An early fourth-century or even Constantinian date is certainly possible given the other exemptions that emperor bestowed upon teachers. Such a date cannot, however, be demonstrably proven.

These were primarily undertaken by various proconsuls of Achaea in response to the escalating student violence. After one fight between the students of the professors Julianus and Apsines around the year 330, a number of Apsines's students charged those of Julianus with assault. When the case went before the proconsul of Achaea, the governor ordered that the students be taken into custody. He also decreed that Julianus should be arrested and imprisoned with his students until the trial.[108] This clearly communicated that student violence was unacceptable and, for the first time, indicated that teachers would be held responsible for the conduct of their students. Nevertheless, during the trial, the proconsul allowed himself to be persuaded to release Julianus and his students without punishment.[109] Even when a dramatic event provoked his anger, the proconsul was hesitant to inflict actual punishment upon a prominent teacher.

This message was sent more forcefully in 339/40 by another proconsul. "As a result of rioting by the students, he dismissed their teachers as being no good shepherds and began to look around for three to take their place as professors."[110] The three dismissed men were likely holders of endowed chairs of rhetoric in Athens.[111] Although the governor had access to lists of those men who claimed to be teaching, he could not as yet control whether or not private teachers continued to teach. He could, however, control who was holding the publicly funded teaching posts. In this circumstance, he chose to punish those teachers for their roles in the riot by stripping them of their public chairs. Though the proconsul enacted these tough measures, Libanius says that, after a time, the governor's anger was placated and the previous teachers were restored to their positions.[112] Libanius gives no reasons for their restoration, but a combination of repentance on the teachers' part, promises of better behavior from their students, and, most importantly, pressure put on the proconsul by Athenian allies of the teachers probably made the man reconsider. In fact, it is likely that the proconsul issued this punishment with the full intention of retracting it once his point had been made. He too was quick with stern gestures but hesitant to take real action.

The reason for this caution is clear. Despite the problems caused by the schools in Athens, teachers had sufficient influence in the city and at court

---

108. *Vit. Soph.* 483.

109. P. Brown, *Power and Persuasion in Late Antiquity,* 43–44.

110. Libanius, *Or.* 1.25.

111. While the rhetorical chairs appear to have survived the Herulian assault, the chairs in philosophy are not mentioned after the third century. The nature of the third chair is a mystery, although one may note K. Brandstaetter's proposal ("De notionum πολιτικός et σοφιστής usu rhetorico," *Leipziger Studien zur classichen Philologie* 15 [1893]: 194–95) of imperial chairs in both sophistic and political rhetoric in Athens. Against this, however, see I. Avotins, "The Chairs of Rhetoric at Athens," 318 n. 13.

112. Libanius, *Or.* 1.25.

to make it impossible for proconsuls to take action against them unilaterally. It is true that, with the backing of other teachers and the Athenian city council, a proconsul could take measures to force a teacher out of the city (as happened to Heracleides of Lycia). In the case Libanius mentions, however, the actions of the proconsul were not directed against an unpopular individual teacher. Instead, they were intended to punish broadly those responsible for the lawless academic culture in the city. Such a measure was certainly within the specified powers of the proconsul, but without wide support from teachers and local councilors, the dismissals of these publicly funded teachers would have been difficult to uphold. When a large group of teachers called for a proconsul to restrain the conduct of a colleague, they welcomed his intervention. They would not, however, support unilateral action taken against them as a group. With their wealth and power, it would not be surprising if, had the proconsul not gracefully yielded in 339/40, Athenian teachers would have stopped co-operating with him on local issues. At the same time, they would probably have begun to use their network of connections to appeal his decision at either the court of the praetorian prefect or, if necessary, that of the emperor.[113] This would imperil both the proconsul's ability to administer the province effectively and his future administrative career.

The "Great Riot" and its aftermath reveal the uncomfortable balance between education's importance in Athens and the government's desire to control it. On the one hand, Athenian teachers and their students were becoming so difficult to manage that they presented a legitimate danger to both members of the city's academic community and average Athenians. This called for provincial authorities to become more involved in regulating the conduct of students. However, the wealth and prominence of teachers made it imperative that any measure a proconsul took to control events in Athens be broadly popular among both the city councilors and the teachers themselves. In essence, though he was technically so empowered, a proconsul could not practically intervene in either public or private teaching in the city unless most of the teachers were themselves calling for him to take action.

While this would seem like a rather ineffective administrative system, it actually had the potential to work quite well. In such a system, no teacher could violate rules with impunity. If he did something wrong, his colleagues

---

113. For this process of appeal see C. Roueché, "The Functions of the Governor in Late Antiquity: Some Observations," *Antiquité Tardive* 6 (1998): 31–36. The risks associated with such appeals are described by P. Brown, *Power and Persuasion in Late Antiquity,* 24, 55. As Ammianus (28.6.1) shows, such appeals did not always work, even when they related to a legitimate complaint.

could unite against him and, when their united support of the complaint was relayed to the proconsul, they could cause action to be taken. This was a political process that all understood. Each teacher could gauge his influence in relation to his rivals and judge the limits of his conduct based upon how likely it was that they would unite against him. Nevertheless, as good as the informal system was at controlling the actions of individual teachers, it was completely unable to reform the general educational culture in the city. For a proconsul to do so, he needed to secure the agreement of all teachers to amend their recruiting process and exert greater discipline on their students. While these seem like reasonable aims, the proconsul had little real leverage to force reform on the teachers. Simply put, because teachers could endanger his position if he chose to endanger theirs, both sides were at a political stalemate. It was much safer for a proconsul to serve his term without worrying about the reform of Athenian teaching. Consequently, for much of the fourth century, the informal yet well-defined system of controls that governed education in Athens persisted. It was, perhaps, the Heruls' most unlikely legacy.

Chapter 3

Prohaeresius and the Later Fourth Century

At the turn of the fourth century, the economic, political, and cultural importance of teachers in Athens had led to the development of an informal system that regulated the city's schools. In it, proconsuls and city councilors placed a set of controls upon teachers and established mechanisms by which teachers could ensure that these controls were applied appropriately. This arrangement had a tendency to punish the less powerful teachers much faster than their more established counterparts, but despite its shortcomings, it enabled teachers to correct the serious problems caused by even the most powerful of rivals. In this way, an understood political process both secured and controlled the dominant position of teachers in the city. However, as the fourth century progressed, the emergence of Christianity as the faith of the governing class of the empire introduced a new, religious element into Athenian scholastic politics. The addition of religion to this relatively well-defined political process had the effect of making the regulation of teaching more arbitrary. In the past, professorial consensus had sufficed to bring sanction against any inappropriate conduct by a teacher. In this new environment, professorial consensus still played an important part in determining when an individual professor was acting inappropriately, but religious policy could trump these political concerns. Hence, when acts of professorial discipline or scholastic regulation conflicted with the aims of imperial religious policy, the needs of the Athenian academic community would be ignored.

The first Athenian teacher to benefit directly from this new emphasis upon religion was the Christian rhetorician Prohaeresius.[1] He spent nearly seventy

1. Contrary to R. Goulet, ("Prohérésius le païen et quelques remarques sur la chronologie d'Eunape de Sardes," *Antiquité Tardive* 8 [2000]: 209–22), Prohaeresius was clearly a Chris-

years in the city as both a student and a teacher and, for much of this time, his career reflected the political developments surrounding Athenian education. When he began teaching in the mid-330s, his school and his professorial activities were still governed by the post-Herulian political structure. An aggressive recruiter of students, Prohaeresius did not thrive in a setting where the consensus opinions of rivals could restrain his instincts. Indeed, not long after he began teaching, Prohaeresius found himself in a great deal of political trouble. His recruiting tactics angered his rivals enough for them to band together and force him out of the city. He was saved from ruin only because his Christianity enabled him to attract direct imperial patronage. After this point, continued imperial support enabled Prohaeresius to circumvent local controls and function more or less independently of their restrictions. The career of Prohaeresius marks a significant turning point in the history of the Athenian schools. An examination of it, then, is a good way to understand the changes that occurred in fourth-century Athenian society. Let us turn now to that task.

PROHAERESIUS THE *HETAIROS*

Prohaeresius was born in 276 to a family living in a Roman-controlled part of Armenia.[2] When he was about eighteen, he and his family were forced to leave Armenia and move on to Antioch.[3] In Antioch, Prohaeresius studied rhetoric under the sophist Ulpian and was among the top pupils in the school. Throughout his time in Syria, Prohaeresius yearned to go to Athens to finish his schooling, but the poverty of his family made it impossible for him to do this immediately. After a period of time with Ulpian, which probably lasted less than ten years,[4] Prohaeresius and his equally poor friend Hephaestion

---

tian. Goulet's alternative, which runs counter to the word of Jerome and the implication of a number of other ancient sources, would create considerable interpretative difficulties. As will be explained, the sources for the life of Prohaeresius create a narrative of his career that is wholly consistent with his being a Christian.

    2. Eunapius, *Vit. Soph.* 485. The *Suda* entry places his birth in Caesarea, Cappadocia (Π 2375). This seems to be erroneous and probably derives from a conflation of information about Prohaeresius and his teacher, Julianus. Julianus was, in fact, born in Caesarea. For this problem see R. Penella, *Greek Philosophers and Sophists in the Fourth Century* A.D.: Studies in Eunapius of Sardis (Leeds, 1990), 83.

    3. The term *neos* (νέος) is used by Eunapius. Based upon general usage of the term, it seems to indicate that Prohaeresius was about eighteen at the time (i.e., 294–95). For this term in Eunapius see R. Goulet, "Sur la chronologie de la vie et des oeuvres d'Eunape de Sardes," *Journal of Hellenic Studies* 100 (1980): 60–72. For a different perspective see R. Penella, *Greek Philosophers and Sophists*, 4.

    4. Eunapius's imprecise "not a short period of time" in *Vit. Soph.* 487 is unhelpful and likely hides his ignorance about the length of Prohaeresius's study under Ulpian. The *Suda* (O 912) de-

were able to collect enough money to leave Antioch. Around the turn of the fourth century, the two men arrived in Athens and began studying under Julianus.

Aside from an amusing anecdote about the poverty of Prohaeresius and Hephaestion, little is known of Prohaeresius's activities as a student.[5] Eunapius does make it clear, however, that Prohaeresius was rapidly recognized as the finest of Julianus's students. While it enhanced his standing within the school, this excellence did not accelerate Prohaeresius's departure into the world of independent teaching. This was perhaps due to Julianus's standing among Athenian teachers. Though it seems that he began teaching in the city before the turn of the fourth century, the *Suda* says that Julianus reached his professional acme in the reign of Constantine.[6] In addition, Eunapius indicates that he held one of the endowed chairs in Athens at the end of his life. It is likely that the "professional acme" described by the *Suda* as occurring during the reign of Constantine came when Julianus assumed an endowed chair in Athens. Prohaeresius, then, had studied and worked under Julianus for between twenty and thirty years before his teacher was recognized as one of the city's premier teachers.

The length of time Prohaeresius spent at the school of Julianus is known only because of a brawl that occurred between the students of Julianus and those of Apsines, a rival teacher. This incident was discussed briefly in the preceding chapter, but its importance to the career of Prohaeresius makes it worth revisiting. The fight erupted between a group of students studying under Julianus and another group affiliated with his rival, Apsines. Although Apsines' group won the struggle, after its conclusion they traveled to the office of the proconsul and filed charges against Julianus's students. The proconsul then ordered that Julianus and every member of his school be ar-

---

scribes Ulpian as a teacher who thrived in the reign of Constantine. If this is true, Prohaeresius had certainly moved on from his school by that time. Though specific evidence of this is lacking, there is also a temptation to identify Ulpian with Libanius's first teacher in Antioch. If Ulpian is so identified, it seems he died in 328 or 329; Libanius tells us that his teacher died shortly after he began to study rhetoric at age fifteen. Though it was not uncommon for a man to become the late antique equivalent of a perpetual graduate student, I know of no case where such a man switched primary teachers when he was older than thirty. Porphyry's transfer from the school of Longinus to that of Plotinus at age thirty occurred late enough in life to puzzle his old master (see *Vit. Plot.* 4 for Porphyry's age at the transfer and *Vit. Plot.* 20 for Longinus's reaction to it).

5. Eunapius writes that the two students were forced to share one set of school clothes and attend classes on alternate days (*Vit. Soph.* 487).

6. *Suda* I 435. *Suda* testimony regarding such things should never be taken as definitive. Nevertheless, in this case, Eunapius indicates that Julianus was a contemporary of Aedesius (*Vit. Soph.* 482), the most important successor of Iamblichus, who taught independently from 330–55. Since Julianus was surely dead by 336, the *Suda* testimony seems correct here.

rested and held pending trial.[7] When the participants came forward to be tried, Julianus was forbidden from making a speech of defense. Instead, he was ordered to send forth one of his *hetairoi*[8] to speak on behalf of the group. Prohaeresius was chosen, made the speech, and was so powerful in his delivery that the judge himself was said to be applauding from his seat.[9]

Eunapius gives no date for these events, but it is possible to determine when the trial took place from outside evidence. The first clue to the trial's date is the age of Apsines, Julianus's accuser. We know that Apsines was the son of Onasimus, a powerful and productive teacher who thrived under Constantine.[10] In cases where a prominent teacher has a son who also goes into teaching, the son usually succeeds the father as the head of his school upon the elder's death.[11] If it is assumed that Onasimus taught early in the reign of Constantine (which began in Athens in 314), then, at the earliest, the trial took place in the later years of this reign, probably between 325 and 335.

The *terminus ante quem* for these events is Julianus's own death. This surely occurred some time before Libanius's arrival in Athens in 336. Both Libanius's future teacher, Diophantus, and Epiphanius, the teacher he had arranged to study under, had been among the members of Julianus's circle who were on trial. By 336, however, both men had become established teachers in their own right. Furthermore, Libanius makes no mention of Julianus in his account of his time in Athens. Given that his former students had already established themselves as teachers, it is quite possible that Julianus had died a few years earlier, possibly as early as 333. Furthermore, Eunapius, who began work on this account in the 390s,[12] used Tuscianus, an *hetairos* of Julianus and an eyewitness to the events, as his source.[13] If Tuscianus were still alive in the 390s, as he seems to have been, then these events cannot have occurred before the 330s.

The trial in which Prohaeresius starred then took place about 330, meaning that he was approximately fifty-five years old when he delivered his impressive speech. This makes for a bizarre sequence of events. The proconsul, who

7. The proceedings are described in *Vit. Soph.* 483–85.

8. ἑταῖροι. Literally the word means "companions." In the past it has been translated as "students" (see, for example, R. Penella, *Greek Philosophers and Sophists*, 78 n. 93), but, as will be outlined below, that translation causes substantial interpretative problems in this case.

9. *Vit. Soph.* 485.

10. *Suda* O 327.

11. This process will be discussed in more detail in chapter 7.

12. For the date of the composition of the *Lives of the Sophists* see T. Banchich, "The Date of Eunapius' *Vitae Sophistarum*," *Greek Roman and Byzantine Studies* 25 (1984): 183–92. He argues that it was composed in late 399, a date Penella also accepts.

13. See *Vit. Soph.* 484.

had prohibited both Julianus and Apsines from speaking for fear that they would turn the trial into a rhetorical contest, allowed a fifty-five-year-old member of Julianus's school to give the defense speech. Surely he could not have expected anything less rhetorical from Prohaeresius. It is equally difficult to believe that Prohaeresius, a man from a family without great means, would agree to remain affiliated with his teacher's school for over thirty years without any immediate opportunity for advancement.

It seems, though, that both of these things were the case. In his discussion of the brawl that precipitated this trial, Eunapius mentions that the fight involved the *mathētai* of Julianus and Apsines.[14] This is a general term that Eunapius uses to describe students. When he speaks of the trial, however, Eunapius says that Prohaeresius was an *hetairos*. This is a term that had a different sense from *mathētai*. In Eunapius's text, the term *hetairoi* usually refers to those people who occupied the inner circle of a teacher.[15] Unlike students who stayed for a time under the teacher and then moved on, these *hetairoi* seem to have been relatively permanent figures in the schools of late antiquity. For an *hetairos*, the decades that Prohaeresius spent at Julianus's school were not exceptional. Indeed, Prohaeresius's thirty-year stint under Julianus is comparable to the twenty-four years Amelius spent in Plotinus's inner circle and the nearly thirty years Marinus spent under Proclus.[16]

One must not, however, think of these decades as time spent studying. Once a man became a part of a teacher's inner circle, he not only participated in intellectual discussions, but also taught and performed other duties within the school. Amelius and Porphyry, both members of Plotinus's inner circle, were responsible for editing the texts written by their master. Marinus, who was one of Proclus's *hetairoi*, taught Aristotelian doctrine at the school while he held that status.[17] Within Eunapius's account, Eusebius and Chrysanthius, the *hetairoi* of Aedesius, were called upon to teach the future emperor Julian when he arrived to study at the school of their master.[18] Though these positions were not as desirable as heading one's own

14. οἳ μαθηταί.

15. Eunapius makes the contrast between *hetairoi* and other grades of students explicit in a number of passages in the text (e.g., *Vit. Soph.* 458, 461, 481, 485). His use of *hetairoi* contrasts with Philostratus (who preferred the term *gnōrimoi*) and Porphyry (who used words with roots like *gnōrizo*). Porphyry also uses other words with a hint of intimacy like *sungignomai* (συγγίγνομαι) to describe Plotinus's inner circle. To avoid repetition, Porphyry does use *hetairos* (ἑταῖρος) to refer to one member of Plotinus's inner circle (*Vit. Plot.* 7.18), but it is not his preferred term. Writing in the late fifth century, Marinus frequently employs *hetairoi* to describe the members of the inner circle of Proclus.

16. For Amelius see *Vit. Plot.* 3.30. Marinus's time under Proclus will be described in the next chapter.

17. *Vit. Is. Ath.* 38A; Z. Ep. 42.

18. *Vit. Soph.* 474.

school, one could certainly make a living working under a successful teacher. Furthermore, the most favored of the *hetairoi* could legitimately expect to be chosen as the new head of the school once his master passed from the scene.[19]

This explains why Prohaeresius, a man approaching sixty, was still a part of the school. As the most gifted of Julianus's pupils, it is likely that he had been marked out as the legitimate successor of Julianus long before the 330s. At the time of the court case, he was just biding his time before the opportunity arose for him to take over his teacher's school. It is less clear why the proconsul allowed Prohaeresius to speak at the trial when he had already prevented both Apsines and Julianus from doing so. In all likelihood, the proconsul was simply ignorant of the rhetorical skill of the middle-aged assistant professor. It must be remembered that, when the proconsul forced Apsines' *hetairos* Themistocles to speak at the trial, the man was unprepared and unable to make a speech.[20] He probably expected the same result when he compelled one of Julianus's circle to speak without any advanced notice. Additionally, one might be forgiven for underestimating the *ex tempore* skill of a fifty-five-year-old who had not yet headed his own school. Many lifelong assistants turned out to be rather mediocre professors in their own right.[21] The proconsul presumably expected Prohaeresius to give an incompetent speech or, more likely, to respond with the same silence that he had gotten from Themistocles. That the speech he heard was eloquent and persuasive shows the unexpected skill of Prohaeresius more than it does a lack of judgment on the proconsul's part.

PROHAERESIUS THE *DIADOCHOS*

Eunapius is unclear about what happened when Julianus died in or around the year 333, but from all indications, Prohaeresius was selected to assume

19. P. Wolf's discussion of assistant teachers (*Vom Schulwesen der Spätantike: Studien zu Libanius* [Baden, 1952], 63–66) is good at establishing the nature of their teaching activities. His contention that they were public employees whose position was not tied to their relationship with the professor is improbable. While he is correct to note that these assistants received public support (Wolf, *Schulwesen der Spätantike*, 63, on the basis of Libanius, *Or.* 31), this was likely due to their affiliation with a professor who also received public support. Some such assistants may have passed from one chairholder to the next, but it is difficult to believe that this happened in cases (like that of Julianus) where the newly named public professor already had established a large inner circle of assistants. Indeed, the fact that Julianus's assistants all began teaching independently following his death seems to indicate that their publicly funded assistantships ended with their master's death.

20. *Vit. Soph.* 484. Eunapius may, of course, be exaggerating Themistocles' incompetence in order to amplify the difficulty of Prohaeresius's achievement.

21. This was the case with Amelius and Marinus. It seems to have been true of Eusebius as well.

control of his school. Eunapius tells us that, when Julianus died, he left his house to Prohaeresius.[22] This was a significant gesture. Julianus taught out of this house and had specifically designed the building to serve as a place of teaching.[23] By handing Prohaeresius possession of the school's teaching center, Julianus also placed him in charge of the teaching done there. There are other Athenian parallels to this kind of transfer. When Plutarch the Neoplatonic scholarch died in the early 430s, he too made sure that his house, the center of teaching for his school, was deeded to Syrianus, his designated successor. Then, when Syrianus died, the same house was transferred to Proclus, the new head of the school.[24] In each case, the man who was given possession of the teaching center was also given control of the school.

Although Prohaeresius assumed control of Julianus's school and the building associated with it, Julianus was not able to select the next occupant of his endowed chair. Julianus's school was a private possession and it was his right to bestow it upon whomever he wanted. The public teaching post, however, was not Julianus's to transfer. Hence, when he died, the chair was left vacant and could not be filled until the town council and proconsul went through the formal appointment process. This was presumably similar to that described by Lucian in the second century and by Augustine in the late fourth.[25] In each case, an initial round of applications was reviewed and finalists were chosen. The selected candidates were subsequently invited to show their mastery of philosophy or rhetoric in a public declamation before the notables who made up the selection committee. This is the set of events one would expect to take place following the death of Julianus, but it is difficult to see how closely the procedure was followed in this case.[26] Eunapius's account, which is usually the best source for the career of Prohaeresius, is so intentionally convoluted as to make almost no sense. It is, however, the only source that speaks of Julianus's death and the events following it. For this reason, one must try to decipher its meaning.

Eunapius begins by saying that Julianus was awed by the greatness of Pro-

---

22. *Vit. Soph.* 483.

23. For Julianus teaching out of his house, see *Vit. Soph.* 483. Later in the same passage, Eunapius describes the theater of polished marble that Julianus had built in order to give his lessons.

24. Marinus, *Vit. Proc.* 29.

25. Lucian's *Eunuchos* is an amusing parody of this procedure. For the process Augustine went through to get appointed in Milan, see *Confessions*, 5.13. In his case, he won the position through a set of influential letters written on his behalf and the successful completion of a test before the prefect.

26. R. Penella's idea (*Greek Philosophers and Sophists,* 85–86) that the selection process involved a prolonged teaching competition has no precedent. Lucian and Augustine make it clear that these competitions were relatively short and designed only to measure a candidate's skill in public declamation.

haeresius's natural gifts and preferred him to all others.[27] Nevertheless, when Julianus died, the Athenian authorities initiated a broad search for a successor.[28] Many men expressed their interest in his public chair and, in accordance with the selection procedure for this chair, the pool of applicants was reviewed. Six from their number were selected by all judges. Four of these six finalists were Julianus's *hetairoi* Prohaeresius, Diophantus, Epiphanius, and Hephaestion. Though Eunapius does not say it, it seems that each of these men had already begun teaching privately in his own school.[29] Two others of less accomplishment and skill joined these four candidates so that the appropriate number of finalists would be available.[30]

After explaining why so many nominees were selected, Eunapius continues:

> When these men [i.e., the finalists] had been elected,[31] the more humble ones held the title of sophist alone, and their influence was present within the confines of the walls and platform upon which they taught. But the city immediately divided itself into the camps of the more powerful. And it was not the city alone [that did this] but all the peoples who lived under Roman rule. Their *stasis* [conflict] was not about rhetoric but, over and above rhetoric, it was on behalf of all peoples in the empire.[32]

Although Eunapius's meaning is again somewhat vague, a close reading of the vocabulary he uses to describe the situation makes the events he is recounting clearer. In the beginning of the passage, Eunapius makes deliberate use of the vocabulary of democratic Athens to show that the selection of the new public professor was done according to a transparent, organized process. This peaceful process enabled the finalists to be chosen, but after their selection, factions within the city and empire caused *stasis* that disrupted the orderly process before it came to its conclusion. Given Eunapius's previous use of *stasis* in connection with the riot between the students of Julianus and Apsines, it seems that he intends to convey that crowds of students took to the front lines of this conflict.

The second part of Eunapius's description indicates that this conflict had a geographical component. This is, of course, rhetorical exaggeration—the selection of a public professor was an Athenian matter and was decided pri-

---

27. *Vit. Soph.* 487. "But nevertheless Julianus inclined his soul towards Prohaeresius and perked up his ears to him, and was awestruck by the stature of his natural gifts."

28. Ibid.

29. All except Hephaestion are known to have been teaching upon Libanius's arrival in the city in 336.

30. *Vit. Soph.* 487. In Eunapius's words, the only reason for the inclusion of these two lesser teachers was a law that required "there to be many to give speeches and many to listen."

31. χειροτονέω. In Athenian democracy, the word was used to indicate one "chosen by lot" (e.g., Plato, *Laws* 755e8) or the act of approving a proposal by a vote (e.g., Thucydides 6.13.1).

32. *Vit. Soph.* 487.

marily by the people in the city. Nevertheless, it seems that each teacher had a recruiting base in a different region of the Eastern Mediterranean. Since the students were the ones creating the *stasis* and they had arranged themselves around individual teachers along geographic lines, it was correct, though disingenuous, to say that their street fights divided the peoples of the whole empire. Far from explaining this hyperbole in the following sentence, Eunapius merely expands upon it by cataloging the peoples each teacher drew to his side. The East (i.e., Syria and Mesopotamia) "granted a certain privilege"[33] to Epiphanius. Diophantus was "allotted"[34] the province of Arabia. Because his place of origin was the same as that of his more distinguished friend, Prohaeresius, Hephaestion left Athens, overawed by his countrymen, and seems to have died not long after.[35] Prohaeresius, we are told, received pupils from the Pontic region and all of Bithynia because he was a native of the region. In Eunapius's metaphorical language, all the teachers acquired their geographic bases by systematic means of allotment. However, as he continues his list of Prohaeresius's supporters, Eunapius switches his vocabulary. He states that Prohaeresius also "appropriated"[36] the province of Asia and later added all of Egypt and Cyrene to his "empire of rhetoric."[37]

In the first part of this passage, Eunapius has described a system in which the teachers were either assigned specific regions from which to recruit students or agreed amongst themselves to limit their formal recruiting to only students from those regions.[38] The regions "assigned" to each teacher were either their home region or some other place to which they were connected. This inevitably reflected the place to which their personal ties were strongest. Epiphanius, for example, had ties to Antioch and he was able to draw Libanius from there in 336, not many years after the death of Julianus. If the *Suda* is to be believed, Epiphanius was the son of Ulpian, the famous Antiochene sophist (and Prohaeresius's teacher when he lived in the city).[39] This would both explain his Antiochene connections and show why he was better connected to people in the city than was Prohaeresius (who had lived and studied in the city as a youth).

33. γέρας.

34. εἰλήχει.

35. Eunapius says he ἀπῆλθεν ἐξ᾿Ἀθηνῶν τε καὶ ἀνθρώπων. This is the same phrase that he uses to describe the death of Julianus.

36. ἀφορίζεται.

37. ἡ ἐπί τοῖς λόγοις ἀρχή.

38. R. Penella (*Greek Philosophers and Sophists*, 86) feels that these regional alignments were a part of the selection process for Julianus's chair. While Eunapius has not clearly signaled to the reader that his account has moved past the selection process for the chair, it seems that he has, in fact, done so.

39. *Suda* E 2741.

As a native of Armenia, Prohaeresius was allotted students from the regions on Anatolia's Black Sea coast that neighbored Armenia. However, Eunapius indicates that he secured those from Asia and Egypt by some other means. Instead of using verbs of allotment, Eunapius switches to vocabulary indicating a different sort of acquisition. Prohaeresius was not given charge over the recruitment of students from these places—he took it. Eunapius's own recruitment gives a good idea as to how Prohaeresius may have "captured" the two regions. Eunapius was from Sardis (in the broadly defined province of Asia)[40] and, when he came to Athens to study, he traveled by ship. When the ship docked at the Piraeus late at night, "the captain, an old friend and guest of Prohaeresius, knocked at his door and led this great crowd of students into his house. The result was that, when so many battles were developing over one or two youths, those who were handed over seemed to be enough to fill a whole sophistic school."[41] A standing arrangement with captains sailing from Asia would have been quite lucrative for Prohaeresius. The cities in this region had been deeply influenced by Athenian intellectual culture and sent many students to the city.[42] If Prohaeresius had been able to attract the majority of them, his school would have done quite well.

These recruitment arrangements were important because the Athenian teachers of the time had apparently agreed to respect their competitors' spheres of influence. Indeed, Libanius indicates that, during the 330s and 340s, movement between teachers was so unacceptable that teachers themselves would refuse to accept defecting students.[43] Even in the 360s, Eunapius says that this system was in place, despite the exceptional cases of "a few youths who either migrated from one teacher to another or sometimes went to another teacher as a result of being deceived upon arrival."[44] Eunapius's experiences, however, date from the 360s, a less turbulent period in the city's schools and, Libanius notes, a time in which movement between teachers was more common. Libanius indicates that, during his time in Athens, such

40. In the fourth century Sardis was part of the province of Lydia but none of the regional titles Eunapius uses in this section correspond to their Diocletianic provinces. Instead, it seems that Eunapius is using the anachronistic regional titles of the Augustan age. In that period, Sardis was, in fact, a part of the province of Asia.

41. *Vit. Soph.* 486.

42. In the case of Cappadocia, Prohaeresius seems to have parlayed Julianus's roots in the province into a steady stream of students, which continued through the 350s. These included both Gregory Nazianzen and Basil of Caesarea.

43. Some of this is clearly designed to contrast the settled situation in his youth with the more unsettled situation Libanius faced while teaching in Antioch. For Libanius's problems with student transfers see *Or.* 43. Augustine experienced similar things when teaching in Rome (*Confessions* 5.12). Libanius's recollection of the time when transfers were discouraged is found in *Or.* 1.16–20.

44. *Vit. Soph.* 488. Eunapius had read Libanius's *Oration* 1, and this passage is probably designed to respond to Libanius's description of the rigidity of the Athenian system.

movement between teachers was not acceptable. At that time, he intimates, a teacher was assured of keeping those students who agreed to study exclusively under him. He was also assured of having students to fight for his interests in street brawls within the city. Most importantly, though, he could expect a handsome profit from their fees. With the reputation of his school (and possibly his connections with ship captains) assuring his drawing power and arrangements with other teachers preventing student transfers, Prohaeresius stood as the most dominant of Julianus's former *hetairoi* in the period immediately following his master's death.

According to Eunapius, the Athenian teaching community had a strong reaction to the growing influence of Prohaeresius. Combining their influence, the teachers "brought about the man's expulsion from Athens by bribing the proconsul. And then they held the kingship[45] with respect to rhetoric."[46] As the school of Prohaeresius quickly became the dominant recruiter in the city, its rival institutions likely began to struggle. The students from Egypt and Asia whom Prohaeresius now secured for his school had previously been available to all teachers. By snatching these students before they had even left the ship, Prohaeresius made them impossible to recruit. His control of student recruitment also put Prohaeresius in a position to deny teachers new students and to limit the number of occasional listeners who paid them fees.[47] This was a grave threat to the financial position of the other teachers and their schools.

It is, then, not surprising that the various Athenian teachers put aside their differences and united against Prohaeresius. In such circumstances, it was in the best interest of every other teacher to file a collective complaint against the dominant teacher. When they did so, the proconsul, who was likely still troubled by the violence surrounding the search for a new public teacher, would have been more than willing to respond to their complaints.

Eunapius is silent about the events of Prohaeresius's exile, but he does give an indication of when Prohaeresius was sent away. Because it is known that he was still teaching in Athens when Libanius arrived in 336, Prohaeresius was exiled sometime between 337 and 340.[48] This did not mean that teaching stopped in his school, however. Eunapius says that *hetairoi* of

---

45. τὴν ἐπὶ λόγοις βασιλείαν εἶχον αὐτοί.

46. *Vit. Soph.* 488.

47. Eunapius uses the term *homilētēs* (ὁμιλητής) to describe such students. Though the Eunapian term does not seem to have been as precisely defined as the Philostratan term *akroatēs* (ἀκροατής), it is clear from both the *Lives of the Sophists* and the Libanian corpus that the distinction between occasional listeners and dedicated students still existed in the time Eunapius chronicles.

48. It is tempting to associate the events preceding his exile with the Great Riot, which Libanius indicates occurred in 339. There is, however, nothing concrete to link Eunapius's account with this event.

Prohaeresius remained in Athens while the teacher was abroad; in all like-lihood, this meant that teaching in Prohaeresius's school was placed in the hands of his inner circle. The institution then continued to function while its master was absent.[49]

If Prohaeresius had been a second- or third-century teacher, he probably would have shared the fate of Heracleides, the Smyrnan teacher who was ex-iled from Athens and forced into an early retirement.[50] Indeed, even in the fourth century, Prohaeresius probably should have expected a similar fate. Prohaeresius escaped obscurity simply because he was a Christian and a teacher of rhetoric who worked within the territory controlled by the West-ern emperor Constans in the 330s and 340s. Though Eunapius, a convinced pagan, is hesitant to say so explicitly, Prohaeresius drew obvious benefits from his religious identity during and after his exile from Athens. Prohaeresius was forced from Athens at a time when the Constantinian dynasty's support of Christianity had become a major part of public life. As a Christian Greek rhetorician, Prohaeresius stood out as a particularly rare breed of individ-ual among Constans's largely Latin-speaking subjects. This made him quite useful in the propaganda of Constans's regime. In the mid-fourth century, when some educated men were still questioning the intellectual potency of Christianity,[51] the appearance of a display piece like the Christian rhetor Pro-haeresius provided an important demonstration of the intellectual creden-tials of the new faith. One can be certain that this status was not something that Prohaeresius desired or something he actively cultivated but, given the weakness of his position, it seems to have been something that he accepted.

Constans's support enabled Prohaeresius to return to Athens in 343.[52] During the time that he was in exile, a younger man replaced the procon-sul responsible for sending him off. Eunapius says that this new proconsul, when he heard of Prohaeresius's fate, worked to overturn the decision of his predecessor. It is possible, though not provable, that this same proconsul also

49. Eunapius does not make this entirely clear, however. The source of the confusion is the vague meaning of *hetairoi* (ἑταῖροι) in this context. Usually in Eunapius's text the term means "members of a school's inner circle." In this circumstance, however, it could also take on the more general meaning of "friends." The identification of Tuscianus as one of these *hetairoi* fur-ther complicates things, because he was both an *hetairos* of Julianus and Prohaeresius in the for-mer sense and a personal friend of Prohaeresius. It is likely, however, that Eunapius was being consistent in his use of the term *hetairoi* and these men served as teachers both when Prohaeresius was present and while he was away.

50. Philostratus, *Vit. Soph.* 613.

51. See, most famously, Augustine, *Confessions* 3.5.

52. This seems to be the only possible date. When Prohaeresius was summoned from Athens to Gaul, Anatolius, the Prefect of Illyricum from c. 344 until 347 was still at the court of Con-stans. On the career of this Anatolius and his distinction from the correspondent of Libanius, see S. Bradbury, "A Sophistic Prefect: Anatolius of Berytus in the Letters of Libanius," *Classical Philology* 95 (2000): 172–86 (esp. 181–84).

awarded Prohaeresius a publicly funded chair in the city.[53] The proconsul was able to do these things on Prohaeresius's behalf "because the emperor was supportive."[54] Given that it comes from Eunapius's pen, the meaning of this phrase is, of course, unclear. Nevertheless, it appears to describe something more significant than a simple bureaucratic necessity. It was not standard procedure for the emperor to approve such a decision. The former proconsul had sent Prohaeresius away without imperial consultation, and proconsuls of Achaea were generally within their powers to exile and recall teachers. They were given substantial autonomy in matters relating to education, and it would be peculiar if a proconsul suddenly needed imperial approval to recall Prohaeresius. It seems instead that Prohaeresius's return was a result of both proconsular and imperial initiative. The latter would certainly be the more important factor.

Constans took more than a passive interest in Prohaeresius's restoration and, in return, he clearly expected Prohaeresius to show his gratitude by supporting the regime. Sometime in the spring or summer of 343, not long after Prohaeresius had shaken off the stigma of exile and returned to Athens, the emperor Constans summoned the rhetor to visit his court in Gaul.[55] Prohaeresius took a part of the spring or summer to travel to Constans and then spent the winter with the emperor in the Gallic provinces. While there, he so pleased the emperor that he was given the great honor of sharing his table. He was also invited to give declamations before the emperor and his courtiers.[56] After his winter in Gaul, Constans sent Prohaeresius to Rome "since he was ambitious to show what sort of men he ruled over."[57] The result, we are told, was that Prohaeresius charmed the people of Rome so much that they erected a life-size bronze statue in his honor.[58] Given the emperor's explicit patronage of Prohaeresius it would have been wise for them to do so. As a final gesture to Prohaeresius before he returned to Athens, the emperor permitted the teacher to ask him for a present. Prohaeresius asked him that several is-

---

53. An incident described by Eunapius suggests that Prohaeresius was awarded the public chair upon his return. When the proconsul visited Athens after Prohaeresius's recall, he called for a rhetorical contest to be held (*Vit. Soph.* 488). As one just returned from exile, Prohaeresius was not allowed to compete (see R. Penella, *Greek Philosophers and Sophists*, 87). Right after this, the proconsul seems to have called a second contest and made a point of announcing that Prohaeresius would be a part of the field. According to Eunapius, Prohaeresius won this competition and silenced his enemies (*Vit. Soph.* 490). The prize is unclear but a publicly funded chair is a possible reward.

54. *Vit. Soph.* 488.

55. The date of 343, proposed on the basis of Himerian evidence by T. D. Barnes, "Himerius and the Fourth Century," *Classical Philology* 82 (1987): 208, seems to be wholly consistent with the evidence found in Eunapius.

56. *Vit. Soph.* 492.

57. Ibid.

58. Ibid.

lands be designated as exclusive grain suppliers to Athens. Constans granted this and also placed Prohaeresius in charge of the Athenian grain supply.[59]

The honors that Constans lavished upon Prohaeresius marked him as a true intellectual superstar. Typically this sort of imperial recognition went to teachers of the imperial family and high-profile intellectuals with the stature of Polemo, Libanius, and Themistius. At this stage in his career, Prohaeresius was a peculiar man to put in such company. Prohaeresius was a sixty-nine-year-old, recently exiled teacher who had only headed his own school for, at most, seven years. The only clear explanation of how such a middling figure shot to the top ranks of teachers in the empire was Constans's desire to recognize and display the Christianity of an Athenian teacher. This factor, which one can be sure Prohaeresius's partisans worked to emphasize to the emperor, explains Constans's efforts to get Prohaeresius recalled to Athens as well as the invitation he extended for Prohaeresius to come to Gaul and Rome. Indeed, even though he tried to characterize Prohaeresius's time at the court of Constans as proof of his remarkable character, Eunapius found it hard to downplay the fact that Constans used his visit to parade Prohaeresius around as a kind of showpiece.[60]

The trip had tangible benefits for Prohaeresius as well. It had come at a crucial time because, despite the emperor's involvement in restoring Prohaeresius, his position in Athens was still not entirely secure. Immediately after his return from exile, the group of teachers who had initially forced him out of the city began working to get him sent away again.[61] Given that the proconsul had just bowed to pressure from the emperor to reinstate the teacher, Prohaeresius's opponents wisely did not try to sway his opinion. Instead, they centered their efforts upon convincing the wealthy members of the Athenian council to work with them to get Prohaeresius sent away again.[62] Eunapius indicates that these were "extreme measures" akin to a defeated army's relying upon "slingers and archers" to win a pitched battle. His classification, however, is a bit unfair. These wealthy men played an important role in the political life of the city, and, when they allied with the city's

---

59. Ibid.

60. Prohaeresius's reception may have resembled the response of Rome's Christian population to the public profession of faith made by the rhetorician Victorinus upon his conversion to Christianity. Augustine describes the event as follows: "Then, as he mounted the platform to make his profession, all who knew him joyfully whispered his name to their neighbors (indeed, who could not have known him?) and a hushed murmur of 'Victorinus, Victorinus' swept across the mouths of all who had gathered. When they saw him, they were quick to let their joy be heard but just as quickly came a hush so that they could hear him speak. He made his declaration of the true faith with splendid confidence, and, seized with love and joy, all would gladly have clutched him to their hearts and taken him with their arms" (*Confessions* 8.2).

61. *Vit. Soph.* 490.

62. Ibid.

teachers, they were still an important group in the city. Though his power trumped theirs, the proconsul of Achaea ignored the wishes of a unified front of teachers and councilors at his peril. The teacher-councilor alliance, then, presented a credible threat to Prohaeresius.[63]

With these events as its background, Prohaeresius's trip to court and the subsequent honors he received secured his position within Athens. They left no question about the degree to which Constans supported the teacher and made it clear that further attempts to remove him would be thwarted by the emperor's personal intervention. For this reason, Constans's explicit intervention on Prohaeresius's behalf upset the regulatory balance in Athenian intellectual politics. Proconsular actions against teachers had usually been taken either in response to major misconduct in the schools or as a reaction to complaints by a large number of councilors and teachers. Now, because of Constans's strong support for Prohaeresius, the proconsul could take no such actions against him, even when other teachers complained. This imposed a strict limitation upon his ability to address a critical issue in his province. Nevertheless, the proconsul had no choice but to act in this way. Constans's protection of Prohaeresius ensured that he and his school now essentially functioned outside of local and provincial control.

Prohaeresius's position was not entirely secure, however. His influence was the result of imperial favor and was subject to the whims of the imperial court. If the wind were to blow differently from Rome, Prohaeresius could not expect that Athenian councilors or his fellow teachers would try to persuade the proconsul to save him. He was a powerful man but not a man who could be secure in his power.

Sources are silent about what happened to Prohaeresius's position after Magnentius overthrew Constans in 350. One would presume that he endured a mediocrity similar to that of Libanius after the death of Julian. Like Libanius, he would have suffered no injury except the loss of his unofficially privileged position and personal influence, but he would now have to be more aware of possible enemies.[64] When Constantius defeated Magnentius, it seems that he did little to restore Prohaeresius to the influential position he had enjoyed under Constans. Our one indication of Prohaeresius's status under Constantius comes from a letter Libanius wrote on behalf of one of Prohaeresius's relatives. In this letter, tentatively dated to 361, Libanius appeals to the governor of Armenia to grant a favor to Prohaeresius's relative Philastrius.[65] The story behind this incident is lost to us, but it seems that the ap-

63. Ibid.
64. Libanius, *Or.* 1.146, describes the challenges he faced as an intellectual who was suddenly deprived of an imperial patron.
65. This is Libanius, *Ep.* 275. Though Constantius died in fall 361 (Ammianus, 21.16 marks the date as October 7, but the accuracy of this has been disputed), this letter surely reflects the

peal was sent by the Antiochene rhetor because Prohaeresius did not have sufficient influence to get the matter decided in Philastrius's favor. Evidently, Libanius now was a more influential patron than Prohaeresius could be.[66]

Despite the diminution of his influence after the death of Constans, it seems that Prohaeresius continued to draw large numbers of students, both pagan and Christian, to his school. His reputation and his network of connections throughout Asia Minor were important reasons for his continued appeal, but his teaching also played an important part in his success. Though he was publicly identified as a Christian teacher of rhetoric, Prohaeresius did little to incorporate Christian elements into life at his school. A sense of this can be gained by looking at the writings of two of his students—Gregory Nazianzen and Basil of Caesarea.[67] Though Gregory and Basil were Christian, the school itself seems to have attracted a mixed population of pagan and Christian students. It may even have had a majority of pagan students. Indeed, although he makes it clear that they had other Christian companions, Gregory remarks that he and Basil were almost unique in attending church regularly.[68]

The curriculum was as traditional as the atmosphere. While Gregory and Basil make no mention of the curriculum that was studied, their own works leave little doubt that the school taught the standard rhetorical curriculum

---

state of things during his reign. Even if Libanius's letter was composed after this date, Philastrius's request for Libanius's help would have been sent in the reign of Constantius. The 361 date, then, should not obscure the fact that the initial correspondence reflects Prohaeresius's position during that reign.

66. This could be due to the fact that Prohaeresius was living in a region of the empire distant from Armenia while Libanius was geographically (and hence politically) closer to the governor. Although Libanius's prominent mention of his name indicates that Prohaeresius was still a figure of known importance, the Athenian teacher was clearly not as powerful as he had been under Constans.

67. Though neither man ever makes it clear that he studied under Prohaeresius, there is abundant evidence to suggest that both did. Both Socrates and Sozomen indicate this (Soc. 4.26; Soz. 6.17), and there are a number of suggestions in Gregory's writings that support this contention. The two men were fellow students and, consequently, wherever Gregory studied, Basil did as well. The first link between Gregory and Prohaeresius is the epitaph Gregory wrote to honor the teacher (*Epitaphia* 5). While this may not signify much, it is worth noting that Gregory also wrote epigrams in honor of Craterius, another of his teachers. In addition, Gregory mentions that a group of Armenians were among his classmates—it would be surprising if these men studied under anyone besides Prohaeresius. Another possible support of the view that Gregory and Basil studied under Prohaeresius is the similarity between the initiation ritual Basil went through (*Panegyric on Basil* 16) and that described by Eunapius. This may have been standard fare in the Athenian schools of the time, however (cf. Olympiodorus of Thebes, fr. 28 = Photius, *Bib.* cod. 80.177–78).

68. Gregory even remarks of Athens, "Hurtful as Athens was to others in spiritual things, and this is of no slight consequence for the pious . . . it is hard to avoid being carried away by [the gods'] devotees and adherents." (*Panegyric on Basil* 21).

of the time.[69] Both were quite skillful in their use of non-Christian rhetorical allusions, when the situation called for such things. Given their later devotion to the traditional educational curriculum and their use of materials gained from it, one can assume that they were both taught in the traditional way. This suggests that Prohaeresius did not adapt his curriculum to de-emphasize the pagan elements within it. Despite his publicly proclaimed Christianity, Prohaeresius's school taught rhetoric according to the same curriculum as his pagan rivals.

PROHAERESIUS AND JULIAN

Prohaeresius was something of a nonentity under Constantius, but he quickly became prominent again when Julian assumed power. Unlike the fame he had enjoyed under Constans, Prohaeresius's new renown did not arise from imperial amity. In fact, Julian was uniquely ill disposed towards the sophist. Julian revealed his opinion of the teacher in a letter he wrote to Prohaeresius soon after his entry into Constantinople. The letter reads as follows:

> To Prohaeresius
>
> Why indeed would I not think to greet the noble Prohaeresius, a man who discharges speeches upon the youth just as rivers discharge floods upon the plains; one who imitates Pericles in his speeches except that he does not throw Greece into confusion and utterly confound it? Indeed, you ought not wonder if I am evincing Laconic brevity towards you. For while it is suitable for you, a wise man, to compose long and impressive speeches, few words will suffice from me to you. You must know also that a great many affairs are inundating me from all quarters. With respect to the causes of my return, if you are going to write a history, I will report back the most specific of details and, by giving you letters, I will produce official documentation [of the incident]. If, however, you are determined to persist in scholastic declamations and exercises until old age, you will perhaps not blame my silence.[70]

In the past, this letter has been understood as a brash and unsolicited request by Julian for Prohaeresius to write a history of his victory over Constantius. With this interpretation there follows an argument that Julian actually continued to favor Prohaeresius through the first part of his reign.[71]

---

69. See chapter 1 for Basil's advocacy of the utility of the standard educational curriculum in the teaching of Christian youths.

70. Julian, *Letter* 31 in the edition of J. Bidez, ed. and trans., *L'Empereur Julien: Oeuvres Complètes*, vol. 1 (Paris, 1972). The translation is my own.

71. For this view see Bidez, *L'Empereur Julien*, vol. 1, 2.36–37. R. Browning, *The Emperor Julian* (Berkeley and Los Angeles, 1976), 172; and G. Bowersock, *Julian the Apostate* (Cambridge, Mass., 1978), 64.

Those who make these assumptions ignore the tone of the letter. When it is read closely, it becomes clear that Julian's letter is, in fact, a highly sarcastic piece written in response to a congratulatory letter sent by Prohaeresius to the new emperor.[72] It was relatively common for rhetoricians to send letters and/or speeches to new emperors. A surviving letter of this type was sent to Julian by Libanius. The short piece reads "To Julian: I have sent you a small oration about great events. You certainly have it in your power to make the oration even greater, if you give me the material for it to grow. If you do, you will show that you regard me as a craftsman of panegyric; if not, you will give reason to think the opposite."[73] It is likely that whatever Prohaeresius sent was framed in similar terms.

In the case of Prohaeresius, a man who owed his position to imperial favor, it would be surprising if he did not send some sort of nervous correspondence to congratulate Julian on his victory. This seems especially likely because Julian's response was composed after his arrival in Constantinople in late 361. He must have entered the capital and found a stack of congratulatory correspondence waiting for him (much of which had been sent by men who had been closely connected to Constantius and now feared for their lives under the new sovereign). An additional urgency was attached to these letters when, following Julian's arrival in the capital, the trials of Constantius's former supporters began in Chalcedon.[74] Indeed, since Prohaeresius asked to hear of Julian's return to Constantinople, these trials could even have been the reason he chose to write in the first place.

When he saw it, the letter from Prohaeresius must have caught Julian's eye. As Julian had spent time in Athens as a student,[75] he would have known Prohaeresius, been aware of his religious background, and acutely understood his ties to the regimes of Constans and Constantius. It is unlikely that any of these things impressed him favorably. Indeed, Julian's first line, "Why indeed would I not think to greet the noble Prohaeresius," seems to be a subtle attack upon Prohaeresius's character as well as a feigned apology to his "friend" Prohaeresius for not being the one to write first. This was mere politeness and neither Prohaeresius nor Julian would have thought to read any warmth into this rather icy greeting.

Julian then comments upon Prohaeresius's oratorical productivity. Here he seems to include something of a warning to the teacher. After mention-

---

72. Libanius *Ep.* 369 (writing to Julian upon his elevation to the rank of Caesar) gives a good idea of what such a letter of congratulations could have looked like. Both the length and the panegyrical tone would be expected in Prohaeresius's letter as well.

73. *Ep.* 610. The accompanying speech was *Or.* 13.

74. For the trials see Ammianus 22.3.1–12. Ammianus indicates that these took place shortly after Julian's entry into the city on December 11, 361.

75. Julian's studies in Athens: Libanius, *Or.* 18.27–28; Gregory Nazianzen, *Or.* 5.23; Eunapius, *Vit. Soph.* 475.

ing the volume of work Prohaeresius produced, Julian compares him to a
Pericles who does not "throw Greece into confusion." This seems to be not
a playful allusion but rather a piece of praise for Prohaeresius's behaving
himself during Julian's conflict with Constantius and, probably, also a notice
to the old Christian teacher to continue to refrain from causing trouble for
the new regime.[76] Julian then makes another cold apology for being "laconic"
by telling Prohaeresius that, while a rhetorician is in the business of composing long works for the emperor's benefit, he ought to be satisfied with
only a few words in return.

At this point in the letter, Julian begins directly responding to the content of Prohaeresius's original correspondence. Indeed, the first line is a
response to the rhetorician's request that Julian tell him something about
his military campaign and victorious return to Constantinople. Julian re-
sponds to Prohaeresius's request for information with more of the chilli-
ness that typifies this letter. He tells Prohaeresius that this information will
be given to him only if the rhetorician agrees to write a history of the campaign. This was, of course, the farthest thing from Prohaeresius's mind.
Whereas a speech in praise of a new emperor was a conventional way of showing one's allegiance to the new regime,[77] a history was a different sort of
undertaking that involved a greater investment of time and personal credibility.[78] Julian surely knew this and he must have amused himself no end
at the absurd thought of an openly Christian rhetor and famous client of
the previous regime writing a history of the young pagan emperor's cam-

76. I thank John Matthews and an anonymous reviewer for this nuanced interpretation of
the Pericles reference.

77. The career of Themistius amply illustrates this. At the beginning of every regime from
Jovian to Theodosius I, it seems that Themistius offered a speech in support of the new emperor that mixed in criticism of the previous regime. On this, see P. Heather and D. Moncur,
trans., *Politics, Philosophy, and Empire in the Fourth Century: Select Orations of Themistius* (Liverpool,
2001), 24–38.

78. Julian himself notes the difference by contrasting a history with "scholastic declamations and exercises." Here too the career of Themistius, who also was a notable supporter of
Constantius, is informative. In Julian, Themistius found an unsympathetic audience for his
rhetorical flattery. The emperor's *Letter to Themistius*, which was written in response to a letter
of congratulations sent by Themistius in 355, chides the addressee for his exaggeration. This
text, which was written when Julian was in a far more politically vulnerable position than he
found himself in 361, shows Julian's polite disdain for the rhetoric of a supporter of Constantius. Once Julian was in power, this disdain may have become less polite. At any rate, it seems
that Themistius's support of the previous regime doomed him to a relative obscurity from which
even the best rhetoric did not enable him to escape (on this, see P. Heather and D. Moncur, *Select Orations of Themistius*, 138–42). Prohaeresius's rhetorical flattery, it seems, received a similar response. The suggestion that Prohaeresius write a history may well have been Julian's attempt to toy with Prohaeresius by offering him the opportunity to compose a less ephemeral
testimony of his allegiance to the new regime. A history, after all, is presumably harder to re-
tract than a speech.

paign to topple Constantius.[79] Julian surely did not think Prohaeresius would accept the task.

At the same time, Julian does not pretend to give Prohaeresius any incentive to write. In the letter, he promises Prohaeresius neither official patronage nor even friendly correspondence in exchange for his history. Instead, Julian only agrees to provide Prohaeresius with access to the letters related to the affair and to forward some official documents connected with the civil war in order to help him write.[80] If Prohaeresius should choose not to write the work, which Julian must have assumed would be his response, then Julian tells the rhetorician in no uncertain terms that no more correspondence would be sent from the palace. He could not be more blunt in conveying his dislike of Prohaeresius.

Presumably drawing from Eunapius's *History*, the *Suda* confirms Julian's dislike of Prohaeresius. "Julian [the Apostate], although he was engaged in such important matters, had a strong streak of rhetorical ambition. He expressed special admiration for the sophist of Antioch who was named Libanius. On the one hand, perhaps, he was really applauding him, but he also honored someone else in order to cause pain to the great sophist Prohaeresius."[81] Between Julian's sarcastic letter and this notice in the *Suda*, it is clear that Prohaeresius was not a friend of the new emperor. The symbolic importance of being a Christian rhetorician had earned him praise in the previous regime, but under a pagan emperor, the same identification made him a target. ·

This change in imperial favor did not affect Prohaeresius adversely, nor did it change the way he ran his school. Kidnappings and other mischief seem to have remained his normal way of recruiting students. Indeed, Eunapius, our source for Prohaeresius's agreement with the Aegean ship captain, arrived to study under him in 362. In spite of these questionable activities, however, it does not seem that there was any further movement among his rivals to get Prohaeresius sent away. One cannot know for certain why this was so, but there are a number of potential explanations. It had been nearly twenty years since Prohaeresius's exile and more than fifteen since he was awarded Julianus's chair. After such a long time, his rivals may have become accus-

---

79. This proposal would have been all the more shocking because Julian had only recently professed his paganism openly. Since Julian did this while in Constantinople (Ammianus 22.5), Prohaeresius's letter would have been sent before the announcement. The Christian rhetor then would have been quite shocked to read Julian's reply.

80. Among these may have been the letter against Constantius that was sent by Julian to the senate (Ammianus 21.10) and the exchanges of letters between Julian and Constantius that began in winter 360 and continued throughout 361 (for these see Ammianus 20.8.9).

81. *Suda* Λ 486. The same passage is paraphrased in the *Suda* entry on Prohaeresius (Π 2375). It states that Prohaeresius "flourished in the time of Julian, at the same time as the sophist Libanius. And Julian marveled greatly at Libanius, so that he could cause pain to Prohaeresius."

tomed to the power and influence that Prohaeresius was able to wield and adapted their recruitment practices to compensate for his dominance of certain regions. It is also possible that the old teacher had agreed to let his students be the *akroatai* of his rivals so that Prohaeresius no longer represented a great threat to them. In addition, Prohaeresius was now in his mid-eighties. An attack against so old a man may have seemed both cruel and unnecessary. Not only was it unlikely that he would live much longer, but he also may already have turned over the day-to-day teaching and administration of his school to his *hetairoi*. This was a common move among teachers. If Prohaeresius had followed this pattern, and there is no reason to suppose that he did not, then his rivals would have little to gain by forcing him out.[82]

In the short term, Julian took no action against Prohaeresius or any other Christian teacher. It seems, however, that he had planned a legislative program that would effectively cripple these men and their schools. This culminated in his famous law prohibiting Christians from teaching. This law, and the larger legislative program of which it was a part, had a specific impact on the career of Prohaeresius. Before considering his specific case, however, it will be informative to examine the progression and universal intent of Julian's legislation.

Julian's legislative attempt to redefine the relationship between the imperial government and professors began with a law issued on June 17, 362. The text of the law itself reads:

> Masters of studies and teachers ought to first excel in personal character, then in eloquence. But since I myself am not able to be present in all the individual municipalities, I command that, if anyone wishes to teach,[83] he shall not leap forth suddenly and rashly, but he shall be approved by the judgment of the municipal senate and shall obtain the decree of the decurions with the consent and agreement of the best citizens. For this decree shall be referred to me for consideration so that such teachers may enter upon their pursuits with a certain higher honor because of our judgment.[84]

Since this is the only preserved law of Julian that relates to the regulation of education, there is a strong temptation to assume that this is the actual text of his law prohibiting Christians from teaching. But this law must rather

---

82. Philostratus states that the second-century teacher Damianus of Ephesus stopped teaching full-time when he got old (*Vit. Soph.* 606). The fourth-century philosopher Aedesius was another teacher who remained head of his school but stopped teaching because of his old age (Eunapius, *Vit. Soph.* 474). The same was true of Plutarch the scholarch in the early fifth century and his protégé Proclus in the later decades of the same century (a process suggested by *Vit. Proc.* 12 and discussed in more detail in chapter 4).

83. Latin: *si quisque docere vult*.

84. *C. Th.* 13.3.5 (trans. Pharr, with slight revisions).

be seen as an act of legislation distinct from the teaching edict.[85] When taken independently, the law makes no mention of Christians. It fails to mention the prohibition of teaching, does not call for the removal of "immoral" teachers, and neglects to establish any procedures for doing such a thing. Instead, the law requires a formal certification of all men teaching in the empire and, most importantly, it requires that information on all of these individuals be forwarded to the imperial court. There, presumably, officials would be delegated the responsibility of collecting this information and making it available for review by the emperor.

This was necessary because, according to all evidence, no such central record of teachers existed. Records of which teachers were eligible for liturgical immunities had been kept locally as far back as the time of Antoninus Pius.[86] Constantine's extension of the exemption from liturgies to all teachers in the empire forced localities to keep even more detailed records of the people who were teaching in their communities.[87] Liturgies were locally delegated duties and localities themselves were responsible for keeping track of the exemptions held by teachers. Though imperial officials did maintain records of individuals in each city who enjoyed exemptions, there is no evidence that this was ever collated into an empire-wide list of active teachers.[88] Indeed, until the reign of Julian, they would have had no need of such records.

While such a list would have had little significance before the 360s, the records his law created would have given Julian a sort of checklist of teachers (and their character evaluations). This, in turn, could be used to ensure that the actions he took against Christian teaching were truly comprehensive. Without such a list, a law banning Christian teaching would have been unenforceable. Except in the most conspicuous cases, Julian would not have known the identities of the Christian teachers in the empire. By establishing a process through which the imperial government could collect the names of all professors, the law of June 362 laid the groundwork for his subsequent action.

---

85. The difference between the Julianic law and the law found in the *Theodosian Code* has been described by J. Matthews, *Laying Down the Law: A Study of the Theodosian Code* (New Haven, 2000), 274–77; and T. Banchich, "Julian's School Laws: *Cod. Theod.* 13.3.5 and *Ep.* 42," *The Ancient World* 24 (1993): 5–14.

86. As per *Dig.* 27.1.6.10. See V. Nutton, "Two Notes on Immunities: *Digest* 27.1.6.10 and 11," *Journal of Roman Studies* 61 (1971): 52–63.

87. See chapter 2 for a discussion of this law, *C. Th.* 13.3.1.

88. For an excellent study of liturgies in a local context see C. Drecoll, *Die Liturgien im römischen Kaiserreich des 3. und 4. Jh. n. Chr.* (Stuttgart, 1997). It seems that lists of exempted people were maintained not only by municipalities but also by professional guilds. The ship owners' guild, for example, was required by Hadrian to certify the exemptions of its members (Justinian, *Digest* 50.6.6).

Despite its eventual use, this law probably would not have seemed particularly unjust at the time. For one thing, the fourth century was a time of increased administrative centralization in the Roman world.[89] Julian's act would have seemed a part of this trend. In addition, though this law cemented in legislation a certification procedure for all the teachers in the empire, the standards it appeared to set for certification had long been accepted in the Roman world. Moral uprightness had been an important qualification for teachers since at least the time of Quintilian.[90] When Julian's law established this as a universally applicable standard for judging who could claim to be a teacher, it was in step with convention. In fact, by creating a specific criterion upon which to evaluate a man's claim to the exemptions due a teacher, the law could actually be seen as beneficial to both teachers and town councils.

While the law seemed benign enough, its malignant intent quickly became clear. Once he had the list of teachers (or even a partial list of teachers) and a description of their character, Julian could now effectively enforce a ban on Christian teachers. The ban itself was issued between July 18 and mid-September 362.[91] Given the administrative challenges of collecting information from localities in the empire, a date in the late summer is most likely.

The text of the teaching law is lost, but a letter of Julian that describes the intent and general workings of the legislation does survive. This letter makes it apparent that the ban was a logical continuation of the idea expressed in the certification legislation of June 362. It must be remembered that, in Julian's earlier law, his certification process privileged personal virtue above even professional ability. Julian's teaching edict built upon this base by defining personal virtue in a new and unexpected way. By Julian's reasoning, the virtuous teacher taught only ideas he believed to be true.[92] This meant that a teacher who taught the traditional school curriculum would have to believe the truth of the pagan religious ideas inherent in this curriculum. The clever emperor then left Christians with a choice: "Either do not teach the things which you do not think honorable or, if you wish to teach, first persuade [your] students that neither Homer nor Hesiod nor any one of these, the authors about whom you lecture and explain, is guilty of any impiety."[93] This choice between God and profession, so simply put by Julian,

89. For a concise description of this process, see A. H. M. Jones, *The Later Roman Empire, 284–602* (Norman, 1964), 401–6.

90. As J. Matthews has pointed out (*Laying Down the Law,* 276 n. 60), this idea was concisely expressed by Qunitilian, *Inst. Or.* 12.1.1, but the notion itself far preceded him.

91. Banchich, "Julian's School Laws," 13.

92. On this idea, see Averil Cameron, *Christianity and the Rhetoric of Empire: The Development of a Christian Discourse* (Berkeley and Los Angeles, 1991), 138.

93. Julian, *Ep.* 61 (Bidez-Cumont). This is the *Ep.* 42 to which Banchich, "Julian's School Laws," refers passim. He is taking his numbers from the Hertlein edition, not that of Bidez-Cumont.

was not really a choice at all. We know of no Christian teachers who chose to keep teaching under these restrictions. This is probably just what Julian expected to happen, at least initially.

The emperor's intent for this law was straightforward. His goal was to eliminate Christian teachers and send all students, both Christian and pagan, to pagan teachers. These teachers would then be expected to emphasize the pagan religious aspects of the traditional curriculum, which Christian teachers downplayed. In the emperor's mind, this type of education would guide any student, regardless of his religious background, to a belief in paganism.[94]

Despite all of the malevolent genius Julian put into the teaching edict, the shrewdest part of its implementation involved Prohaeresius. Eunapius is uncharacteristically terse about how Julian's teaching laws affected Prohaeresius. He says only that Prohaeresius "was shut out of the teaching because it was thought he was a Christian."[95] Eunapius's relative silence in the *Lives of the Sophists* obscures the much more compelling story[96] preserved in Jerome's *Chronicle*. It reads as follows: "Prohaeresius the Athenian sophist abandoned his school of his own accord after the enactment of the law which forbade Christians from teaching the liberal arts. This was in spite of the fact that Julian had made an exception for him so he could teach as a Christian."[97]

On the surface, Julian's exemption for Prohaeresius looks like an act of charity done for a friend who would be adversely affected by the teaching edict. There is no doubt that Julian intended this to look like an act of compassion, but in this case, there was no genuine good feeling behind it. The emperor extended this offer to make the law look less oppressive to Christians. However, even in making the offer of an exemption, Julian knew that

---

94. This reflects Julian's own biography. The future emperor was first taught classical texts by Christian teachers. Some of these, like Mardonius, were teachers capable of refined thought (for Mardonius, see *Misopogon* 252a–254c, W. C. Wright, ed. and trans., *Julian*, vol. 2 [Cambridge, Mass., 1913], a revision based on C. Hertlein's Teubner text, *Juliani imperatoris quae supersunt* [Leipzig, 1875–76]; and G. Bowersock, *Julian the Apostate*, 24). Others, like the eunuchs who kept guard over Julian in Cappadocia, were less able (Eunapius famously derides them in *Vit. Soph.* 473). It is upon the latter group that one should probably pin responsibility for Julian's idea of "immoral" Christian teachers. Much to Julian's dismay, these men carefully constructed their lessons to prevent the prince from thinking seriously about the pagan content of the texts he was reading. This was only undone when Julian was allowed to begin studying classical philosophical texts with the pagan Maximus of Ephesus. Then, in response to the "correct" training he received in that school, Julian became a convert to paganism. See Libanius, *Or.* 12.34 and 13.12, for a discussion of Julian's conversion and its significance. See also G. Bowersock, *Julian the Apostate*, 29 ff.

95. *Vit. Soph.* 493.

96. It is conceivable that he spoke more about Prohaeresius and Julian's teaching edict in his now-fragmentary *Histories*.

97. Jerome, *Chronicle* 242–43.

Prohaeresius would probably not accept it. As one of the most prominent Christian teachers, Prohaeresius would have destroyed all personal credibility if he had continued to teach while other Christians were forced out. It is likely that this offer, like the emperor's earlier request for Prohaeresius to write a history, reflects Julian's low opinion of the teacher's integrity. In a way that parallels his earlier invitation, Julian gave the teacher two options.[98] He could keep teaching and break ranks with other Christian professors, or he could refuse Julian's exemption and stop teaching. The first option, while something of a propaganda victory for the emperor, would have been a personal setback for Prohaeresius. Given his symbolic importance to Christians, they would not have been particularly forgiving of his compromise. Prohaeresius's only real choice was to stop teaching voluntarily in solidarity with others affected by the ban. If this happened, it was no great loss for Julian. He would still have accomplished his original goal of making the schools better able to facilitate conversions to paganism.

A number of questions have been raised about what exactly happened to Prohaeresius and his school after he turned down Julian's offer of an exemption. These problems arise because Eunapius's arrival at the school of Prohaeresius seems to have happened at almost the same time that Julian's teaching edict was being sent out to the cities.[99] This is a rather strange convergence of events because, if Prohaeresius were forbidden from teaching, it would presumably be impossible for Eunapius to be enrolled at his school.

Proposed resolutions to this confusion range from revisions of Eunapius's text to a new chronology of his life.[100] Such exotic explanations are unnecessary. A close reading of Eunapius's own account of his arrival in Athens explains away this apparent paradox. When Eunapius arrived at Piraeus, he and the rest of his shipmates were handed over to Prohaeresius. Prohaeresius immediately transferred the crowd of new arrivals to the care of his relatives[101] so that they could be housed for the night. In the morning, Prohaeresius's

98. To this day scholars have been taken in by Julian's mischief and have seen this exemption not as a cynical ploy on the emperor's part but as an act of genuine goodwill (see for example R. Browning, *The Emperor Julian*, 172). Browning also suggests that *Confessions* 8.5 raises the possibility that Julian made a similar offer to Victorinus. It seems, instead, that Victorinus had merely obeyed Julian's existing law and was not offered a special exemption. Augustine is, however, not clear on this.

99. Against this see R. Goulet, "Eunape de Sardes," 60–72. He proposes a date of 364. For the 362 date, see T. Banchich, "On Goulet's Chronology of Eunapius' Life and Works," *Journal of Hellenic Studies* 107 (1987): 164–67.

100. See, for example, R. Goulet, "Eunape de Sardes," 60–72; C. Fornara, "Eunapius' *Epidemia* in Athens," *Classical Quarterly* 39 (1989): 517–23; R. Penella, *Greek Philosophers and Sophists*, 2–4; T. Banchich, "Eunapius in Athens," *Phoenix* 50 (1996): 304–11. Also T. Banchich, "Julian's School Laws," 10–11.

101. συγγενεῖς ἴδιοι. Unlike other occasions when familial vocabulary is used to describe members of a school, it seems likely that this term refers to actual relations of Prohaeresius.

students came and took the new arrivals through a hazing process before they swore an oath of allegiance to the school.[102] At this time, Eunapius was quite sick and could not go along with the other students. He spent this day and a number of following days recovering from his illness. He did not see Prohaeresius once in all that time.[103] Then, when the teacher learned of his recovery, Prohaeresius sent the "strongest and most noble of his students" to initiate Eunapius in the gentlest way possible.[104] Throughout all of this Prohaeresius had no direct contact with Eunapius. Instead, he preferred to delegate tasks to those relatives and older students who were affiliated with the school.

In this brief sketch, Eunapius paints a picture of a teacher who had little contact with his new students. Some of this detachment may have been due to the fact that Eunapius had not yet gone through the initiation procedure. Most of it, however, was probably due to Prohaeresius's age (he was eighty-six or eighty-seven at this point). As was mentioned above, teachers who reached that age were often just the titular heads of their schools. Real responsibility for almost all of the teaching done in their schools had been given to members of their inner circle.

Eunapius's experience confirms this impression. Once Eunapius was in school, it does not seem that he had much more direct contact with his famous "teacher." Eunapius says that he studied under Prohaeresius for five years,[105] but aside from the teacher's special care in delegating strong students for his initiation, there is little evidence of any personal bond between the men.[106] This stands in stark contrast to the way Eunapius presents his relationship with Chrysanthius, his teacher of grammar and philosophy. This was a true friendship in which both men spent a great deal of time together and expressed their affection for one another.[107] Furthermore, Eunapius's writings relied heavily upon Chrysanthius as a source for narrative material

102. *Vit. Soph.* 486. The hazing ritual is also mentioned by Gregory Nazianzen, *Or.* 19.16. For more on this hazing process see E. Watts, "The Late Antique Student's Perspective on Education Life," *New England Classical Journal* 27.2 (2000): 73–77.

103. *Vit. Soph.* 486. Eunapius says that "as his sickness got worse, he was wasting away having seen neither Athens nor Prohaeresius."

104. οἱ κρατίστοι καὶ γενναιοτάτοι τῶν ὁμιλητῶν.

105. In my view, T. Banchich ("Eunapius in Athens") has fully refuted the textual emendation proposed by C. Fornara ("Eunapius' *Epidemia*") that would drastically reduce the amount of time Eunapius spent in Athens.

106. His mention that "Eunapius was loved by Prohaeresius like his own child" (*Vit. Soph.* 493) seems more an evocation of the traditional familial language associated with late antique education than evidence of a close personal relationship between the men. For more on the use of this language see chapter 1.

107. As noted by an anonymous reader, some of their closeness would have been due to the fact that family ties linked the two men. Chrysanthius had married Eunapius's cousin Melite (*Vit. Soph.* 477).

about the philosophical circles of Iamblichus and Aedesius.[108] By contrast, none of the material about Athenian academic life is explicitly derived from Prohaeresius. Instead, Eunapius's account relies upon his own experiences in the city and, when another source is named, the testimony of Tuscianus.[109] Prohaeresius is mentioned as a source just once—as a witness to verify his own age.[110] Indeed, Eunapius seems to have used Tuscianus even for information about the events of Prohaeresius's life. This is interesting because Tuscianus was one of the *hetairoi* of both Julianus and Prohaeresius. It has been assumed that he left teaching for a career in government in the 350s,[111] but it seems more likely that he was still an *hetairos* of Prohaeresius in 362. In fact, one is left with the impression that Eunapius, though formally a student of Prohaeresius, was actually taught by Tuscianus most of the time. This would explain the closeness of their relationship and the fact that they remained in contact long after Eunapius left Athens.[112] It would also explain why Eunapius classifies Tuscianus as one "who would have been Prohaeresius, if Prohaeresius had not existed."[113] This must mean that, had Prohaeresius not been the head of the school, Tuscianus would have taken this position and the honor that came with it.

Eunapius describes a school in which, perhaps aside from lectures to his *hetairoi*, Prohaeresius was doing little actual teaching. The little bit he did do

---

108. See *Vit. Soph.* 458, 477, 481. For a discussion of Eunapius's sources see R. Penella, *Greek Philosophers and Sophists*, 23–32 (esp. 30–32); and J. Dillon, "Iamblichus of Chalcis," *Aufstieg und Niedergang der Römischen Welt* 2.36.2 (1987): 874.

109. Tuscianus was the source for the events of Julianus's trial (*Vit. Soph.* 484–85) and Prohaeresius's return from exile (*Vit. Soph.* 488).

110. *Vit. Soph.* 485. It is possible that Prohaeresius had described his encounter with the Eleusinian hierophant (*Vit. Soph.* 493), but it seems more likely that Tuscianus was Eunapius's source.

111. R. Penella, *Greek Philosophers and Sophists*, 137–38, 138 n. 49. Penella's identification of Tuscianus with the assessor of the praetorian prefect of Illyricum is based upon Libanius's comments about the latter's rhetorical ability (*Ep.* 345.3; 348.4; 353.1). A. H. M. Jones, J. R. Martindale, and J. Morris, *Prosopography of the Later Roman Empire*, vol. 1 (Cambridge, 1971), however, distinguish this Tuscianus from the rhetorician, and tentatively propose that the prefect be identified with a *Comes Orientis* mentioned in a law dating from 381 (*C. Th.* 16.2.26). This seems to me to be more likely. As for the idea that the lack of a full biography of Tuscianus in the *Vit. Soph.* was due to his later career in administration, it need only be added that he may also have been denied a biography because he never was able to establish himself successfully as a teacher in Athens. This seems to have been the reason that Eunapius says so little about Hephaestion. One need only recall Libanius's comment about the difficulty a perpetual student had in getting a teaching position in Athens to know that it is very possible that Eunapius could not write anything substantial about Tuscianus without offending his friend.

112. It also eliminates the necessity of explaining how Eunapius, who does not seem to have traveled widely, would have gotten to know Tuscianus so well if the latter man was serving in an administrative post.

113. *Vit. Soph.* 488.

was presumably not for the newest students to arrive at his school. It follows that Eunapius and the other students who arrived in 362 could continue to be taught at the school even after Prohaeresius had decided to stop teaching in response to Julian's edict. It is likely, then, that Julian's action forced Prohaeresius to assume a purely administrative role at the school. He also must have been forced to resign from the publicly funded chair he had held since the 340s. The edict did not, however, close Prohaeresius's school.[114] Eunapius and others could have continued to study at the old teacher's school under the tutelage of *hetairoi* like Tuscianus.

If Julian's law on Christian teachers did not immediately affect Prohaeresius and his school, the old teacher was surely concerned about the long-term impact of the emperor's measure. The personal reputation of Prohaeresius drew students to his school and, if it were known that there was no possibility that students would hear him teach, few would have an incentive to enroll. For some Christian teachers at this time, the response to the emperor's edict was simple—they avoiding its teeth by creating a teaching curriculum filled with texts presenting Christian themes. Indeed, it seems that Victorinus, Prohaeresius's Latin-speaking contemporary, turned to the exposition of Christian themes after Julian's law.[115] The Apollinarii father and son tandem did the same.[116] However, given his age, the small native Athenian Christian community, and his reliance upon the recruitment of both pagan and Christian students, Prohaeresius attempted no such radical revision of his curriculum. Besides, if, as it seems, the majority of the teaching at his school was done by his pagan *hetairoi,* they would not have been willing to teach a Christian curriculum. For all of these reasons, Prohaeresius decided to wait out the edict. This carried a risk, however. Despite older teachers' reliance upon their *hetairoi* for teaching help, they were still expected to hold some classes with their most promising students. If Prohaeresius could not do this, he could expect his school to slowly whither away—just as Julian would have wanted.

Prohaeresius was unable to teach from the fall of 362 until the early part of 363. There was simply nothing that he could do. After turning down Julian's exemption offer, Prohaeresius could not teach furtively. There was also

114. The edict does seem to have closed schools with fewer *hetairoi.* The law of Jovian that overturned Julian's edict allows teachers to reoccupy vacant teaching spaces (*C. Th.* 13.3.6). These were presumably the sites of smaller schools that less accomplished Christian teachers were forced to abandon in the face of Julian's law.

115. This is based upon the idea of P. Hadot (*Marius Victorinus, recherches sur sa vie et ses oeuvres* [Paris, 1971], 286) that Victorinus's commentary on the Pauline epistles dates from 362–63. See also T. Banchich, "Julian's School Laws," 11.

116. For the Apollinarii see Socrates, *HE* 3.16, and Sozomen, *HE* 5.18. T. Banchich's concern over whether these men were public or private teachers ("Julian's School Laws," 11) seems unnecessary, given the fact that Julian's law was to have applied to *quisque docere vult*—anyone who wishes to teach.

no chance that he could assemble local support to change his fate. Julian had singled Prohaeresius out in this matter, and it would be treasonous to try to overturn such a clear expression of imperial will. Bereft of his teaching post, Prohaeresius was left to anxiously hope that Julian would quickly pass from the scene. Eunapius explains that, despite his Christianity, the teacher consulted the hierophant of Eleusis during this time and asked about the duration of a law of Julian's that gave pagans a favorable tax status.[117] Because Prohaeresius was legally prohibited from asking for information about the length of Julian's reign, this was not really a question about taxes. It was instead a thinly veiled demand for information about the length of time the emperor had left to live. Prohaeresius was certainly pleased to learn that tax reform was coming.

We are not informed about Prohaeresius's reaction when the hierophant's prediction of Julian's quick death came true. For all the controversy that surrounded Julian's reign, the emperor's actions against Christian teachers ended rather innocuously. Julian died on campaign in 363 and, in January of 364, the emperor Jovian issued a law overturning Julian's teaching edict with the simple provision that "If anyone is found equally suitable in character and eloquence to educate students, let him either set up a new teaching space or return to one that has been abandoned."[118] When Jovian's edict was issued, Prohaeresius was able to resume teaching. He continued to do so, without incident, until his death in 366 at the age of ninety.[119] His funeral oration was given by his former rival Diophantus and, except for Eunapius's account of his life, he passed quietly out of history.[120]

The turns of Prohaeresius's career reveal a great deal about how political relationships evolved in the Athenian schools of the fourth century. Nevertheless, it is only when we turn our attention to the later stage of his teaching career that we begin to see the increased role that religion played in the educational disputes of the time. In Athens, religious concerns had not been a part of educational politics until Constans began to support Prohaeresius

117. *Vit. Soph.* 493. Though it was not exactly orthodox Christian practice, there is no inherent problem with assuming that someone who identifies himself as a Christian would consult a pagan priest in a time of extreme emotional distress. For something of a parallel, note Zacharias Scholasticus, *Life of Severus* 37–39.

118. The law is *C. Th.* 13.3.6. It reads: *Impp. Valentinianus et Valens AA. ad Mamertinum praefectum praetorio. si qui erudiendis adulescentibus vita pariter et facundia idoneus erit, vel novum instituat auditorium vel repetat intermissum. dat. iii id. ian. divo ioviano et varroniano conss. (364 ian. 11).* Though the law states that it was issued under Valens and Valentinian, the date places it in the reign of Jovian.

119. *Vit. Soph.* 493.

120. Ibid., 494.

in the 340s. This support came only because of the teacher's willingness to demonstrate his Christianity publicly. It was in no way contingent upon his introduction of Christian themes in his teaching or a de-emphasis on pagan aspects of the standard curriculum. In exchange for the emperor's clear support, Prohaeresius was only to serve as a rather conspicuous example of a culturally accomplished Christian. This did not differ from the favor the imperial court sometimes showed to Christians in the civil service. Nevertheless, because such highly accomplished Christian teachers seem to have been something of a rarity in the early 340s, Prohaeresius was an important symbol of Christian accomplishment to the emperor's subjects. By attracting such favoritism, Prohaeresius's religion made his position in Athens untouchable. For the first time, an Athenian teacher's religion insulated him from being called to account by his fellow teachers, the Athenian council, and the proconsul.

Julian's law on Christian teaching represents a second sort of religious intrusion into the management of the Athenian schools. This law, for the first time, specifically defined education in religious terms—in pagan religious terms.[121] Prohaeresius, as a Christian teacher, was unable to teach under this law because, in the mind of the sovereign, his Christianity prevented him from correctly emphasizing the pagan elements in the curriculum. This action was very different from Constans's overt patronage of Prohaeresius. Constans expressed his favoritism of Prohaeresius in a way consistent with established custom. He granted Prohaeresius honors and made sure that his position in the city was secure. In no way were his actions designed to harm any other teacher or affect the content of teaching. Though dangerous insofar as it exempted one person from the controls of the political system, this favoritism did not revolutionize education in the city.

Julian, on the other hand, took action that was directly intended to limit the options of Christian teachers. More significantly, under Julian's program, the goal of education also changed. In Julian's redefined system, education was supposed to teach students about the pagan gods and convince them of the correctness of pagan religion. Education became a tool to promote religious conversions. This obliterated the religious inclusiveness of the old system. Of all the disquieting elements of Julian's legislation, this must have been the one that caused the most reaction.

The experience that Prohaeresius had under this law shows why Julian's educational redefinition so upset people.[122] Despite his importance as a sym-

---

121. For the religious significance of Julian's law interpreted in a different context, see S. Elm, "Hellenism and Historiography: Gregory of Nazianzus and Julian in Dialog," *Journal of Medieval and Early Modern Studies* 33.3 (2003): 493–515.

122. For Christian responses to the law see Gregory Nazianzen, *Or.* 4.12; Socrates 3.5–6; Sozomen 5.12; and Theodoret 3.4.2 and 5.1.

bol of Christian intellectual attainment, Prohaeresius continued to teach the same curriculum as his pagan rivals. Indeed, if he had not, his school would not have succeeded; there was little demand for someone who taught exclusively Christian themes and texts in fourth-century Athens. At the time the law was enacted, Prohaeresius had pagan students, Eunapius soon to be among them, and presumably Christian ones as well. This mixed environment apparently had little impact upon students' faith. Eunapius came to Athens a pagan, studied at the school of the Christian teacher for more than four years, and emerged as much a pagan as before. Almost a decade before, the Christians Gregory and Basil had studied under the same curriculum and remained steadfast Christians. At this point in their lives, Eunapius, Gregory, and Basil, like most people of the time, clearly thought that education had no defined religious identity. The schools were settings in which pagans and Christians could equally interact with a common culture. Most people, the emperor excluded, simply did not see, or want to see, the schools as places to which young men were sent to be converted. By challenging this identity, Julian's religious redefinition threatened to change education in a way that prevented it from performing the function people expected.

Although Julian's program failed, future imperial policy regarding education showed a continued awareness of the potential link between education and conversions to paganism. In Athens, too, concern about the political and protreptic importance of a teacher's religious loyalties would only grow as the fifth century dawned. Julian made people most acutely aware of the enormous (though usually latent) potential teachers had to shape religious opinion. He also revealed the power of the government to affect their use of that potential. After his law, pagan teachers would forever remain suspect figures in the eyes of some Christians. Hence, when control of the empire shifted permanently to Christian emperors after Julian's death, it was pagan teachers, not their Christian counterparts, who suffered because of this policy. This is Julian's final legacy to the schools.

Chapter 4

Athens and Its Philosophical Schools in the Fifth Century

The early years of the fourth century represented the moment of greatest political power for Athenian teachers. By the turn of the fifth century, the dominance that Athenian teachers had once enjoyed over the political life of the city was only a memory. Much of this was due to the rapid evolution of Athenian public life in the late fourth century. The Athenian councilor class, which had been devastated by the Herulian invasion, began to recover economically and, in the later half of the fourth century, it was prosperous enough to engage in large-scale civic euergetism again. From all indications, pagans comprised the majority of this group, and, as the fifth century progressed, the institutions of civic government became particular sources of pride for both pagans in the city and prominent pagans from abroad. As a result of this interest, local Athenian government, which, in the fourth century, had seemed to be slipping into oblivion, regained a surprising vitality and political potency.

At the same time, however, the Athenian Christian community was beginning to emerge as a force in the early fifth century. Evidence of the considerable growth of Athenian Christianity becomes impossible to ignore by the 420s and, as one would expect, these Christians seem to have combated non-Christian elements of the Athenian population. Despite its numerical growth, the Christian community seems to have exercised local influence only when its efforts were backed by imperial resources. Such intervention, while effective, came without any great regularity.

Teachers, most of whom were pagan, had to determine how best to adapt to a new political environment in which their independence was diminished and religious concerns could never be ignored. Amidst these changes in the city, there is a distinct shift in the focus of the extant sources describing Athenian education. While third- and fourth-century sources largely chronicle the careers of Athenian rhetoricians, fifth-century sources are concerned primarily with Athenian philosophers. This is not a disadvantageous development, however. These texts reveal the closed world of private philosophical schools at a very significant moment: when Athenian teachers of philosophy first introduce Iamblichan Neoplatonism to the Athenian educational environment.

Though broadly based upon Platonic philosophy, the Iamblichan system of thought also contained pagan religious teachings and encouraged participation in elaborate pagan religious rites. This development is significant because Plutarch the scholarch, the most prominent early exponent of Iamblichan Neoplatonism in Athens, came up with a particularly effective way to function in this new political environment. Given the nature of Plutarch's teaching, he could not be under any illusions about how Christians would see his activities. In order to protect his enterprise, he needed to ensure that his teaching was seen as a rather innocuous part of the Athenian cultural landscape. Contrary to what one might expect, he did not choose to withdraw from the established order or downplay his activities. Instead, Plutarch found ways to remain active in the city and, in so doing, made the local pagan power establishment inclined to protect his interests. The story of his school allows one to understand how a pagan teacher could effectively adapt to the challenges this new educational landscape presented.

LATER FOURTH-CENTURY ATHENS

To understand the challenges faced by Plutarch's school, one must first explore the economic and religious changes Athens underwent in the later fourth and fifth centuries. Both archeological and epigraphic sources indicate that, contrary to the trend of the previous century, relatively widespread prosperity took hold among the Athenian upper classes in the later fourth century. The most striking evidence for the new wealth of the city comes from the ruins of a number of large houses constructed in the mid- to late fourth century on sites scattered throughout the city.[1] The remains of the most elaborate of these houses were found grouped together on the north slope of the Areopagus hill. Dating from the last quarter of the fourth century, these houses were extraordinary in both their size and their layout.[2] At a time when the average Athenian house occupied something in the neigh-

---

1. For these see P. Castrén, "General Aspects of Life in Post-Herulian Athens," in *Post-Herulian Athens: Aspects of Life and Culture in Athens, A.D. 267–529*, ed. P. Castrén (Helsinki, 1994), 8. Among the examples he cites are those found beneath Kekropos 7–9 (findings published by O. Alexandre, *Archaiologikon Deltion* 24 [1969]: 50–53; plans 19–20) and those uncovered below Basilisses Sophias/Herodikou Attikou Streets (published by E. Spatharē and M. Chatziotē, *Archaiologikon Deltion* 38 [1983]: 23–25).

2. A. Frantz, *The Athenian Agora XXIV: Late Antiquity; 267–700* (Princeton, 1988), 37–47, discusses these houses in detail.

borhood of 130–150 square meters, the Areopagus houses ranged in size from 1000 to 1350 square meters.[3] These large houses had distinctive architectural features (like apsidal rooms)[4] and elaborate interior decorations such as were common to urban and suburban villas of the time.[5] Broad upper-class prosperity is seen from the remains of other Athenian buildings as well. These include the massive Palace of the Giants in the Agora,[6] an elaborately decorated complex of buildings and enclosed gardens that occupied over 13,500 square meters of space,[7] and public construction of a stoa complex containing a mysterious round building.[8]

Epigraphic evidence from the later fourth and early fifth centuries tells a similar story. Inscriptions describing the efforts of private individuals to pay for the physical rehabilitation of the city begin to appear in the mid-fourth century. In the later fourth century, a new gateway to the Acropolis was constructed.[9] Similarly, private funding paid for the renovation of the theater of Dionysus, the erection of a sundial, and the carving of a set of honorary statues to a prefect responsible for renovating the Library of Hadrian.[10] The inscriptions mark some of the men responsible for these pro-

3. Ibid., 37.

4. For these features see A. Frantz, *The Athenian Agora XXIV*, 39. Their similarity to urban villas in other cities has been noted by P. Castrén, "General Aspects of Life," 8; and G. Fowden, "The Athenian Agora and the Progress of Christianity," *Journal of Roman Archeology* 3 (1990): 494–500.

5. In the past, it has been speculated that the Areopagus houses were the residences and schools of teachers operating in the city (A. Frantz, *The Athenian Agora XXIV*, 39–41). This notion derives from a passage in the *Lives of the Sophists* in which Eunapius states that the house of Prohaeresius contained a marble theater in which he held class (*Vit. Soph.* 483). On the basis of this description, it has been assumed that the apsidal rooms in the Areopagus houses were constructed to serve the same purpose as the private theater that Eunapius mentions (e.g., A. Frantz, *The Athenian Agora XXIV*, 45). Such features are typical of later Roman villas found throughout the empire, and consequently it is likely that they had some domestic function. On this see, G. Fowden, "The Athenian Agora," 496. J. P. Sodini ("L'habitat urbain en Grèce à la veille des invasions," in *Villes et peuplement dans l'Illyricum protobyzantin, Actes du colloque organisé par l'École française de Rome 78* [Paris, 1984], 344–50, 359–60, 375–83) discusses the possibility that such rooms were, in fact, dining areas. Furthermore, when one examines the apses in the Areopagus houses, one is struck by their relatively small sizes and their dissimilarity in shape to a theater. With the exception of that found in the school of Proclus, these semicircular apses are quite narrow (with a maximum diameter of less than three meters).

6. A. Frantz, *The Athenian Agora XXIV*, 111–12; and J. Burman, ("The Athenian Empress Eudocia," in *Post-Herulian Athens*, ed. P. Castrén, 83) give a good survey of the site. P. Castrén ("General Aspects of Life," 10–12) is probably correct in thinking this a typical urban villa of the time.

7. Frantz, *The Athenian Agora XXIV*, 98.

8. Ibid., 60–61.

9. *IG* II/III² 5206. For discussion see E. Sironen, "Life and Administration in Late Roman Attica," in *Post-Herulian Athens*, ed. P. Castrén, 28–29.

10. *IG* II/III² 5021; 5208; 4224; 4225. For discussion see E. Sironen, "Late Roman Attica," 43–53.

jects as teachers, but it seems best to see this public spending less as an indication of the wealth of teachers and more as proof of the general prosperity of the period.

The source of this activity is particularly interesting because many of the people responsible for this renewed public euergetism were demonstrably pagan. Traces of this can be seen in several well-known public inscriptions. One such inscription honors the prefect Herculius. It marks him as a defender of the city whose image rests beside that of Athena.[11] Another inscription records civicly sanctioned honors for Dexippus, who is "dear to the gods."[12] These references ought not be taken as mere rhetorical convention. Wealthy Athenians in the late fourth and early fifth centuries worked hard both to maintain the vitality of pagan worship in their city and to demonstrate this vitality publicly. On May 27, 387, a man of senatorial rank named Musonius celebrated a taurobolium, an initiatory rite that culminated in a very public acclamation of the devotee's piety, and displayed an inscribed commemoration of this act.[13] Another (undated) taurobolium memorial also survives from this period.[14] As was the case with taurobolia commemorations in fourth-century Italy, these monuments were intended to preserve the memory of specific public acts of pagan religious self-expression.[15] Less exotic public manifestations of pagan devotion also occurred. Wealthy pagans continued to pay for the Panathenaiac procession[16] and, through their influence, the Athenian temples remained intact until the middle of the fifth century.[17]

Given the general decline of city councils in the fourth-century Roman East, the vigor shown by the Athenian councilor class is remarkable.[18] Indeed, its vitality is particularly notable because this Athenian recovery occurred despite the fact that most historically prominent families had been devastated by the Herulian attack. It seems, however, that this activity was due as much to a sense of pagan civic patriotism as to a re-emergence of economic power among Athenian city councilors. Simply put, fifth-century pa-

---

11. *IG* II/III² 4225.

12. Ibid., 4008.

13. Ibid., 4842. For ancient descriptions of the event, see Firmicus Maternus, *Carmen contra paganos,* 60; and more spectacularly (though less reliably), Prudentius, *Peristephanon* 10.1036–40.

14. *IG* II/III² 4841.

15. For the significance of the event as a public display of piety, see N. McLynn, "The Fourth Century Taurobolium," *Phoenix* 50 (1996): 312–30.

16. *IG* II/III² 3818 is a late fourth/early fifth century monument honoring Plutarch for three times sponsoring the Panathenaic procession.

17. Indeed, Marinus (*Vit. Proc.* 29) indicates that the Asclepius temple was still ἀπόρθητον in the middle fifth century, a probable indication that it still contained its religious sculpture at that time.

18. The decline of the councils is a much discussed and thoroughly analyzed point. For typical ancient complaints, see Libanius, *Or.* 49.

gans valued Athenian civic institutions and were willing to assume certain extraordinary burdens to keep them viable. There was a reason for this. At a time when imperial and provincial administrators were pursuing policies largely favorable to Christianity, the city council could serve as a governing organ that preserved certain features of pagan civic life. Possibly because of this continued relevance, participation in civic government remained a source of pride to Athenian pagans. Civic office in general and the archonship in particular remained an important achievement in one's political career, even in the later fifth century,[19] and evidence suggests that the archonship was an office that was often tied to prominence in the pagan community.[20] Beyond simply valuing the office, Athenian pagans also respected the continuity of the institution. In some cases, pagans even continued to mark each year with the name of the eponymous archon, a deliberate contrast to the system of dating employed by the Christian court.[21]

Pagan interest in ensuring the continued vitality of city councils was not confined exclusively to Athens, but the Athenian situation was still remarkable.[22] Athens represented something of an administrative peculiarity. Since the division of the empire that followed the appointment of Valens as co-emperor in 364, the city had been governed primarily from the West.[23] As

19. The continued prestige attached to involvement in Athenian public life has been described, briefly, by G. Fowden, "The Athenian Agora," 497. In light of this, it is not insignificant that the *Suda,* when paraphrasing Damascius's portrait of Theagenes, begins by identifying him as an Athenian archon (*Suda* Θ 78).

20. Hegias, a late fourth- or early fifth-century archon, is commemorated for both his archonship and his involvement in organizing the Panathenaic procession (*IG* II/III² 3692). P. Athanassiadi, ed., *Damascius: The Philosophical History* (Athens, 1999), 251–53 n. 277, discusses his involvement in the Panathenaea. Theagenes, archon in the later fifth century, was a prominent Athenian pagan. Nicagoras, archon in 485/6, may well have been a descendant of the Eleusinian priest sent to Egypt by Constantine (F. Millar, "P. Herennius Dexippus: The Greek World and the Third Century Invasions," *Journal of Roman Studies* 59 [1969]: 16–18; for the earlier Nicagoras see chapter 2 above). P. Graindor, *Chronologie des archontes athéniens sous l'empire* (Brussels, 1922), 268–74, records only four post-Herulian archons, a number to which Hegias must be added. The religious identities of these figures are either unclear or certainly pagan.

21. The best example is *Vit. Proc.* 36. In this text, the archon year is used deliberately to distinguish Marinus's dating scheme from that employed by Christian emperors.

22. Symmachus, while visiting Benevento in 375, notes with pleasure the great energy shown by the pagan notables in the city (*Letters* 1.3.4, ed. Callu). In North Africa, a similar situation seems to have existed in the late fourth and early fifth centuries (for this, see C. Lepelley, *Les cités de l'Afrique romaine au Bas-Empire* [Paris, 1979–81], 1.293–303, 357–69). As Lepelley's study shows, this activism could support pagan actions, but need not always have done so. The euergetism and civic officeholding of pagans in Aphrodisias is also notable (for this, see C. Roueché, *Aphrodisias in Late Antiquity: The Late Roman and Byzantine Inscriptions* [London, 1989]). Some of these figures assumed the cost of this involvement even though they were legally exempt from such financial burdens (see the examples of Asclepiodotus and Pytheas in Roueché, *Aphrodisias,* #53–58).

23. Sozomen 7.4 indicates that the diocese of Macedonia (the Athenian administrative region) was transferred to Theodosius upon his accession in 378. Theodosius himself turned ad-

a result, Athenian temples and religious institutions emerged untouched from the officially sanctioned anti-pagan violence that destroyed a number of prominent pagan monuments in the East in the 380s and early 390s.[24] Consequently, when the administration of Athens was finally transferred to Constantinople for good following the death of Theodosius in 395, its public and religious life retained a decidedly pagan flavor that could prove attractive to a certain population.

The Athenian council was also helped by the traditional prestige that non-Athenians attached to officeholding in the city. In the imperial period, men came from abroad, were given Athenian citizenship, and, through their office-holding, played an important role in sustaining many traditional Athenian civic institutions.[25] Though the events of the later third century seem to have diminished the frequency of such actions, there are signs of a similar process developing in the fourth and early fifth centuries. Flavius Septimius Marcellinus, who paid for the construction of a new gateway to the Acropolis, was likely a western transplant. Nevertheless, he also served as an *agonothete* in the city and, as such, played an important role in one of its pagan religious festivals.[26] Another likely western transplant was Rufinus, a man of high rank and a notable pagan supporter in the mid-fifth century.[27] While the number of examples is not great, these figures seem to indicate that the vitality of Athenian civic and pagan religious life both attracted and benefited from the attention of non-Athenians.

The persistence of paganism in Achaea, however, overshadows the steadily increasing influence of Athenian Christians in the period. While scattered textual references to an Athenian Christian population exist from the first

---

ministration of the area back to Valentinian II, probably following his recognition of Magnus Maximus in 384 (for details on this see A. H. M. Jones, *The Later Roman Empire, 284–602* [Norman, 1964], 1099 n. 51). Theodosius assumed control of it again only following his defeat of Eugenius in 394.

24. A process described most memorably in Libanius, *Or.* 30.

25. Although an imprecise measure, the number of Latin names on second- and third-century archon lists is a sign of the attraction the office held (see P. Graindor, *Chronologie,* 291–300, for a complete list). Non-Athenian interest in Athenian civic institutions of this period is further confirmed by large numbers of foreign students enrolled in the yearly ephebe classes. For the ephebic numbers, see J. Day, *An Economic History of Athens Under Roman Domination* (New York, 1942), 254 ff.

26. *IG* II/III² 5206. For his status as a former *agonothete,* see line 2. While there were many different types of *agonothetai* in Roman Athens, the most prominent were those responsible for the Panathenaic festival. On their role, see D. Geagan, *The Athenian Constitution After Sulla,* Hesperia Supplement 12 (Princeton, 1967), 132–36.

27. *Vit. Proc.* 23. He is simply described as ἀνὴρ τῶν ἐπιφανῶν ἐν τῇ πολιτείᾳ. His paganism is beyond dispute.

three centuries of our era,[28] the church seems to have kept a very low profile. This began to change in the fifth century. Under apparent imperial initiative, a major program of public construction was begun under Theodosius II and his (Athenian-born) wife, Eudocia.[29] Their efforts included the construction of a basilica in the center of the recently reconstructed Library of Hadrian and, possibly, the erection of a basilica beside the Ilissus River.[30] In the years following this imperial initiative, significant congregations of Athenian Christians began meeting within the walls of the city, evidently for the first time.[31]

The rising profile of the Christian community coincided with a number of successful efforts to limit the activities of Athenian pagans. By the middle of the fifth century the Panathenaea had ceased to be celebrated and the city's temples had closed.[32] Not long afterward, the cult statues associated

28. There were three Athenian bishops who were said to have been martyred in the second century (A. Frantz, *The Athenian Agora XXIV*, 8–9). There are also selected references to the community in Eusebius (*HE* 4.23.2, 6.32). This includes a mention that the church was upbraided for laziness in the second century.

29. K. G. Holum (*Theodosian Empresses: Women and Imperial Dominion in Late Antiquity* [Berkeley and Los Angeles, 1982], 112–21) has questioned her Athenian origins, a doubt which has not been echoed elsewhere. Against this, see E. Sironen, "An Honorary Epigram for Empress Eudocia in the Athenian Agora," *Hesperia* 59 (1990): 371–74.

30. For the Library of Hadrian basilica, see A. Karivieri, "The So-called 'Library of Hadrian' and the Tetraconch Church in Athens," in *Post Herulian Athens,* ed. P. Castrén, 89–115; and G. Fowden, "The Athenian Agora," 498–99. Though it functioned as a library for much of its useable life, the Library of Hadrian also served as a sort of imperial forum that, in its classical incarnation, contained the Library, a pond, and a temple of the imperial cult (Karivieri, 108–9). The placement of the tetraconch church in the center of this complex conveyed the very powerful message that the Christian church had replaced the imperial cult as the correct way to show one's devotion to the regime. For Eudocia and the Ilissus basilica, see Fowden, "The Athenian Agora," 497; and L. K. Skontzos, "*Η παλαιοχριστιανική Βασιλική τοῦ Ιλισσοῦ*," *Αρχαιολογία* 29 (1988): 50.

31. Relatively large numbers of Christian tombstones dating from the fifth and sixth centuries have been found within Athens. For a survey, see E. Sironen, *The Late Roman and Early Byzantine Inscriptions of Athens and Attica* (Helsinki, 1997), 119–271. This evidence, which seems to show the sudden fifth-century emergence of an Athenian Christian community from a nonexistent base, is slightly misleading. As G. Fowden ("The Athenian Agora," 495) rightly remarks, Christian churches remained *extra muros* in many cities throughout the fourth century. The nearly complete lack of Athenian Christian tombstones before c. 400 can be partially explained by their placement alongside undiscovered Athenian churches. One such tombstone (*IG* III 3521), which may date from the fourth century, appears to have been originally erected outside a suburban church. It was moved in the mid-fifth century when a new basilica was constructed beside the Theater of Dionysus. On this stone, see E. Sironen, "Inscriptions," 124.

32. It is not possible to determine an exact date for the cessation of the procession, but the *Life of Isidore* (*Vit. Is.* Ath. 105A; Z. fr. 273) seems to indicate that it was no longer possible to sponsor the festival in the later 460s.

with many of these temples were also removed.[33] Nevertheless, these initiatives did not prefigure the emergence of the Athenian Christian community as a dominant local political force. In fact, these Christian successes seem to have resulted from direct imperial intervention.

The picture is more complicated than this statement would suggest, however. While the imperial government was clearly involved, these actions are better understood as occurring in response to Christian demands.[34] In the same way that proconsular action against teachers usually occurred only when a broad professorial and curial consensus demanded it, broad support among powerful Christians was the only reason that an imperial official would consider taking such a provocative act as closing the Athenian temples.

By the same token, Athenian Christian demands would only attract an imperial response if they were heard at a time when the court had an interest in either the local Athenian political situation or the activity upon which the complaint was based. Action against Athenian pagan cult centers seems to have occurred when the religious use of the temples was first restricted (probably in the 420s) and again when pagan cult images were removed (probably in the late 430s or early 440s). In both instances, Athenian Christians seem to have succeeded in taking action only because imperial officials were keenly interested in the Athenian religious affairs that were being brought to their attention. In the 420s, the impetus would have been the attention the empress Eudocia had recently paid to her home city. The removal of the cult statues is a bit more mysterious. Still, imperial involvement in this removal seems likely. The presence in Constantinople of a bronze statue of Athena that was said to have come from Athens and bore a compositional similarity to the Promachos suggests quite strongly that at least one cult image from the Acropolis was transferred to Constantinople under imperial order.[35] This may well have been the event to which Marinus refers. Such imperial con-

---

33. The *Life of Proclus* 29–30 indicates that the temples remained intact, if not open, into the later part of the fifth century. A. Frantz (*The Athenian Agora XXIV*, 75–76) thinks that the Athena Promachos statue on the Acropolis remained until c. 462, a date that may be too late.

34. The suggestion of A. Frantz ("From Paganism to Christianity in the Temples of Athens," *Dumbarton Oaks Papers* 19 [1965]: 187) that these actions occurred in response to *C. Th.* 16.10.25 fails to acknowledge the time gap between the closing of the temples and the removal of the cult statues. Christian responsibility for the closing of the temples and, especially, for the removal of their cult statues is suggested by *Vit. Proc.* 30, where it is said that "the statue from the Parthenon was transferred by those who move things that ought not be moved (τὸ ἄγαλμα ἐν Παρθενῶνι ὑπὸ τῶν τὰ ἀκίνητα κινούντων μετεφέρετο)."

35. Marinus's use of the term μεταφέρω in *Vit. Proc.* 30 makes it clear that he is speaking of a physical transfer of the image of Athena. The bronze Athena in Constantinople is mentioned in Arethas's scholia on Aristides, *Or.* 50.408, line 15; Cedrenus 1.565; and Nicetas Choniates 738–40. Scholars linking the bronze Athena in Constantinople with the Athena Promachos include R. J. H. Jenkins, "The Bronze Athena at Byzantium," *Journal of Hellenic Studies* 67 (1947): 31–33; as well as H. D. Saffrey and L. G. Westerink, *Proclus: Theologie Platonicienne* (Paris, 1968–

cern was desultory and, under normal conditions, not a factor in the religious life of the city. As a result, while it was never possible to overturn the restrictions Athenian Christians were able to get imposed, when imperial attention was directed elsewhere, an effective combination of personal discretion and political connections enabled Athenian pagans and their foreign supporters to use civic institutions to protect elements of their religious life.

EARLY ATHENIAN NEOPLATONISM

These religious developments are doubly interesting because of the effect that they had upon the Athenian intellectual community. The nature of the community had begun to change in the early fifth century. Fourth-century Athenian intellectual culture had been known largely for the excellence of its teachers of rhetoric. In philosophy, the city had fallen far behind the intellectual avant-garde. In the fifth century, however, an Athenian philosophical school again emerged as a vital center of contemporary philosophical thought. Much of this was due to its inclusion of Iamblichan Neoplatonism in its teachings. As its name implies, Iamblichan Neoplatonism derived from the philosopher Iamblichus's interpretation of Plato and his ideas. It differed in a number of important ways from traditional Platonic education. This new curriculum emphasized the study of the divine in its everyday courses and, at its highest level, functioned as a sort of pagan religious training. It taught not only the ideas of Plato, Aristotle, and (supposedly) Pythagoras but also elements culled from quasi-philosophical religious works like the Chaldean Oracles and the Orphic writings.

The most distinctive feature of this brand of thought was its emphasis upon theurgy. Theurgy, in its most basic form, was a set of rituals designed to assist the human mind in apprehending something of the ineffable divine presence. These enabling rituals made it possible for man to come into contact with divine elements that were beyond his natural intellectual grasp. The essential goal of the theurgist was to purify his soul to such a degree that the individual would fall into a state in which his mind could not only overcome the limitations and imperfections of the material world, but even ascend for a time to the heavenly world of pure thought.[36]

Inherent in the practice of theurgy were purificatory rituals, religious rites,

---

97), xxiii n. 1. Disagreeing on rather unconvincing grounds is A. Frantz, "Did Julian the Apostate Rebuild the Parthenon?" *American Journal of Archaeology* 83 (1979): 401 n. 54. The statue remained in Constantinople until it was destroyed in a riot in 1203.

36. The best (though far from most accessible) description is that of Iamblichus, *De Myst.* 2.11.98, 3.7.114–8.117, 25.158–59. Among the many contemporary scholars who have written about theurgy are P. Athanassiadi, "The Chaldean Oracles: Theology and Theurgy," in *Pagan*

and invocations of the divine that resembled mainstream pagan religious practice. Sacrifice, for example, was essential as a way to spiritualize matter and to recognize the chain linking the spiritual world to that of humans.[37] At the same time, however, theurgy was also tinged with additional active elements that, to outsiders, resembled magic.[38] These active elements were intimately linked to a theoretical understanding of the divine expressed in the Chaldean Oracles. This work, said to be a set of divine teachings revealed to a Syrian named Julian the Theurgist, was seen by Iamblichan Neoplatonists as a holy book that provided clear statements about the divine and its relationship to the world.[39] To many Neoplatonists, the Chaldean texts even provided a clear theoretical explanation of theurgy's essential necessity as a tool to enable ascent to the divine.[40] As a result, it was held that any true philosopher needed to understand their teachings.[41]

While it was controversial, theurgy held a strong appeal for those with a philosophical inclination.[42] In some Iamblichan-influenced schools, theurgy had such importance that teaching came to emphasize the ways in which Platonic philosophy was in harmony with texts like the Chaldean Oracles.[43] Aside from this curricular emphasis, theurgy had a more basic appeal for students. The theurgists' particular ability to facilitate a mystical union with the divine and, in some cases, to do so in a spectacular manner convinced students of its potency and drew them to teachers who knew the art. The emperor Julian, for example, became a devotee of Maximus of Ephesus after learning

Monotheism in Late Antiquity, ed. P. Athanassiadi and M. Frede, 149–83 (Oxford, 1999); G. Shaw, "Theurgy: Rituals of Unification in the Neoplatonism of Iamblichus," *Traditio* 41 (1985): 1–28; A. Sheppard, "Proclus' Attitude to Theurgy," *Classical Quarterly* 32 (1982): 212–24; A. Smith, *Porphyry's Place in the Neoplatonic Tradition* (The Hague, 1974), especially 81–99; and Y. Lewy, *Chaldean Oracles and Theurgy*, 2nd ed., edited by M. Tardieu (Paris, 1978).

37. Iamblichus, *De Myst.* 5.10.214–5.22.231.

38. The use of strange invocations is defended in *De Myst.* 3.24.157–3.25.159. Iamblichus (*De Myst.* 2.11.98, 3.17.140–3.21.152) emphasizes that the gods who assist in divination or other theurgic activities do so willingly and, contrary to the practices of magic, they are not compelled in any way.

39. For this idea see most recently P. Athanassiadi, "The Chaldean Oracles," 165–66.

40. The most notable exponent of this position was Proclus. For his views and the contrasting perspective of Damascius, see P. Athanassiadi, "The Chaldean Oracles," 175–76.

41. See Damascius, *Vit. Is.* Ath. 85A; Z. Ep. 126. See also P. Athanassiadi, "The Chaldean Oracles," 181.

42. The controversial nature of theurgy is revealed clearly enough by Iamblichus's *On the Mysteries of the Egyptians*, a book that is intended in part to serve as an explanation (and something of a defense) of theurgy.

43. I thank Bert van den Berg for his thoughts on this matter. See as well, H. D. Saffrey, "Accorder entre elles les traditions théologiques: une caractéristique du Néoplatonisme Athénien," in *On Proclus and his Influence in Medieval Philosophy*, ed. E. P. Bos and P. A. Meijer, 35–50 (Leiden, 1992).

that his theurgic activities had caused a cult statue to smile.[44] Theurgy functioned on an earthly level as well. Iamblichan Neoplatonists could use theurgic techniques to prevent natural disasters, control the weather, and even heal people whose sicknesses were untreatable by doctors.[45]

Although much of the impact of these deeds on potential students is unknown (and unknowable) to us, there are reasons to suspect that the abilities of theurgists played a great role in developing a loyal group of student followers. Eunapius, for example, describes a rumor that circulated among the students of Iamblichus and described how Iamblichus used to levitate when he prayed.[46] Despite Iamblichus's own denial, this rumor and others like it continued to inspire awe among his students.[47] Within a school's inner circle, these accounts served to illustrate the potential benefits of Neoplatonic teaching and to validate a student's commitment to the school.[48] Some of this testimony also spread beyond the immediate circle of students and, through either the writings of authors like Eunapius or the oral testimony of interested observers, it circulated freely in the outside world.[49] To some young outsiders, these stories could affirm their pagan religious commitment and excite them about the possibility of religiously tinged philosophical study.[50] Theurgic ability was seen as an advantageous skill by both engaged and potential students and, as word of its possibilities spread, its appeal to students of philosophy certainly grew as well.[51]

Iamblichan Neoplatonism represented a philosophical system that was innovative both in its textual interpretation and in the active religious demands it placed upon its followers. Nevertheless, as the system developed, Athens had no discernable connection to either Iamblichus or the system of thought that he pioneered. Indeed, Neoplatonism in its Iamblichan form probably did not take hold among Athenian intellectuals until it was introduced to the city by a nephew of the philosopher Iamblichus in the 360s.[52] Once in-

44. Eunapius, *Vit. Soph.* 475.

45. *Vit. Proc.* 28–29. For theurgy as a form of "white magic," see A. Sheppard, "Proclus' Attitude to Theurgy," 218.

46. *Vit. Soph.* 458.

47. Eunapius mentions that even more marvelous (but less reliable) testimony about Iamblichus circulated among his students (*Vit. Soph.* 460).

48. Eunapius's source for most of his anecdotes about Iamblichus and his followers was Chrysanthius, a student of Iamblichus. On this, see, for example, *Vit. Soph.* 458, 459.

49. For an example of the latter type of dissemination, see the discussion of Asclepiodotus and the miraculous birth of his son (chapter 8, below).

50. This, at any rate, seems to have been the effect of these stories in the later fifth century. On this, see the cases of Paralius, Epiphanius, and Euprepius described in chapter 8.

51. Indeed, making such activities more widely known (and hence more appealing) may have been part of the reason that Eunapius chose to write so extensively about them.

52. Alan Cameron, "Iamblichus at Athens," *Athenaeum* 45 (1967): 143–53. The notion, advocated by H. D. Saffrey and L. G. Westerink, eds. (*Proclus: Théologie Platonicienne,* [Paris, 1968–97],

troduced, however, it grew into an important part of Athenian intellectual life. By the 370s, an eccentric named Nestorius is recorded using Neoplatonic theurgic rites to prevent an earthquake in Athens[53] and Iamblichan-influenced psychotherapy to cure a woman of the depressive memories of her past lives.[54]

While Nestorius is significant as the first known Athenian Neoplatonist, Neoplatonic doctrines took firm root in the city through the efforts of his descendant Plutarch.[55] Unlike Nestorius, Plutarch was committed to both the practice and the teaching of the Iamblichan Neoplatonic system.[56] He was a gifted exegete and able teacher, whose effectiveness was enhanced by a strikingly charismatic personality.[57] Plutarch's academy was founded in the last decades of the fourth century[58] and, by the year 400, the school and its founder had gained such notoriety that a steady stream of students began arriving from around the eastern Mediterranean to study under him.[59] He is known to have attracted students of philosophy from Athens, Syria, and

---

xlii–xliii), that Priscus, a disciple of Iamblichus, was at least partially responsible for the introduction of Iamblichan teachings into Athens seems to conflate Eunapius's account of Priscus's life in Greece (*Vit. Soph.* 482) with a description of the horrors of Alaric's raid on Athens. Eunapius never specifies that Priscus took up residence in Athens; consequently, it is impossible to assume that he did so.

53. Zosimus 4.18.

54. Proclus, *In Rep.* II. 324.12–325.10. This too was done under divine guidance. For the Iamblichan connection to such practices, see Iamblichus, *On the Pythagorean Life,* 14.

55. Their relationship is ambiguously described by ancient sources. Marinus, *Vit. Proc* 12 and 28, as well as Proclus, *In Rep.* II. 64.6, seem to suggest Nestorius was Plutarch's grandfather. On the basis of Damascius (*Vit. Is.* Ath. 64; not included in Zintzen), P. Athanassiadi (*Damascius: The Philosophical History* [Athens, 1999], 173 n. 149) has suggested that Plutarch was Nestorius's son.

56. Hierocles, *On Providence* 214.173a is the most concise statement of Plutarch's place in the tradition of Iamblichan thought.

57. Plutarch authored a number of philosophical commentaries, but these survive only as fragments quoted by other Neoplatonists. For a collection of the sources related to his career, see D. Taormina, *Plutarco di Atene* (Rome, 1989), 107–44.

58. The date of foundation is not clear but its impact can begin to be seen by the late 390s. É. Évrard ("Le maître de Plutarque d'Athènes et les origines du Néoplatonisme Athénien," *L'Antiquité Classique* 29 [1960]: 109) places Plutarch's birth around the year 350, a date that suggests an early date of foundation for the school. This approximation is based upon the imprecise notice in *Vit. Proc.* 12 that Plutarch died an old man in 434. This makes a date of birth in the late 350s or early 360s just as likely. Despite some claims to the contrary, the academy of Plutarch was a new foundation that bore no direct connection to the famous school of Plato. For this, see J. Glucker (*Antiochus and the Late Academy* [Göttingen, 1978], 322 ff.) and H. J. Blumenthal ("529 and its Sequel: What Happened to the Academy?" *Byzantion* 48 [1978]: 369–85).

59. For this process, see E. Watts, "Student Travel to Intellectual Centers: What Was the Attraction?" in *Travel, Communication, and Geography in Late Antiquity,* ed. L. Ellis and F. Kidner, 11–21 (Aldershot, 2004).

Lycia. He also taught students who were enrolled at the schools of the rhetoric in the city but wanted philosophical training.[60] It seems, however, that Plutarch's most fruitful recruiting ground was Alexandria.[61] Hierocles, Syrianus, and Proclus, his three most prominent students, all came to his school from that city.

Hierocles and Syrianus must have arrived in Athens sometime around 410, and the fact that they undertook such a journey seems to suggest that there was a significant difference between the teaching that went on in Plutarch's school and the sort of philosophy presented in Alexandria at the turn of the fifth century.[62] In the seventh book of Hierocles' *On Providence* (now preserved only in the epitome of Photius), he describes "the doctrine professed by Ammonius, Plotinus, and Origen as well as Porphyry and Iamblichus and their successors (all a part of a holy race). This is true through the time of Plutarch, who taught me these doctrines. All of these men were in agreement with the philosophy of Plato and celebrated the doctrines in a pure state."[63] To Plutarch and his followers, those teachers who did not follow the Iamblichan set of teachings diverged from this holy race and the pure interpretations of Platonic doctrine that they professed.

This difference was the cause of the best-documented transfer of a stu-

60. His one known Athenian student, his own daughter Asclepigeneia (*Vit. Proc.* 28), obviously represents a special case. The Lycian rhetor Nikolaos was trained by Plutarch. This was probably additional training that he received during his rhetorical studies (*Vit. Is.* Ath. 64; not included in Zintzen; cf. *Suda* N 394). Likewise, the Syrian Odaenathus was also attracted to Plutarch's school and trained there (*Vit. Is.* Ath. 65; Z. fr. 142). Domninus, known primarily as a student of Plutarch's successor Syrianus, was probably initially attracted to the school while Plutarch was presiding over it. A fragment from the *Life of Isidore* (*Vit. Is.* Ath. 89A; Z. fr. 218) describing a visit that he made with Plutarch to the Athenian shrine of Asclepius seems to support this.

61. The close relationships between the Athenian and Alexandrian philosophical communities is also concisely described by M. Vinzent, "'Oxbridge' in der ausgehenden Spätantike oder: Ein Vergleich der Schulen von Athen und Alexandrien," *Zeitschrift für Antikes Christentum* 4 (2000): 52–55. See as well the discussion of G. Ruffini, "Late Antique Pagan Networks from Athens to the Thebaid," in *Ancient Alexandria between Egypt and Greece*, ed. W. V. Harris and G. Ruffini, 241–57 (Leiden, 2004). The application of network theory to these intellectuals is intriguing but, absent a wider collection of data, this theory does little to take us beyond the narrow network of prominent intellectuals deliberately constructed by the authors of our sources.

62. The character of Alexandrian teaching at the turn of the fifth century will be discussed in more detail in chapter 7. Nevertheless, a vivid (although unscientific) indication of the non-Iamblichan focus of its best-known school comes from the citations in the letters of Synesius, one of its former students. In his writings, one hundred and twenty-six references come from Plato, twenty from Aristotle, nine from Plotinus, three from Porphyry, and none from Iamblichus (see A. Fitzgerald, trans., *The Letters of Synesius of Cyrene* [Oxford, 1926], 16). This is, of course, quite distinct from the overt links made between Plutarch and Iamblichus in the works of Plutarch's followers.

63. Photius, *Bib.* cod. 214.173a.

dent from the philosophical schools of Alexandria to the institution headed by Plutarch. The student involved was Proclus and the reason for his move is revealed in his biography. "After passing his time with the teachers in Alexandria and enjoying their company in so far as they were able, Proclus looked down upon them when, in a common reading of something, it seemed to him that they no longer bore true to the intention of the philosopher in their interpretations."[64] He then left for Athens, "with the escort of all oracles, the gods of philosophy, and the good spirits. The gods led him to the guardian of philosophy so that the pure, unadulterated teaching of Plato would be saved."[65] Proclus did not leave for Athens because of a lack of skill among Alexandrian philosophers. He left because they were unwilling or unable to teach the true meanings of the texts. Proclus knew that what he considered the true, pure teaching of Plato was preserved only with Plutarch in Athens.[66]

For pagans like Proclus, Plutarch's school represented the foremost institute of Iamblichan Neoplatonic learning in the eastern Mediterranean. This is not to say that the school was solely devoted to the religious aspects of Neoplatonism. While, at its highest levels, the Iamblichan system had a deeply religious character, the lower levels of Iamblichan teaching focused upon more basic philosophical instruction. As a result, in his school, Plutarch propounded non-religious elements of philosophy as well.[67] The general courses of philosophy taught at Plutarch's school were probably uncontroversial and designed to give the student a basic grounding in philosophical traditions. At its highest level of teaching, however, Plutarch's school seems to have catered to a particular audience of pagan students in search of a philosophical training that emphasized the religious aspects of the discipline. Plutarch succeeded because he was able to provide this type of teaching with unmatched skill.

If this was the character of the people affiliated with Plutarch's school, it strikes one as rather strange that such an institution was able to thrive in Athens at a time when the influence of teachers had declined and that of Christianity was increasing markedly. Plutarch's unique personal identity made this possible. Plutarch was the descendant of a well-established Athenian family with a history of involvement in local cultic activities.[68] His Athenian roots meant that he and his family were known both in Athenian curial circles and within the province of Achaea. This also meant that Plutarch

64. *Vit. Proc.* 10.
65. Ibid.
66. Ibid.
67. *Vit. Is.* Ath. 59E; Z. fr. 134.
68. On Plutarch and his family, see A. H. M. Jones, J. R. Martindale, and J. Morris, *Prosopography of the Later Roman Empire*, vol. 1 (Cambridge, 1971), Stemma 35. If the identification of the Plutarchus commemorated by *IG* IV² 436–37 with an ancestor of Plutarch the scholarch is correct, one can see a family involvement with the cult of Asclepius reaching back into the early fourth century.

naturally inherited a network of Athenian friends and associates from whom he could draw support. These things would have given him a measure of personal and professional security as he worked to establish his school as a major center of pagan learning.

Plutarch clearly benefited from his social status, and he diligently fulfilled the civic responsibilities appropriate to a man of his station. Three fifth-century monuments connected to men named Plutarch have been found in Athens.[69] In recent years, scholars have generated a lively debate about which of these, if any, can be attributed to Plutarch the scholarch. In the case of two of them, the identification is relatively secure. The first (and least controversial) of these, is an extremely fragmentary inscription found near the site of the Lyceum, Aristotle's long since vanished school. When reassembled, its three pieces yield a fragmentary dedication, in typically philosophical language, that was erected to commemorate gifts given to a temple by Plutarch.[70]

The second inscription is more informative. It reads: "The people of the Erechtheus put this up for Plutarch, the king of words, the mainstay of firm prudence, who drew the Sacred Ship to the temple of Athena three times spending all his wealth."[71] The drawing of the Sacred Ship formed the central element of the Panathenaic procession, one of the most important events of the Athenian civic and pagan religious calendar. Even in the fifth century, this event remained an important (and expensive) local festival, which demanded that its sponsor be a well-respected member of the city's upper class. By taking such a prominent role in paying for the procession, Plutarch reaped considerable personal honor. Besides the religious role the procession played, the Panathenaea was an important civic festival as well. Its sponsorship was a notable civic benefaction to perform and, by taking responsibility for it on three occasions, Plutarch reveals himself to have been one of the community's leading citizens.[72]

These two monuments reveal the important role that Plutarch played in

69. These are *SEG* 31, no. 246 and *IG* II/III² 3818, 4224.

70. The three pieces are cataloged as Epigraphic Museum 4878, 4713, and 8572. They were first put together by M. Mitsos, Ἀπὸ τοὺς καταλόγους Ἀθηναίων Ἐφήβων κλπ. (III), *Archaiologikē Ephēmeris* 1971, 64–65. I have disregarded the fanciful reconstruction of the entire inscription by W. Peek, "Zwei Gedichte auf den Neuplatoniker Plutarch," *Zeitschrift für Papyrologie und Epigraphik* 13 (1974): 201–4. The stone also mentions Plato and Telesphorus, a deity connected with the cult of Asclepius. The reference to Plato immediately suggests that Plutarch the scholarch was the man honored by this monument. The connection with the cult of Asclepius is another marker that confirms the identification. Plutarch himself was involved with this cult (*Vit. Is.* Ath. 89A; Z. fr. 218), as was one of his ancestors. While this Athenian inscription is impossible to date and explains little about Plutarch's activities, it does at least speak to his interest in providing financial support for pagan public cults.

71. *IG* II/III² 3818.

72. While the social status of the dedicant is certain, the identity of the Plutarch commemorated in this inscription has been the subject of recent scholarly contention. Opinions

sponsoring Athenian pagan cults and festivals. A third monument demonstrates his willingness to involve himself in the political affairs of the city. This is a dedicatory inscription, carved above a statue of the praetorian prefect Herculius, that was erected in the Library of Hadrian after the building's restoration in the years 408–10. It reads: "Plutarch the sophist, steward of words, erected this for Herculius the holy prefect, steward of laws."[73] The identification of this Plutarch with the scholarch has been questioned on the basis of terminology. Given the efforts that philosophers and sophists made to differentiate themselves from one another in previous eras, the presence of the word *sophistēs* in the inscription is enough to make many hesitate to identify the dedicant with Plutarch the scholarch.[74] However, scholars have made a number of valid points that should eliminate this hesitation. The most important of these concerns the relative lack of distinction made between philosophers and sophists in the late antique period.[75] In this period, the significance of the term depended upon the context in which it was used; often it could mean simply "a wise man." In polemical pieces, the anachronistic distinction could be used for emphasis, but in general usage the terms seem to have become almost synonymous.[76]

In this particular case, it is clear that, for reasons of meter, the anonymous author of this epigram apparently found the terms sufficiently close to permit the substitution of the shorter *sophistēs* for the more precise *philosophos*.[77] This epigram is in the dactylic hexameter common in later imperial epigrams

---

range from the unquestioning acceptance of H. Blumenthal ("529 and its Sequel," 373) to the rejection of any link by L. Robert (*Épigrammes du Bas Empire (Hellenica IV)* [Paris, 1948], 91–94) and E. Sironen ("Life and Administration in Late Roman Attica," in *Post-Herulian Athens: Aspects of Life and Culture in Athens, A.D. 267–529*, ed. P. Castrén [Helsinki, 1994], 46–48). Others in support of the identification of this honorand with the philosopher include G. Fowden, "The Pagan Holy Man in Late Antique Society," *Journal of Hellenic Studies* 102 (1982): 51 n. 147 and "The Athenian Agora," 499; as well as A. Frantz, *The Athenian Agora XXIV*, 64–65. Despite the controversy, this inscription does appear to honor Plutarch the scholarch. As is suggested by *Vit. Is.* Ath. 105A; Z. fr. 273, Plutarch likely had both the wealth and the desire to support the Panathenaic festival. In addition, contrary to the assertions of Robert, the language of the stone (including the controversial phrase βασιλεὺς τῶν λόγων) was perfectly appropriate in late antique descriptions of philosophers. In the mid-fourth century, Gregory Nazianzen (*Ep.* 24 B–C) describes Themistius as βασιλεὺς τῶν λόγων while also taking the time to compliment his philosophical way of life.

73. *IG* II/III² 4224.

74. As it did to E. Sironen, "Life and Administration," 50–51.

75. This was the point made by G. Fowden, "The Athenian Agora," 499. Themistius, mentioned above, is only one of many examples that prove Fowden's point. Themistius was, practically speaking, both a philosopher and a rhetorician, but in most contexts he would have been displeased to be termed a sophist.

76. A particularly interesting case is that of Synesius, *Ep.* 136.

77. H. Blumenthal, "529 and its Sequel," 373, first pointed to the importance of metrical concerns. Many thanks are owed to Ann Hanson for her help in articulating the metrical limi-

and, as such, it could never have accommodated the inclusion of the three consecutive short syllables of *philosophos*. Given this restriction, *sophistēs* must have seemed a more than adequate substitution to make. As a result, the use of this term ought not to preclude identifying Plutarch the scholarch with the dedicant of this statue. In fact, in light of the public activities that Plutarch the scholarch seems to have had a hand in, it is natural to assign responsibility for this inscription to him as well.[78]

The monument he erected to Herculius gives a true picture of the depth of Plutarch's involvement in the political life of early fifth-century Athens. The statue for which this stood as a base was erected to commemorate the role that Herculius had played in renovating the complex built around the Library of Hadrian. This renovation was a major project, and it had great importance for both Athenian intellectuals and the rest of the Athenian population. Hence, the man who erected this statue did so both as an agent of the Athenian intellectual community and as a representative of the entire city.[79]

These three monuments reveal that, far from being on the Athenian political margins, Plutarch served as an important patron in the political and religious affairs of the city. Although deep involvement in the pagan religious festivals of Athenian life may have seemed a bit anachronistic to some of his fellow Athenians, Plutarch's behavior was consistent with the traditional activities expected of a wealthy and well-placed member of the community. This activity would also have had a positive impact upon the political position of his school. Since Plutarch was one of the more important figures in Athenian civic government, he could rest assured that the friendships and connections he secured through his public activity would line up the obstructive powers of the largely pagan Athenian civic order in support of himself and his educational enterprise.

The importance for Plutarch of cultivating good local relations cannot be overstated; these prevented local opposition from bubbling up against his school. These relationships also made it unlikely that the general impe-

---

tations of this text. The epigram centers upon the parallelism between the two ideas of stewardship and, given the brevity of the text, the need to emphasize this parallelism requires the author to be less than precise. The line referring to Plutarch in the inscription does not allow for much metrical tinkering. It reads Πλούταρχος μύθων ταμίης ἔστησε σοφιστής. Of these words, the name of Plutarch, the two words relating to stewardship (μύθων ταμίης), and the verb are all essential. Hence, the lack of compositional flexibility may have forced the poet to choose the shorter term "*sophistēs*."

78. Regardless of their feelings about whether or not this man was Plutarch the scholarch, most scholars are inclined to identify the dedicant here with the man honored for paying for Panathenaic procession.

79. Another statue base similarly inscribed with a creative epigram honoring Herculius was erected at the same time by Apronianus, an otherwise unknown man who is also styled a sophist (*IG* II/III² 4225).

rial discontent with aspects of paganism would be detrimental to his school. In the same way that local outcry could attract imperial attention, quiet local support could shield one from it. The imperial government itself knew this clearly enough, and repeatedly threatened harsh penalties to local officials who hid pagan activity "through favoritism . . . or connivance."[80] Even when such things were made known, the imperial government could show a lack of interest in taking action against known pagans if such action threatened important people or posed a danger to social order.[81] By becoming a visible fixture of the Athenian political scene, Plutarch could count on favoritism and connivance preventing his activities from ever coming to the attention of the imperial authorities.

THE NEOPLATONIC SCHOOL AFTER PLUTARCH

The integral role that the figure of Plutarch played in securing the continued functioning of his school gave greater than normal importance to the question of his successor. Even in Athens, the religious and political climate for pagans like Plutarch and his students was becoming unpredictable.[82] For his school to continue teaching the doctrines that he held to be true, Plutarch needed to choose a capable successor and ensure his orderly assumption of power. Consequently, in the years before his death, Plutarch anointed his successor and stepped from teaching into retirement.

Plutarch chose Syrianus, one of his Alexandrian students, to be his successor. The arrival of Proclus during the time when this transition was taking place means that we are uncommonly well informed about how this process affected the functioning of Plutarch's school. Proclus left Alexandria for Athens in 429 or 430 with the desire to study at the Neoplatonic school in the city (then headed by Syrianus).[83] When Proclus arrived in Athens, he met Syrianus and enrolled under him. At the age of nineteen,

80. As, for example, *C. Th.* 16.10.12.4.

81. Theodosius, Honorius, and Arcadius, the emperors by whom the law cited above was issued, all knew and did not prosecute a number of pagans (including Themistius, the teacher of the latter two men). Indeed, their reputation as selective opponents of paganism may have contributed to the incident in the *Life of Porphyry, Bishop of Gaza* in which Arcadius hesitates to sanction an attack on the temples of Gaza because the natives of the city paid their taxes regularly (*Vit. Por.* 41).

82. Late in Plutarch's life, for example, he would have seen the construction of the tetraconch church in the area of his beloved Library of Hadrian.

83. Proclus's trip was clearly planned well in advance. When he arrived in Athens, Proclus was immediately taken in by Nikolaos (*Vit. Proc.* 11). Nikolaos, a rhetorician, was a friend of Proclus who had studied some philosophy at Plutarch's school. Despite Marinus's pretensions, it was no matter of chance that Proclus happened upon Syrianus (*Vit. Proc.* 11). He had clearly contacted Nikolaos to meet him at the port. It would be surprising indeed if, in this correspondence, Proclus had not also asked about Plutarch's school and the possibility of enrolling in it.

Proclus was already something of an advanced student.[84] He had excelled in the rhetorical curriculum that he had followed in Alexandria and had taken some courses in philosophy in that city as well.[85] Although most of his philosophical training likely consisted of courses designed to give students of rhetoric a grounding in the discipline, Proclus did enter into some more serious philosophical study with Alexandrian teachers.[86] It is likely that Syrianus, enrolling a young man with such a background, did not know whether to treat Proclus as a new member of the school's *hetairoi* or to place him in the introductory classes with other new students. To resolve this question, Syrianus brought Proclus to meet Plutarch.

Plutarch seems to have interviewed the youth and come away quite impressed with him. Marinus states: "When Plutarch saw the youth . . . he was greatly pleased by Proclus, so much so that he was eager to give himself to Proclus for philosophical discussion, although, as he was already well into senescence, such activities were hindered by his age."[87] Plutarch apparently decided that, because Proclus showed such eagerness and promise, he would take a role in his instruction. Plutarch read two texts with Proclus, Aristotle's *De Anima* and Plato's *Phaedo*. He also made him a member of the school's inner circle.[88] Nevertheless, it seems that Syrianus had most of the responsibility for Proclus's teaching and supervision. We know, for example, that Syrianus was especially concerned about Proclus's vegetarian diet and his ability to endure the rigors of his classes on such a strict regimen.[89] Syrianus discussed this concern with Plutarch and, after Plutarch echoed the concern but showed no alarm, Syrianus deferred with bemusement to the opinions of his mentor.[90]

The early training of Proclus reveals how the transfer of power was handled in Plutarch's school. Before the time of Proclus's arrival, the old scholarch had already turned over most of the day-to-day teaching and administrative responsibilities to Syrianus. Syrianus was placed in charge of the

84. His age is known from *Vit. Proc.* 12.

85. *Vit. Proc.* 8–10.

86. This is perhaps the best way to understand the "common readings" he had with Alexandrian teachers that are described in *Vit. Proc.* 10. It was, after all, his dissatisfaction with these that had led him to transfer to Athens.

87. *Vit. Proc.* 12.

88. Ibid. Usually a young student of Neoplatonism needed to complete his study of Aristotle before moving on to the study of Plato. It is worth noting, however, that two of the four commentaries known to have come from Plutarch's pen were on *De Anima* and the *Phaedo*. It is possible that these were the texts Plutarch could teach to the eager student without much effort. For the remains of his commentaries, see D. Taormina, *Plutarco di Atene*, 137–38.

89. *Vit. Proc.* 12.

90. After hearing Plutarch's advice, Syrianus replied, with obvious frustration, "Let [Proclus] learn how much I desire, while he follows harsh dietary laws, and then, if he wishes, let him die" (*Vit. Proc.* 12). On the theological significance of this exchange, see M. Edwards, *Neoplatonic Saints: The Lives of Plotinus and Proclus by their Students* (Liverpool, 2000), 75 n. 121.

recruitment and interviewing of students as well as most introductory teaching. Plutarch appears to have continued to do some upper-level teaching but,
for the most part, his role was to mentor Syrianus and teach him how to handle the difficult situations that presented themselves at the school. Hence,
when Proclus appeared, Plutarch was there to advise Syrianus about how to
handle the young man and his motley background. Although retired, Plutarch
maintained a presence in the school so that he could teach his successor how
to deal with the mundane aspects of running such an institution.

   The preparation that Plutarch gave Syrianus to handle issues of school administration must have been matched by an effort to prepare him for the political challenges he would face as the new head of such an institution. No text
like the *Life of Proclus* exists to give a glimpse of these discussions, but it is not
hard to imagine the advice that Plutarch would have given Syrianus. Because
Syrianus was not a native Athenian, it would be harder for him to play the
prominent public role Plutarch had. Nevertheless, Plutarch could have ensured
that Syrianus was introduced to all of the important friends and benefactors
of the school. He would also have advised his successor to maintain these relationships and refrain from antagonizing people into opposition to the school.

   From the available evidence, it seems that Syrianus was well prepared to
lead the school when Plutarch died in or around 432.[91] Upon Plutarch's
death, Syrianus inherited the building in which the school was housed,[92] a
collection of skilled *hetairoi*,[93] and (presumably) a group of students who took
introductory philosophy courses. Perhaps the most important bequest left to
Syrianus, however, was the school's reputation among the pagans of the empire for teaching "the pure and true" Platonism of the Iamblichan tradition.
Even under a new head, the school remained the foremost center for the
teaching of religious Neoplatonism. As it had done for Plutarch, this reputation seems to have made the recruitment of students relatively easy for Syrianus. From our meager evidence, there is no indication that the succession
lessened the willingness of students to travel to Athens. Indeed, in the case
of Alexandrian youths, the regime of Syrianus seems to have increased the
appeal of the school. Syrianus was a member of a pagan intellectual family
native to Alexandria. After he left for Athens, Syrianus had remained in close

---

91. The date is based upon an assumption that Proclus was born in 412. Because the horoscope of Proclus provided by Marinus in the *Life of Proclus* contradicts some biographical details he provides in the same text, this date has been the subject of a great deal of scholarly dispute. For a date of 412, see the compelling arguments of A. Jones, "The Horoscope of Proclus,"
Classical Philology 94 (1999): 81–88. For a date of 410, see L. Siorvanes, *Proclus: Neo-Platonic Philosophy and Science* (New Haven, 1996), 26–27. See as well M. Edwards, *Neoplatonic Saints*, 112
nn. 377, 378.
   92. *Vit. Proc.* 29.
   93. Ibid., 12. These included Proclus, Archiades (the grandson of Plutarch), and the Syrian Domninus.

contact with individuals in his home city.[94] Not coincidentally, soon after Syrianus assumed control, a fresh group of Alexandrian students arrived in Athens to study philosophy at his school.[95]

Under Syrianus, the teaching in the school does not seem to have changed markedly from that done by Plutarch. Syrianus followed a standard Iamblichan curriculum. The program began by teaching students math, astrology, and other subjects. They were then led through the works of Aristotle before beginning the study of Plato.[96] This served as an introduction to philosophy that gave students skills useful in higher philosophical study. It also provided them with a moral and ethical training that emphasized the virtues appropriate to a philosopher. These virtues were themselves organized according to a scale of virtues introduced by Plotinus in *Ennead* 1.2, systematized by Porphyry, and adapted by Iamblichus.[97] In the Athenian Neoplatonic school, this scale was further developed and molded into a system in which the virtues were divided into physical, ethical, political, purifying, theoretical, and theological categories.[98] Platonic dialogs were found that corresponded to and gave instruction in the last four of these six virtues (the physical and ethical were not covered because philosophy could not help develop them), and the scale of virtues came to form the basic organizing principle of Neoplatonic education.[99]

94. His brother Ammonianus was a grammarian in Alexandria (*Vit. Is.* Ath. 47; Z. Ep. 60, fr. 111).

95. The Alexandrians known to have been attracted by Syrianus are Hermeias (*Vit. Is.* Ath. 54; Z. Ep. 74), Gregory (*Vit. Is.* Ath. 55; Z. Ep. 75, fr. 123) and Ulpian (*Vit. Is.* Ath. 123A; Z. fr. 324). In light of this, the contention of R. Lamberton ("The Schools of Platonic Philosophy of the Roman Empire: The Evidence of the Biographies," in *Education in Greek and Roman Antiquity,* ed. Y. L. Too [Leiden, 2001], 450–51) that Syrianus may have had only two students at the end of his life seems to understate the student population.

96. Syrianus's teachings seem to have greatly influenced some of Proclus's own interpretations of Platonic texts. On his contribution, see M. Edwards, *Neoplatonic Saints,* 72 n. 105; and A. Sheppard, *Studies on the 5th and 6th Books of Proclus' Commentary on the Republic* (Göttingen, 1980).

97. Plotinus initially created these ideas out of a concern for whether, and how, virtues exist at the various levels that the soul could occupy. He created the scale by taking passages of the *Phaedo* and *Republic* out of context to create the political and purifying virtues. In his *Sententiae,* Porphyry then elaborates on the hierarchy and creates two more kinds of virtue, the theoretical and paradigmatic. Iamblichus was the first to correlate the first three of these virtues and three orders of knowledge.

98. Proclus added the ethical virtues. Marinus, his successor, describes theurgic virtues for the first time. Besides playing a large role in Marinus's *Life of Proclus,* the scale of virtues was also mentioned by John Philoponus (*In. Cat.* 141.25–142.3); Damascius (*In Phaedo* I.138–44); and Olympiodorus (*In Phaedo* 1.5.1–9, 8.2.1–12). All of these men were students of Proclus's student Ammonius. For more on the scale of virtues see J. Pépin, *Théologie cosmique et théologie chrétienne* (Paris, 1964), 380–86. See also D. O'Meara, *Pythagoras Revived: Mathematics and Philosophy in Late Antiquity* (Oxford, 1989), 97–99, for Iamblichus and his role in establishing the hierarchy.

99. Physical virtues were acquired at birth while ethical virtues were developed during the pre-philosophical education. The system is laid out in the *Prolegomena to Platonic Philosophy,* on

Syrianus taught his *hetairoi* subjects that extended beyond the basic philosophical canon. Marinus says that "he offered to guide both Proclus and the Syrian philosopher Domninus in either the Orphic writings or Chaldean Oracles and he offered the choice of either one to them."[100] Nevertheless, the small class size and the fact that, after Syrianus's death, almost no one remained in Athens who knew theurgic doctrines indicates Syrianus's hesitancy to make this training widely available. Along with some of the dialogs of Plato,[101] Orphic and Chaldean writings were the most important religious texts to Athenian Neoplatonists. They were central to Iamblichus's theology, but not a part of the system of *paideia*. They were purely pagan, religious in nature, and outside of the common educational culture.

Despite the dangers of doing such religiously defined teaching in the fifth century, there is no evidence that Syrianus or the school suffered any adverse effects from offering overt pagan religious instruction. Much of the credit for this must go to Plutarch and the efforts he made to prepare Syrianus for the challenges he would face as the head of the school. The school probably would have done well in his hands. It is unfortunate, then, that Syrianus died not more than six years after being designated the head of the school.[102] The school would never enjoy the full benefits of his training. More importantly, though, because Syrianus had not yet been able to train his successor, his unexpected death meant that many of the advantages he enjoyed were not passed on to his successor.

THE PROCLAN SCHOOL

The school was fortunate that, despite the suddenness of Syrianus's death, there was little question that Proclus would succeed him.[103] Syrianus had

---

which see L. G. Westerink, ed., *Prolégomènes à la Philosophie de Platon* (Paris, 1990). Note, however, the comment of M. Edwards, *Neoplatonic Saints*, 60 n. 31, that there seems to be no "prevailing orthodoxy" for how these divisions were understood.

100. *Vit. Proc.* 26.

101. Marinus describes Proclus's jump from Aristotle to Plato as "initiation into the Mysteries of Plato" (*Vit. Proc.* 13).

102. Syrianus died while in the midst of giving a course of lectures on Orphic doctrines to Proclus (*Vit. Proc.* 26), but Marinus's text does not give an explicit date of death. We do know, however, that Proclus completed his *Timaeus* commentary in 438 at the age of twenty-eight (*Vit. Proc.* 13). In the Neoplatonic curriculum the *Timaeus* was the second to last Platonic dialog taught. One would presumably begin the study of Orphic texts after the completion of the Platonic curriculum. Given the time it must have taken Proclus to revise the *Timaeus* commentary, it is likely to have been completed at about the time Syrianus died.

103. Proclus's classification of Syrianus as his "father" and Plutarch as his "grandfather" (*Vit. Proc.* 29) seems to indicate a direct succession from the two. Marinus's remark that Domninus was also a διάδοχος or "successor" (*Vit. Proc.* 26) must not be understood as implying direct

made this clear in a number of ways. The attempt to arrange a marriage between Proclus and Aedesia, a member of Syrianus's family, was one indication of Proclus's high profile in the school.[104] Nevertheless, nothing indicated Proclus's position as designated successor more than the tomb Syrianus had constructed for himself. In providing for its construction, Syrianus ordered that it be built as a double tomb that would hold both his own body and, when the time came, that of Proclus as well.[105]

Through such action, Syrianus had expressed his will quite clearly and, upon his death, Proclus inherited the building in which the school was housed and took charge of the teaching of its *hetairoi*.[106] It also seems that he took some responsibility for the education of the other, less advanced students who came to the school.[107] In these ways, Proclus's quick succession meant that the death of Syrianus caused little disruption in the functioning of the school.

The event did have a real effect upon the teaching done in the school. Proclus continued to teach the same ordered curriculum of Aristotelian and Platonic texts that had existed under Syrianus,[108] but his advanced course of study went well beyond these basic texts. Both Marinus and Damascius make it clear that Proclus did not confine himself to the texts of Plato and Aristotle. Though Syrianus was reluctant to teach Orphic and Chaldean texts, even to his inner circle of students, Marinus recounts that he and a group of his fellow *hetairoi* took a course in Orphic texts with Proclus.[109] Indeed, the texts and meanings of these hymns were well enough known among the students that, when Proclus lay dying, the *hetairoi* of the school

---

succession after Syrianus's death. The explanation of J. Glucker (*Antiochus and the Late Academy*, 155 n. 122; echoed and expanded by P. Athanassiadi, *Damascius*, 43 n. 73) that a deputy διάδοχος was always appointed when a new scholarch took control of the school seems a particularly prudent measure and probably is correct. If so, Domninus did not succeed Syrianus but was designated by Proclus to be his own successor if something unfortunate were to happen.

104. *Vit. Is.* Ath. 56; Z fr. 124. This is described in more detail in chapter 8.

105. *Vit. Proc.* 36.

106. For the building see *Vit. Proc.* 29. His control of the teaching of the *hetairoi* can be seen only in the case of Archiades. It is said by Marinus that, upon Syrianus's death, Proclus went from being the fellow *hetairos* of Archiades to being his teacher (*Vit. Proc.* 17).

107. We are told that he taught five courses a day and also gave daily lectures that were not based upon any prepared text (*Vit. Proc.* 22). It would be hard to explain such teaching activity if at least some of it was not directed towards introductory students.

108. The similarity of the Proclan curriculum to that in which Proclus himself was educated is revealed in Marinus's *Life of Proclus*. For this idea, see H. J. Blumenthal, "Marinus' *Life of Proclus:* Neoplatonist Biography," *Byzantion* 54 (1984): 471–93. The *Life of Proclus* is organized around the scale of virtues described above. Each of these virtues represented a stage in Proclus's own philosophical training, and their emphasis makes it apparent that they had an important role in the curriculum as it was taught when Proclus lived.

109. *Vit. Proc.* 27.

crowded around his bed and sang Orphic verses to comfort him.[110] The teaching of the Chaldean Oracles also had an important role in the Proclan school and it seems that they were a required part of the upper-level course of study.[111]

Proclus's regular teaching of both the Chaldean and Orphic texts was a dramatic departure from the state of affairs under Syrianus. Though Syrianus had been trained in and had written about these religious texts, he was apparently hesitant to teach them. Even Proclus, his appointed successor, "acquired only some rudiments of Orphic and Chaldean theology" because "Syrianus did not speak about or discuss them with Proclus."[112] It seems that he agreed to teach these subjects only after Proclus implored him to do so and, even then, Syrianus limited the class to just two students. Clearly, in making these teachings more widely available to his students, Proclus had a different set of priorities.

Proclus also explored other religious subjects with his students. The *Life of Proclus* contains a remarkable description of the religious rituals he performed on a regular basis. It also indicates that these things were taught in the school.[113] In addition, the same text contains discussion of miraculous deeds performed by Proclus through the use of theurgy.[114] Because these activities were quite controversial, Marinus does not indicate how well known they were within the school. He is also silent about how widespread theurgic training was among Proclus's students. It is clear, however, that Marinus and his contemporaries had witnessed many of Proclus's theurgic activities and, presumably, learned something of his techniques.

This again contrasts with the situation under Syrianus. Before Proclus ar-

110. Ibid., 20. These were sung along with other songs of a similar type. M. Edwards (*Neoplatonic Saints*, 89 n. 220) suggests that, on this occasion, these verses were read and not sung from memory.

111. This is known from an amusing story that Damascius tells about his teacher Isidore. Isidore apparently resented some of Proclus's requirements and, "sometimes during the Chaldean rituals, he gave a display of his imitation of sparrows and hens and other birds flapping their wings as they prepare themselves for flight." Needless to say, "Proclus was bemused by Isidore's imitations of the cries and other noises produced by birds" (*Vit. Is.* Ath. 59F; Z. fr. 200).

112. *Vit. Proc.* 26.

113. "The purifying virtues distinguish these things [emotions and desires] entirely and remove the lead weights of birth, thus completing the unhindered flight [of the soul] from affairs here. Indeed, the philosopher practiced these same virtues throughout his entire life in philosophy . . . day and night he would use sacrifices to avert evil and ritual cleansings and other purification techniques, either Orphic or Chaldean, and he tirelessly went down to the sea once or even two or three times each month" (*Vit. Proc.* 18). A more complete list of his religious activities is found in *Vit. Proc.* 19.

114. They are, at any rate, exhibited as examples of his theurgic virtues. For these see *Vit. Proc.* 28–29.

rived, Marinus says, "The entire theurgic teaching of the great Nestorius was preserved in [one woman] alone."[115] Not only had Syrianus downplayed theurgy, it seems that Plutarch himself was hesitant to teach it in his school. The emphasis on theurgy in Proclus's school, then, reflected a shift in the school's focus that coincided with Proclus's elevation to the position of scholarch. Unlike Syrianus, and Plutarch before him, "Proclus put theology before any other branch of philosophy."[116] Given the sort of teaching for which Plutarch's school was known and the type of student it seems to have attracted, it was perhaps natural for Proclus to place more emphasis upon the school's religious elements. The young pagans attracted there must have welcomed this religious redefinition because it enabled the school to serve their religious needs better. It seems, however, that Proclus may have gone too far, even for some of their tastes. Isidore, for example, appears to have been uncomfortable with his teacher's zeal and set limits for himself so that he was not overwhelmed by religious doctrines at too young an age.[117] Others may well have felt the same way.

Proclus's interests were an even more uncomfortable fit for the world outside of his school. He had appeared to shift from training young men to be virtuous to training them to be good pagans. This was an important change. Even though the school had served as a safe haven for youths to learn about philosophical paganism under Plutarch and Syrianus, it had also served the general educational needs of students who wished for a general introduction to philosophy. Athens still had a vibrant group of rhetorical schools during Proclus's career and, presumably, a substantial student population.[118] While Proclus still seems to have attracted some of these students,[119] those who knew of his emphasis upon religion must have sensed that the school was less devoted to general education than it had appeared under his predecessors. This was a danger because, while both pagans and Christians could theoretically accept a school designed to train young men to act virtuously, it was much harder to do so when the emphasis upon virtuous conduct was inextricably combined with pagan religious training.

It is impossible to judge how widely understood Proclus's new curriculum was, but whatever response it generated was compounded by an extreme lack of subtlety in Proclus's own conduct. Proclus was surely aware that the changes he had instituted in the school would prove disconcerting to Athe-

115. *Vit. Proc.* 28.
116. *Vit. Is.* Ath. 59E; Z. fr. 134.
117. *Vit. Is.* Ath. 59C, D; Z. fr. 136, 137.
118. Mid-fifth-century Athenian rhetorical schools were led by men like Superianus (*Vit. Is.* Ath. 61; Z. Ep. 83, fr. 140) and Salustius (*Vit. Is.* Ath. 60; Z. Ep. 81–82, fr. 138).
119. Nikolaos, the rhetorician who studied under Plutarch and Syrianus, also seems to have continued his studies under Proclus (*Vit. Is.* Ath. 64; not included by Zintzen).

nian Christians. All the same, it seems that Proclus still made himself and his students visible in Athenian public life. Proclus urged his students to wear a *tribon*, the coarse cloak traditionally associated with philosophers.[120] In doing this, he aimed to heighten the visible distinction between his students and the rest of the men in the city. Like his students, Proclus himself cut a distinct figure. His appearance perhaps mirrored that which he demanded of his students and, in his diet, he was noticeably frugal.[121] His devotion to pagan religious activities also distinguished him. Marinus is unclear about how public Proclus made his religious activities, but his periodic processions to various holy places must not have gone unnoticed in a city of perhaps twenty thousand. Some, but not all, of his theurgic activities must have been public knowledge, while the Chaldean rites that Proclus performed to alleviate droughts in Attica and save it from earthquakes would probably have been publicized as well.[122]

Proclus also took it upon himself to be politically active. Marinus states that "sometimes the philosopher himself went to the city assembly . . . sensibly guided the discussions, [and] conversed with the leaders about matters of justice."[123] Indeed, despite a personality that even his friends admitted was prickly,[124] Proclus became the self-appointed social gadfly of fifth-century Athens. In this, he could not have proven more tiresome to the city's Christians.

All of this personal distinctiveness made the newly installed Proclus uniquely ill suited to gain the indulgence of those in power in fifth-century Athens. He was a young man who had suddenly been elevated to the top position in the school. The unexpected death of Syrianus had left Proclus without any real training in how to handle the administrative and political challenges that came along with running the Athenian Neoplatonic school. It had left him equally devoid of the personal friendships that could gain the school political support within the city. Whereas Syrianus could turn to Plutarch for help during the first years in which he ran the school, Proclus was left to make decisions by himself. This was a dangerous position. An un-

120. "Proclus ordered Isidore to change his appearance and wear a *tribon* (τρίβων) for the purposes of a higher life. Isidore did not obey, although he revered Proclus just as a god" (*Vit. Is.* Ath. 59B; Z. fr. 135—trans. Athanassiadi, with amendments). Olympiodorus (Olympiodorus of Thebes, fr. 28 = Photius, *Bib.* cod. 80.177–78) describes a fourth-century ceremony in which students were given the privilege of wearing the τρίβων. His ceremony, however, seems to be distinct from what is described in this passage of Damascius.

121. *Vit. Proc.* 19.

122. Ibid., 28.

123. Ibid., 15.

124. Marinus even says that he would upbraid those whom he judged to be lazy in their professions (*Vit. Proc.* 16). One may, however, doubt the extent to which Proclus actually played this public role.

compromising person by nature, Proclus's relative youth and his deep religious feelings must have made him resolute and unwilling to bow to the political and religious forces that pressed upon the school in the 430s and 440s.
Without an elder to restrain his more provocative impulses, Proclus seems
to have acted in accordance with his philosophical and religious inclinations.
This was an admirable principle, no doubt, but, given the increasing power
of Christians in fifth-century Athens, it was not the wisest of ideas.

With Proclus evincing such a contentious personality, it was only a matter of time before he found himself and his school in a great deal of trouble. Marinus describes this moment in vague language. "In a difficult circumstance [Proclus] retired from certain vulture-like men and went away
from Athens, obeying the revolution of all things, and made a journey to
Asia . . . after spending only one year in Lydia, he came back again to Athens
by the design of the philosophic god."[125] Despite the deliberate lack of clarity in Marinus's account, one should not imagine that Proclus's journey to
Asia was anything but an exile from Athens, even if it was a voluntary one.
This must have been a shocking experience for the young scholar, but there
is no information in his works that allows one to date this event. With this
noted, there can be little doubt that the exile occurred early in Proclus's career. Given the political influence that Proclus seems to have wielded later
in life[126] and the overwhelmingly positive portrayal of him in sixth-century
sources like John Malalas,[127] it is unlikely that his exile occurred during Proclus's scholarly maturity.[128] There is equally little solid information about the
identities of the "vulture-like men" responsible for this exile. It is not hard
to imagine that Proclus would have made a great number of enemies within
the city. It is known, for example, that Proclus quarreled about a student
with Salustius, an Athenian philosopher/sophist.[129] Salustius, however,
ended his days at the court of Marcellinus in Dalmatia, an unsuccessful
usurper. If he had been responsible for Proclus's exile, there would not be
any reason for Marinus to hide that fact with the colorful yet indefinite term

125. *Vit. Proc.* 15. For the identification of the "philosopic god" with Apollo, see M. Edwards, *Neoplatonic Saints*, 80 n. 159.

126. See *Vit. Proc.* 16 for a description of his later influence.

127. John Malalas is notable for his remarkable attribution of the invention of a sort of na-
palm to Proclus (*Chronicle* 16.16) in the year 515. Proclus, of course, died in 485. Ignorant of
that fact, but aware of the philosopher's reputation, Malalas made this rather comical historical error.

128. Though a one-year exile would be hard to find given the poor state of our chronological information for Proclus's school, there is a steady string of students known to have studied under him from the 450s forward. It seems best to place such an exile early in his career.
L. Siorvanes's connection of Proclus's return with the death of Theodosius II in 450 (*Proclus,*
28) rests on no concrete evidence. Given the progression of Proclus's career, it seems to me
better to imagine that the exile occurred in the early 440s instead of later in the decade.

129. *Vit. Is.* Ath. 68; Z. fr. 143.

"vulture-like men." The obscure phrase he chooses seems instead to point to Christian opponents. Throughout the *Life of Proclus,* Christians are referred to by allusive phrases such as "those who move things that ought not be moved."[130] For the most part, the same hesitancy to call a Christian a Christian is shown in the *Life of Isidore.* Given this fact, it seems quite likely that Proclus's exile was caused by the activities of Athenian Christians.[131]

Following his exile, it seems that Proclus became far more politically savvy and, taking advantage of the particular interest that wealthy pagans had taken in traditional Athenian religious institutions, Proclus worked to get external political support for his school.[132] One individual who seems to have responded was the pagan grandee Rufinus, styled by Marinus "a man among the elite in the state."[133] Rufinus was a particularly impressed admirer of Proclus who, following the latter's return from exile, offered the teacher a great sum of money to support the school and its endeavors.[134] Perhaps not wishing to mortgage his philosophical independence in such a way, Proclus rejected this money out of hand. He would not, however, have so quickly rejected whatever political support Rufinus could lend him. Marinus and Damascius make other passing mentions of pagan barons who lent financial and political support to Proclus's school. There were men like the Aphrodisian magnate Asclepiodotus (to whom Proclus dedicated his *Commentary on the Parmenides*) and the Athenian senator Theagenes (whom Marinus styles "a benefactor towards us").[135] They were keenly interested in using their wealth and influence to ensure that Proclus could continue teaching. Even in the face of Christian opposition the school was not without powerful friends who were interested in its survival.

130. *Vit. Proc.* 30. This phrase evokes both Herodotus 6.134 and Porphyry, *Abst.* 87.16, causing M. Edwards (*Neoplatonic Saints,* 105 n. 332) to suggest that it is proverbial. The fear of Christians is obvious in Proclus's hesitancy to publicize his miraculous cure of Asclepigeneia. Given the age of the girl and the identity of her father this event must have occurred after Proclus's exile.

131. It is unlikely that Proclus's response to the deconsecration of the Parthenon led to his exile. We know that Proclus was very much troubled by this event. Marinus even recounts that Proclus had a vision in which he was asked by Athena to take her into his house. Nevertheless, there is nothing in the text to suggest that Proclus publicly protested the action. The *Life of Proclus* in fact gives one the impression that these were two completely separate events. Indeed, if Proclus had vehemently protested the statue's removal, this would have been a heroic resistance. One would expect to see at least a mention of it in Marinus's text.

132. On the Athenian school and its external supporters see also M. Vinzent, "'Oxbridge,'" 58.

133. The text reads ἀνὴρ τῶν ἐπιφανῶν ἐν τῇ πολιτείᾳ. For more on Rufinus, see above.

134. *Vit. Proc.* 23.

135. Asclepiodotus is described by C. Roueché, *Aphrodisias,* 86–92. His wealth and influence are attested to by a set of inscriptions put up in his honor in Aphrodisias (Roueché, *Aphrodisias,* #53, 54). Theagenes was probably a child when Proclus was exiled, but he eventually married a descendant of Plutarch and, given the connections he had to the family of Plutarch, it would be surprising if his family were not among the supporters of the school in this period.

These men quieted some of the outcry Proclus had provoked, but it seems that his difficulties made Proclus realize that he also needed to restrain his conduct. When he performed a theurgic cure of Theagenes' future wife, Asclepigeneia, in the 450s,[136] for example, Proclus did so in a way that "escaped the notice of most people and provided no pretence to those who wished to lay an accusation against him."[137] Among these potential accusers were no doubt Christians eager to charge the philosopher with the practice of magic. After his exile, it seems that Proclus was much more aware of the Christian opposition to his school and its real political power. From that point forward, Proclus was careful to be as inconspicuous as possible.

The position of the school in the wake of his exile also caused Proclus to work on again joining the interests of his school to those of the pagan councilors who dominated Athenian political life. He did this by anointing Plutarch's grandson Archiades as the school's political advocate.[138] Marinus says that Proclus "summoned Archiades, the one dear to the gods, to this occupation. At the same time he taught that man and showed him the political virtues and methods, and he guided him, just as ones calling out to runners."[139] Archiades was to serve as the public voice of the Proclan school, and he was a good choice for this position. Since Proclus was an outsider in the city, the council of Athens probably had little initial interest in listening to the scholarch's opinions and little patience for his attempts to express them. Archiades, however, came from the wealthy, established, and influential Athenian family of Plutarch. Like his grandfather, he too was born into the Athenian aristocracy and, because of this, he was a more acceptable spokesman than the outsider, Proclus. His lineage alone would have allowed Archiades to express the school's positions on issues pertaining to it in a way that the council would approve (or at least listen to). This was made easier by the fact that Archiades, like his ancestors, actively served as a public benefactor within Athens.[140] In a sense, Archiades came to reprise the role that

136. Hegias, the son of Asclepigeneia, was an adolescent when he took classes from Proclus in the early 480s. If one assumes that he was eighteen in 480 (an exceptionally early age to begin the study of high-level philosophy), his mother was likely born sometime between 440 and 450. When Proclus cured her she was a girl who still lived with her parents (*Vit. Proc.* 29). This suggests that her illness occurred sometime in the late 440s or (more probably) in the mid-450s.

137. *Vit. Proc.* 29.

138. M. Edwards, *Neoplatonic Saints*, 75 n. 124, raises the possibility that "grandson" may be best understood metaphorically. Nevertheless, the later activities of Archaides' descendants seem to suggest that he was connected to the family of Plutarch.

139. *Vit. Proc.* 14. It is possible that Proclus envisioned Archiades playing this role even before his exile. Proclus's difficulties may then have been caused in part by his own choice to act in Archiades' stead while he taught the young man what would be expected of him.

140. *Vit. Proc.* 14. On this interpretation of the passage, see M. Edwards, *Neoplatonic Saints*, 77 n. 137.

his grandfather had played. He was both an active member of the local aristocracy and an influential local face who could use his involvement in Athenian political affairs to protect the interests of the school.

As Archiades grew into his public role, the school became stronger and better protected. This support freed Proclus from worries about again being forced into exile. He became somewhat disengaged politically and spoke at the assembly meetings only on the rare occasion when he was forced to advocate the rights of his students.[141] Aside from such instances, Proclus served mainly as a passive public figure who wrote letters to governors on his friends' behalf and generously gave money to Athenians.[142]

Proclus's delegation of the school's political representation to Archiades and his close relationships with other wealthy pagans gave the school enough political and financial support to survive unmolested. In this safety, Proclus composed commentaries on theological works like the Chaldean Oracles, worked on treatises examining pagan theology, and wrote texts designed to disprove Christian doctrines about creation.[143] In addition to the advantages that the school received from their political patronage, the financial support given by these patrons was equally important.[144] It enabled Proclus to employ assistants and, in all probability, also made it possible for him to offer scholarships to interested pagan students who may not have been able to afford the trip to Athens.[145] The attraction of as many new students as possible was important both in ensuring the school's continued prominence and in spreading its doctrines.[146] The more such students it could attract and teach, the better the chance that the type of philosophy it taught would be preserved and spread.

141. *Vit. Proc.* 16.

142. Ibid., 16–17.

143. This last work is the provocative *De Aeternitate Mundi,* which was later attacked by John Philoponus.

144. Though Marinus says that Rufinus's gift to Proclus was turned down, Damascius says that the income from the school's estates totaled a thousand *solidi* in the time of Proclus. The reason was that "as pious lovers of learning died at various times they left to the philosophers enough money to ensure the leisure and tranquility for a philosophical life" (*Vit. Is.* Ath. 102; Z. Ep. 158, fr. 265; trans. Athanassidi). It is clear, then, that Proclus did not look askance upon all gifts to the school, especially when the deaths of their donors would have freed the school from any potential meddling.

145. J. Glucker (*Antiochus and the Late Academy,* 254) has figured that the thousand *solidi* were sufficient to fund fifteen teachers. Nowhere near this number of teachers is ever mentioned in our sources, so it is likely that some of this money was also given to students as scholarships (as was the case in many fourth-century schools).

146. This is not to say that he accepted every student who wished to enroll. The notorious Hilarius of Antioch, turned away by Proclus because of his dissolute lifestyle, was probably only one of many such people (*Vit. Is.* Ath. 91A; Z. fr. 222–23). Marinus does speak of the generosity Proclus showed to family members of his associates (*Vit. Proc.* 17) and it is possible that Am-

The school's popularity masked the fact that it was in many ways quite out of touch with an Athenian political and religious reality in which Christianity played an ever-increasing role. The network of supporters Proclus was able to attract both within Athens and outside of the city was the only factor that enabled it to thrive in such an environment.[147] Nevertheless, when Proclus was at the height of his powers, the school thrived. Proclus's school had the capacity to attract and train a great number of students from all over the empire. Once in Athens, the best of these could be included among his *hetairoi*. Indeed, by the later stages of his career, the number and influence of his associates caused Proclus to request publicly that the city increase the political status of his *hetairoi* and make them eligible for public funding for their meals.[148] This was an old convention followed in the *Mouseion* of Alexandria and elsewhere in the Mediterranean world.[149] It gave a special sort of recognition to the most accomplished scholars. Though perhaps a bit tongue-in-cheek, Proclus's request that his pagan associates be treated in the same way as great intellectuals of the past reflects a different reality from that which he knew earlier in his career. In spite of his earlier missteps, Proclus had ultimately developed a remarkably effective administrative strategy.

The repute and security that the school appeared to enjoy at the height of Proclus's career depended upon Proclus's reputation as a scholar and the relationships he had established with influential pagans. In a sense these two things reinforced each other. Proclus was able to establish a great reputation because he had the political savvy to survive and actively teach for nearly fifty years. At the same time, his longevity and renown attracted the attention and support of pagan aristocrats like Rufinus, Theagenes, and Asclepiodotus. These factors did much to obscure the fact that the way he taught was ob-

---

monius and Heliodorus, two students whose father had died and left the family deep in debt, may have received some preferential financial treatment. It is additionally possible, though I do not think it likely, that Olympiodorus's statement about the Athenian schools being free of tuition (*In. Alc.* 140–41) describes Proclus's school.

147. It is likely that Rufinus fits this profile, but the best example of an outside supporter of the school is the Aphrodisian Asclepiodotus.

148. Marinus's description of this is worth quoting in full: Proclus "encouraged the growth of the study of reason, for he aided those who pursued it and demanded that food allowances (σιτηρέσια) and other honors be correctly given to each according to his merit" (*Vit. Proc.* 16). Though Eunapius uses the term σιτηρέσια to describe the corn dole Constans placed under the control of Prohaeresius, the statement that Proclus demanded both σιτηρέσια and appropriate honors seems to hearken back to a similar, earlier term. This is the σίτησις that Philostratus describes as a reward given to prominent scholars at Alexandria's *Mouseion*. For it, see Philostratus, *Vit. Soph.* 524, 533.

149. For more on this convention at the *Mouseion*, see chapter 6.

jectionable to an increasingly large segment of the Athenian population. The Christian forces that had initially forced him into exile were still present in the city and, in all likelihood, still eager to force him from the city again. Their efforts amounted to nothing because of the steps that Proclus had taken to secure his position.

Proclus's decision to train Archiades to serve as an advocate on behalf of the school represents the most crucial of these steps. In a sense, this replicated the formula that had allowed Plutarch to found his school with so little visible objection. Most members of the council would have known little about what went on in the inner circle of Proclus's school. Most would not have cared but, for the suspicious or Christian among them, what knowledge they had of Proclus's religious activities could have proved worrying. When represented by the friendly face of the Athenian Archiades, the school became less sinister than when Proclus, the terse and ascetic Lycian, spoke for its interests. When others like Theagenes and Rufinus also spoke on its behalf, the school likely became even more acceptable. As time passed and Proclus too became a familiar face to Athenians, the subtle reassurances of these men would have been less important. Nevertheless, if their support were to be withdrawn, people would again look suspiciously at the school and its leaders. As Plutarch would have understood, the survival of Proclus's school was decided by the local perception of his influence and his activities. The positive public face that Archiades, Theagenes, and others lent to Proclus's enterprise protected him from the attention of local Christians and allowed provincial officials to pretend to be unaware of his activities. It also helped Proclus to develop his public presence from that of a weak young man into that of a secure and respected philosopher. Ultimately, the survival of Proclus's school is testimony to the strength of this political arrangement and the resilience of his character.

Chapter 5

The Closing
of the Athenian Schools

When one looks at the Athenian Neoplatonic school in the first three-quarters of the fifth century, its success in a potentially unfriendly religious and social climate is particularly notable. This success was due in large part to the political sensibilities of the institution's heads. In the early fifth century, the scholarch Plutarch used his deep ties to the Athenian aristocracy to protect the school from the negative attention of Christian and provincial officials. Under Proclus, the position of the school within the community improved. Though political weakness had once forced Proclus into exile, he eventually managed to make the school more politically potent than even his predecessor had. He did this by deliberately adopting a low political profile and selecting Archiades, an Athenian and the grandson of Plutarch, to serve as the public face of the school. While Archiades gave the school a potent local presence, Proclus also managed to secure the support of a number of wealthy and prominent pagan landholders both within Attica and in other parts of the empire. This collection of supporters gave the school effective political protection for as long as Proclus remained at its head.

Proclus was the key to the success of this arrangement. The respect he commanded as a person of great intellectual accomplishment and spiritual knowledge both attracted the attention of prominent pagans and restrained them from trying to influence events in the school. Once he slipped away from the scene, his successor would have to earn the same sort of personal respect. If he could not, there would be nothing to prevent these men from fighting amongst themselves over the direction of the school.

This chapter draws in part on E. Watts, "Justinian, Malalas, and the End of Athenian Philosophical Teaching in A.D.529," *Journal of Roman Studies* 94 (2004): 168–82.

PROCLUS AND THE PROBLEM OF SUCCESSION

Proclus himself seems to have realized the dangers inherent in such a situation and, late in his life, he became quite concerned about the choice of a capable successor. In his time at the school, Proclus had twice witnessed the transfer of power between a scholarch and a successor. Once, when Syrianus had followed Plutarch, the process had worked well. Syrianus took control of the school only after a thorough training process during which Plutarch ceded increasing amounts of administrative responsibility to him.[1] At the same time, he instructed his successor in how best to handle the challenges the school faced. Plutarch's careful training, then, made for an easy transition between his regime and that of Syrianus.

In the same way that the transition from Plutarch to Syrianus was an ideal transfer of authority, that between Syrianus and Proclus was a good example of a situation to be avoided. Syrianus died unexpectedly and had not yet had an opportunity to train his successor. Proclus, a young man with great intellectual gifts but no administrative experience, was thrust to the head of the school. Without any training or any real sense of how to handle the political relationships his position entailed, Proclus had a very unsuccessful first few years at the school's head. It was only with time that Proclus came to be a skillful manager of the affairs of the school.

With the lessons of his own early years as scholarch in mind, Proclus devoted a great deal of time and attention to the selection and training of a possible successor. The Athenian Neoplatonic school had a rather well-defined order of succession. Each retiring scholarch appears to have chosen both his actual successor and a deputy who assisted that man.[2] When Proclus became head of the school in his late twenties, his classmate Domninus seems to have been appointed as his deputy.[3] Perhaps because of the difficulty the two men had co-existing under this arrangement, Domninus was gradually marginalized by Proclus.[4] By the 460s, and probably earlier,

1. This process is described in more detail in chapter 4.

2. See chapter 4. Because the deputy would probably help in the initial stages of the change in administration, it is possible that he was chosen only when a change in administration appeared imminent. He would also, presumably, be the successor designate if the new scholarch were to die unexpectedly.

3. *Vit. Proc.* 26. The amusing story of the visit Domninus and Plutarch paid to a shrine of Asclepius (*Vit. Is.* Ath. 89A; Z. Ep. 134, fr. 218, 227) seems to indicate that Domninus was at the school while Plutarch was still relatively young. Domninus was the other student (along with Proclus) in the class on the Orphic hymns that Syrianus was teaching when he died (*Vit. Proc.* 26).

4. Domninus's attempts at philosophical writing received such a hostile reaction within the school that Proclus wrote a work refuting many of his interpretations (*Vit. Is.* Ath. 89A; Z. Ep. 134).

Domninus had broken with the Proclan school, left Athens, and begun teaching on his own in Syria.[5]

The next man known to have been designated as Proclus's deputy was Marinus. Marinus had an interesting pedigree. Though born a Samaritan, Marinus had converted to paganism in adolescence and then traveled to Athens to study under Proclus.[6] In Athens, Marinus developed into a capable mathematician and astronomer with additional training in advanced philosophy.[7] Because mathematics and astronomy played an important part in the early stages of the Neoplatonic curriculum, these specialties made Marinus an asset to the school. In addition to this sort of teaching, Marinus is also known to have lectured on Aristotle.[8] These teaching competencies were useful at the school, but even more crucial to Marinus's advancement was his loyalty to Proclus. Unlike Domninus, Marinus had no question about how he ranked in relation to Proclus and had no interest in disputing his teacher's ideas. He could be counted on to work patiently under his mentor and be prepared to succeed him in due course.

Despite this arrangement, by the early 470s it had become clear that, in the selection of Marinus as his successor, Proclus had made one of the few miscalculations of his later career. Marinus was of limited ability as a Platonic philosopher.[9] This was an obvious handicap, but it appears not to have alarmed Proclus as much as Marinus's health. In the early or mid-470s Marinus was stricken by a chronic illness. He would never fully recover and the

---

5. Domninus taught the Alexandrian Asclepiodotus in Syria, probably in the late 460s (*Vit. Is.* Ath. 93; Z. fr. 228).

6. For his birth and conversion see *Vit. Is.* Ath. 97A; Z. Ep. 141. On his Samaritan origins, see K. Hult, "Marinus the Samaritan: A Study of *Vit. Isid.* Fr. 141," *Classica et Mediaevalia* 43 (1993): 163–75.

7. Marinus's mathematical and astronomical work can be seen in the commentary he composed on Euclid's *Data*. He is also known to have lectured on Pappus's commentary to Book V of the *Almagest* (O. Neugebauer, *A History of Ancient Mathematical Astronomy* [New York, 1975], 1036–37).

8. *Vit. Is.* Ath. 38A; Z. Ep. 42. Marinus taught Isidore Aristotelian philosophy when Isidore arrived in the 470s. Though, in this passage, the clause "he took over the school of Proclus" is linked to the clause "he instructed Isidore in the philosophy of Aristotle" by a καί, it is incorrect to assume that these events are temporally related. Isidore had himself taught philosophy for over ten years when Marinus took over the school of Proclus. Since Aristotle was a basic precursor to higher philosophical study in the Neoplatonic curriculum, Marinus must have taught this to Isidore long before he assumed the leadership of the school.

9. This is Damascius's assessment (*Vit. Is.* Ath. 97I; Z. Ep. 245) and may reflect his experiences when he knew Marinus. As such, it is somewhat unfair. Damascius's description of Marinus's philosophical production is based upon texts written late in the latter's life when he was quite ill and unable to engage in debate. One wonders how representative they were of the man when he was at his height. Nevertheless, even if this characterization is merely attributed to Damascius's own experience, one is still struck by how intellectually insecure Marinus seems to have been.

disease came to take an ever greater toll on his health. Given his plans for Marinus, one can understand why Proclus was alarmed when he "saw the wasting away of his body."[10] Proclus himself was ageing (he would have been in his mid-sixties by this time) and was becoming less able to complete the many tasks he set out to do on a routine basis.[11]

Both Proclus and Marinus seem to have realized that there was an urgent need to find and train a capable philosopher who could be appointed as Marinus's deputy and eventual successor. There were two ways they could have approached this search. First, they could attempt to find an exceptional philosopher among Proclus's inner circle of *hetairoi*.[12] This was always the preferred method in ancient schools, but Proclus seems to have had problems keeping members of his inner circle at the school once they had completed their studies. Many of Proclus's students had traveled to his school from abroad, and most of these returned home and began teaching when they had finished their studies.[13]

Beyond the in-house candidates, Proclus's other option was to convince one of his former *hetairoi* to come back to Athens. This was more problematic than simply choosing one of the school's current *hetairoi*. From Proclus's perspective, there was a real danger that, in his time away from the school, such a student could have come to question some of the doctrines Proclus had taught. The school's abhorrence of unorthodox teaching made this a real concern,[14] but the candidates too would have had concerns in this situation. Once established, a professor of the stature that Proclus sought would naturally have been hesitant to leave a secure position in order to come to Athens.

Proclus and Marinus initially decided to approach an inner-circle student about the position. Their attention immediately turned to Isidore, an Alexandrian who had just completed his studies at the school. Isidore had come to Athens to fill out the philosophical training he had begun in Alexandria and intended to return to his home city after his time studying with Pro-

---

10. *Vit. Is.* Ath. 97K; Z. Ep. 147.

11. For the brutality of Proclus's daily schedule see *Vit. Proc.* 22, 26. By the time Proclus turned seventy (in the year 480), he was no longer able to perform his duties as scholarch with any real vigor (*Vit. Proc.* 26).

12. For this pattern of succession, see the discussion of Prohaeresius's early career in chapter 3.

13. The phenomenon of students traveling to the school of Proclus has been discussed in chapter 4. Among those who returned and began teaching in the city from which they originated are Ammonius, Heliodorus, Asclepiodotus, and Isidore.

14. As the fate of Domninus shows, this concern about philosophical orthodoxy played an important role in defining the intellectual climate of the Athenian Neoplatonic school (cf. P. Athanassiadi, "Persecution and Response in Late Paganism," *Journal of Hellenic Studies* 113 (1993): 11–12; and "Philosophy and Power: The Creation of Orthodoxy in Neoplatonism," in *Philosophy and Power in the Graeco-Roman World*, ed. G. Clark and T. Rajak [Oxford, 2002], 271–91.).

clus. Before his planned departure, Isidore was approached by someone, possibly Marinus, and asked to serve as successor designate. When Isidore initially balked at this, Proclus approached him.[15] Despite this direct appeal, Isidore was especially concerned about the religious duties of the position and his inability to measure up to them.[16] Isidore expressed these reservations to Proclus and declined the invitation.[17]

Isidore's refusal left Proclus even more concerned about the school's future. In two unfortunately abbreviated fragments of the *Life of Isidore*, we learn that "Proclus was fearful that the truly Golden Chain of Plato might abandon our city of Athens," and "he was fearful also on account of the bodily weakness that afflicted Marinus."[18] It seems that he then decided to expand the search for a deputy so that it included more of the members of his inner circle, both past and present. This led Proclus to summon Asclepiodotus to Athens. This man, who was engaged to the daughter of Proclus's benefactor Asclepiodotus of Aphrodisias, had also once studied under Proclus.[19] Proclus and Asclepiodotus thought highly of each other and, when he received word of Proclus's summons, Asclepiodotus hastened to Athens.[20] Pro-

---

15. *Vit. Is.* Ath. 98C; Z. Ep. 150, fr. 250–52. The *Life of Isidore* records three trips that Isidore made to Athens. The first of these, undertaken about 470, was his trip to begin study with Proclus. The second was a trip he made in 485 when news reached him that Proclus was on the verge of death (*Vit. Is.* Ath. 125A, B; Z. Ep. 188, fr. 327). The third follows his flight from Alexandria in 488 (*Vit. Is.* Ath. 141B; Z. Ep. 207). Since Proclus figures prominently in this episode, his appeal to Isidore must have occurred during the first of his visits to Athens. Marinus indicates that Proclus was unable to follow a conversation at the end of his life (*Vit. Proc.* 20). This makes it highly unlikely that he would have made such an appeal to Isidore at that time. Because Proclus died in 485, Isidore's third visit is clearly not a possibility.

16. "Yet the more the importance of the Succession was emphasized in Proclus's words, the less disposed to persuasion Isidore became since he felt that the burden was too great for him to bear" (*Vit. Is.* Ath. 98C; Z. fr. 252.)

17. *Vit. Is.* Ath. 98D; Z. fr. 253.

18. Ibid., Ath. 98E, F; Z. Ep. 151–52. Despite the apparent relationship of the two fragments, they are not syntactically connected. The second fragment contains a δέ while the first has no reciprocal μέν. In addition, the participle δεδίως is repeated in each. The fragments are concurrent in Photius's text, however, and while their direct relationship is highly questionable, the thematic relationship between the two is undeniable. It is likely, then, that Proclus's fear for the disruption of the Athenian Platonic tradition arose from both his concern about Marinus's physical weakness and some other unknown cause (which could have been represented by a missing μέν clause preceding the second fragment).

19. For his engagement and marriage see *Vit. Is.* Ath. 86 A–G; Z. fr. 202, 204, 205, 208, 210, 211, 130. He and his wife, Damiane, also figure prominently in the *Life of Severus* by Zacharias Scholasticus.

20. This seems to be the case based upon P. Athanassiadi's understanding of *Vit. Is.* Ath. 99A; Z. Ep. 153, fr. 255. Given the sequence of the fragments in Photius's text, it is clear that Proclus summoned someone to Athens after Isidore refused his invitation. As Athanassiadi apparently surmised, Asclepiodotus's portrayal in the text strongly suggests that he was this second-choice candidate.

clus had confidence that Asclepiodotus was the right person for the position but, when he arrived in Athens, it seems that Asclepiodotus was something of a disappointment. As a result, Proclus decided not to ask Asclepiodotus to fill the open position.[21]

After the rejection of Asclepiodotus, Proclus turned his search back within the ranks of his own school. A fragment of the *Life of Isidore* indicates that Zenodotus, a man described as "the darling of Proclus,"[22] was eventually chosen to occupy the third position in the hierarchy of the school. Though very little is known about him, it seems that Zenodotus was a good fit for this position. Marinus specialized in mathematics and Zenodotus was interested in theoretical philosophy.[23] His selection ensured that the school would continue to have a conventional philosopher at the top of its hierarchy.

Proclus had great affection for Zenodotus and Marinus, but he seems to have realized that both men had their limitations. These two men were loyal but mediocre candidates. Late in his life, however, Proclus did find a young student who had the potential to be a thinker on par with himself and his predecessors. This young man, Hegias, was the grandson of Archiades and the son of Theagenes, a senatorial patron of the Athenian Neoplatonic school. Along with this notable genealogy, Hegias had uncommon scholarly potential. Damascius writes of him: "When he was still but an adolescent,[24] [Hegias] had hopes for himself and gave hope to everyone else that he would not fall short of the great Plutarch. Indeed, Proclus thought him worthy, when he was still a youth,[25] of [participating in] his seminar on the Chaldean Oracles."[26]

Hegias entered the school as the 480s dawned. At this point, Proclus was

21. Asclepiodotus may have been the candidate about whom Damascius recalled, "He was enraged because he was not chosen, but he did not show it at that time" (*Vit. Is.* Ath. 99C; Z. fr. 148).

22. *Vit. Is.* Ath. 99B; Z. Ep. 154. P. Athanassiadi's use of "darling" for παιδικά seems especially appropriate. The placement of this fragment within the Photian epitome of the *Life of Isidore* seems to indicate that Zenodotus was not only considered as a possible successor but even put among the finalists. The fragment seems to be the second half of a comparison, quite possibly between Zenodotus and Asclepiodotus.

23. The contrast between the interests of Marinus and those of Zenodotus is suggested by their teaching competencies. When Damascius studied in Athens, Marinus taught him mathematical and scientific courses while Zenodotus taught the more conventional philosophical courses (for this see Photius, *Bib.* cod. 181.83–85). Based on this, P. Athanassiadi (*Damascius: The Philosophical History* [Athens, 1999], 44 n. 74) has suggested that Marinus died before Damascius had reached the stage where he was learning theoretical philosophy. This is a possibility, but not something we can be certain about. It is interesting, however, that we have no evidence that Marinus ever taught theoretical philosophy.

24. μειράκιον—this word conventionally refers to a youth around the age of twenty.

25. νέον—though less specific in meaning than μειράκιον, it seems to indicate that Hegias was still unusually young to undertake this type of training.

26. *Vit. Is.* Ath. 145B; Z. fr. 351.

nearing seventy, and signs of his physical and mental decline had become evident.[27] When a professor reached such an age and condition, it was customary for him to turn over many of the responsibilities incumbent upon the head of the school to his successor.[28] Proclus, however, seems to have allowed Hegias's astounding potential to disrupt his retirement. "Although he was so weak, the youth Hegias made [Proclus] more enthusiastic about his lectures . . . [and] Proclus carefully discussed with him both Platonism and the other studies of the divine."[29]

This is, of course, a familiar pattern within the Athenian Neoplatonic school. Plutarch, Hegias's great-great-grandfather, had made the same sacrifice so that he could teach Proclus in the 430s.[30] As Plutarch had done for him, Proclus made a special effort to teach the young Hegias. He must have sensed that this young student had the potential to be the best he had ever taught. This must have had a powerful effect upon Proclus. If such a student fulfilled his potential, he would further secure Proclus's reputation as a great teacher. More importantly, by instructing Hegias, Proclus could ensure that the doctrines he had taught would continue to be understood by another generation of teachers. Because the stakes were so high, Proclus allowed Hegias to begin advanced courses in philosophy and theology, including his capstone seminar on the Chaldean Oracles, without completing the early stages of the curriculum.

As Proclus entered the last years of his life, he had reasons to be both optimistic and pessimistic about the future of his school. He had managed to create a succession structure that, at least in theory, guaranteed the institutional and doctrinal continuity of the Athenian school. Marinus was secured as his successor and, should anything happen to him, Zenodotus was prepared to assume control. Succession struggles were the greatest threat to late antique schools and Proclus could hope that his efforts in the late 470s had eliminated the possibility of such a struggle's occurring.[31] Beyond his immediate successors, Proclus also had found in Hegias a young student who was capable of leading the school in the generation following Marinus. The potential stability that came from this clear path of succession seemed to bode well for the future of the school.

This clarity had come at quite a price. The selection process that Proclus

---

27. *Vit. Proc.* 26. See chapter 4 for a more detailed discussion.

28. Marinus remarked as follows about this stage in Proclus's life: "He fell into a state unequal to all of his activities. Although he was in such a state, he prayed, composed hymns, wrote sometimes, and had discussions with companions, but he did all these things more feebly" (*Vit. Proc.* 26). Marinus and Zenodotus must surely have taken up the administrative and educational slack.

29. *Vit. Proc.* 26.

30. Ibid., 12.

31. The dangers of a succession struggle can be seen in chapter 3.

had used to choose Marinus's deputy alienated both former students and, more importantly, some of the influential men upon whom the school relied for political support. This seems to have been especially true of Asclepiodotus of Aphrodisias. His son-in-law had come to Athens expecting that Proclus would offer him the position and had returned in disappointment. One cannot suppose that, in those circumstances, Asclepiodotus would have continued to spend much time trying to help the school. Even Hegias, the great hope for the future of the school, was not an entirely unproblematic figure. While he was a direct descendant of Plutarch the scholarch and Archiades, Hegias was the product of a marriage arranged by the socially respected but poor Archiades and the wealthy family of Theagenes.[32] Theagenes was the wealthier and more influential partner in the marriage and, as such, he had little patience for the protocol of the philosophical school.[33] Hegias seems to have inherited some of his sense of entitlement. There was a very real possibility that Hegias would get restless while waiting for both Marinus and Zenodotus to pass from the scene.

Even so, when Proclus died in April of 485, his grieving associates were probably optimistic that his efforts to ensure an orderly succession would prevent the school from being torn apart by internal struggles. The problems that his efforts had caused must have seemed rather distant. As it turned out, these problems arrived at the school more rapidly than anyone might have expected. In a short time, Proclus's orderly arrangement was completely undone.

THE NEOPLATONIC SCHOOL AFTER PROCLUS

The events that followed the death of Proclus are even less clear than those that preceded it. Our only account of them comes from the *Life of Isidore* and, without supporting evidence, its fragmentary nature makes it nearly impossible to establish a chronology of events. Nevertheless, from the pieces of the text that survive, one can see that the succession plan arranged by Proclus was put into effect. Marinus did, in fact, succeed Proclus as the head of the school and Zenodotus seems to have served immediately under him.[34] Each one assumed the teaching duties that Proclus hoped they would. But problems were evident. Perhaps feeling the need to expand his competen-

---

32. For Archiades' financial state at the time see *Vit. Is.* Ath. 105A; Z. fr. 273.

33. *Vit. Is.* Ath. 100A; Z. fr. 261.

34. Marinus's authorship of the *Life of Proclus* is indication enough of his status. Zenodotus is marked as a "successor" by Photius in the ninth century. Photius may have been relying upon a lost portion of the *Life of Isidore* for this information, but it is also possible that he took it from an independent source.

cies to suit his new status as scholarch, Marinus began work on two Platonic commentaries, both unsuccessful works derided by his contemporaries.[35] This intellectual blunder was matched by a political misstep. Not long after this, Marinus managed to alienate Theagenes, the father of Hegias, who had become the school's richest and most influential supporter in the later years of Proclus's life.[36] While helpful, Theagenes was also notoriously hot-tempered and interested in using his patronage activities to increase his own reputation.[37] Theagenes was initially restrained in his dealings with the school by his great respect for the powerful personalities of Proclus and Archiades.[38] With the passing of Proclus and, not much later, that of Archiades, his attitude began to change.[39] Between the composition of the *Life of Proclus* in 485–86 and the arrival of Isidore in Athens in 489, the relationship between Theagenes and the caretakers of the Neoplatonic school rapidly deteriorated.[40] Marinus was younger and less imposing than Proclus and, freed from the watchful eye of Archiades, Theagenes began to expect a degree of flattery from the philosopher.

Marinus would not flatter Theagenes. Although Theagenes fancied himself a student of philosophy and craved the approval of philosophers, Marinus refused to acknowledge him as a philosophical compatriot. Marinus would give Theagenes the honors appropriate to a man who held high rank in the empire, but he consciously withheld any recognition of his philosophical pretensions.[41] Marinus felt that Theagenes had become so involved

35. Marinus's discomfort in his new position is clear from the introduction of the *Life of Proclus*. Though many authors claim to be inadequately prepared for the task they are about to undertake, Marinus seems more convinced of his own inadequacy than most ancient writers. For the reaction to his commentaries, see *Vit. Is.* Ath. 97J; Z. fr. 245.

36. The school was not the only pagan institution that benefited from his attention. Theagenes also served as a patron to the poet Pamprepius and to other teachers. It seems best to attribute the poem written in honor of Theagenes to Pamprepius (see E. Heitsch, *Die griechischen Dichterfragmente der römischen Kaiserzeit* [Göttingen, 1961–64], xxxv). This poem mentions his great wealth and then dubs him, a bit disingenuously, "a calm shelter for the race of poets."

37. Given Damascius's flair for focusing upon a subject's negative characteristics, it is not surprising to find this noted in the *Vit. Is.* Ath. 100A; Z. fr. 258. In this case, however, Damascius may not have misrepresented Theagenes. Malchus (fr. 23, Blockley) describes the violence with which Theagenes investigated a charge leveled against his former client Pamprepius.

38. One immediately recalls the touching scene where the young Theagenes tries to comfort Archiades after the loss of much of his family property (*Vit. Is.* Ath. 105A; Z. fr. 273).

39. It is known that Archiades died after Proclus because Proclus left property to him and his family (*Vit. Proc.* 14). He was still living when the *Life of Proclus* was composed but was dead by the time Damascius arrived in Athens in 489. Given the way that he is described in the *Life of Isidore*, Damascius apparently did not know him personally.

40. In the *Life of Proclus*, Marinus still described Theagenes as "a benefactor." By the time Damascius arrived in Athens, however, Theagenes and Marinus had an extremely icy relationship.

41. *Vit. Is.* Ath. 100A; Z. fr. 261.

in public life that he was no longer a philosopher, and, as such, he merited none of the respect Marinus would accord to a peer.[42]

Theagenes was sensitive to this sort of implicit criticism. He cherished his philosophical pedigree[43] and he made such an effort to live a life of restraint that even Marinus, presumably in one of his weaker moments, recognized that he was the most distinguished of Roman senators in this regard.[44] Furthermore, outside of the Athenian school, there were many philosophers who were not as particular in their definitions of suitable philosophical conduct as Marinus happened to be.[45] To Theagenes, the approving words of these men would have confirmed his suspicion that Marinus was being unduly prickly and unkind.[46]

Though Marinus was perhaps justified in taking such a position from a purely philosophical standpoint,[47] there were ways for a philosopher to criticize an individual without resorting to such an extreme measure. By falling back into the crouch of philosophical propriety, Marinus had managed to emphasize his own integrity as a philosopher (a thing which, despite his many shortcomings, was never in doubt). In the process, he had chosen to alienate the school's most important political backer when there were ample means for him to be gracefully placated.

These problems with the supporters of the school led to a dramatic transformation in the political position of the school and its professors. In 480, the school was headed by a respected philosopher, protected in Athens by Archiades and Theagenes, and supported by wealthy people throughout the eastern empire. By 487, the succession debacle, the death of Proclus, and the social missteps of Marinus left the school and its teachers in a much less secure position. This is not to say that the school faced any major external threat.

---

42. Damascius had a similar reaction. "Since he valued new honors before the traditional piety, he separated himself from the Hellenes and his ancestors and fell into the life of the multitude in a way that escaped even his own notice" (*Vit. Is.* Ath. 100 A; Z. fr. 258). This passage has often been understood as an indication that Theagenes converted to Christianity in return for high government positions, but this ignores the force of "it escaped his own notice." Clearly one could not convert without realizing it. Instead, Damascius's meaning seems to be that, in choosing to assume some of the highest honors in the Roman state, Theagenes did not realize that he had moved away from the philosophical ideal. On the hazards of identifying Hellenism as a religious instead of a cultural category, see G. Bowersock, *Hellenism in Late Antiquity* (Ann Arbor, 1990), 7–11.

43. Pamprepius is careful to acknowledge this in his panegyric by establishing a fictional familial link between Theagenes and Plato.

44. *Vit. Is.* Ath. 100B; Z. fr. 261.

45. Characteristically, Damascius styles these philosophers as "flatterers" (*Vit. Is.* Ath. 100A; Z. fr. 258).

46. This would be understandable given the perception that Marinus was socially awkward (*Vit. Is.* Ath. 101A; Z. fr. 260).

47. So Damascius suggests (*Vit. Is.* Ath. 100A; Z. fr. 258).

It did not. But the extreme misgivings that the school's patrons had about the current administration meant that any internal disagreements that arose would not be easily settled. The school lacked a powerful leader and, with a number of wealthy, dissident supporters, was now susceptible to internal conflicts.

It was not long after the death of Proclus that an internal dispute did break out in the school. The *Life of Isidore* is silent about the cause, but it does describe the result. Marinus chose the wrong side in the dispute and quickly ended up with powerful enemies arrayed against him. "On account of this strife Marinus withdrew from Athens to Epidaurus since he suspected that plots were being directed against his very life."[48] Marinus returned after a time of exile, but his departure had caused the major supporters of the school to fix their gaze upon the academic hierarchy. Marinus's exile had placed the regime that he headed in an exceedingly weak position. When Marinus came back to the school, Hegias had assumed a much higher profile. Hegias had both political and philosophical differences with Marinus, and his new influence within the school caused real doctrinal dispute to erupt. The *Life of Isidore* preserves various fragmentary *aporiai* in which Hegias takes unorthodox positions only to see them refuted by other thinkers.[49] Despite these thorough refutations and the custom that unorthodox thinkers should be separated from the community, no one was able to force Hegias out of the school.

Eventually, it seems that Marinus and Hegias settled into something of an uneasy coexistence, but an unexpected development changed the Athenian school's internal dynamics in early 489. At that time, Isidore, Proclus's first choice to be Marinus's successor, came to Athens as an exile from Alexandria.[50] With him came Damascius. The future scholarch was at that time simply a young rhetorician who had received only basic philosophical training.[51] He was, however, eager to broaden his training. When they arrived, Isidore and Damascius seem to have gravitated immediately towards Marinus and his supporters. Damascius was turned over to Marinus and Zenodotus for a fuller and more proper philosophical education.[52] Isidore, for his part, be-

---

48. *Vit. Is.* Ath. 101C; Z. Ep. 77. On this passage note as well P. Athanassiadi, *Damascius,* 247 n. 273.

49. See, for example, *Vit. Is.* Ath. 149A; Z. fr. 364. The late antique period is not without the sort of doctrinal factionalism that characterized the administration of Hellenistic philosophical schools. While Hellenistic professors who disagreed with the rest of the school would eventually disassociate themselves from the institution (J. Glucker, *Antiochus and the Late Academy* [Göttingen, 1978], 13 ff.), it was not uncommon for differing philosophical opinions to exist for a time in the same school. In late antiquity, teachers were just as prone to disagreement, but they were also quicker to leave such situations (as happened with Domninus).

50. For the specific events leading to his journey, see chapter 8.

51. Damascius's early education is known from Photius, *Bib.* cod. 181.80 ff.

52. Photius *Bib.* cod. 181.84–85.

came the voice that opposed Hegias in the debates within the school.[53] In this matter Isidore's leadership was crucial. By the time Isidore arrived, Marinus had become too frail even to take difficult questions from students.[54] He certainly could not continue to contend with Hegias.

Isidore, by contrast, brought energy to the faction opposing Hegias and, as Marinus became increasingly ill, the scholarch began rethinking the selection of Zenodotus as his successor.[55] Untainted by the events of the mid-480s and vigorous in his opposition to Hegias, Isidore seemed to be a much better candidate than Zenodotus in the present circumstances. Apparently in recognition of this, Marinus renewed Proclus's plea that Isidore agree to be appointed as deputy scholarch.[56] Despite his reservations, this time Isidore relented and agreed to accept the position but not the actual responsibilities attached to it.[57]

It is not immediately clear how Isidore became a deputy scholarch while remaining exempt from the accordant responsibilities.[58] The position was a great honor and one cannot imagine that Marinus bestowed it upon Isidore in a purely ceremonial sense. It is likely, in fact, that some sort of compromise was reached, possibly one in which Isidore held the honors of a deputy scholarch without the administrative responsibilities that came with running the school (which would perhaps be left to someone else). In return, Isidore may have agreed to use the authority of his new position to oppose Hegias and his party in the school's internal disputes.

Isidore's acceptance of the position initially cheered the partisans of Marinus.[59] Their hope was that Isidore could restore peace in the school and defend the integrity of its teachings. Unfortunately, this hope was not realized. Isidore took the position with great reluctance and was not terribly effective in it. In fact, once he assumed the mantle, it seems that the situation got much worse for the Marinian party. Damascius remarks about this time:

53. In the philosophical discussions that P. Athanassiadi has reconstructed from the fragments of the *Life of Isidore*, Isidore and Hegias are the disputants. In these, Isidore remains civil yet quite firmly opposed to Hegias. These fragmentary discussions are found in *Vit. Is.* Ath. 149A, B, C, 150; Z. fr. 364, 366, 61, Ep. 227.

54. *Vit. Is.* Ath. 97D; Z. fr. 241. This fragment seems to be based upon Damascius's personal experience and, therefore, must date to the late 480s when he was himself a student of Marinus.

55. *Vit. Is.* Ath. 148A; Z. Ep. 224.

56. Ibid., Ath. 148B; Z. Ep. 225.

57. Ibid., Ath. 148C; Z. Ep. 226.

58. Damascius uses the curious phrase ἐψηφίσθη διάδοχος ἐπ᾽ ἀξιώματι μᾶλλον ἢ πράγματι.

59. *Vit. Is.* Ath. 148D, E; Z. Ep. 303, 304. As P. Athanassiadi has noted (*Damascius*, 325 n. 389), the image of light overcoming darkness that Damascius uses to describe the hopes aroused by Isidore's decision contrasts with the image of darkness overcoming light that Marinus uses to describe the death of Proclus. This was supposed to be the closing of a particularly dark chapter in the school's history.

"He had deluded even himself into trying to correct an incorrigible situation, one which had advanced to an excessively bad state. He did not accomplish anything more."[60] Both Isidore and Marinus had underestimated the resistance Hegias could put up and, with their efforts failing, Isidore decided to leave Athens. As he was making these preparations, Marinus finally succumbed to his long illness. He died leaving Isidore as his successor.

His experience as the ceremonial successor had left Isidore with no desire to assume the actual leadership role in the school. He knew the situation was one in which he could not easily prevail and wanted no further part in it. After the death of Marinus, then, Isidore seems to have decided not to suspend his departure. Further recognizing the reality of the circumstances, Isidore handed power not to the discredited Zenodotus but to Hegias and his own appointed successor, Syrianus. As his parting words to his former adversaries, Isidore advised: "It is necessary for [you] to restore philosophy which is now wasting away."[61] His couched criticism of his adversaries' doctrines and actions no doubt amused Isidore as much as it angered Hegias, but, in the end, this mattered little. Hegias had prevailed.

THE ATHENIAN SCHOOL UNDER HEGIAS AND DAMASCIUS

Hegias had won this political battle, but he now headed a divided school. Although he was no longer in a high position in the hierarchy, Zenodotus was still teaching in the school.[62] The students of Marinus who had acclaimed Isidore upon his selection as honorary successor were also still on the premises. Foremost among them was Damascius, Isidore's friend and a staunch opponent of Hegias. It is reasonable to believe that these men made life as difficult for Hegias as his supporters had made it for Isidore. Unfortunately, we cannot know the degree to which internal disaffection affected Hegias's ability to manage the school. The only information that has come down to us about Hegias comes from the unfriendly pen of Isidore's disciple Damascius. But his assessment is characteristically blunt: "We have heard that philosophy in Athens was never so despised as we had seen it when it was dishonored under Hegias."[63]

Damascius elaborates upon the condition of philosophical teaching under Hegias and the picture he paints, though biased, shows a school that was

60. *Vit. Is.* Ath. 151B; Z. Ep. 228. Though it seems more like a description of the problems Isidore faced, it is possible that this remark refers to Marinus.

61. *Vit. Is.* Ath. 151E; Z. Ep. 230.

62. It is probably in this period that he taught Damascius. For this relationship, see Photius, *Bib.* cod. 181.84.

63. *Vit. Is.* Ath. 145A; Z. Ep. 221. Given Hegias's continued role in the school, J. Glucker's suggestion (*Antiochus and the Late Academy*, 307 n. 23) that this statement refers to Hegias as a political figure is almost certainly mistaken.

run with little regard for what the city around it would find palatable. Like Proclus, Hegias emphasized the religious elements of philosophical teaching more than any other part of the school's curriculum. Damascius records that Hegias led pagan religious rituals and, as a result, came into conflict with local authorities.[64] From Damascius's account, it appears that these religious rites were of two types. The first type, "the rites of his ancestors" were secretly celebrated "throughout Attica"[65] and may well be the theurgic type of rituals that had been a part of Hegias's family for over a hundred and fifty years. These rituals probably included any number of things, such as crop blessings and healings, and may have resembled those performed by Nestorius to avert earthquakes and those employed by Proclus to bring about rainstorms.[66] The second sort of religious activity, the revitalization of dormant religious rituals, is again consistent with the historical activities of the Athenian scholarch.[67]

Insofar as they corresponded to philosophic ideals, Hegias's activities were defensible. By emphasizing religious ritual beyond all else in the school, Hegias was broadly following the pattern established by his mentor, Proclus. In reality, however, Hegias's actions differed in a crucial way from previous scholarchs. Unlike Proclus and his predecessors, Hegias had little interest in doing these things discreetly.[68] In fact, he was particularly ostentatious in the pagan rituals he performed.

Hegias's ostentation was particularly ill advised in the early-sixth-century Athenian political climate. Much of the school's external support had dissolved following the disastrous succession battles of the 480s and 490s. With Hegias in power, the school's political and financial support must have come overwhelmingly from the family of Theagenes. Financially, the family was probably able to continue supporting the school for long into the future.

---

64. "From these actions scandal arose in the city and he attracted angry hatred and was plotted against both by those who longed for the abundant possessions, of which he was the master, and by some of the men who established the laws" (*Vit. Is.* Ath. 145B; Z. fr. 351).

65. This passage is quite obscure. The Greek reads τά τε τῶν κηδεστῶν ἱερὰ λαθὼν ἐτελειώσατο κατὰ τὴν Ἀττικήν. P. Athanassiadi (*Damascius*, 319 and n. 382) has translated the phrase as "he completed work on the shrines of his relatives all over Attica, secretly" and, alternatively, "he performed all over Attica holy rites on behalf of his in-laws secretly." It seems best to understand the genitive κηδεστῶν as a simple possessive genitive. The rites then become not simple rituals intended to honor dead relatives, but the rites favored by these ancestors.

66. See chapter 4 for these activities.

67. Proclus's work to reestablish traditional cults is especially notable in this way. The most memorable example of this activity came during his exile in Asia (*Vit. Proc.* 15). P. Athanassiadi, *Damascius*, 320 n. 382, has also noted the similarity between the activities of Hegias and those of Proclus.

68. Damascius says that his actions were "more reckless than pious" (*Vit. Is.* Ath. 145B; Z. fr. 351). Peter Brown (letter of August 29, 2003) has suggested that Hegias's "recklessness" may refer to an overly aggressive "probing of the divine," possibly through divination. If this is the case, this would have attracted unwanted official attention to his activities.

Politically, however, the situation was different. Despite being a rather prickly man, Theagenes had been an individual who maneuvered quite well in political circles. Hegias, by contrast, had few of the direct political contacts of his father and even less of his political acuity. Even worse, his ostentatious paganism increased his political inefficacy. This was a dangerous situation for both Hegias and the school. Absent the political cover provided by his father, Hegias's public religious activities provided his enemies with an attractive and relatively easy target.

In fact, Hegias's actions attracted the attention of both informers within the city and the Achaean provincial magistrates.[69] Though he escaped with his life and property, Hegias was publicly chastised.[70] Nothing is known about what followed, but one cannot imagine that circumstances were comfortable for either the school or the scholarch. However, there was another, more important consequence of Hegias's troubles. For the first time since Proclus had assembled his powerful patrons in the 450s, the opponents of the Neoplatonic school had managed to win a victory against the philosophers who taught in the city. The actions taken against Hegias had made the vulnerability of the school and its scholarch apparent to everyone in Athens.

The eventual fate of Hegias is unknown to us but, through either death or dismissal, Damascius replaced him as scholarch.[71] Whatever the circumstances, the change from the administration of Hegias to that of Damascius led to a remarkable shift in the direction of the school. This becomes clear enough in the way that Damascius chose to present his predecessor in the *Life of Isidore*. On the most basic level the descriptions of Hegias contained within the text are far from flattering. Hegias was bright and eager, but prone to following bad advice.[72] Eventually, these characteristics led him to behave in a way that was almost entirely unphilosophical and, when Damascius took control of the school, he was eager to disavow Hegias's actions.

Beyond simply criticizing Hegias's activities, Damascius also initiated a reevaluation of the doctrines that were taught in the school. Damascius differed greatly from his predecessor in his understanding of Platonic teaching and its significance. Indeed, when Damascius assumed control of the

69. This must be the identity of the "people who establish the laws" described in *Vit. Is.* Ath. 145B; Z. fr. 351.

70. Ibid.

71. The *Life of Isidore* is the only source that provides any information about the school in the first two decades of the sixth century. It does not mention how Hegias's tenure ended or who was selected to replace him. The date at which this occurred is equally unclear. A date of 500 is just as plausible as a date of 520 (see L. G. Westerink, *The Greek Commentaries on Plato's Phaedo*, vol. 2, *Damascius* [New York, 1976–77], 8). A date of c. 515 has been proposed by J. Combès, *Damascius, Traité des premiers principes*, vol. 1 (Paris, 1986), xix, xxxvi, and accepted by P. Athanassiadi, *Damascius*, 43.

72. *Vit. Is.* Ath. 145B; Z. fr. 351.

school he initiated a type of teaching that called into question not only the doctrines and interpretations of Hegias, but even those favored by Proclus himself. His approach to Proclan teachings becomes clear in two written treatises. These two works, a commentary on Plato's *Parmenides* and a monograph on the argument from opposites found in the *Phaedo,* have a common structure.[73] They use Proclus as a starting point for discussion and proceed to develop the ideas in a way that either supplements or, from time to time, refutes Proclus.[74] These works were clearly written for only the most educated readers because, in spite of the quantity of references to Proclus in the work, Damascius often neglects to give a full description of Proclus's position on certain topics. Only an audience of initiates who had access to both Damascius's text and the writings of Proclus to which he refers could effectively make use of these teachings.[75]

The critical examination of Proclan positions was not confined to Damascius's theoretical treatises and the inner-circle discussions of the school. One sees it as well in his commentaries on the *Phaedo* and the *Philebus.* These were originally lecture notes taken down by Damascius's students and, as such, they show the manner in which he taught his seminars. In each lecture, when the lesson called for it, Damascius introduced the Platonic text. Then he gave Proclus's explanation of the passage, followed by his own analysis of both the Platonic text and Proclus's interpretation.[76] In contrast to the way Proclan ideas are introduced in Damascius's written works, in his lectures Damascius cites the Proclan interpretation, explains it, and examines its meaning in a way that suggests the listeners were unfamiliar with it. This indicates that the critical evaluation of Proclus's ideas represented an important part of Damascius's more elementary teachings as well as his inner-circle discussions.

In each context, Damascius was especially diligent about examining Proclus's interpretations of Iamblichus. Iamblichus had played a crucial role in helping to form the ideas of the Athenian school, yet Proclus seems to have misunderstood large parts of the Iamblichan system.[77] Recognizing this, Dam-

---

73. The *Parmenides* commentary forms the second part of the manuscript that contains *On First Principles.* The monograph is found within the commentary on the *Phaedo* (1.207–52 in the edition of L. G. Westerink, 1977). That "commentary" is really a series of lecture notes into which Damascius's monograph has been copied. For a more detailed discussion of these two selections and their relationship to the texts in which they are found, see L. G. Westerink, *The Greek Commentaries on Plato's Phaedo,* vol. 2, 10–14.

74. Ibid., 10.

75. Such is Westerink's understanding of this peculiarity in the texts.

76. Westerink, *Commentaries on Plato's Phaedo,* vol. 2, 11. For a typical example of this structure see *In Phaedonem* 1.100.

77. P. Athanassiadi, "The oecumenism of Iamblichus: Latent knowledge and its awakening" *Journal of Roman Studies* 85 (1995): 247; and "Dreams, theurgy and freelance divination: The testimony of Iamblichus," *Journal of Roman Studies* 83 (1993): 128–29.

ascius worked to bring the true meaning of Iamblichus's teachings back to the school. In the words of his student Simplicius, Damascius "did not hesitate to oppose many of Proclus's doctrines because of his industriousness and his appreciation of Iamblichus's ideas."[78] Instead, he aimed to improve the teaching of the school by fixing some of the problematic elements of Proclan teaching and placing the school back upon a solid Iamblichan doctrinal foundation.[79]

Though the disavowal of Hegian conduct and the refutation of some Proclan philosophical positions were important elements of Damascius's administration, the changes he brought extended even further. From what one can tell of his fragmentary corpus of work, Damascius set out to establish a comprehensive new system of philosophical understanding in Athens along broadly Iamblichan lines. This was laid out in a series of works, nearly all of which have since been lost, that discussed Aristotle, Plato, and the Chaldean Oracles.[80] As these titles suggest, Damascius had a remarkably productive mind. Alongside his critical capacities, however, Damascius had a predilection for accounts of the paranormal. In two other works, the *Life of Isidore* and the *Paradoxa*, these interests are more fully explored.

As we have seen, the *Life of Isidore* was not primarily devoted to the description of wonders. However, in addition to its descriptions of the character of various intellectuals, the *Life of Isidore* contains vivid accounts of pagan religious sites and miraculous events.[81] The *Paradoxa* takes this one step further. The text originally contained four books that described (in succession) extraordinary actions, marvels relating to the gods, the appearances of the souls of the dead, and miscellaneous unnatural phenomena.[82] Though the text itself is completely lost, the religious implications of these stories are clear from Photius's incredulous review: "In all of this work there are only impossible, unbelievable, ill-conceived marvels and folly as are truly worthy of the godlessness and impiety of Damascius."[83] While probably not reflected in the formal curriculum, these personal interests certainly colored the school's in-

78. Simplicius, *Commentary on Aristotle's Physics*, in *CAG* IX.795, 15–17.

79. P. Athanassiadi, "The oecumenism of Iamblichus," 247, and H. D. Saffrey, "Neoplatonist spirituality II: From Iamblichus to Proclus and Damascius," in *Classical Mediterranean Spirituality: Egyptian, Greek, Roman*, ed. A. H. Armstrong (New York, 1986), 264.

80. Among Damascius's extant works are commentaries on Plato's *Parmenides, Phaedo*, and *Philebus*. Additional commentaries on Aristotle's *Meteorology* and Plato's *Republic, Phaedrus, Sophist, Timaeus*, and *Laws* are also known. For these see J. Combès, *Damascius*, vol. 1, xxxiv. His Chaldean Oracles commentary is mentioned in Damascius, *In Parmenidem* (ed. Ruelle), 9.21–22, 11.11–15, 132.9–10.

81. E.g., *Vit. Is.* Ath. 52; Z. Ep. 69 (a strange divination technique); Ath. 72E; Z. Ep. 93 (a supernaturally long lock of hair); Ath. 81; Z. Ep. 116 (a miraculous escape from a whirlpool).

82. The text is known only from Photius, *Bib.* cod. 130.

83. Photius, *Bib.* cod. 130.7–12.

tellectual environment in the same way that Damascius's doctrines shaped the curriculum.

Damascius's radical re-appraisal of Neoplatonic philosophy proved popular with his immediate peers. In the works of Olympiodorus, a much younger Alexandrian contemporary, the teachings of Damascius figure prominently.[84] The Christian John Philoponus also knew them (although he accorded Damascius much less respect than Olympiodorus did).[85] While Damascius's teachings helped to rehabilitate the reputation of the school, they had another important effect. After nearly three decades in which few students are known to have journeyed to the school for philosophical study, under Damascius it began to attract student travelers again. Eight such students are known. Two of them came from Syria and five journeyed from Asia Minor.[86] Another student, Simplicius, came to Damascius's school after spending the late 510s studying in Alexandria.

UNDERSTANDING 529

By the 520s, Damascius's powerful new teachings (complete with overt pagan religious content) enabled the Athenian school to thrive in an otherwise stagnant city.[87] The revitalization of the school, however, occurred within a province, Achaea, where Christians were increasingly dominating the political culture.[88] This was crucial because, in the early sixth century, the Roman provincial system was itself evolving. For centuries, the Roman imperial system for governing provinces had been based upon the idea that the governor was the representative of imperial power and, as such, he presided over a web of local city governments. These were usually controlled by *curiae* (or councils) that elected officials, managed affairs in the city, worked

---

84. L. G. Westerink, ed., *Prolégomènes à la philosophie de Platon* (Paris, 1990), xv.

85. Philoponus, *Commentary on the Meteorologia* (ed. M. Hayduck, *CAG* XIV.1, 1901), 44.21–36; 97.10–11; 116.36–117.31. See also J. Combès, *Damascius*, vol. 1, xxxix–xl.

86. The Syrians are Theodora (to whom the *Life of Isidore* is dedicated) and her sister. The other six are the philosophers whom Agathias (2.29–31) mentions as having journeyed to Persia with Damascius in 531.

87. The prosperity that typified early fifth-century Athenian life seems to have come to an end by the beginning of the sixth. This may have been due in part to the Vandal attack of the 460s, which destroyed the fortunes of Archiades, among other things (*Vit. Is.* Ath. 105A; Z. fr. 273; for the impact on the city see A. Frantz, *The Athenian Agora XXIV: Late Antiquity;* 267–700 [Princeton, 1988], 78–79).

88. R. Rothaus's recent study of religious change in Corinth (*Corinth: The First City of Greece* [Leiden, 2000], 93–104) demonstrates the influence of the Achaean Christian community in the sixth century. Their control over Athenian affairs was ensured by the shift of formal authority in cities from the council to a collection of notables that included bishops and priests. On this development generally, see M. Whittow, "Ruling the Late Roman and Early Byzantine City," *Past and Present* 129 (Nov. 1990): 3–29.

with governors, and, in extreme circumstances, sought punishment for unjust ones. This placed a check on governors that, in theory at least, prevented them from governing in ways that conflicted with the desires of the most important of their subjects.[89]

In the fourth and fifth centuries this system came ever closer to collapse. Within the cities, the positions of *curiales* (or councilors) were under threat. On one side, they faced the increasingly onerous financial responsibilities that accompanied the holding of office. On the other, the administrative and religious changes of the time had created powerful classes of men, both churchmen and former government officials, who were wealthy, well connected, and legally exempt from the curial system.[90] As the size of this class of men continued to increase, the councilors in the city became men of ever more modest means and influence.[91]

As civic and provincial authority increasingly concentrated around these new centers of power, emperors worked to adapt provincial government to suit this new reality. In the West, the central government had begun to respond in the early part of the fifth century. In 409, the emperor Honorius moved the responsibility for the selection of civic offices from the *curia* to a council of bishops, clergy, provincial assemblymen, landholders, and councilors.[92] It seems that the emperor Anastasius implemented a similar system in the East through which the clergy and local notables chose local officials.[93] Anastasius's reforms went beyond this, however. It appears that, sometime after 505, he curtailed the administrative functions of local *curiae*[94] and transferred many appointments of local officials to this council of bishops and

89. On the evolution of the role of a governor see C. Roueché, "The Functions of the Governor in Late Antiquity: Some Observations," *Antiquité Tardive* 6 (1998): 31–36 and 83–89.

90. For this system of exemptions and its functioning in the sixth century, see A. Laniado, *Recherches sur les notables municipaux dans l'empire protobyzantin*, Travaux et Mémoires: Monographies 13 (Paris, 2002), 102–29.

91. This process has been much discussed. For a summary, see A. H. M. Jones, *The Later Roman Empire, 284–602* (Norman, 1964), 758–60. A typical ancient complaint about the situation is that of Libanius, *Oration* 49. For an assessment of the role of councils under Justinian, see A. Laniado, *Notables municipaux*, 47–62.

92. Jones, *Later Roman Empire*, 758, bases this upon Honorius's law of 409 transferring responsibility for the appointment of the *defensor civitatis* from the *curia* to this council (*C. Just.* 1.55.8).

93. *C. Just.* 1.55.11. This law related specifically to the *defensor civitatis*, but other evidence suggests that clergy and local notables chose other officials as well (e.g., *Monumenta Asiae Minoris Antiqua* III 197). For discussion, see A. Laniado, *Notables municipaux*, 38–40.

94. Because *C. Just.* 1.55.11 mentions *curiales*, it seems that the councils still existed when the law was issued in 505. John Lydus, writing in the 550s, remembers a time in his youth when councils used to administer the cities (*De Magistribus*, 1.28), but implies that such a time had long passed. As J. H. W. G. Liebeschuetz (*The Decline and Fall of the Roman City* [Oxford, 2001], 106–9) has recently demonstrated, the councils did continue to bear certain heavy financial burdens in the cities long after they had lost governing responsibility.

landholders.[95] Though the intention was to resurrect civic government by reincorporating the wealthiest and most prominent people into the government of the cities, it seems that these measures did little to resurrect the councils. A subsequent reform of Anastasius that created a new office through which the central authority could control civic revenues indicates that the cities continued to rely upon imperial authorities to regulate their affairs.[96]

By the late 520s, the administration of Roman provinces had changed dramatically. The official center of local power in the provinces had shifted from the councilors in cities to a smaller group of local notables that included clergymen.[97] Indeed, by the 520s and 530s, legislation had begun to reflect this fact. Following the reconquest of Italy, Justinian ordered the governors of the reconquered areas to be nominated by provincial assemblies of bishops and principal landowners.[98] In 569, this measure was extended to include the whole empire.[99]

The political developments of the late fifth and early sixth centuries were problematic for both Athens and the school of Damascius. Since the fourth century, Athens had enjoyed a distinctly pagan religious character that the Roman system of provincial government had essentially protected.[100] Pagan aristocrats had worked to maintain the vitality of the Athenian council and, through it, the continuity of the city's pagan institutions. The Neoplatonic school had traditionally benefited from the support of these elite pagans. Now, with the formal power of its patrons diminished by sixth-century reforms designed to bring Christian figures into the formal decision-making process in the city, the school was left somewhat exposed. In the previous

95. For the identity and significance of these *honorati* see A. Laniado, *Notables municipaux,* 133–69; and J. H. W. G. Liebeschuetz, *Roman City,* 115–16. In contrast to the Western law of Honorius, it is unlikely that the reforms put in place by Anastasius placed much formal weight upon provincial assemblies. Indeed, provincial assemblies do not appear in sources for the later sixth century. On this, see A. Laniado, *Notables municipaux,* 229.

96. This was the *vindex.* For a discussion of the *vindex* see A. Chauvot, "Curiales et paysans en orient à la fin du Ve et au debut du VIe siècle: Note sur l'institution du *vindex,*" in *Sociétés urbaines, sociétés rurales dans l'Asie Mineure et la Syrie hellénistique et romaine,* ed. E. Frézouls, 271–81 (Strasbourg, 1987). Ancient sources are mixed in their verdict about the success of Anastasius's reform. In his panegyric of Anastasius, Priscian praises the innovation for helping the poor resist the greed of local landholders (lines 193–95). Evagrius, however, charges that the *vindex* ruined the prosperity of cities (*HE* 3.42).

97. Laniado, *Notables municipaux,* 211–14 and, with a different type of evidence, note M. Whittow, "Ruling the Late Roman City," 20–29.

98. Roueché, "The Functions of the Governor," 36. Justinian's law is *Novellarum Appendices* 7.12.

99. Jones, *Later Roman Empire,* 766; Roueché, "The Functions of the Governor," 36. For a more detailed treatment of *Novel* 149, see A. Laniado, *Notables municipaux,* 225–52.

100. See chapter 4.

century, Christians in Achaea had shown an alarming tendency to attack prominent pagan philosophers when they saw signs of political weakness. In the fifth century, Proclus had been exiled, probably for speaking out in favor of pagan practice.[101] In the early sixth, Hegias had been strongly reprimanded for displaying his paganism too openly.[102]

This was, then, the political and social setting for one of the best known events in ancient intellectual history—the final closing of the Athenian school.[103] Traditionally this event has been understood as the action of an interventionist emperor against the austere philosophers of Athens. In fact, political circumstances and historical precedent suggest that the final closing of Damascius's school, which occurred in 529, was caused by local and not specifically imperial concerns. It seems likely that the closing was simply the most serious of a series of opportunistic actions taken by Athenian and Achaean Christians against Athenian pagan intellectuals. It would then have come about in the same way as these earlier Christian triumphs.

The political situation in Achaea makes it probable that the closure of Damascius's school came about as an imperial response to a complaint forwarded by Christian notables in Achaea. Nevertheless, when one turns to the *Chronicle* of John Malalas, the one source that records the closing of the school in Athens, a different picture seems to appear. His brief notice reads as follows:[104]

> During the consulship of Decius, the emperor issued a decree and sent it to Athens ordering that no one should teach philosophy nor interpret astronomy nor in any city should there be lots cast using dice; for some who cast dice

101. *Vit. Proc.* 15.

102. Hegias's troubles are described above.

103. Numerous articles have been written arguing about the identity of the institution, the course of its closure, and the extent of activities prohibited. The school has been called the Platonic Academy by Alan Cameron, "The Last Days of the Academy at Athens," *Proceedings of the Cambridge Philological Society* 195 (1969): 7–29, an identification echoed by P. Chuvin, *A Chronicle of the Last Pagans*, trans. B. A. Archer (Cambridge, Mass., 1990), 135–39. This identification has been called into question by J. P. Lynch, *Aristotle's School: A Study of a Greek Educational Institution* (Berkeley and Los Angeles, 1972), 184–88; J. Glucker, *Antiochus and the Late Academy*, 322–23; and H. J. Blumenthal, "529 and its Sequel: What Happened to the Academy?" *Byzantion* 48 (1978): 369–85. Reasons for the closing also vary. For a description of the divergent scholarly attitudes, see G. Hällström, "The Closing of the Neoplatonic School in A.D. 529: An Additional Aspect," in *Post-Herulian Athens: Aspects of Life and Culture in Athens, A.D. 267–529*, ed. P. Castrén, 141–60 (Helsinki, 1994); J. Beaucamp, "Le philosophe et le joueur: La date de la fermeture de l'école d'Athènes," *Mélanges Gilbert Dagron*, Travaux et Mémoires 14 (2002): 21–35; and E. Watts, "The End of Athenian Philosophical Teaching," 168–82.

104. Ἐπὶ δὲ τῆς ὑπατείας τοῦ αὐτοῦ Δεκίου ὁ αὐτὸς βασιλεὺς θεσπίσας πρόσταξιν ἔπεμψεν ἐν Ἀθήναις, κελεύσας μηδένα διδάσκειν φλοσοφίαν μήτε ἀστρονομίαν ἐξηγεῖσθαι μήτε κόττον ἐν μιᾷ τῶν πόλεων γίνεσθαι, ἐπειδὴ ἐν Βυζαντίῳ εὑρεθέντες τινὲς τῶν κοττιστῶν καὶ βλασφημίαις δειναῖς ἑαυτοὺς περιβαλόντες χειροκοπηθέντες περιεβωμβίσθησαν ἐν καμήλοις. Malalas, *Chronicle*, 18.47 (ed. Thurn).

had been discovered in Byzantium indulging themselves in dreadful blasphemies. Their hands were cut off and they were paraded around on camels.

The present state of Malalas's text makes the daunting task of making sense out of his account even more difficult. The preserved version of Malalas's text is an extremely abbreviated epitome of the original chronicle.[105] Malalas's epitomator was economical even in his description of major events like the Nika Riot.[106] For something like the closing of Damascius's school, which was considered insignificant even by Malalas's later imitators, he may have been more brief.[107]

Malalas's account is abbreviated, but it does follow a deliberate structure and establishes a clear sequence of events. It indicates that, in 529, Justinian sent an edict to Athens declaring that no one was to teach philosophy nor explain astronomy nor cast lots using dice. Then there is an explanation of what provoked this—some blasphemies were uttered by men using dice in Constantinople—followed by a description of the punishment they suffered. Initially, one may be tempted to separate the passage that concerns the teaching of philosophy and astronomy in Athens from that which concerns dice in Constantinople.[108] Malalas, however, makes it clear that this ought not to be done. He uses a μηδένα... μήτε... μήτε construction to link the teaching edict with that which concerns dice. It is clear that Malalas, or his epitomator, understood each of these events to be connected to the edict that Justinian sent to Athens.[109]

While it may seem unlikely that these actions are connected in the way

---

105. B. Croke, "The development of a critical text," in *Studies in John Malalas*, ed. E. Jeffreys et al., 311–24 (Sydney, 1990). For a discussion of the textual difficulties and their specific impact on this passage, see E. Watts, "The End of Athenian Philosophical Teaching," 171–72.

106. See J. B. Bury, "The Nika riot," *Journal of Hellenic Studies* 17 (1897): 92–119 (esp. 95–106). Despite its age, Bury's work is remarkable for the clarity with which it demonstrates the various ways Malalas's original text has been abbreviated and the manner in which one can begin to reconstruct the original.

107. All other ancient sources, including those that rely upon Malalas, are silent about the incident. The *Chronicon Paschale* and the *Chronicle of John of Nikiu* both derive most of their sixth-century material from Malalas. Later Byzantine authors such as Theophanes, Zonaras, Cedrenus, and Constantine Porphyrogenitus also relied heavily upon Malalas. None of these sources mentions the closing.

108. Among those doing so are B. Croke, "Critical text," 202 n. 19; and G. Hällström, "The Closing of the Neoplatonic School," 144–45.

109. The significance of this syntactical unity becomes even clearer when one compares it to Malalas 18.20, a passage in which a series of different laws are described. These laws are introduced as νόμους and further distinguished from one another by a δέ... καί construction that precedes each new mention. A similar, though less clear, division is seen in 18.67. The μηδένα... μήτε... μήτε construction is paralleled in two other passages of Malalas (305.11–20, 401.14–19), each of which unifies different elements of one piece of legislation.

that Malalas suggests, there are good reasons to think that Malalas did intend for his readers to link them. In his accounts of Justinianic legislation Malalas generally preserves the content and structure of the original laws.[110] In all, Malalas preserves eleven references to laws issued by Justinian and, in the cases where his notice can be linked to a known law, he follows the structure and, at times, the vocabulary of the original.[111] There is no reason to suspect that the passage describing the prohibition of philosophical teaching in Athens is an exception to that rule.

One must, then, explain how the teaching of philosophy and astronomy in Athens could be prohibited by a law that also forbade the use of dice. The common thread linking all of these activities seems to be the act of divining the future. Divination was a skill that greatly interested Damascius and his associates, especially when it could be done in a novel way.[112] Astronomy, through its derivative, astrology, was also useful in foretelling the future and, as it was taught in the Athenian Neoplatonic school, its astrological element was neither separated nor downplayed.[113] Although one would not immediately think it, dice too could be used for fortune telling. The use of dice to divine the future is well attested in antiquity.[114] It worked in a number of different ways but, on its most basic level, the practice relied upon a con-

110. The structural similarities between the legal notices in Malalas were first noticed by R. Scott, "Malalas and Justinian's Codification," in *Byzantine Papers*, ed. E. Jeffreys et al., 12–31 (Canberra, 1981); and elaborated upon in R. Scott, "Malalas, *The Secret History*, and Justinian's Propaganda," *Dumbarton Oaks Papers* 39 (1985): 99–110.

111. The eleven references are *Chronicle*, 17.18; 18.11, 18, 20 (a summary of four laws), 38, 42, 47, 64, 67, 78, 142. Examples of such summaries are Malalas 18.11 (a summary of *C. Just.* 1.3.41) and 18.67 (an apparent summary of a larger law from which *C. Just.* 3.2.4–5 are excerpts). The best example of this phenomenon is Malalas, 18.78. The epitomized text preserves the heading of the law and the instructions for its public posting. The *Chronicon Paschale*, quoting from a more complete version of Malalas than our manuscript tradition preserves, records these details and provides a complete text of the law (*Chronicon Paschale* 630–33). This leaves open the possibility that each of Malalas's Justinianic legal notices originally included the full text of the legislation. These may have been abbreviated by subsequent epitomizers.

112. The *Life of Isidore* celebrates a woman who arrived at a method of divining the future and interpreting dreams from cloud patterns (*Vit. Is.* Ath. 52; Z. Ep. 69). Despite Damascius's denial of the connection of divination to philosophy (*Vit Is.* Ath. 88A; Z. Ep. 131), it certainly remained an element that was discussed in detail at his school.

113. For the interest in astronomy among Athenian teachers, see E. Watts, "The End of Athenian Philosophical Teaching," 172 n. 29. Though Damascius himself expresses reservations about the utility of astronomy (e.g., *In Phileb.* 225.20), he did have some astronomical training (Photius, *Bib.* cod. 181.90–91).

114. For the use of dice oracles in antiquity see R. Lane Fox, *Pagans and Christians* (New York, 1986), 209–10; and the more extensive treatment of C. Naour, *Tyriaion en Cabalide: Épigraphie et géographie historique* (Zutphen, 1980), 22–37. Additional epigraphic evidence for the practice has been found in Pamphylia, Pisidia, and Lycia.

version chart that joined each set of numbers to a corresponding fortune. A number of examples of such charts are known from late antiquity (the most famous likely being the *Sortes Sanctorum*) and, in their attempts to arrive at a fortune, they often invoked pagan deities.[115] There is even a late example of dice divination that involved using a twelve-sided die to create a horoscope.[116] To the emperor Justinian, this type of activity would likely seem objectionable, especially if it included the invocation of pagan deities.

There is reason, then, to suppose that divination is the common thread stringing together philosophy, astronomy, and dice throwing in the first part of Malalas's statement. However, it is still necessary to explain how the punishment of dice throwers in Constantinople relates to a law restricting the teaching of divination practices in Athens. Again, Malalas provides a basic explanation. Malalas recalls that the action in Constantinople was precipitated by a report that some people who were throwing dice were engaged in "dreadful blasphemies." While this phrase could certainly refer to the act of using dice to divine the future, the punishment described by Malalas makes one suspect that his dicers were doing more than gambling. Justinian issued a law in 529 that prescribed a simple monetary penalty for people who were found to gamble with dice.[117] Malalas, by contrast, says that the Constantinopolitan dice throwers were mutilated and paraded around the city on camels. This penalty was clearly not assessed for violating the Justinianic gambling law. It is, however, nearly identical to a punishment that Procopius says Justinian inflicted upon astrologers.[118] These dice players appear to have violated the same law as those astrologers (if they were not, in fact, the same

115. Among the late antique and medieval examples, see A. Dold "Die Orakelsprüche im St. Galler Palimpsestcodex 908," *Österreichische Akademie der Wissenschaften* 225.4 (Vienna, 1948); and E. Kraemer, *Le Jeu d'Amour: Jeu d'aventure du moyen âge*, Commentationes Humanarum Litterarum 54 (Helsinki, 1975): 1–66. I thank Peter Brown for these references. On the *Sortes Sanctorum*, see W. Klingshirn, "Defining the *Sortes Sanctorum*: Gibbon, Du Cange, and Early Christian Lot Divination," *Journal of Early Christian Studies* 10 (2002): 77–130. For further discussion, see E. Watts, "The End of Athenian Philosophical Teaching," 173.

116. The earliest attestation of this is from the fifteenth century. On this particular game, see E. Kraemer, *Le Jeu d'Amour*, 5–7.

117. Justinian's gambling law of 529 is *C. Just.* 3.43.1. This Latin law (part of which is repeated in Greek as *C. Just.* 1.4.25) placed restrictions upon the types of dice games that could be played in Constantinople and limited the amounts that could be bet. J. Beaucamp ("Le philosophe et le joueur," 31–4) has recently proposed linking this law with the closure of the Athenian school. She is correct to try to connect a law on dice and the measure closing the school, but her attempt to reconstruct that law using *C. Just.* 3.43.1 and two other texts seems overly optimistic. While *C. Just.* 3.43.1 mentions blasphemy as a consequence of the excessive bets placed in these games, blasphemy is clearly not the problem that this law tries to solve. In addition, this law does not have the same penalties as that which was described by Malalas.

118. Procopius, *Secret History* 11.37. They are μετεωρολόγοι who are σοφοὶ τὰ περὶ τοὺς ἀστέρας. Procopius does, however, differ from Malalas in saying that the astrologers were flogged before

people). Malalas's account, then, seems to describe a series of events that were all connected to a Justinianic law against divination.[119] An examination of Malalas's text, then, allows one to establish a rough sequence of events leading to the cessation of teaching in Damascius's school. The process probably began when Justinian became aware of the blasphemies connected to the divination by dice that were occurring in the capital. A law prohibiting such activity was then issued and sent to the praetorian prefects. It seems, however, that the law sent to the prefect of Illyricum contained some specific instructions that focused upon the elimination of philosophical and astronomical teaching that could be connected to divination. These instructions would have been tailored to respond to the particular situation in the prefecture to which they were sent. As such, they may have been a product of a dialog in which local concerns were expressed to the imperial court and legislation acknowledging these concerns was returned.[120] Once the law was delivered to the prefect, it would then have been

---

being placed upon the camels. Parading religious deviants was not an uncommon practice in the late Roman world (cf. Socrates Scholasticus 3.3 on George the Cappadocian), but, judging by Procopius's tone, it appears to have been a relatively rare event in Constantinople.

119. While no text of a Justinianic law against divination or astrology or the teaching of philosophy exists, divination and astrology were concerns of Justinian. This allows for the possibility that a law on this subject was issued and not included in the code. B. Croke ("Critical text," 202) catalogs a number of Justinianic laws described by Malalas but not included in the *Codex Justinianus*. In fact, a set of fourth-century laws about these subjects remained valid in 529 and were quite comprehensive in their prohibitions (these are *C. Th.* 9.16.4 and 8; see E. Watts, "The End of Athenian Philosophical Teaching," 174–75). Given Justinian's explicit instruction that the editors of the *Codex Justinianus* were to exclude new laws that restate the prohibitions of old ones (e.g., *C. Haec* 2), it is not surprising that his own recent law reaffirming these precedents is not included. To this, one can add one other factor that may have encouraged the emperor to avoid issuing a new sort of restriction on divination. By the early sixth century, the nuanced interpretation of what did or did not constitute acceptable divination had become largely an activity of the church (on this see M. T. Fögen, "Balsamon on Magic," in *Byzantine Magic*, ed. H. Maguire [Dumbarton Oaks, 1995], 103–5; as well as Zacharias Scholasticus, *Life of Severus* (57–65, 70–74). Justinian's law may, then, have just reiterated the terms of this existing legislation in order to provide a legal basis for the punishment of those who had clearly violated its terms.

120. While, by their nature, late Roman law codes obscure much of the specific regional content in imperial legislation, clear evidence of this dialog is found in *Sirmondian Constitution* 6 and textually similar laws in the *Theodosian Code* (variations of the law preserved in *Sirm.* 6 make up *C. Th.* 16.2.47, 16.5.62 and 16.5.64). These texts represent regional variations of one law, which addressed issues concerning clerical rights and placed restrictions on unorthodox religious groups. For a discussion of these specific texts and the phenomenon they illustrate, see E. Watts, "The End of Athenian Philosophical Teaching," 174–75; and J. Matthews, *Laying Down the Law: A Study of the Theodosian Code* (New Haven, 2000), 155–60. For the *Sirmondian Constitutions* in general, see M. Vessey, "The Origins of the *Collectio Sirmondiana*: A New Look at the Evidence," in *The Theodosian Code*, ed. J. Harries and I. Wood (Ithaca, 1993), 187–99.

sent down to the governor of the province of Achaea with instructions about how it was to be implemented.[121]

Generally speaking, this process produced a number of local variations of one law. In some cases, the instructions included on a text would be specifically tailored to the situation in one province. In others, the instructions would be more generally framed.[122] Whatever the nature of these instructions, however, once a governor received this communication, he would be responsible for disseminating the law within his province and, if necessary, providing instructions for its local implementation.[123] This means that, in the case of the Athenian Neoplatonic school, the prohibition of philosophical and astronomical teaching would have been contained in the law handed down from the imperial court, but the actual closing of the school would have been ordered by either the prefect or the provincial governor. However, although the words ordering the cessation of Athenian philosophical teaching were those of a lower official, the edict to which they were attached was issued in Justinian's name and, as Malalas suggests, the emperor bore ultimate responsibility for the actions taken under its terms.[124] Nevertheless, as suggested by the century of strained relations between teachers and Christians, the clauses relating to Athens would have been precipitated not by the events in the capital but by the specific complaints of Achaean authorities.

The improved condition of the Athenian Neoplatonic school under Dam-

121. While rare, some laws preserved solely based upon texts of such communications from provincial governors to civic administrators are preserved in *Theodosian Code* laws (e.g., *C. Th.* 7.13.11). On this process, see J. Matthews, "The Making of the Text," in *The Theodosian Code*, ed. J. Harries and I. Wood (1993), 27.

122. *C. Th.* 16.5.63, a variation of the same law as *Sirm.* 6 that was addressed to the proconsul of Africa, provides only a derivative summary of the law's general restrictions on heretics and pagans. In that case, the process of implementation would have been far less clear than in *Sirm* 6.

123. This process of final dissemination and local action was, of course, often problematic. For this, see, S. Mitchell, "Maximinus and the Christians in A.D. 312: A New Latin Inscription," *Journal of Roman Studies* 78 (1988): 113.

124. J. Harries, "The Background to the Code," in *The Theodosian Code*, ed. J. Harries and I. Wood (Ithaca, 1993), 15. On the basis of Malalas's use of the term πρόσταξις, J. Beaucamp ("Le philosophe et le joueur," 29–30) has argued that Malalas is describing one legislative moment. The gambling law and the prohibition of teaching were both issued from Justinian at the same time. In one sense, this is correct. Malalas (or his epitomator) evidently did conceive of this as one legislative moment, hence his use of πρόσταξις (on this word in Malalas see Beaucamp, "Le philosophe et le joueur," 30 n. 56; and Watts, "The End of Athenian Philosophical Teaching," 174 n. 47). Nevertheless, the constitution itself and the communication between a prefect and a governor seem to have been conflated by Malalas. The specific implementation instructions for a law were a part of the text of that law and were treated as a part of the text of the constitution by both Malalas and, more significantly, the compilers of law codes. In Malalas, the term πρόσταξις seems to refer to the texts that he drew upon—including local versions of laws containing communications from the prefect.

ascius and the type of teaching that was pursued there likely precipitated this action. For this reason, the prefect's action and the appeals coming from Achaea that provoked it should not be seen as anti-intellectual. Indeed, Malalas's statement makes it clear that this edict was not intended to extinguish all teaching in the city. The only subjects that are expressly forbidden, philosophy and astronomy, were those taught in Damascius's school. The teaching of rhetoric in Athens, for example, was still permitted and one can presume that teachers of it remained active in the city.[125] Contrary to the modern idea, Justinian and his deputies did not close the *schools* of Athens. They did not really act against a school at all. Instead the legislation was designed to eliminate one type of teaching—Neoplatonic philosophy as it was presented in Athens.

This is a crucial distinction. It shows that Athenian notables and the emperor acted against professors not because of their religion but because of the content of their curriculum. Damascius and his school were particularly able to incite this sort of feeling. His teaching was unapologetically pagan in content, subtly anti-Christian in tone, and complemented by stories and practices that any good Christian would consider blasphemous. Even more problematic was Damascius's aversion to compromise, especially when the compromise involved religion. In the *Life of Isidore* he wrote: "Nothing human is worth as much as a clear conscience. A man should . . . never give great importance to anything other than Truth—not the danger of an impending struggle nor a difficult task from which one turns away in fear."[126] His harsh criticism of the men who had compromised with Alexandrian Christians in the 480s is further evidence that Damascius was unwilling to adapt his teaching in the face of Christian protests.[127] Damascius's school was out of touch with the religious reality surrounding it, but he was unwilling to make his teaching any less abrasive. This inflexibility would have forced concerned Athenian Christians either to ignore its activities (an unlikely event) or to forward complaints about the philosopher and his school to imperial authorities. The response, the edict forbidding philosophical teaching in Athens, was then issued to address Athenian complaints about the anti-Christian content of philosophical teaching in the city.

The prohibition of teaching that this law put in place would have had little immediate impact upon the intellectual life of Damascius's philosophical circle, but it would eventually have strangled the school.[128] Since the time

125. The *Life of Isidore* indicates that the teaching of rhetoric in Athens continued at least into the early sixth century. The fact that Malalas does not mark rhetoric as a forbidden subject shows the limited scope of the edict.

126. *Vit. Is.* Ath. 146B; Z. fr. 69. The translation is that of P. Athanassiadi.

127. This will be described below in chapter 8.

128. The activities of the inner circle would have been largely hidden from others in the city. *Vit. Proc.* 11 captures this attitude most vividly. Indications of the nature of the inner circle

of its foundation, the school had managed to be philosophically relevant only when its head was able to do three things. First, he needed to attract a group of students to study in his introductory classes.[129] Next, he needed to draw from these students enough highly capable youths to form a bright and active inner circle. Finally, he needed to find a suitable successor from within the ranks of his current or former inner-circle students. Ultimately, even at its highest levels, the long-term health of the school was dependent upon the size of the group of students that the school could introduce to philosophy. If the flow of new students was cut off entirely, however, Platonic thought in Athens would not survive the death or departure of the last member of the school's inner circle.

THE AFTERMATH

While the events of 529 had caused a long-term problem for the school, a later set of legislation further hastened the demise of the Athenian Neoplatonic community. It seems that, in about 531, the emperor Justinian issued two laws that were intended to eliminate the behaviors and institutions that had permitted the personal practice of paganism. The first of these laws, *Codex Justinianus* 1.11.9, prevented pagans and pagan institutions from receiving bequests. The second law, *C. Just.* 1.11.10, exhorted pagans to be baptized, prohibited them from teaching and receiving a municipal salary,[130] mandated the confiscation of property and exile of recalcitrant pagans, ordained that children of pagans should be forcibly instructed in Christian teaching, specified penalties for those who accept baptism disingenuously, and extended similar penalties to Manichees.[131] These laws, then, established some quite

---

are found throughout the *Life of Proclus* and *Life of Isidore.* For the special studies of inner-circle students see *Vit. Proc.* 20, 27. Their unique style of dress is described in *Vit. Is.* Ath. 59B; Z. fr. 135. *Vit. Is.* Ath. 59F; Z. fr. 200 contains a humorous account of a student acting up in an inner-circle meeting.

129. The necessity of active student recruitment appears to have been recognized quite early in the history of the institution. Resentment of Plutarch's recruitment efforts seems to lie beneath Synesius's famous remark about the "pair of Plutarchan sophists who draw the young to their lecture room not by the repute of their learning but by jars [of honey] from Hymettus" (*Ep.* 136). The identification of these teachers with the Athenian Neoplatonic school has been made by G. Fowden, "The Athenian Agora and the Progress of Christianity," *Journal of Roman Archeology* 3 (1990): 500; as well as by Alan Cameron and J. Long, *Barbarians and Politics at the Court of Arcadius* (Berkeley and Los Angeles, 1993), 409–11.

130. This is the probable meaning of δημοσίος σιτήσις.

131. Though one may be tempted to link this law to the events of 529 in Athens, the likely dating argues against such an identification. In terms of dating, the law itself is undated but, from the slight indications that are available to us, it seems unlikely that this law was, in fact, issued in 529. The final chapter of *C. Just.* 1.11.10 equates Manichees with Borboritai and alludes

severe penalties for the activities in which Damascius and his circle were engaged. In fact, it seems that it was their implementation and not the prohibition of teaching in 529 that brought about the final suspension of activity at the Athenian Neoplatonic school. In 531, two years after the teaching of philosophy was prohibited, Damascius and six members of his inner circle decided to leave Athens and travel to Persia. Their journey is known from an account by the historian Agathias.[132] Agathias speaks of them as the best philosophers of his age and indicates that they chose to emigrate because their religion made it "impossible for them to live without fear of the laws" in the Roman Empire.[133] To protect their freedom to live as they pleased, Damascius and his associates traveled to the Persian court of Chosroes.[134]

Damascius's decision to leave Athens was very much in character. Damascius's writings praise pagan thinkers who remained philosophical (i.e., uncooperative) even in the face of violent persecution.[135] Indeed, at an ear-

---

to a previous decree that already established this fact. That previous decree, *C. Just.* 1.5.18, slaps restrictions upon a range of unorthodox religious groups and is the fifth undated law following a law of 527. It immediately precedes a law issued sometime after October 529, suggesting a probable date of 529. Terms of *C. Just.* 1.5.18 also resemble those mentioned by Malalas in an entry describing events of 529 (18.42). *C. Just.* 1.11.10 is, then, likely the second phase of a persecution that did not work as well as planned. Consequently, it is unlikely to date to 529. On these laws and their dating to 531, see E. Watts, "The End of Athenian Philosophical Teaching," 178–82. The recent study of M. Meier (*Das andere Zeitalter Justinians. Kontingenzerfahrung und Kontingenzbewältigung im 6. Jht. N. Chr.*, Hypomnemata 147 [Göttingen, 2003], 202–9) highlights these laws and their particular focus upon individual pagans. While it is debatable whether Justinian primarily intended for these laws to exclude specific political figures from office (e.g., Meier, *Das andere Zeitalter Justinians*, 205–6), there is certainly something new about their focus upon personal aspects of pagan practice.

132. Alan Cameron, "The Last Days of the Academy," 18. E. Zeller, *Philosophie der Griechen*, vol. 3.2 (Leipzig, 1876–89), 916 n. 3, sees Damascius as a possible author of the account used as a source by Agathias. Averil Cameron, *Agathias* (Oxford, 1970), 101–2, thinks it more likely that Simplicius is Agathias's source.

133. Agathias, *Histories* 2.30.3–4.

134. For the journey itself and the activities of the philosophers while in Persia, see J. Walker, "The Limits of Late Antiquity: Philosophy between Rome and Iran," *Ancient World* 33 (2002): 45–69; and U. Hartmann, "Geist im Exil: Römische Philosophen am Hof den Sasaniden," in *Grenzüberschreitungen: Formen des Kontakts zwischen Orient und Okzident im Altertum*, M. Schuol, U. Hartmann, and A. Luther, eds. (Stuttgart, 2002), 123–60. This journey had to occur in 531 because Chosroes did not ascend to the Persian throne until September 13, 531. Despite Agathias's explicit statement to the contrary, I. Hadot (*Simplicius: Commentaire sur le Manuel d'Épictète* [Leiden, 1996], 12) has argued that Agathias makes no attempt to attribute the trip to a desire to see Chosroes. It seems better to understand the passage as an attempt to highlight Chosroes' own inability to differentiate between true philosophers like Damascius and charlatans like Uranius. For this idea see Averil Cameron, *Agathias*, 101–2.

135. Among the many he praises are Hierocles (*Vit. Is.* Ath. 45B; Z. fr. 106), Horapollo and Heraiscus (*Vit. Is.* Ath. 117C; Z. fr. 315), and Julian (*Vit. Is.* Ath. 119J; Z. Ep. 185).

lier point in his life, Damascius himself chose voluntary exile over the possibility of interrogation and forced religious compromise.[136] This choice was
made because he deemed the latter course to be akin to philosophical and
religious apostasy. In 531, the situation was far more dire and, in Damascius's
mind, likely far more unjust. *C. Just.* 1.11.9 and 10 changed the legal status
of pagans in a way that particularly threatened the lifestyle of his school and
his followers. Although the prohibition of teaching had made it impossible
to collect student tuition, the school could still receive financial bequests
from supporters.[137] *C. Just.* 1.11.9 eliminated this possibility and forced
Damascius to consider running his philosophical circle without any financial support.[138]

Even more severe were the terms of *C. Just.* 1.11.10. According to it, the
houses in which the philosophers lived and the property upon which they
were supporting themselves were now subject to seizure.[139] Based upon their
earlier experience, Damascius and his colleagues must have known that both
the Athenian Christian community and the provincial notables had sufficient influence to convince the governor of Achaea to enforce these laws.
In fact, the remains of a group of houses next to the Areopagus show that
the provisions of these laws *were* enforced in Athens. Excavation has shown
that, at some point in the early decades of the sixth century, the largest of
these houses underwent a major renovation in which statues of pagan gods
were desecrated and a pagan image in a floor mosaic was replaced by a
cross.[140] Indicating that this house was not willingly given to Christians, a
well outside of the house contained a further seven statues, all in a good
state of preservation, that apparently had been hidden before the previous
owner fled the property. It has been suggested that these houses were connected with Damascius's school.[141] Even if this speculative idea is not accepted,

---

136. In this earlier persecution, Damascius and others were initially willing to wait for circumstances to change (*Vit. Is.* Ath. 126B; Z. Ep. 190). It quickly became apparent that this would
not happen (*Vit. Is.* Ath. 126C–E; Z. fr. 285, 319, 328) and, when it did, Damascius chose exile
over any form of cooperation. For details on these circumstances, see chapter 8.

137. Olympiodorus implies (*In Alc.* 140–41) that Athenian teachers were never particularly diligent in collecting fees. By contrast, the school did benefit greatly from bequests (*Vit.
Is.* Ath. 102; Z. Ep. 158, fr. 265).

138. *C. Just.* 1.11.9.1.

139. Ibid., 1.11.10.3.

140. See A. Frantz, *The Athenian Agora XXIV*, 88–89; and, for a more detailed discussion,
T. L. Shear, "The Athenian Agora: Excavations of 1971," *Hesperia* 42 (1973): 156–64.

141. The link was initially proposed by A. Frantz ("Pagan Philosophers in Christian Athens,"
Proceedings of the American Philosophical Society 119 (1975): 36–37, and, later, *The Athenian Agora
XXIV*, 44–47). Recently P. Athanassiadi (*Damascius*, 343–47) has suggested linking House C,
the largest of the Areopagus houses, with Damascius. As she admits, this is a "necessarily speculative theory."

their fate and that of the property belonging to Damascius would have been similar.[142]

Given the timing of the abandonment of the house, it is reasonable to assume that its fate is linked to Justinian's anti-pagan measures. Those laws provided the bishop of Athens, to whom the redecorated house may be linked,[143] both an opportunity and a legal justification to seize the property. The renovation of this house, then, strongly suggests that the most valuable of the properties belonging to the philosophers would have been confiscated, whether or not they remained in Athens.

After a brief stay in Persia, Damascius and his colleagues returned to the Roman empire in 532 with the freedom to practice their religion secured by the Romano-Persian peace treaty of that year.[144] The eventual fate of Damascius and his circle of associates after their return has become a subject of intense but unresolved debate.[145] It is now clear, however, that the closing of their school and their Persian exile resulted from two different causes. The prohibition of philosophical teaching in Athens represented a regional response to a complaint about the Athenian Neoplatonic school. This was the final event in a struggle between Athenian Platonists and Athenian Christians that had endured for over a century. In its last stages, the struggle had been characterized by an increasing unwillingness on the part of Athenian teachers to moderate the pagan religious elements in their school. In 529, Damascius refused to compromise his principles in this matter, even when

142. Writing in the 560s, Olympiodorus (*In Alc.* 140–41) seems to indicate that the school's property was touched by Justinianic confiscations (cf. Blumenthal, "529 and its Sequel," 370; Glucker, *Antiochus and the Late Academy*, 323–25; and Alan Cameron, "The Last Days of the Academy," 9–11).

143. A. Frantz (*The Athenian Agora XXIV*, 88) sees the redecoration as "a transition [of the house] to Christian use of an official character" because the nymphaeum had been converted into a baptistery.

144. Agathias 2.31.4.

145. Athens has been suggested as their eventual destination by Alan Cameron, "The Last Days of the Academy," 22–23. The Syrian city of Harran is the choice of M. Tardieu ("Sābiens Coraniques et 'Sābiens' de Harrān," *Journal Asiatique* 274 (1986): 1–44, and *Les Paysages reliques. Routes et haltes syriennes d'Isidore à Simplicius*, Bibliothèque de l'École des Hautes Études, Sciences Religieuses, vol. 94 [Louvain-Paris, 1990]). Against Tardieu, see C. Luna, review of *Simplikios und das Ende der neuplatonischen Schule in Athen*, by R. Thiel, *Mnemosyne* 54 (2001): 482–504; J. Lameer, "From Alexandria to Baghdad: Reflections on the Genesis of a Problematical Tradition," in *The Ancient Tradition in Christian and Islamic Hellenism*, ed. G. Endriss and R. Kruk, 181–91 (Leiden, 1997); and, on an aspect of his argument, D. Gutas, "Plato's Symposium in the Arabic Tradition," *Oriens* 31 (1988): 44 n. 34. The earlier idea of an Alexandrian stay is no longer given any weight.

his school lay unprotected and vulnerable to the attack of local authorities. As a result, when Justinian's edict about divination was received by the prefect, it was a natural step for it to be turned into an edict prohibiting teaching at Damascius's school.

While the closing of the Athenian school was indeed an event with local implications that was caused by local concerns, the flight of Damascius and his colleagues to Persia resulted from central governmental policies. The prohibition of teaching was an institutional deathblow, but one that would not be felt fully for many years. Indeed, it seems that the philosophers responded to this initial set of restrictions by keeping a low profile and waiting for circumstances to change.[146] The severe personal and property restrictions issued in 531 were a different matter. By depriving the school of its meeting space and the philosophers of their personal property, *C. Just.* 1.11.9 and 10 posed an immediate threat to their continued pursuit of the philosophical life. As the Athenian archeological evidence suggests, these laws would not have permitted the philosophers to survive simply by keeping a low profile. Perhaps sensing the inevitability of this fate, they left Athens for Persia. And this was, for all practical purposes, the end of Athenian philosophy.

146. If Alan Cameron ("The Last Days of the Academy," 16–17) is right to place the composition of Simplicius's *Commentary on the Encheiridion* in the years 529–31, Simplicius's statements (*In Ench. Epict.* 32.120 ff.) about the necessity for a philosopher to maintain a low profile and teach furtively may indicate the circle's collective state of mind at the time. Against Cameron, see I. Hadot, *Simplicius,* 8–20.

Chapter 6

Alexandrian Intellectual Life in the Roman Imperial Period

The rhetorician Dio Chrysostom came to Alexandria sometime in the later first century A.D. and delivered a speech to the people of the city. This speech, which upbraided the Alexandrians for being induced to riot by a performance in the theater, criticized the people and their conduct in rather firm tones.[1] But, while his subject made it difficult to compliment the people of Alexandria, even Dio could not resist praising the wealth, size, and beauty of the city itself.[2]

Alexandria was worthy of this praise. Its physical location was ideal. It was perched atop a limestone ridge at the western edge of the Nile Delta. Its uniquely solid foundation, so distinct among the marshy lands of that part of Egypt, was crisscrossed with canals linking the city both to the Nile and to the large freshwater lake (Lake Mareotis) that lies to its south. To the north of the city lay the Pharos Island, a rocky spit of land that was connected to the mainland by a long promontory in the Hellenistic period. This promontory bisected what was once the harbor of the city and, in its place, created two

---

1. For this speech and its context see C. P. Jones, *The Roman World of Dio Chrysostom* (Cambridge, 1978), 36–44. Although more conventionally the speech has been placed in the reign of Trajan, Jones ("The Date of Dio of Prusa's Alexandrian Oration," *Historia* 22 [1973]: 302–9) rather convincingly argues that it was given during the reign of Vespasian. This dating has been accepted by J. L. Moles, "The Career and Conversion of Dio Chrysostom," *Journal of Hellenic Studies* 98 (1978): 84 n. 48; W. D. Barry, "Aristocrats, Orators, and the 'Mob': Dio Chrysostom and the World of the Alexandrians," *Historia* 42.1 (1993): 82–103; and B. Winter, *Philo and Paul Among the Sophists: Alexandrian and Corinthian Responses to a Julio-Claudian Movement*, 2nd ed. (Cambridge, 2002), 40–42. On the Alexandrian tendency to riot following theatrical performances, see H. Musurillo, ed., *Acts of the Pagan Martyrs* (Oxford, 1954), 247–48.

2. Dio Chrysostom, *Or.* 32.35–36. This was, of course, also a way to give the praise of the city expected of a visiting orator while still highlighting the negative qualities of its people.

ports: the Great Harbor in the east and the smaller Eunostos Harbor in the west. These were the two great seaports of Alexandria and at their head was the famous Pharos lighthouse. The lighthouse was both one of the wonders of the ancient world and, it seems, a trendy place to dine during the Roman period.[3] Alexandria's seaport was no doubt magnificent but, of the city's two sets of harbors, those on the sea were actually the less crowded. The busier harbor was located on Lake Mareotis and handled products, both Egyptian and foreign, that had been transported to the city by ships traveling down the Nile.[4] As one might expect, the imports coming to that harbor were greater in size than those which came by sea but, surprisingly, the exports from the city leaving by this channel also exceeded those sent from the seaport.[5]

Perhaps excluding the Pharos, the most spectacular sites in Roman Alexandria were its temples. The city possessed many and a number of them were quite elaborate. The most impressive, however, seem to have been the Caesareum and the Serapeum. The Caesareum was perched on the shore near the southernmost point of the Great Harbor. The structure was begun by Cleopatra to honor Julius Caesar. It was finally completed under Augustus and, from that time forward, it came to serve as the Alexandrian center of the imperial cult. Even in such a central location, the temple and its precinct dominated the surrounding area. Indeed, it was so striking that, in the fourth century, it was given to the church of Alexandria to become the city's most prominent cathedral.

As grand as the Caesareum was, its impact could not exceed that of the Serapeum. The Serapeum was perhaps the most impressive sacred compound in the entire eastern Mediterranean.[6] The temple was set atop Alexandria's highest hill at a location in the extreme southwest of the city. Although always a grandiose structure, the Serapeum endured periods of both poverty and prosperity. By the first century B.C., it appears that the site of the original Ptolemaic temple was in a state of disrepair.[7] Nonetheless, the Ptolemaic sanctuary remained an impressive monument that survived until destroyed

---

3. Achilles Tatius, *Leucippe and Clitophon* 5.4.

4. Alexandria was the site through which most of the exports of Egypt were shipped to the rest of the Roman world. Though a canal linking the Red Sea to the Nile accounted for much less volume of material, its opening also made Alexandria a natural transit point for the shipment of goods from locations on the Indian Ocean. See P. Fraser, *Ptolemaic Alexandria* (Oxford, 1972), 800–801, for an assessment of the size of this trade.

5. Strabo, *Geography* 17.1.7. This presumably does not include the large volume of grain that was shipped out by sea.

6. Such is the view of Ammianus Marcellinus (22.16.12), who ranks it second in the world to the Capitolium in Rome. On the Serapeum site, see now the study of J. S. McKenzie, S. Gibson, and A. T. Reyes, "Reconstructing the Serapeum in Alexandria from the Archeological Evidence," *Journal of Roman Studies* 94 (2004): 73–121.

7. Strabo's description of the site (17.1.10) indicates its downtrodden state in the first century B.C.

by fire around 181 A.D.[8] A larger and more impressive temple complex was erected on its ruins sometime between 181 and 217.[9] It had such an impact that, even in the late fourth century, a Christian visitor was forced to describe it with awestruck admiration.

The whole edifice is built with enormous vaults, above which are immense windows. The hidden inner chambers are separate from one another and provide for the enactment of various ritual acts and secret observances. Sitting courts and small chapels with images of gods occupy the edge of the highest level. Lofty houses spread across this height in which the priests, or those which they call *agneuontas*, this is, those who purify themselves, had been accustomed to live. Beyond these buildings, a portico raised on columns and facing inward runs around the periphery. In the middle of all of this stands the temple, rising on precious columns and constructed on a magnificent scale out of marble. Inside there was a statue of Serapis so vast that the right hand touched one wall and the left the other.[10]

The temple dominated a large precinct that was filled with stoas and other open spaces.[11] Also within this precinct were shrines to other gods and an important Nilometer, the remains of which have survived to the present day.[12] In addition to the temple, the precinct surrounding the sanctuary contained lecture halls and a large library.[13]

CENTERS OF ALEXANDRIAN SCHOLARSHIP

In other ancient cities, a library like that of the Serapeum would have been the most important center of scholarship. In Hellenistic and Roman Alexan-

---

8. For the date of the fire, see McKenzie, Gibson, and Reyes, "Reconstructing the Serapeum," 86 n. 47. The late-second-century destruction of the temple is described by Clement of Alexandria (*Protrep.* 4.42) and dated to 181 in Jerome's version of Eusebius's *Chronicle*.

9. Traditionally this reconstruction has been dated to the Trajanic period (e.g., Fraser, *Ptolemaic Alexandria*, 803). On this new dating see McKenzie, Gibson, and Reyes, "Reconstructing the Serapeum," 98–99. Note as well their description of the rebuilt Roman complex.

10. Rufinus, *HE* 11.23.

11. For a concise description of the archeology of the site, see B. Tkaczow, *Topography of Ancient Alexandria: An Archeological Map* (Warsaw, 1993), 68–70. On the stoa-like structure and associated buildings, see McKenzie, Gibson, and Reyes, "Reconstructing the Serapeum," 82–84, 89.

12. C. Haas, *Alexandria in Late Antiquity: Topography and Social Conflict* (Baltimore, 1997), 166. The remains and functioning of the Ptolemaic Nilometer are most evident. The location of the Roman Nilometer is more obscure, though it is mentioned by Socrates Scholasticus (*HE* 1.18.2) and Sozomen (*HE* 5.3.3). On these Nilometers generally, see McKenzie, Gibson, and Reyes, "Reconstructing the Serapeum," 90, 96.

13. Ammianus 22.16.12 says it contained seven hundred thousand volumes. This is a wild exaggeration but, nonetheless, it does hint at the immense size of the collection. On the Serapeum library, see McKenzie, Gibson, and Reyes, "Reconstructing the Serapeum," 99–100; and

dria, however, the Serapeum library was of secondary importance. The city's two largest and best-known intellectual centers were the Royal Library and *Mouseion*. Both of these were public cultural institutions that had been established under Ptolemaic patronage.[14] Their establishment culminated a process that began when the first Ptolemaic king, Ptolemy I Soter, provided incentives for Greek intellectuals to come to his court. In the third century, royal support for intellectuals was expanded to provide an endowment for two institutions, the *Mouseion* and the famous Royal Library, in which they could work. Of these two, the *Mouseion* is the better attested. While the prestige of the Alexandrian *Mouseion* was unmatched in the Hellenistic world, the institution itself was not an innovation.[15] *Mouseia* had existed in a number of other Greek cities. In these cities, they served both as ritual centers devoted to the cult of the Muses and as centers of literary and cultural activity.[16] Despite these institutional parallels, the Alexandria *Mouseion* seems to have been modeled more on the Hellenic philosophical schools in Athens.[17] Plato's Academy, for example, may have been officially organized as a body of people devoted to the worship of the Muses.[18] In addition, the wills of the heads of Aristotle's school mention that there was a *Mouseion* on the grounds of the school and made provisions to ensure that the successor had access to the tableware that was used for the common meal one enjoyed at the shrine.[19]

In fact, at its inception, the Alexandrian *Mouseion* likely bore a strong resemblance to the Lyceum. Both possessed a common meeting room in which a meal was served. They also had space devoted to the worship of the Muses. The Alexandrian *Mouseion* even had a priest of the Muses as its head.[20] As was common for both schools and religious institutions, the *Mouseion* also

---

L. Canfora, *The Vanished Library: A Wonder of the Ancient World*, M. Ryle trans. (Berkeley and Los Angeles, 1990), 61–63.

14. An exceptional and concise description of the founding of these institutions is found in P. Fraser, *Ptolemaic Alexandria*, 305–35.

15. For the cultural significance of the *Mouseion* in the Ptolemaic period see A. Erskine, "Culture and Power in Ptolemaic Egypt: The Museum and Library of Alexandria," *Greece and Rome* 42 (1995): 38–48. Note as well the description of scholarly activities given by Canfora, *The Vanished Library*, 37–44.

16. P. Fraser, *Ptolemaic Alexandria*, 312–13. At least some of these *Mouseia* were endowed. A boundary stone has been found on land near Thespiae once "dedicated to the Hesiodic society of those who sacrifice to the Muses" (*IG* VII.1785).

17. Such is the (probably correct) supposition of P. Fraser, *Ptolemaic Alexandria*, 314.

18. P. Boyancé, *Le culte des muses chez les philosophes grecs: Études d'histoire et de psychologie religieuses* (Paris, 1937), 261 ff.

19. The wills are preserved in Diogenes Laertius, 5.51–57, 61–64, 70–74. Theophrastus, Aristotle's direct successor, refers to a *Mouseion* on the property of the school. For discussion, see H. B. Gottschalk, "Notes on the Wills of Peripatetic Scholarchs," *Hermes* 100 (1972): 314–42.

20. Strabo 17.1.8.

was given an endowment over which it had control.[21] Much of this endowment was, of course, derived from the royal treasury. It is possible, however, that distinguished families with connections to the institution also gave funds.[22] This endowment was used to attract scholars to Alexandria and to provide them with support while they were in the city.

The Hellenistic *Mouseion* was an intellectual center in which scholars could research and discuss their ideas. At the same time, the institution also appears to have been a center for teaching. Its members gave public lectures, presumably from lecture halls within the compound, and many men in Ptolemaic Egypt claimed to be *akroatai* of distinguished members.[23] In these capacities, the *Mouseion* was intended to introduce, produce, and perpetuate a high level of intellectual culture in Alexandria. In so doing, it ensured that Alexandria remained at the forefront of Hellenistic intellectual life.[24] It also made the city attractive to a wide range of accomplished scholars and a diverse group of students.[25] Even with the general decline of the city in the first century B.C., the institution still managed to sustain a vigorous intellectual life until the end of the Ptolemaic dynasty.

In the Roman period, government support for the *Mouseion* continued. The Roman government assumed responsibility for the stipends paid by and the common meals held in the institution. It also gave tax exemptions to scholars who were members.[26] In addition, the Roman emperor took control of the selection of the members of the community.[27] Some Roman emperors undoubtedly had little interest in the institution. Others, however, took a very active role in the affairs of the *Mouseion*. Claudius, for example, paid for the refurbishment and enlargement of the physical space.[28] More than a century later, Caracalla, in a fit of pique, suspended the subsidy for the common meal.[29] This appears to have been a temporary measure and the support may have been restored soon after.[30]

Under the emperors, membership in the *Mouseion* came to be seen as a

21. Ibid.

22. A second century B.C. Delian inscription dedicated to Chrysermus, a member of a prominent Alexandrian family, calls him the "*Epistates* of the *Mouseion*" (*Ins. Dél.* 1525). For this see P. Fraser, *Ptolemaic Alexandria*, 316.

23. Fraser, *Ptolemaic Alexandria*, 318.

24. This reflected a larger Ptolemaic concern with visibly emphasizing the Greek cultural identity of the city. On this see, A. Erskine, "Culture and Power in Ptolemaic Egypt," 42–43.

25. Strabo 14.5.13 contrasts the provincial scholastic environment of Tarsus with the cosmopolitan atmosphere of Alexandria.

26. Fraser, *Ptolemaic Alexandria*, 316–17.

27. Strabo 17.1.8

28. Suetonius, *Claudius* 42.

29. *Historia Augusta*, Caracalla 6.2–3.

30. A member of the *Mouseion* who received such a stipend appears in a papyrus (*SB* VIII 9898) of the 220s. For discussion, see N. Lewis, "The Non-Scholar Members of the Alexan-

sort of reward to be given both to prominent Greek-speaking intellectuals and to important men of affairs.[31] Philostratus records that Hadrian enrolled both Dionysius of Miletus and Polemo of Smyrna, despite the fact that neither man is known to have spent any significant time in Alexandria.[32] In the case of Polemo, the honor of attending was extended not only to him but to all of his descendants as well.

The memberships given to Dionysius, Polemo, and important non-teachers are indicative of the changes that the *Mouseion* underwent in the first two centuries of Roman rule. While Ptolemaic kings used the honor of a *Mouseion* stipend to attract scholars to their capital, Roman emperors saw little reason to link residence in Alexandria with this honor. All the same, as the ones in charge of the *Mouseion,* emperors were not disinclined to use a *Mouseion* membership to reward scholars and supporters, even if there was no chance that they would ever spend much time engaged in intellectual pursuits in Egypt.[33]

The other great intellectual institution of Ptolemaic Alexandria was its Royal Library. Although often considered separately, the original Library was affiliated with the *Mouseion,* seems to have been located on its grounds, and, probably, held a private collection of literature available only to a select group of scholars.[34] At the same time, the collection was intended to be as extensive as possible and its curators aspired to acquire a copy of every work in the Greek language.[35] This was never accomplished, but, in addition to its substantial collection of Greek manuscripts, the library also appears to have commissioned translations of major works in other languages.[36] Altogether,

---

drian Museum," *Mnemosyne* 16 (1963): 257–61, and republished in N. Lewis, *On Government and Law in Roman Egypt: Collected Papers of Naphtali Lewis,* American Studies in Papyrology 38 (Atlanta, 1995), 94–98.

31. For this see N. Lewis, "*Literati* in the service of Roman Emperors: Politics before culture," in *Coins, Culture and History in the Ancient World: Numismatic and Other Studies in Honor of Bluma L. Trell,* ed. L. Casson and M. Price, 149–66 (Detroit, 1981), republished in N. Lewis, *On Government and Law in Roman Egypt,* 257–74.

32. Philostratus, *Vit. Soph.* 524 (Dionysius), 533 (Polemo).

33. N. Lewis ("*Literati* in the service of Roman Emperors," 155–57) includes a list of known *Mouseion* members in the Roman period. In addition to the individuals cited above, Fronto is among the non-Egyptian intellectuals so honored (cf. *Suda* Φ 735).

34. This is hinted at by Strabo's failure to mention the Library building in his description of the city. As D. Delia ("From Romance to Rhetoric: The Alexandrian Library in Classical and Islamic Traditions," *American Historical Review* 97 [1992]: 1449–67) has noted, this may be simply because the Library consisted of a book repository. The reading rooms and other things associated with a modern library building would have been already available for readers in the *Mouseion.*

35. Fraser, *Ptolemaic Alexandria,* 329.

36. The most famous of these is, of course, the Septuagint. The apocryphal story of its commissioning is recounted in the *Letter of Aristeas.* There also were works translated from original texts written in hieroglyphics, probably including Manetho's *Aegyptica.*

the collection was said to hold upwards of four hundred and ninety thousand papyrus scrolls.[37]

The Royal Library began to decline in the late second century B.C. For a part of the troubled reign of Ptolemy VIII Euergetes II, Cydas, an army spearman, served as its head.[38] By the first century B.C., the librarians were so insignificant that the exact dates of their terms of office were of little interest, even to contemporaries.[39] Further difficulties occurred when Julius Caesar arrived in the city in 48/7 B.C. and burned the Ptolemaic fleet as it lay docked in the harbor. Wind carried the blaze into the city and the ensuing fire destroyed storehouses along the waterfront as well as a large number of books belonging to the Royal Library.[40] The building itself, however, along with the rest of the structures in the Bruchion quarter, seems to have survived the fire. The damage done to its collection may also have been repaired by Antony's gift to Cleopatra of the holdings of the other great Hellenistic library, that of the kings of Pergamum.[41]

Little is known of the Library and its functioning during the Principate. Because the *Mouseion* continued to exist, one must presume that the Library did as well. Its collections, however, seem to have been dispersed among other libraries in the city. By the end of the first century A.D., there were apparently major libraries within the precincts of the Caesareum and the Claudianum temples. These may have been stocked with surplus materials from the old Royal Library.[42] The most important annex library, however, was the one located in the Serapeum. This facility had long predated Roman sovereignty over the city—its foundation probably occurred in the third century B.C.[43] In the Hellenistic period, the Serapeum was called "the daughter library"

37. Tzetzes (*Prolegomena de comoedia Aristophanis* 2.10) remarks that there were four hundred thousand books described as συμμιγεῖς (which were apparently rolls containing a number of different works) and ninety thousand ἀμιγεῖς (rolls containing only one work).

38. *P. Oxy.* 10.1241.ii. N. Lewis ("*Literati* in the service of Roman Emperors," 154–55) speculates that this Cydas's tenure may indicate not the degradation of the institution but simply the fact that, even under the Ptolemies, the *Mouseion* membership had a "political ambience."

39. Fraser, *Ptolemaic Alexandria*, 333–34.

40. Although Caesar's account of the Alexandrian war understandably leaves out any mention of this destruction, Livy described the impact of this event upon the collections of the Library. Accounts derived from Livy appear in Aulus Gellius, *Noc. Att.* 7.17.3; Seneca, *De Tranq.* 9.5; and Cassius Dio, 43.38.2. These mention thousands of volumes being destroyed, but do not say anything about the impact upon the building itself.

41. Plutarch, *Antony* 58. The significance of this gift and the question of whether it actually occurred are discussed by P. Fraser, *Ptolemaic Alexandria*, 335; and D. Delia, "From Romance to Rhetoric," 1462.

42. For the Caesareum, see Philo, *Legatio* 151. The Claudianum is mentioned in Suetonius, *Claudius* 42. For comment on this see D. Delia, "From Romance to Rhetoric," 1458 n. 37.

43. Fraser, *Ptolemaic Alexandria*, 323. Note, however, the questions recently raised by McKenzie, Gibson, and Reyes, "Reconstructing the Serapeum," 99–100.

and was clearly comprised of duplicate books that could not be housed in the main library.[44] Even so, its collection was estimated at nearly forty-three thousand papyrus rolls in the later Ptolemaic period. In the Roman period, it undoubtedly grew even larger.

The *Mouseion* and the Royal Library both disappear from the historical record in the mid-third century. The last reference to *Mouseion* membership appears in materials dating from the 260s.[45] By the tetrarchic period, it appears that both the *Mouseion* and the Royal Library had been destroyed,[46] probably during the emperor Aurelian's campaign against Zenobia in 272 A.D.[47] Sometime in the fourth century, the *Mouseion* appears to have been reestablished on a different site,[48] but, despite scattered mentions of *Mouseion* members, nothing is known about the exact characteristics of this later organization.[49] The fate of the library after the third century is equally mysterious, but, by the fourth century, the Serapeum and its library likely had become the biggest repository of literature in the city. The *Mouseion* may have con-

44. For the daughter library see Epiphanius, *De Mens. Et Pond.* 11. Tzetzes (19–20) also mentions a second library that he calls "the Outer Library."

45. Lewis, "*Literati* in the service of Roman Emperors," 157.

46. A stone statue base that was originally dedicated to the rhetor Aelius Demetrios, a member of the *Mouseion*, was reused in the reign of Diocletian. For this, see E. Breccia, *Catalogue générale des antiquités du Musée d'Alexandrie (nos. 1–568): Iscrizioni greche e latine* (Cairo, 1911), no. 146; and D. Delia, "From Romance to Rhetoric," 1455. His *Mouseion* connection was reaffirmed by C. P. Jones, "A Friend of Galen," *Classical Quarterly* 17 (1967): 311–12.

47. Aurelian's forces completely destroyed the Bruchion quarter in which the *Mouseion* was situated. The later sack of the city in the reign of Diocletian would have completed what was begun twenty-five years before. For this see A. J. Butler, *The Arab Conquest of Egypt*, 2nd ed. by P. M. Fraser (Oxford, 1978), 411. Eusebius (apparently wrongly) attributes the destruction of the quarter to Claudius II (7.32.7–12).

48. Zacharias Scholastiicus and Aeneas of Gaza both speak of a physical space known as the *Mouseion* in the later fifth century. This may well be connected to the lecture halls recently excavated in the city that are close to, but not on, the presumed site of the Hellenistic *Mouseion*. On these, see M. Rodziewicz, "A Review of the Archeological Evidence Concerning the Cultural Institutions in Ancient Alexandria," *Graeco-Arabica* 6 (1995): 317–32 (esp. 325–26); and, for a detailed plan of the site, B. Tkaczow, *Topography of Ancient Alexandria*, Plans IIIa–b. See also M. Vinzent, "'Oxbridge' in der ausgehenden Spätantike oder: Ein Vergleich der Schulen von Athen und Alexandrien," *Zeitschrift für Antikes Christentum* 4 (2000): 59–60.

49. Two of the new *Mouseion* members, Theon and Horapollon, will be discussed in more detail in chapters 7 and 8. Although almost nothing is known about the nature of *Mouseion* membership in this later period, the recent attempt by M. Vinzent ("'Oxbridge' in der ausgehenden Spätantike," 59, 63) to link *Mouseion* membership with the possession of a publicly funded professorship seems incorrect. As has been described above, *Mouseion* membership in the Roman period was open to an increasingly diverse group that included many men who were not Alexandrian teachers (or even intellectuals). It is difficult to imagine any circumstances under which the resurrected institution would exclude such men and transform itself back into the exclusive Hellenistic institution where membership, scholarly achievement, and teaching were closely connected.

tinued, but whatever bibliographic resources it had probably did not compare to those available to its predecessor.

THREE *LAOI* ONE CULTURE

Surrounding these intellectual centers was a large population as diverse and vibrant as any in the Roman world. Alexandria was a Greek foundation and a large percentage, if not a clear majority, of its population was of Greek descent. Nevertheless, contained within Alexandria were large populations of Jews and native Egyptians. There were also smaller enclaves of immigrants from Lycia, Phrygia, and, presumably, other parts of the Mediterranean world.[50] The members of these communities dwelled in ethnic neighborhoods that were geographically distinct. A large community of Alexandrian Jews, for example, were known to have lived in the Delta quarter, one of the five sectors into which the Hellenistic and early Roman city was divided. A smaller though still significant community of native Egyptian weavers is known to have lived in Rhakotis, an area located in the extreme southwest of the city.[51]

In a city as confined and crowded as Alexandria, it is not surprising that this diverse mixture of people could become combustible. Indeed, as great as the reputation of its monuments and intellectual culture was, most characterizations of Alexandria in the Roman period focus upon its propensity for civic violence. The anonymous author of the fourth-century *Expositio Totius Mundi et Gentium* is typical in this respect. He notes, "One finds that Alexandria is a city that imposes its will upon its governors; the people and the city itself are easily moved to rebellion . . . Among them there is no hesitation to bring torches and rocks against those governors who are guilty of faults."[52]

The city had earned this reputation long before it became a part of the Roman empire, but Alexandria's history under Roman rule had done little to dispel this idea.[53] Despite Strabo's optimistic declaration that "the Romans,

50. For the Lycian and Phrygian communities see C. Haas, *Alexandria in Late Antiquity*, 49; and *IGRR* 1.1078; *SEG* 8.359; *OGIS* 658.

51. Strabo 17.1.6; Q.Curtius 4.33; Tacitus, *Histories* 4.83–84; Clement, *Protrepticus* 4.42. For discussion see C. Haas, *Alexandria in Late Antiquity*, 49.

52. *Expositio Totius Mundi et Gentium*, ed. J. Rougé, *Sources Chrétiennes* #124 (Paris, 1966), 37.1–8.

53. In the Hellenistic period, there were numerous riots touched off by government policy. The fury of the Alexandrian mob was first directed against Agathocles, the head of a junta, in 204–203 B.C. Much of the reign of the unpopular king Ptolemy VIII Euergetes II (145–127 B.C.) was spent in either the suppression of revolts within the city or the prevention of further uprisings. After describing the political violence of that reign, Strabo, who was writing in the first years of the Roman administration, remarked, "Such then, if it was not worse, was the state of things under the later kings as well" (Strabo 17.1.13).

according to their ability, have corrected many things," Alexandrians in the Roman period were often moved to revolt by political and religious concerns.[54]

While communal differences could provoke outbreaks of violence like the attacks on the Jewish community in 38 A.D.[55] and those on Alexandrian Christians in 248,[56] it is incorrect to assume that Alexandria's various ethnic and religious groups were constantly at odds. A series of social and economic relationships inextricably tangled the lives of Alexandrian pagans, Christians, and Jews of all backgrounds. Indeed, the social and economic status of individuals was as much of a unifying factor as their religious allegiance. Alexandria was filled with *collegia,* associations of individuals who worked at a common craft.[57] *Collegia* are attested for a wide range of industries including sailors, shopkeepers, and even gravediggers.[58] These groups had a developed hierarchy that spread out beneath the collegial elders and their stewards.[59] Individual members, regardless of where they ranked, were often quite proud of their involvement in these associations, and this pride in membership even crossed religious lines. *Collegia* put up collective dedications to emperors and, from the fourth century forward, were collectively required to perform certain public duties.[60] Indeed, their collective identification was so important that worshippers in the main Alexandrian synagogue were seated according to *collegia.*[61]

Cultural bonds were equally strong among members of Alexandria's upper classes. In the same way that similar interests cemented ties between members of the city's *collegia,* the culture of *paideia* provided educated Alexan-

54. An undercurrent of dissatisfaction with Roman rule appears to have been a constant feature of Alexandrian life at least until a city council was created by Septimius Severus. The texts that have come to be called the *Acts of the Pagan Martyrs,* ed. H. Musurillo (Oxford, 1954) indicate how constant the simmering of these tensions was. In the third century, the city backed two different usurpers and suffered the retribution of both Aurelian and Diocletian.

55. Philo, a witness to the event, describes it in vivid terms. "They overran our houses, expelling the owners with their wives and children . . . then they stole the furniture and cherished valuables." Philo, *Legatio ad Gaium* 121–22.

56. Eusebius, *Ecclesiastical History* 6.41. According to Eusebius, a pagan mob apparently set upon a number of prominent Christians in the city and tried to compel them to show allegiance to pagan gods. When the Christians resisted, the mob beat them and dragged along the main street in the city. Once they were outside of the city wall, they were stoned to death.

57. This brief discussion owes much to the account of C. Haas, *Alexandria in Late Antiquity,* 57–59.

58. Sailors: *C. Th.* 13.5.32, Philostorgius, *HE* 2.2. Shopkeepers: Leontius, *Life of John the Almsgiver* 16. Gravediggers: Epiphanius, *Haer.* 76.1.6–7. For a more detailed list, see C. Haas, *Alexandria in Late Antiquity,* 382–83 nn. 33–35.

59. Haas, *Alexandria in Late Antiquity,* 58.

60. *IG* XIV.198, an honorific inscription erected by the association of Alexandrian *naukleroi,* shows this collective spirit. The public duties of the *collegia* are discussed in *C. Th.* 14.27.2. For both see C. Haas, *Alexandria in Late Antiquity,* 59.

61. Haas, *Alexandria in Late Antiquity,* 59.

drians of all faiths with a common set of interests and a universally accepted pattern of behavior. As leaders of their individual communities, upper-class men knew their peers of other faiths and, in many cases, became friendly with them. The Jewish philosopher Philo, for example, was deeply attached to Greek culture and his brother, Alexander, even held public office in Alexandria.[62] Later, Alexander developed a sincere friendship with the future emperor Claudius and served as the steward of that emperor's mother.[63]

Despite their official condemnation, the leaders of Alexandria's Christian community also appear to have had political relationships with their social peers. Alexandria's large Jewish population and its proximity to Judea meant that a Christian community had been established in the city quite early on. From this point, Alexandrian Christianity enjoyed a steady (and, apparently, a relatively undisturbed) period of growth. By the end of the third century, Christians too were likely playing an important role in Alexandrian public life.[64]

Regardless of religious allegiance, men of high social status were expected to participate in the political life of their city. These men recognized their public influence, understood the responsibilities that came along with this position, and acknowledged the importance of fulfilling their social obligations, regardless of the inconvenience.[65] This sort of activity, predicated upon the culture of *paideia* and conducted in the language of that system, brought these individuals into daily contact with peers of different faiths. Despite their religious differences, shared political concerns ensured that friendships and other social relationships developed between these men.

The common interests of Alexandria's educated men were not solely defined by events in the political arena. Indeed, many shared a great inter-

---

62. Josephus, *Jewish Antiquities* 18.259.

63. For more on Alexander, see E. Goodenough, *The Politics of Philo Judaeus: Practice and Theory* (New Haven, 1938), 64–65. His son, Tiberius Julius Alexander, had an even more spectacular career. He served as procurator of Palestine, prefect of Egypt, and, finally, as the second in command during the final stages of the Jewish war (Josephus, *BJ* 2.309). Before this, however, he apostatized from Judaism.

64. The *History of the Patriarchs of Alexandria* (1.6) states that members of the municipal council organized an elaborate burial for Peter, the martyred bishop of the city, in 311. While this notice is undoubtedly problematic, it suggests the possibility that Christians were holding municipal offices by the turn of the fourth century.

65. This sense of unshakeable duty gains clear expression in Philo's *De Specialibus Legibus*. Early in his life, Philo concentrated upon the study of philosophy, but, like many men of his stature, Philo was drawn away from literary pursuits by the duties that wealthy men of learning were supposed to play in Roman society. "And yet envy, which is hateful of noble things, suddenly fell upon me and did not stop violently dragging me until it threw me into a great sea of political concerns . . . although I groan, nevertheless I withstand the event because the love of *paideia* was implanted in me as a youth." *De Specialibus Legibus* 3.3.1–7.3. For a discussion of this passage see E. Goodenough, *The Politics of Philo Judaeus* 66–68.

est in rhetoric, philosophy, and the ways in which religious traditions could be understood philosophically. As one might expect, the same sort of networks that had been established to foster political cooperation also encouraged intellectual exchange. Word of the latest compositions of prominent rhetoricians, philosophers, and doctors would have passed along the same channels as letters of reference and requests for favors.

In Alexandria, this occurred at a very high level of sophistication. As the site of the *Mouseion* and Library, Alexandria naturally attracted a great number of prominent intellectuals in the first three centuries A.D. Not only could the *Mouseion* and Library induce distinguished scholars to come to Alexandria, but the prospect of a visit also would have encouraged prominent authors to get their works circulating in the city.[66] Like Dio, many men with no intention of moving to the city still welcomed the opportunity to lecture there (and collect the lucrative gifts that surely accompanied such a visit). In addition, prominent teachers would have written epistles or short treatises to their friends in the city. While these were not intended for general circulation, it was common for the recipient to have them copied and sent around to his circle of correspondents.[67]

One must imagine that a great deal of original literary and philosophical material passed through the social networks that bound upper-class Alexandrians. This flow would not have been impeded by religious differences. Men of all faiths attended some of the same schools for rhetoric and philosophy.[68] Their mutual interest and similar educations meant that certain intellectual approaches were shared between them. This is especially apparent in the points of intersection between Alexandrian Christianity and contemporary Greek culture. Rhetoric and grammar played an undeniable part in shaping the expression of early Alexandrian Christian doctrine, and Greek philosophy gave Alexandrian Christian teachers a set of philosophical models around which they could shape their learned explanations of Christian cosmology and psychology.[69]

66. The example of Synesius (discussed in chapter 1) provides a later example of an intellectual with such concerns.

67. Apparently this happened frequently. For example, Galen (*De libris propriis liber* 19.11.8) complains that some private correspondence of his entered into circulation in this way. Similar complaints can be found in Cicero (*De Or.* 1.94) and Tertullian (*Adversus Marcionem* 1.1). On this problem, primarily in relation to Galen, see J. Mansfeld, *Prolegomena: Questions to be settled before the study of an author or text* (Leiden, 1994), 118 n. 208, 126–27.

68. Despite Alexandria's nearly complete absence from the text of Philostratus's *Lives of the Sophists*, it is clear that the city remained an important center of rhetorical study in the second and third centuries. On this, see P. Schubert, "Philostrate et les sophistes d'Alexandrie," *Mnemosyne* 48.2 (1995): 178–88. Particularly important for the argument is *P. Oxy.* 18.2190, a document discussed in chapter 1.

69. No text better shows the importance of rhetoric in the Alexandrian Christian environment than the *Paedagogus* of Clement. Written c. 200 to urge Christians to follow a simple lifestyle,

THE SCHOOL OF AMMONIUS SACCAS

While similarities in language and philosophical concepts make the interaction between philosophy and Christian intellectual culture easy to see, one Alexandrian intellectual circle provides a glimpse into the relationships that facilitated such interaction. This was the circle of intellectuals involved with the school of the pagan teacher Ammonius Saccas. The intellectuals associated with his school reveal how pagan schools facilitated philosophical discussion between Alexandrian Christians and pagans.

Although a figure of great importance in the history of Greek thought, Ammonius is quite mysterious. He appears to have written no works of his own and, consequently, Ammonius is known only through the accounts of his students.[70] But his associates included some of the most prominent pagan and Christian intellectuals of the third century and, for this reason, the school of Ammonius Saccas provides a unique window on the type of intellectual discourse that occurred between the most educated pagan and Christian scholars.

While he has been the subject of exhaustive (though often inconclusive) modern studies, Ammonius is mentioned in only four roughly contemporary ancient sources.[71] The earliest witness to Ammonius's teaching is found in Porphyry's *Life of Plotinus*, a biography of one of the most accomplished students of Ammonius. In speaking about Plotinus's education, Porphyry tells his readers that Plotinus was extremely hesitant to provide his associates with any details of his life. Even so, occasional references to his biography did leak out. One of these concerned his choice of a philosophical teacher. Porphyry writes:

> In his twenty-eighth year Plotinus became eager to study philosophy and it was recommended that he go to the most renowned teachers in Alexandria at that time. He came away from their lectures so full of sadness that he communicated

---

the work was filled with the powerful rhetoric and arcane erudition typical of pagan literary set pieces. The text also shows the great importance philosophy played in this cultural world. On this text see, R. Lane Fox, *Pagans and Christians* (New York, 1986), 305–6; S. Lilla, *Clement of Alexandria: A study in Christian Platonism and Gnosticism* (Oxford, 1971), 96–97, 111–13; H. I. Marrou, ed., *Le pédagogue [par] Clément d'Alexandrie*, 3 vols. (Paris, 1960), 78–93.

70. On the biography and its aims, see the introduction and translation by M. Edwards, *Neoplatonic Saints: The Lives of Plotinus and Proclus by their Students* (Liverpool, 2000), as well as his intriguing discussion of this text, "Birth, Death and Divinity in Porphyry's *On the Life of Plotinus*," in *Greek Biography and Panegyric in Late Antiquity*, ed. T. Hägg and P. Rousseau, 52–71 (Berkeley and Los Angeles, 2000).

71. F. M. Schroeder ("Ammonius Saccas," in *Aufstieg und Niedergang der Römischen Welt* 2.36.7 [1987]: 493–526) has collected and summarized most of the modern scholarship. Since the publication of Schroeder's piece, M. Edwards ("Ammonius, Teacher of Origen," *Journal of Ecclesiastical History* 44 [1993]: 169–81) has added a new twist to the discussion.

his experiences to a friend. That friend, who understood the desire of his heart, sent him to Ammonius, whom he had not yet tried. Plotinus, upon going and hearing him speak one time, told his friend "This is the man I was seeking."[72]

Plotinus then became a member of Ammonius's inner circle of students, and, from that day forward, "he stayed continually beside Ammonius" and ended up spending eleven years at the school.[73]

Porphyry's text also contains another note about Ammonius that is derived not from Plotinus but from the Athenian philosopher Longinus. Porphyry recorded the preface of a book that Longinus wrote to refute the teachings of Plotinus. In this, Longinus described a number of contemporary philosophers. Of Ammonius, he notes, "[of the philosophers who did not write] were the Platonists Ammonius and Origen, beside whom [pl.] I studied for a great time.[74] These were men who surpassed their contemporaries in their knowledge."[75]

Although brief, these two passages reveal a number of important details about Ammonius Saccas and the arrangement of his school. First, it is clear that Ammonius was not one of the mainstream Alexandrian teachers. Plotinus began his philosophical studies in the 230s, a time when the *Mouseion* was still functioning as an institution. Indeed, it is likely that the "most renowned teachers in Alexandria" first visited by Plotinus were either *Mouseion* members or, possibly, other publicly funded professors. Ammonius clearly did not fit into this group.[76]

While Ammonius did not enjoy the prestige of such rivals, he clearly did have quite a reputation. Not only was he known in Alexandria, but it seems that he managed to attract students from abroad as well.[77] These students could enroll in basic courses in philosophy or, if they were sufficiently skilled, they could enter Ammonius's inner circle of students and become involved in more advanced discussions. Though it is somewhat controversial, there is good evidence for this sort of twofold division in Ammonius's

72. *VP* 3.7–13.

73. Ibid., 3.14–17. The verb Porphyry uses is παραμένοντα, a word that connotes personal intimacy. G. Fowden, "The Platonist Philosopher and His Circle in Late Antiquity," Φιλοσοφία 7 (1977): 363 n.15, supposes that their association ended with Ammonius's death. D. O'Brien, "Plotinus and the Secrets of Ammonius," *Hermathena* 157 (1994): 117–53 (esp. 123–24), suggests that Plotinus left the circle before Ammonius's death. Porphyry is silent about this, but his account seems to support Fowden's position.

74. προσεφοιτήσαμεν. In this context, the verb seems to indicate habitual but informal study. It is the verb used to describe Plotinus's study under the teacher of letters (*VP* 3.2) as well as the habitual but inattentive attendance of the painter who covertly painted Plotinus while pretending to listen to his lectures (*VP* 1.14).

75. *VP* 20.36–39.

76. On Ammonius's outsider status see, for example, J. Dillon, *The Middle Platonists*, 381–82.

77. Longinus is one such student.

school.[78] For example, in true Pythagorean fashion, Plotinus made a pact with Origen and Erennius (two other initiates of the circle) never to write or speak about Ammonius's teaching.[79] If the Pythagorean parallel is any indication, this pact was an agreement between members of the school's inner circle.[80] A further indication that Ammonius's students were divided into two groups with different responsibilities and privileges comes from Longinus's statements about his experience in the school. Longinus notes that he studied informally at the school[81] and mentions that, while he was there, both Ammonius and a Platonist named Origen taught him.[82] Because Longinus must have begun teaching long before Origen left the school of Ammonius, it seems that, while Longinus attended the school of Ammonius, Origen gave some of his instruction as a part of his duties as a member of Ammonius's inner circle. As has been discussed above, members of a philosophical school's inner circle were expected to do introductory teaching in the fourth and fifth centuries.[83] There is no reason to assume that things would have been different in the third.

What is known of his philosophical work also suggests that Longinus received a philosophical training that differed significantly from that given to Plotinus and other inner-circle students. While Longinus claims that Ammonius and Origen had a great influence on his thought, his own work appears to be rather conventional.[84] It certainly bore none of the imprint of Ammonius's originality that one can presume to see in Plotinus.[85] Furthermore, Longinus also gives no indication that he knew about the teachings that Ammonius's inner circle students agreed to keep secret.[86]

78. This division of students has been questioned by M. Edwards, "Ammonius, Teacher of Origen," 176 n. 16.

79. *VP* 3.24 ff. As will be discussed below, this Origen is distinct from the Christian thinker of the same name.

80. For the Pythagorean idea that initiates were not to reveal any of the school's doctrines see Iamblichus, *Vit. Pyth.* 17.

81. As implied by the verb προσεφοιτήσαμεν (on which, see discussion n. 74 above).

82. Again, it is clear that this is not the Christian Origen.

83. Chrysanthius and Aedesius (Eunapius, *Vit. Soph.* 474) are the most prominent such students. For a discussion of this phenomenon, see chapter 3 above.

84. In *VP* 14.18–19, Plotinus described Longinus as "a scholar (φιλόλογος) but not a philosopher."

85. There has been significant debate about the degree to which Plotinus's thought depends upon the teaching of Ammonius. Numenius (*De Natura Hominis* 3.20) indicates that Ammonius presented some proto-Neoplatonic doctrines. On the other hand, it has been argued by H. Dörrie (*Platonica Minora* [Munich, 1976], 393–95) that the title of Origen's lost work, *That the King is the Only Maker*, reveals a Middle Platonic interpretation of the doctrine of creation. If this is the case, then Ammonius's teaching may have been much less revolutionary than Plotinus's work. Nevertheless, when Origen visited his school, Plotinus was embarrassed and wanted to stop lecturing because "his audience already knew what he was going to say" (*VP* 14.24). Clearly Origen had already learned a great deal about some of the Plotinian doctrines.

86. One need only compare Plotinus's dismissal of Longinus's knowledge with his feelings about Origen.

The *Life of Plotinus* tells nothing more about Ammonius. The rest of our knowledge concerning him and his circle comes from excerpts of other works that are introduced by the Christian author Eusebius in the midst of a pseudo-biography of the Christian thinker Origen.[87] The most important reference found in Eusebius is lifted from Porphyry's lost work *Against the Christians*. In it, Porphyry begins by criticizing Christian writers who, "in their efforts to find a way" to explain away "the depravity of the Jewish scriptures", resort to "interpretations which cannot be reconciled with these Scriptures. 'Enigmas' is the pompous name they give to the perfectly plain statements of Moses, glorifying them as oracles full of hidden mysteries."[88]

Porphyry then claims that a teacher named Origen was the man most responsible for this and, through his numerous writings, "he attained great fame among the teachers of these doctrines."[89] He then discusses Origen's education.

> Origen was a hearer[90] of Ammonius, who had the greatest proficiency in philosophy of our day; and, in his familiarity with philosophy, he owed a great debt to his master. But, as regards the right choice[91] in life, he took the opposite course. For Ammonius was a Christian who was brought up in Christianity by his parents. However, when he began to think and study philosophy, he immediately changed to a way of life that conformed with the laws. But Origen, who was a Hellene educated in Hellenic doctrines, pressed forward to barbarian recklessness . . . and while in his life he lived abnormally and as a Christian, in his opinions about material and divine things, he played the Hellene and introduced Hellenic ideas into foreign fables.[92]

87. On the larger nature of this piece, see the study of P. Cox (*Biography in Late Antiquity: The Quest for the Holy Man* [Berkeley and Los Angeles, 1983], 69–101) as well as R. M. Grant, "Eusebius and His Lives of Origen," in *Forma Futuri: Studi in onore del Cardinale Michele Pellegrino* (Turin, 1975), 635–49; and P. Nautin, *Origène: Sa vie et son oeuvre* (Paris, 1977).

88. Porphyry in Eusebius, *Ecclesiastical History* 6. 19.4.

89. *HE* 6.19.5.

90. ἀκροατής.

91. προαίρεσις. This is a play on the word used to indicate one's philosophical allegiance.

92. *HE* 6.19.6–7. For the significant contrast between upbringing and education in this passage, see P. Cox, *Biography in Late Antiquity*, 92–93; and W. C. Van Unnik, *Tarsus or Jerusalem?* trans. G. Ogg (London, 1962), 32–33. Porphyry's text is additionally interesting in light of contemporary discussions about the relationship between "Hellenism" as a cultural and religious identifier in late antiquity (see, for example, the discussions of G. Bowersock, *Hellenism in Late Antiquity* [Ann Arbor, 1990]; R. Lyman, "Hellenism and Heresy," *Journal of Early Christian Studies* 11.2 [2003]: 209–22; and S. Elm, "Hellenism and Historiography: Gregory of Nazianzus and Julian in Dialog," *Journal of Medieval and Early Modern Studies* 33.3 [2003]: 493–515). Because he aims to criticize Origen on both intellectual and religious grounds, Porphyry consciously exploits two possible understandings of the term "Hellene." He is, in essence, linking the cultural significance of Hellenism with the possible religious connotation of the term "Hellene." According to Porphyry's construction, Origen was born a Hellene (one with a pagan

Eusebius then inserts his own comments. While he agrees that Porphyry is correct about Origen's education, Eusebius maintains that he lied about Origen's pagan birth and Ammonius's conversion to paganism. As proof of the first claim, he mentions that his work has already made clear that Origen's father was a Christian martyr. Then, to demonstrate the second point, Eusebius produces the title of a work called *On the Harmony of Moses and Jesus* that he claims Ammonius wrote.

One final piece of evidence that Eusebius introduces is a fragment of a letter that Origen himself wrote. In this, Origen states:

> As I was devoted to the word, and the fame of our abilities was spreading abroad, heretics and men familiar with Greek learning and, most of all, philosophy, approached me. I thought it right to examine the doctrines of the heretics and also the claims philosophers make to speak about the truth. And we did this, imitating both Pantaenus, who, before us, helped many and acquired no small attainment in these matters, and also Heraclas (the one now seated among the Alexandrian presbyters) whom I found with the teacher of philosophy and who had been his follower[93] for five years before I began to hear[94] his teachings. And though he formerly wore ordinary dress, on his teacher's account, he put it off and assumed a philosophic garb, which he keeps to this day, all the while never ceasing to study the books of pagan scholars.[95]

When reading these Eusebian passages, it is natural to attempt to connect the Christian Origen with the inner-circle student described in the *Life of Plotinus*. But the evidence argues strongly against such an identification. For one thing, as both Porphyry and Eusebius indicate, the Christian Origen wrote voluminously. The pagan Origen, by contrast, wrote only two texts, neither one of which has ever been attributed to the Christian Origen. In addition, some of the details of their lives are impossible to reconcile. Origen the Christian died in the Decian persecution of the 250s.[96] The pagan Origen, however, visited the school of Plotinus while Porphyry was a student there.[97] This visit, then, must have occurred in the later 260s, well after the death of Ori-

---

religious identity) and was educated in Hellenic doctrines (a sort of cultural training). Unlike Ammonius's conversion from Christianity to philosophy, Origen's conversion to Christianity represents a repudiation of both the religious and the cultural aspects of his Hellenism. This is a particularly damning indictment of his intellectual projects.

93. προσκαρτερήσαντα. This word is often found in the New Testament. In Origen's other writings, it frequently connotes a strong personal devotion to a superior (e.g., *Fr. In Lamentationem* 109.6, where it describes the Israelites' devotion to God).

94. ἀκούειν.

95. *HE* 6.19.12–14.

96. Eusebius, *HE* 6.39.

97. *VP* 14.24.

gen's Christian counterpart. Origen was a common name in third century Egypt and it is not surprising that there were multiple men of that name involved in Ammonius's school.[98]

If, as seems clear, the *Life of Plotinus* passages and the references in the *Ecclesiastical History* describe two different men named Origen, one must consider how deeply involved the Christian Origen was in the activities of the school. Both Porphyry and Origen help to answer this question. Porphyry describes Origen as an *akroatēs* or casual student of Ammonius.[99] Origen himself echoes this when he compares the deep devotion that Heraclas had to Ammonius with his own rather casual experience of listening to the lectures at the school.[100] This meant that Origen's level of involvement in the school likely mirrored that of Longinus. Indeed, if Eusebius is correct that Origen was also serving as a teacher of grammar at the time, it is difficult to imag-

98. Dillon, *The Middle Platonists*, 449 n. 84.

99. H. R. Schwyzer (*Ammonios Sakkas, der Lehrer Plotins* [Opladen, 1983], 36) first called attention to the importance of Origen's being called an ἀκροατής (or casual student). M. Edwards, "Ammonius, Teacher of Origen," 174–76, has recently argued that no distinction existed between the status of Plotinus and that of Origen while both men studied philosophy. He maintains that this is the case because Origen is called an ἀκροατής and Plotinus agreed not to share the teachings expressed in the ἀκροάσεις of Ammonius. According to this reasoning, both men were simply hearers of lectures. This reconstruction, however, ignores a crucial distinction between the meanings of the two words. As we have seen earlier, ἀκροατής was a technical term that was understood to indicate a casual student (a modern equivalent may be something like "underclassman"). ἀκρόασις had no such clear meaning. It could be either the lectures given to the general student population or special doctrines discussed only among the inner circle of the school. Philostratus in *VS* 585 mentions that the members of Herodes Atticus's inner circle listened to a special, exclusive ἀκρόασις that followed the ἀκρόασις open to all! In Porphyry's work a clear distinction is made between an ἀκροατής and a ζηλωτής (Ἔσχε δὲ ἀκροατὰς μὲν πλείους, ζηλωτὰς δὲ καὶ διὰ φιλοσοφίαν συνόντας, *VP* 7.1), but the term ἀκρόασις carries no such distinguishing feature. It seems to be a general term simply used to describe the teachings in a philosophical school (on this term, see as well C. Scholten, "Die alexandrinische Katechetenschule," *Jahrbuch für Antike und Christentum* 38 [1995]: 26). Because Plotinus and the other close associates of Ammonius took a vow not to reveal this teaching, it is clear that these particular ἀκρόασεις of Ammonius could not have been accessible to the general public. However, in *VP* 20.67, the philosopher Heliodorus is criticized for never going beyond the teachings his elders expressed in their ἀκρόασεις. For such a criticism to be leveled, the teachings of his mentors must have been publicly available. Another use of the term, in the *Life of Pythagoras*, reveals that Porphyry thought it appropriate to use for even the most basic summary of a teacher's ideas. Porphyry remarks that Pythagoras converted a crowd of people to his way of thought through one ἀκρόασις (*Vit. Pyth.* 20.3). Consequently, the idea that Plotinus and Origen had the same status in the school is not sustainable.

100. F. M. Schroeder, "Ammonius Saccas," 508, questions whether Origen's letter even refers to Ammonius. While Eusebius is not well informed about Origen's philosophical training (P. Cox, *Biography in Late Antiquity*, 94), he does introduce this text into a discussion about Origen's education. Nowhere else in the account does he mention Origen's having any other teachers. It then seems reasonable to assume that the teacher it describes is Ammonius.

ine him being anything more than a casual student.[101] As Porphyry separately indicates, both men received a thorough training in the teachings of Plato as well as an introduction to Pythagorean and Stoic doctrines. But, as casual members of the school, both men likely did not know about some of the more revolutionary teachings of Ammonius.[102]

While one might be tempted to assume that Origen's Christianity excluded him from the inner circle of the school, the experience of Heraclas suggests that this was not the case. Heraclas was an affluent pagan with a thoroughly classical education when he began attending the school of Ammonius. After a number of years at the school, Heraclas became intrigued by Christianity and approached Origen to learn more about the faith.[103] The instruction he received led to his conversion. Despite his Christianity, Heraclas apparently retained an intimate personal relationship with Ammonius. Origen also suggests that, before he left the school to become a presbyter in the church, Heraclas was a member of the same inner circle that Plotinus later joined and that he remained involved with philosophy even following his entrance into ecclesiastical office.[104] Heraclas's experience, then, suggests quite strongly that Christians were welcome in the circle of Ammonius. More generally, it also reveals the depth of elite Christian engagement in high-level Alexandrian intellectual culture.

Heraclas's case also suggests that Christian teachers could capitalize upon the ties between Christian and pagan intellectuals to attract intellectually inclined converts. Origen, for example, understood philosophical explanation to be a gateway through which students could be led to Christianity.[105] For him, a philosophically tinged, religious education became a method to bring about conversion and the teacher became a type of missionary. In this, Origen was drawing upon a well-established Alexandrian tradition that mixed

101. Eusebius, *HE* 6.2. Origen was still a teacher of grammar when he was approached by the future converts Plutarch and Heraclas, each of whom he had encountered during his study with Ammonius.

102. The recent suggestion of M. Edwards (*Neoplatonic Saints: The Lives of Plotinus and Proclus by their Students* [Liverpool, 2000], 14 n. 75) that an ἀκροατής was able to attend all the meetings of the inner circle but not permitted to speak, is not supported by the sources.

103. "While Origen was lecturing . . . some of the Greeks came to him to hear the word of God. The first of them was Plutarch . . . the second was Heraclas, the brother of Plutarch." *HE* 6.3.1–2.

104. The emphasis that Origen places upon Heraclas's wearing the garb of a philosopher indicates the difference in their status at the school. The privilege of wearing the *tribon* was a rite of passage granted to a mature philosopher (on this, see chapter 4). While Ammonius granted this honor to Heraclas, the Christian Origen apparently never attained this level.

105. E.g., Origen, *Homilies on Jeremiah*, 15.2.8. On this idea, see P. Cox, *Biography in Late Antiquity*, 94; P. Nautin, "Origène Prédicateur," in *Origène: Homélies sur Jérémie 1–11*, ed. P. Nautin, Sources Chrétiennes 232 (Paris, 1976), 152.

Christian teaching and pagan intellectual approaches. In the second century, for example, the Christian teacher Pantaenus, who had reportedly led missionary trips to areas as distant as India, seems to have drawn upon his background in Stoic philosophy and textual analysis to add a specifically intellectual flavor to Christian mission activity in Alexandria.[106] Pantaenus and his younger contemporary Clement were so successful in attractively combining the techniques of pagan philosophical learning with Christian doctrine that the intellectual missionary efforts of each appear to have been given official sanction by the bishop of Alexandria.[107]

While both Pantaenus and Clement filled the dual roles of Christian teacher and missionary by mixing elements of Christianity and Alexandrian intellectual culture, Origen's efforts represent the most developed such program. Indeed, in its organization, Origen's teaching bore a strong resemblance to that seen in pagan philosophical schools during his lifetime. For the interested pagan intellectuals who approached him, Origen set up a plan of study that began with preliminary courses explaining the building blocks of philosophical study.[108] In Platonic schools, students who passed through this elementary instruction would then begin a type of spiritual training through the study of Platonic dialogs. In Origen's circle, students who had completed this elementary training (either with him or with some other

106. On Pantaenus's philosophical training, see Eusebius, *HE* 5.10.1. On his teaching in general, see A. Tuilier, "Les evangelistes et les docteurs de la primitive église et les origines de l'École (didaskaleion) d'Alexandrie," *Studia Patristica* 17.2 (1982): 738–42.

107. This sanction came through the controversial institution that has been called the Catechetical School of Alexandria. The Catechetical School is not clearly described by any ancient source (for a typical description, see Eusebius, *HE* 5.10), and modern opinions about its nature vary widely. For a survey of some not entirely modern opinions, see A. Le Boulluec, "L'École d'Alexandrie. De quelques aventures d'un concept historiographique," in Ἀλεξανδρινά. Hellénisme, judaïsme et christianisme à Alexandrie, Mélanges offerts à C. Mondésert, 403–17 (Paris, 1987). A particularly convincing picture of the early institution is that found in C. Scholten, "Die Alexandrinische Katechetenschule." Scholten's notion (p. 34) that the "professors" of the school were often independent teachers whose teaching and missionary activities were sanctioned by the church hierarchy seems correct. See also the portraits of R. van den Broek, "The Christian 'School' of Alexandria in the Second and Third Centuries," in *Centres of Learning: Learning and Location in Pre-Modern Europe and the Near East*, ed. J. W. Drijvers and A. M. MacDonald, 39–47 (Leiden, 1995); and A. van den Hoek, "The 'Catechetical' School of Early Christian Alexandria and its Philonic Heritage," *Harvard Theological Review* 90 (1997): 59–87. van den Hoek's attempt to identify the liturgical role of these prominent Alexandrian teachers is particularly interesting. It is unlikely, however, that their liturgical and evangelical roles overshadowed their intellectual pursuits. It seems more likely that, in their identity as Christian "teachers," they headed small circles of intellectually inclined individuals who understood their teaching and preaching as complementary activities.

108. On this course of study see, C. Scholten, "Die Alexandrinische Katechetenschule," 24–25; and I. Hadot, "Les Introductions aux commentaires exégétiques chez les auteurs néoplatoniciens et les auteurs chrétiens," in *Les Règles de l'Interprétation*, ed. M. Tardieu, 99–123 (Paris, 1987), esp. 110–11.

teacher of philosophy) would also begin a spiritual training. In his case, however, the training was based upon a study of the Bible, which was organized so as to correspond to specific philosophical disciplines.[109] These Biblical texts were closely examined, commented upon, and explained in a fashion similar to that seen in later Platonic circles. Students who completed Origen's training were then left with a truly Christianized philosophical education.[110]

Gregory, a student who joined Origen's circle while he taught in Caesarea, provides even more details about how Origen used philosophy to attract educated men to Christianity.[111] Gregory came to Origen's school as a pagan with training in philosophy and law. He was a visitor alone, drawn to Origen's side by a recommendation from a family friend. Nevertheless, through constant exhortations to value philosophy and daily engagement in philosophic dialectics, Origen made Gregory begin to consider the Christian significance of pagan philosophy.[112] Origen taught him Christian interpretations of physics, astronomy, geometry, and ethics.[113] He did this, in Gregory's words, by "picking out and placing before us everything that was useful and true in each of the philosophers . . . [while] counseling us not to pin our allegiance to any philosopher, even if all men swear that he is all-knowing, but to attach ourselves only to God and the Prophets."[114] This program, with its use of philosophy to underpin Biblical study, produced a religious conversion in Gregory that was firmly based upon intellectual training.

Eusebius leaves no doubt that Origen's activities as a Christian teacher of and missionary to pagan intellectuals were done on his own initiative. Indeed, one must imagine that, while Origen was the most successful such Christian teacher, other less famous Christian teachers with ties to pagan intellectual circles also existed.[115] This fact may explain why it was only later, after the great appeal of his program had become apparent, that Origen was

109. Scholten, "Die Alexandrinische Katechetenschule," 24–27.

110. Ibid., 27, and I. Hadot, "Les Introductions aux commentaires exégétiques," 115–16.

111. The similarity between Origen's methods in Caesarea and those used in Alexandria is affirmed by J. W. Trigg, "God's Marvelous *Oikonomia:* Reflections of Origen's Understanding of Divine and Human Pedagogy in the *Address* Ascribed to Gregory Thaumaturgus," *Journal of Early Christian Studies* 9 (2001): 34; and by R. van den Broek, "The Christian 'School' of Alexandria," 45–47.

112. Gregory Thaumaturge, *Address to Origen* 6–8. The identification of this Gregory with the Thaumaturge has been questioned by P. Nautin, *Origène: Sa vie et son oeuvre,* 161, 184. Against this, see J. W. Trigg, "God's Marvelous *Oikonomia,*" 29.

113. *Address to Origen,* 8–11. On this ordering of teaching see J. W. Trigg, "God's Marvelous *Oikonomia,*" 28–29; P. Cox, *Biography in Late Antiquity,* 95; and, more generally, H. Crouzel, "L'École d'Origène à Césarée," *Bulletin de littérature ecclésiastique* 71 (1970): 15–27.

114. *Address to Origen,* 14–15.

115. C. Scholten ("Die Alexandrinische Katechetenschule," 36) lists the names of some earlier such teachers.

the teacher approached by Demetrios, the bishop of Alexandria, to become an officially supported Christian teacher; Origen's efforts were only officially recognized when he had proven himself the city's most competent Christian teacher.[116]

The young, intellectually inclined pagans who were converted by Origen did not lose interest in traditional philosophy. Heraclas, for example, still remained involved in Ammonius's school after his encounters with Origen. Indeed, even after his career pulled him away from the teacher and his circle,[117] Heraclas continued to wear the robes of a philosopher and allowed his philosophical identification to be recognized.[118] He also maintained an active interest in philosophical discussion.

Heraclas and others like him show that, for some of the most cultivated Alexandrians, philosophy and Christianity were seen as perfectly compatible. The continued interest in intense philosophical study among Christian intellectuals meant that the Christian teaching tradition needed to show how this training complemented Christianity. When Christian leaders could not do this, there was a real risk that a Christian student would be led away from the church, a danger amply illustrated by the biography of Ammonius Saccas. Ammonius was born to Christian parents and raised as a Christian. As a youth, he was given a thorough classical education and, when he learned about philosophy, Ammonius converted to paganism.[119] For Ammonius (and probably for others like him), philosophical study had demonstrated the superiority of paganism. In such circumstances, it was the responsibility of Christian teachers to provide compelling intellectual instruction that prevented such conversions from happening.

116. Eusebius makes this clear in *HE* 6.3. See also C. Scholten, "Die Alexandrinische Katechetenschule," 19. Unless one wishes to posit the existence of some unknown interim administrator, the significant gap between Clement's tenure and Demetrius's recognition of Origen's ability suggests that the "Catechetical School" was not an institution in any formal sense. Its head was probably a prominent Christian intellectual who, like a poet laureate, was given the title to reward his teaching and missionary work with the expectation that he would continue to serve as the official intellectual voice of the city's Christian community. If the head of the "Catechetical School" is so understood, it is likely that Eusebius is correct in suggesting that Origen was given this title.

117. *HE* 6.15.1 indicates that Heraclas eventually served as a teacher at the Alexandrian school of Christian instruction that Origen once headed. This is impossible to date, however.

118. It is worth noting with C. Scholten ("Die Alexandrinische Katechetenschule," 24) the possible polemical intent of Origen's comment to this effect.

119. As noted above, Eusebius argues against the claims made by Porphyry that Ammonius had converted. Eusebius's arguments are not of the same strength as those of Porphyry. While Eusebius evidently knew Ammonius only from his writings, Porphyry had a close relationship with Ammonius's student Plotinus, as well as encounters with others of Ammonius's inner circle. Given these personal interactions with Ammonius's followers, it is reasonable to assume that Porphyry could have confidently and accurately relayed a fact as basic as Ammonius's religious self-identification.

In this respect, Origen was one of the best Christian teachers. He headed a group devoted to the study of Christian scriptures and led discussions that drew heavily upon the philosophical tradition. Although his writings bear the unmistakable imprint of his philosophical training, one need not indulge in a systematic evaluation of Origen's theology to see the role that philosophy played in his religious teaching.[120] Origen himself describes this in a letter to his student Gregory:

> Your natural ability enables you to be made an esteemed Roman lawyer or a Greek philosopher of one of the most notable schools. But I hoped that you would entirely apply your ability to Christianity. Indeed, in order to bring this about, I beg of you to take from your studies of Hellenic philosophy those things such as can be made encyclic or preparatory studies to Christianity.[121]

He then asks Gregory to:

> Apply the things that are useful from geometry and astronomy to the explanation of the Holy Scriptures, so that, as the philosophers say about geometry, music, grammar, rhetoric, and astronomy (namely that they are assistants to philosophy), we may say such things about philosophy in relation to Christianity.[122]

Origen concludes by drawing upon a story in Exodus that mentions the Israelites' using Egyptian gold to make items used for the worship of their God. His message in this is clear. Intellectual approaches and doctrines learned in philosophical schools played an integral role in creating an intellectually defined Christian teaching.

Indeed, the role of Origen's circle was not simply to produce converts. It also helped converted Christians like Heraclas and Gregory to understand how their faith was complemented by the teachings of pagan philosophy. It provided them with a comfortable setting in which they could discuss philosophy, Christianity, and the Christian utility of philosophical culture. Origen helped such reflection by giving public lectures each Wednesday and Friday.[123] A skilled teacher like Origen would use this setting to show his students that pagan philosophy was an asset to Christianity and not an inherently dangerous subject.

---

120. Among the many studies describing the philosophical content of Origen's writings see H. Chadwick, *Early Christian Thought and the Classical Tradition* (Oxford, 1966), 66–95; and the specific but telling study of J. M. Rist, "The Importance of Stoic Logic in the *Contra Celsum*," in *Neoplatonism and Early Christian Thought*, ed. H. J. Blumenthal and R. A. Markus, 64–78 (London, 1981).

121. Origen, *Philocalia* 13.1.2–11. This Gregory seems to be distinct from Gregory the Thaumaturge.

122. *Philocalia* 13.1.12 ff.

123. Socrates Scholasticus, *HE* 5.22.

This was an important contribution because, while schools like that of Ammonius Saccas included Christians among their students, they were not particularly accepting of Christian intellectual culture.[124] A number of third-century intellectuals wrote anti-Christian polemics that relied upon philosophy to demonstrate their points. While none of the surviving texts seem to have been composed in Alexandria, two philosophers with ties to the school of Ammonius did use philosophy to attack Christianity. Plotinus, the student of Ammonius Saccas, wrote a series of refutations of doctrines advocated by the Gnostics.[125] While Plotinus attacked some teachings of one Christian group, his student Porphyry composed a comprehensive refutation of Christianity in c. 270.[126] Both of these works were probably written in Rome, but the links between the Roman and Alexandrian cultural worlds at this time were strong, and these texts, which may or may not have been inspired by the Alexandrian cultural milieu, certainly circulated in the city.

The leaders of Christian study circles represented an important counter in these intellectual exchanges. They not only could teach Christians how to respond intelligently to these criticisms, but they could also circulate classically structured texts that contained reasoned rebuttals to pagan attacks. Clement of Alexandria, for example, wrote the *Protrepticus,* a tract designed to encourage pagans to approach Christianity on intellectual grounds.[127] Origen, too, wrote a different sort of work that aimed to convert by refuting the criticisms of Christianity leveled by the physician Celsus.[128]

Origen's activities, then, reveal the interesting role a Christian teacher had to play. He was essentially the head of a sub-group of intellectuals. These men participated in the general Alexandrian philosophical and cultural

124. Origen himself alludes to the hostility with which Christian thought was received initially by his pagan contemporaries (*Homilies in Jeremiah* 20.5).

125. Plotinus, *Enneads,* 2.9, 3.8, 5.5, and 5.8. These writings are mentioned by Porphyry at *VP* 16. Porphyry mentions that they were written to rebut the ideas of followers of two unknown teachers. For more on this, see J. Igal, "The Gnostics and 'The Ancient Philosophy' in Plotinus," in *Neoplatonism and Early Christian Thought,* ed. H. J. Blumenthal and R. A. Markus, 138–49 (London, 1981).

126. Now preserved only in fragments. On this see A. von Harnack, *Porphyrius "Gegen de Christen"* (Berlin, 1916). See as well as the insightful comments of T. D. Barnes, "Porphyry *Against the Christians:* Date and Attribution of Fragments," *Journal of Theological Studies* 24 (1973): 424–42; and A. Smith, *Porphyry's Place in the Neoplatonic Tradition: A Study in Post-Plotinian Neoplatonism* (The Hague, 1974). For the implications of a date in the 290s, see in part E. DePalma Digeser, "Lactantius, Porphyry, and the Debate over Religious Toleration," *Journal of Roman Studies* 88 (1998): 129–46.

127. On the *Protrepicus,* see the recent edition of M. Marcovich (*Clementis Alexandrini Protrepicus* [Leiden, 1995]).

128. For the philosophical content of the *Contra Celsum* see, among many others, J. M. Rist, "The Importance of Stoic Logic in the *Contra Celsum,*" 64–65; and L. Roberts, "Origen and Stoic Logic," *Transactions of the American Philosophical Association* 101 (1970): 433–44.

world, but they also remained sensitive to the religious implications of their participation. Teachers like Origen steered young intellectuals towards Christianity and kept them secure in the faith through constant instruction. Though subsequent generations of Alexandrian Christian teachers seem to have abandoned Origen's Platonically derived syllabus, the use of elements of pagan learning to introduce intellectually inclined converts to Christianity remained popular into the fourth century.[129]

Equally significant is the role played by schools like that of Ammonius Saccas. Ammonius himself had experience with both paganism and Christianity, and his school seems to have attracted students from both religious traditions. In his general classes, it seems that Ammonius was willing to provide a firm grounding in traditional philosophical methods to every one of his students (regardless of their religious identity). Among his inner circle, the teaching may have been less conventional and, perhaps, more religious in character. Nevertheless, the training that students received in Ammonius's school provided a common set of concepts and philosophical approaches that greatly facilitated cultural exchanges. At times, these techniques were used to convert people from one faith to another. On other occasions, they were used to criticize elements of either Christianity or paganism. But, although our sources sometimes obscure the fact, most often the philosophical training that both pagans and Christians received enabled them to constructively communicate ideas between one another. Philosophy was a social as well as a polemical tool and, in Alexandria, it served the former purpose much better.

The free intellectual exchange between Alexandrian pagans and Christians extended far beyond the school of Ammonius. Before Ammonius began teaching, Christians like Clement had introduced philosophical ideas of varying sophistication into their writings. This trend also continued long after Ammonius passed from the scene. In the 290s, for example, the Platonist Alexander of Lycopolis wrote a polemical tract against the Manichees that was so full of Christian teaching that many modern scholars assumed he was himself a Christian.[130] The intellectual discourse between educated Christians and pagans that this presupposes seems to have been a natural part of the Alexandrian cultural world.

129. For a survey of such teachers (most of whom are noted as heads of the Catechetical school), see C. Scholten, "Die Alexandrinische Katechetenschule," 32–34.

130. He was not a Christian, however. On Alexander see G. Fowden, "The Platonist Philosopher and His Circle," 367; and, especially, J. Mansfeld, "Alexander and the History of Neoplatonism," in *An Alexandrian Platonist Against Dualism: Alexander of Lycopolis' Treatise "Critique of the Doctrines of Manichaeus,"* trans. P. W. van der Horst and J. Mansfeld, 6–48 (Leiden, 1974), and reprinted in J. Mansfeld, *Studies in Later Greek Philosophy and Gnosticism* (London, 1989), ch. 13.

While a certain level of engagement between pagan and Christian intellectuals can be seen in many of the major urban centers of the Roman empire, some of Alexandria's specific attributes made it especially able to nurture such ties. Alexandria's historic status as an important center of teaching certainly played a role. The large community of scholars attracted by the *Mouseion* and the Library had long sustained a sophisticated cultural life in the city. We do not know of any Christians who joined either institution but, through their networks of correspondents, it is likely that they had access to the works produced in them. Furthermore, Christians would have had access to teachers, like Ammonius Saccas, who worked outside of these institutions. The quality of teaching in their schools was sometimes even better than what was available in the public schools.

Christian teachers like Origen played a significant role in making this system work well for Christians. The intellectual circles these men headed provided a forum within which the material taught in schools could be incorporated into Christian understandings of religion. Just as importantly, they taught Christian intellectuals how their philosophical education could complement their Christianity. While schools like that headed by Ammonius Saccas accepted Christians as students, they had little interest in respecting their religious ideas and, in the case of particularly illogical ideas like allegorical scriptural interpretation, they were met with harsh criticism.[131] In the minds of these teachers, Christianity had little positive impact upon their teaching. It was left to men like Origen to show Christian students how philosophy could complement and not inherently compete with their religious values. This was a job they readily accepted and performed throughout the second and third centuries.

Despite their religious differences, educated Christians and pagans shared a great deal in Roman Alexandria. They shared a geographic space, a collection of educational institutions, and a common intellectual culture. Indeed, because conversions between the two faiths were not uncommon, they even shared people. It was inevitable that mixed intellectual circles comprised of pagans and Christians would develop, both in the Alexandrian schools and outside of them. This was only natural in Alexandria, a city abundant in diversity and erudition.

---

131. Such as that of Porphyry. See, however, C. Scholten ("Die Alexandrinische Katechetenschule," 27 n. 75) for the similarity of Origenistic allegory and some Platonic traditions of exegesis.

Chapter 7

The Shifting Sands of Fourth-Century Alexandrian Cultural Life

The fourth century was one of the most dramatic periods in the history of ancient Alexandria. In the year 300, Alexandria retained the culture of intellectual exchange that had characterized the vigorous philosophical debates of the second and third centuries. To a large degree, Christians and pagans were partners in these discussions. While they disagreed about the divine, educated Christians and pagans saw philosophy as a common intellectual framework around which they could construct their understandings of God.

In the course of the fourth century, all of this changed. Alexandria underwent the startling (and often violent) change from a pagan city to one in which the majority of its citizens were Christian. While the Alexandrian Christian community grew, its character changed as well. There was always a strong intellectual component within the Christian community in the city. In the second and third centuries, it was common for circles of classically educated Christian men and women to form around wise or charismatic Alexandrian teachers like Clement and Origen. The discussions these teachers led were often theological in nature, frequently incorporated contemporary philosophical ideas, and naturally led to a wide range of theological interpretations. In the third century, the diversity of opinions that came from such circles was a nuisance to the Alexandrian church hierarchy. Attempts were made to control them, but the resources were not available to do this with any great success.[1] However, when the emperor Constantine linked Christianity and imperial policy, Christian doctrinal disputes, which had once been hidden by the sect's relative obscurity, gained a new impor-

---

1. The most notable attempt to control the activities of these teachers was the forced exile of Origen by bishop Demetrius in 231 (Eusebius, *HE* 6.26).

tance.[2] The most significant such dispute centered upon the teaching of Arius, an Alexandrian presbyter with intellectual (if not personal) ties to pagan philosophy. In response to his ideas, direct ecclesiastical action was undertaken to eliminate the speculative environment created by these classically educated circles. These efforts, which were effectively combined with other naturally evolving Christian intellectual trends, largely decoupled Christian theological speculation and contemporary pagan philosophy.

The first part of this chapter will explore the ecclesiastical and intellectual causes of the Alexandrian Christian community's movement away from the philosophically influenced Christian intellectual circle. Two causes are evident. The first, the Arian controversy, redefined the relationship between pagan philosophical culture and Christianity. This process is shown by the literary program of bishop Athanasius, which was designed to discredit both philosophically inclined Christian teachers (teachers like Arius) and the philosophy upon which their doctrines depended. As his project developed, Athanasius's writings began to capitalize upon a developing strand of Christian thought that tied Christian teaching and ascetic practice ever closer together. At the center of this was the *Life of Antony*, a landmark text that identified asceticism as a new type of Christian wisdom, marked the ascetic as a new breed of Christian teacher, and defined asceticism's superiority to traditional learning.

Athanasius's substitution of ascetic practice for the learning formerly expected of a Christian teacher did not, in practical terms, eliminate the philosophically inclined Christian teacher. But, at the same time (and largely independent of Athanasius), the formal practice of asceticism, usually in a coenobitic monastic environment, did become an important attribute of the later fourth-century Alexandrian Christian teacher. Philosophically influenced theologians like Evagrius Ponticus and the Tall Brothers continued to run teaching circles, but these teaching circles interacted with monasteries and not, as in the past, with pagan philosophical schools.

The efforts to eliminate much of the free-ranging discussion of Christian intellectual circles neither affected Christian enthusiasm for classical learning nor decreased the Christian presence in pagan schools. For this reason, the second part of this chapter will examine Alexandrian pagan schools and the role they played in the education of Christians in the second half of the fourth century. Like the city's Christian community, Alexandria's pagan schools underwent a transformation in this period. Two major strains of Platonic philosophical interpretation contested with one another in later fourth-century Alexandria. One, the Platonism developed by Plotinus and

2. This is an often-repeated assertion. The significance of Constantinian patronage in the Alexandrian environment is concisely explained by R. Williams (*Arius: Heresy and Tradition* [London, 1987], 86). See also D. Brakke, *Athanasius and the Politics of Asceticism*, 2nd ed. (Baltimore, 1998), 58–60.

Porphyry, was a favorite of some pagan teachers.[3] The other strain, the theurgically influenced interpretation of Iamblichus, was the doctrine of choice for another group of intellectuals in the city.[4]

Although it began among pagans, the contest between these two groups was to be decided not by the relative philosophical merits of each system but by the actions of the Alexandrian Christian establishment. In this way, the church unwittingly enabled Iamblichan teaching to become dominant. This created a situation in which Christian students of philosophy, cut off from Christian intellectual instruction by the decampment of religious study circles into monasteries, were sent into schools directed by unapologetically pagan teachers. Consequently, after the demise of the Christian study circle, the events of the later fourth century caused the nature of intellectual interactions between pagan teachers and Christian students to change.

ARIANISM AND THE ATHANASIAN RESPONSE

The Arian controversy, perhaps the most significant doctrinal conflict in the fourth-century Greek world, began in Alexandria sometime around 318.[5] At its root was the teaching of Arius, an Alexandrian presbyter in charge of the church in the Alexandrian parish of Baucalis.[6] In addition to his sacramental duties, Arius, like Origen before him, gave lectures on scriptural interpretation on Wednesday and Friday of each week[7] and served as both a spiritual and an intellectual guide for his hearers.[8] But Arius's message was a unique one. He taught that Christ was of a different nature from God and, because (like humans) he was a creature of God, he provided Christians with a model that showed how salvation could be achieved.[9]

This attractive view of salvation was supported by a number of intellectual

---

3. Plotinian-type teaching had been a feature in Alexandria from the time of Ammonius Saccas. Alexander of Lycopolis apparently continued the trend in the later third century. In the fourth century, Hypatia and her father Theon are the most prominent Plotinian teachers.

4. These were men like Antoninus. For him, see below.

5. For a detailed reconstruction, see R. Williams, *Arius¹*, 48–81.

6. Epiphanius, *Panarion* 3.153.16.

7. Ibid. See also D. Brakke, *Athanasius and the Politics of Asceticism*, 64; and W. Telfer, "St. Peter of Alexandria and Arius," *Analecta Bollandiana* 67 (1949): 117–30. For Origen's twice weekly lectures, see Socrates, *HE* 5.22.

8. As R. Gregg has emphasized (review of *Arius: Heresy and Tradition*, by R. Williams, *Journal of Theological Studies* 40 [1989]: 252), one cannot look at Arius's appeal without focusing upon his appeal as a religious figure as well as his insight as a thinker.

9. This is the compelling reconstruction of R. Gregg and D. Groh (*Early Arianism—A View of Salvation* [Philadelphia, 1981]). Although their conclusions have recently been called into question (e.g., C. G. Stead, "Arius in Modern Research," *Journal of Theological Studies* 45 [1994]: 26, 36), the idea they present seems sound and has won some tentative acceptance (e.g., R. Lorenz, "Die Christusseele im arianischen Streit," *Zeitschrift für Kirchengeschichte* 94 (1983): 1–51).

arguments designed to demonstrate that Christ was distinct from God. Arius maintained that there was a clear and unbridgeable distinction between God, the creator, and the world he created. This was upheld in both a formal and a chronological sense. Formally, Arius held that God had a distinct identity from everything in the world. Because of this, God's nature could never be mingled with the nature of something in the world. Christ, who had been incarnated into a human body, could not therefore share the fully divine nature of God.[10]

Arius also maintained that Christ came into being as a result of a process of generation initiated by God. This process occurred before time but, because Christ came into being through this process that God had begun, God had a certain precedence over Christ.[11] While God has no beginning or end, the existence of Christ must be said to have a beginning.[12] Consequently, God and Christ must be two distinct entities with two different natures.[13]

Another idea concerned Christ's ability to understand God. Arius taught that God, as the origin of all things, had a uniquely unified nature. The son that he created, however, had no capacity to understand the unique nature of God.[14] God's nature was not something that could be seen, nor something that could be described. Consequently, Christ could not conceive of what it would be like.[15]

All of these notions have echoes in the ideas of philosophers who were Arius's contemporaries.[16] But Arius also used philosophical terminology to ex-

10. Arius's idea about the substantial differences between God and Christ are explored by R. Williams, "The Logic of Arianism," *Journal of Theological Studies* 34 (1983): 63–66. Against this, see the objections of C. Stead, "Was Arius a Neoplatonist?" *Studia Patristica* 32 (1997): 43–44; and the response of R. Williams, *Arius: Heresy and Tradition,* 2nd ed. (Grand Rapids, 2002), 263–65.

11. These ideas were conveyed in a letter Arius wrote to Eusebius of Nicomedia. For more discussion of the ideas contained in the letter, see R. Williams, *Arius¹*, 188–90.

12. Arius, *Thalia* (quoted in Athanasius, *De synodis Arimini in Italia et Seleuciae in Isauria* 15.3.6).

13. Arius apparently also used arguments about Christ's role in the rational structure of the world, how God's fundamentally unified nature differs from the multiplicity of natures in other entities, and how the distinct qualities of God and Christ indicate that they must have different natures. R. Williams, *Arius¹*, 181–233, describes these assumptions in great detail.

14. "For the son is unable to understand the magnitude of his father, who exists beside him, for the son himself does not understand the nature of his own father." (Arius, in Athanasius, *De synodis* 15.3.36–37). For a more detailed explanation of this point see R. Williams, *Arius¹*, 231.

15. Arius in *De synodis* 15.3.2–6.

16. For the similarities to the writings of Plotinus, see R. Williams, *Arius¹*, 208–209. Plotinus speaks about the divine mind in *Enn.* 5.3.1–8 and the inability of the created divine mind to understand the one in *Enn.* 5.3.11. While admitting the similarities between some of Arius's thought and that of Plotinus, C. Stead ("Was Arius a Neoplatonist?" 46–47) thinks it more likely that some of these similarities had an Alexandrian origin derived from the writings of bishop Alexander. Although T. D. Barnes expresses skepticism about how widely known Plotinian texts would have been in Alexandria at the time (*Athanasius and Constantius* [Cambridge, Mass., 1993],

press the distinction between God and Christ. In the *Thalia*, he writes, "You should understand that the Monad [always] existed but the Dyad did not exist before it came into being."[17] The particular significance of the term "Dyad" has been debated,[18] but Arius's use of it seems consistent with the pagan philosophical conception of the Dyad as the divine entity that emanated from the One and occupied the first level of existence below the One.[19]

Arius's apparent familiarity with the ideas and language of contemporary philosophy did not distinguish him from previous generations of Alexandrian Christian teachers.[20] Historically, Alexandrian teachers like Clement and Origen had knowledge of basic philosophical themes. They also had some awareness of the philosophical interpretations their contemporaries were debating in the pagan schools. Indeed, the nature of the Christian study circle encouraged the introduction and discussion of these contemporary ideas. The teacher, with his deep understanding of Christianity and his divinely inspired intellectual training, was expected to determine if these ideas were relevant to Christianity. If they were, he needed to show how they increased one's understanding of the religion. This is just what Arius did.

Besides the interest in philosophy that Arius shared with these previous teachers, he also seems to have consciously presented himself as a successor to this trend in Christian scriptural interpretation.[21] In the *Thalia*, Arius describes his intellectual pedigree as follows:

These are the things I have learned from the men who partake of wisdom,
The keen-minded men, taught by God, and in all respects wise.
In the steps of such men I have walked, advancing in thoughts like theirs,

---

245 n. 50), it is worth noting that elements of Plotinian thought turn up in Alexander of Lycopolis (on which, see J. Mansfeld, "Alexander and the History of Neoplatonism," in *An Alexandrian Platonist Against Dualism: Alexander of Lycopolis' Treatise "Against the Doctrines of Manichaeus,"* trans. P. W. van der Horst and J. Mansfeld [Leiden, 1974], 13–14). This suggests that these ideas were current in Alexandrian intellectual and religious discourse at the turn of the fourth century.

17. Arius in *De synodis* 15.3.21.

18. For this debate, see R. Williams, *Arius¹*, 191; and, against Williams, C. Stead, "Was Arius a Neoplatonist?" 45–46.

19. Williams, *Arius¹*, 191–92.

20. It was not unique in the Alexandrian Christian environment. C. Stead ("Was Arius a Neoplatonist?" 46) has shown some similarities between Arius's ideas and those of bishop Alexander. This ought not be taken as evidence that Arius's ideas were wholly conventional and framed exclusively by discourses within the Alexandrian Christian community. In truth, while Arius's approaches were overwhelmingly shaped by the intellectual concerns of Alexandrian Christians, R. Williams (*Arius²*, 265) is certainly correct to see these ideas as the product of a fertile intellectual discussion that drew from both Christian and pagan philosophical trends.

21. D. Brakke, *Athanasius and the Politics of Asceticism*, 64–65.

A man much spoken of, who suffers all manner of things for God's glory,
And, learning from God, I am now no stranger to wisdom and knowledge.[22]

As this suggests, Arius staked a large part of his credibility upon his intellectual descent from wise Christian teachers.[23] This sort of self-presentation was common among past leaders of Alexandrian Christian intellectual circles like Clement.[24] It also served to highlight how Arius's ideas fit within the Christian intellectual tradition.

This was a necessary strategy because, despite Arius's claims, his teachings were not conventional.[25] In fact, they caused a great deal of controversy in the church. Many clergymen and, eventually, the bishop of Alexandria, questioned the orthodoxy of Arius's teachings. The major objections to Arius's doctrines centered upon their innovative nature and their difference from the teaching of the church hierarchy. By presenting both himself and his ideas within the context of an established thought tradition, Arius could counteract the force of these accusations and suggest that his critics' disagreement with his teachings only arose out of their own ignorance.[26]

This type of response forced the church to decide whether the ultimate authority in a Christian community depended upon individual wisdom or one's position in the hierarchy. This was not a new question and, perhaps anticipating the difficulty of answering it, Alexander, the bishop at the time of

22. Arius, *Thalia* in Athanasius, *Orationes tres contra Arianos* 26.20.44–21.3 (trans. R. Williams, *Arius¹*, 85).

23. R. Williams, *Arius¹*, 85–86. This notion is based upon Arius's use of the term θεοδιδάκτων in the *Thalia*. R. Gregg, review of *Arius*, 253, sees this term differently and calls attention to *Vit. Ant.* 66 to show that Williams has overemphasized its significance in an early fourth-century context. This need not follow, however. The usage in the *Life of Antony* may instead represent an attempt by Athanasius to transform the term into one that favors his ideas about the nature of divine teaching.

24. Clement, in *Stromateis* 1.11.3, describes himself as an heir of "[those] teachers [who] preserved the true tradition of the blessed doctrine directly from the holy Apostles Peter, James, John, and Paul . . . By God's will did they come also to us to deposit those ancestral and apostolic seeds." On this, see as well R. van den Broek, "The Christian 'School' of Alexandria in the Second and Third Centuries," in *Centres of Learning: Learning and Location in Pre-Modern Europe and the Near East*, ed. J. W. Drijvers and A. Macdonald (Leiden, 1995), 42–43. Compare as well the claim of apostolic sanction offered by the "Gnostic" teacher Valentinus (cf. B. Layton, *The Gnostic Scriptures* [New York, 1987], 217).

25. While not universally accepted, ideas that the Son was subordinate to the Father had been broached many times before Arius. On this broad topic, see W. Marcus, *Der Subordinatianismus als historiologisches Phänomen* (Munich, 1963).

26. Other Christian thinkers had complained that a higher ecclesiastical rank did not always mean that an individual possessed a higher wisdom. Origen makes this point in *Homily on Numbers* 2.1. In a moment of particular disgust, the anonymous author of the *Apocalypse of Peter* even called bishops "waterless canals" (79.30–31) because of their ignorance. See D. Brakke, *Athanasius and the Politics of Asceticism*, 62.

the conflict's outbreak, was deliberately slow to take sides. While aware of the theological difficulties of Arius's teachings, he respected the priest's intelligence. In the hope of reaching a compromise, Alexander arranged a series of intellectual debates about the matter (thus acknowledging, in principle, the authority of expressed wisdom). Arius too seems to have hoped for a compromise. Pursuant to this, he asked two Libyan bishops to contact Alexander and express their support.[27] It was hoped that these men, who could claim to be equal in rank to Alexander, would convince the bishop that men who were on his own level in the church also agreed with Arius.[28] In trying to avoid an open confrontation, Alexander approached Arius in a way that respected his authority as a Christian intellectual. Arius, for his part, tried to reach an agreement by acknowledging Alexander's hierarchical authority. Unfortunately, no compromise was reached and, as hostilities developed, each side increasingly called the authority of its opponents into question.[29]

As the head of the Alexandrian church hierarchy, it was expected that Alexander would use the power of his position to attack Arius.[30] Even so, as the conflict progressed, the response to Arius was not simply confined to an assertion of the bishop's primacy within the Christian hierarchy. Under Athanasius, Alexander's successor, the arguments against Arius became increasingly distinct and, by the 350s, had expanded into an attack upon the very validity of the philosophically influenced Christian intellectual tradition.

One sees this stage of the argument reflected clearly in Athanasius's festal letter of 352, in which he lays out the notion that human wisdom had little relationship to true Christian wisdom. There was, Athanasius wrote, a need to distinguish between "the words of the saints" and the "fancies of human invention."[31] The "saints" relied solely upon the words of God that are transmitted through the scriptures. Other teachers relied upon contrived notions like philosophy. As a result, the teachings of the saints were grounded in truth while the others, who relied upon their own ideas to create a fanciful interpretation of God, strayed from the truth. Consequently, of the saints, "the Word wants us to be disciples, and they should be our teachers, and it is necessary

27. This was not coincidental. Arius seems to have had ties to Libya (Epiphanius, *Panarion* 3. 152.19).

28. On the relative rank of the Alexandrian bishop see R. Williams, *Arius*[1], 41.

29. For a more detailed explanation of this process, see C. R. Galvão-Sobrinho, "The Rise of the Christian Bishop; Doctrine and Power in the Later Roman Empire, A.D. 318–80," PhD diss., Yale University, 1999, 91–107.

30. What follows is only the most superficial of surveys of this event. Many more detailed reconstructions exist. See, for example, W. Schneemelcher, "Zur Chronologie des arianischen Streites," *Theologische Literaturzeitung* 79.7–8, (1954): 393–99; and C. R. Galvão-Sobrinho, "The Rise of the Christian Bishop," 86 ff.

31. Brakke, *Athanasius and the Politics of Asceticism*, 66.

for us to obey only them."[32] But teachers of the other sort, of whom Arius was one, had no place in determining a Christian's understanding of the divine.

In a later letter, Athanasius makes his attack on academic Christian teachers even more explicit.[33] Calling to mind Matthew 23.8–10, Athanasius reminds his followers that Christ had commanded his disciples to call no one else teacher.[34] In fact, Athanasius argues that Christ is the only source for knowledge about the divine and the only one who expresses divine truth.[35] Human teachers, even those with an academic pedigree, cannot properly be called teachers. Either they teach false doctrines or the wisdom they proclaim was taught to them by Christ.[36] For this reason, only Christ can be seen as a Christian teacher,[37] and, because Christ's teaching was communicated through the scripture, these are the only works one should use for instruction in Christian religion.[38]

These two ideas were direct attacks upon the legitimacy of intellectual Christianity. First, by emphasizing that true Christian wisdom derived only from a Biblical canon, Athanasius excluded all ideas that entered into Christianity from a non-Biblical source.[39] Arius's philosophical influences, for example, became evidence of his folly and not proof of his knowledge. In addition, the idea that Christ alone was the true teacher of Christian wisdom worked to eliminate any authority that a teacher could claim from an intellectual pedigree. If all teachers were really disciples of Christ, Arius's claim to an intellectual descent from a long line of Christian wise men meant nothing. Indeed, because these wise men presumably included non-Biblical elements in their teaching, Athanasius could present Arius's intellectual heritage as nothing more than a legacy of generations of arrogant folly.[40]

Athanasius had a long and productive career in which to write against Arius and the intellectual tradition from which he came. Many of his works contained reasoned denunciations of Arius and attacks upon the sources of

32. *Ep. fest.* (syr.) 2.7 (24.12; 24.22–25). Festal letter 24 has been wrongly transmitted as Festal letter 2. The translation comes from D. Brakke, *Athanasius and the Politics of Asceticism,* 66; note as well 320 n. 26 on the text's transmission.

33. *Ep. fest.* 39. For a more detailed discussion of this letter see D. Brakke, "Canon Formation and Social Conflict in Fourth Century Egypt," *Harvard Theological Review* 87 (1994): 395–419 (esp. 399–410).

34. *Ep. fest.* 39 = Brakke, *Athanasius and the Politics of Asceticism,* 327.

35. Brakke, "Canon Formation and Social Conflict," 405.

36. Athanasius writes: "Even if it is Paul who is teaching, it is nevertheless Christ who is speaking in him. And even if he says that the Lord has appointed teachers in the churches, the Lord nevertheless first teaches them and then sends them out." (*Ep. fest.* 39, trans. Brakke, *Athanasius and the Politics of Asceticism,* 328).

37. *Ep. fest.* 39 = Brakke, *Athanasius and the Politics of Asceticism,* 328.

38. Ibid.

39. Brakke, "Canon Formation and Social Conflict," 409–10.

40. Ibid., 404–5.

his authority. In these works, however, Athanasius did not simply respond to claims made by Arius. He also produced an original and carefully designed program in which Christian wisdom was positively defined. It was described not as the scholastic understanding of Arius but as the practice of Christian ascetics. This was, of course, not an Athanasian invention. Origen, for example, saw asceticism as an important part of his identity as a Christian thinker.[41] As Athanasius evolved as a thinker, however, his ideas grew increasingly nuanced and asceticism became not a complementary part of the identity of a Christian teacher but a defining characteristic. His ascetics became individuals who listened to God's words and practiced the discipline God advocated. This made them superior teachers of truth and their teaching was true Christian philosophy.

THE LIFE OF ANTONY

In Athanasius's writings, the clearest identification of the ascetic as a Christian philosopher was made in the *Life of Antony*, a text that he wrote around 356.[42] This work described, in narrative form, the education, conduct, and lifestyle of Antony, the prototypical Egyptian solitary ascetic.[43] In keeping

41. On Origen's asceticism, see Eusebius, *HE* 6.8.1–3. While Origen was certainly motivated by traditional Christian ideas of renunciation, it is also important to consider the role that asceticism played in the philosophical circles of Origen's pagan contemporaries. On this, see C. Scholten, "Die Alexandrinische Katechetenschule," *Jarbuch für Antike und Christentum* 38 (1995): 20; and, on pagan circles, D. A. Dombrowski, "Asceticism as Athletic Training in Plotinus," in *Aufstieg und Niedergang der Römischen Welt* 2.36.1 (1987): 701–12.

42. Despite the arguments of T. D. Barnes ("Angel of Light or Mystic Initiate? The problem of the *Life of Antony*," *Journal of Theological Studies* 37 [1986]: 353–67; also review of *The Letters of St. Antony* by S. Rubenson, *Journal of Theological Studies* 42 [1991]: 723–32), the contention that the *Life of Antony* was a Coptic text written by someone other than Athanasius is most unlikely. The text has substantial formal similarities to Greek biographic texts and, as will be described below, it was designed to interact with this Greek literary genre. In addition, the manuscript tradition argues against a non-Athanasian authorship. All of the over one hundred and sixty manuscripts of the *Vita* attribute it to Athanasius. This is further supported by the fourth-century references to Athanasian authorship in both Gregory Nazianzen's *Oration* 21 (datable to c. 380— a bit more than two decades after the work's probable composition) and Jerome's *De viris illustribus* (87; 88; 125 datable to 392). For a different sort of argument against Barnes see A. Louth, "St. Athanasius and the Greek Life of Antony," *Journal of Theological Studies* 39 (1988): 504–9. The recent discussion of P. Rousseau ("Antony as a Teacher in the Greek Life," in *Greek Biography and Panegyric in Late Antiquity*, ed. T. Hägg and P. Rousseau, 89–109 [Berkeley and Los Angeles, 2000]) raises interesting questions about the consistency between the ideas in this text and the larger goals Athanasius seems to be advancing in other works. These questions will be addressed below.

43. *Vit. Ant.*, Prologue. Athanasius's portrait of Antony differs significantly from other fourth-century traditions about the saint. The seven letters of Antony represent the most notable divergent tradition. An extensive discussion of the letters and their significance is that of S. Rubenson, *The Letters of St. Antony: Origenist Theology, Monastic Tradition and the Making of a Saint* (Lund, 1990).

with Athanasius's own theological and political purposes, his Antony was an ascetic who deferred to bishops[44] and participated in the fight against Arianism.[45] The most important element of the portrait, though, was Athanasius's identification of Antony as a Christian philosopher who demonstrated the irrelevance of classical intellectual approaches to an exemplary Christian life. Athanasius's demonstration of this took an ingenious form. Instead of simply composing an oration or a treatise, Athanasius used a biography to make his argument. As its title suggests, the *Life of Antony* is structured in accordance with the classical biographic form.[46] By the mid-fourth century, biographies of philosophical holy men had become quite well developed as a form of persuasive writing. The power of such a biography, as opposed to that of a philosophical commentary, lay in its ability to use the deeds of a philosopher to convince the reader about the truth of his teachings.[47] For the text to be effective, the biographic subject needed to be presented as both an individual who was capable of explaining important ideas and as one whose actions showed the truth of his ideas.

A typical example of how the biographic genre enabled the words and deeds of a sage to work together to convince readers about the wisdom of his teaching can be found in Iamblichus's portrait of Pythagoras.[48] Iamblichus begins his text by recounting the traditions of Pythagoras's birth, his education under the best teachers, his travels abroad, and the beginning of his active teaching. Before speaking in any detail about Pythagoras's teachings, however, Iamblichus first describes their practical effects. He tells how they liberated a number of occupied cities and led these cities to excellent govern-

44. Brakke, *Athanasius and the Politics of Asceticism*, 245–46. P. Rousseau ("Antony as a Teacher in the Greek Life," 99–100) compares the work to other Egyptian non-clerical writings and sees Antony's attitude to clerics as one of deference born from an awareness of the political realities of the time. Some of the actions Antony takes in the text can fit with this portrait (e.g., Antony's bowing of his head before clergy in *Vit. Ant.* 67) while others (e.g., Antony's deathbed gift of his possessions to Athanasius and other clergy in *Vit. Ant.* 91) suggest voluntary submission instead of "cautious tact."

45. *Vit. Ant.* 69. P. Rousseau's characterization ("Antony as a Teacher in the Greek Life," 100) of heresy as a concern because of its harm to the soul is particularly good.

46. For the development of biography as an ancient literary form, see A. Momigliano, *The Development of Greek Biography* (Cambridge, Mass., 1971); and, earlier, D. R. Stuart, *Epochs of Greek and Roman Biography* (Berkeley, 1928). The late antique manifestation of the form is discussed by P. Cox, *Biography in Late Antiquity: The Quest for the Holy Man* (Berkeley and Los Angeles, 1983). Its position as a part of the teaching curriculum is explored by J. Mansfeld, *Prolegomena: Questions to be settled before the study of an author or text* (Leiden, 1994). For a more general treatment of the relationship between ancient biography and Christian hagiography, see M. Van Uytfanghe, "L'Hagiographie: un genre chrétien ou antique tardif?" *Analecta Bollandiana* 111 (1993): 135–88.

47. On the interaction of traditions regarding the actions and doctrines of holy philosophers, see P. Cox, *Biography in Late Antiquity*, 49–51.

48. Iamblichus, *de vita Pythagorica liber*, ed. L. Deubner (1937), rev. U. Klein (Stuttgart, 1975).

ment that was free from internal strife. It is only later, after Pythagoras, his education, and the effect that his teachings had on others have been described, that Iamblichus introduces his actual ideas.[49] The effect of this is subtle but powerful; the accounts of Pythagoras's actions have prepared the reader and made him predisposed to look positively upon the sage's teaching.[50]

In the *Life of Antony*, Athanasius similarly relies upon this interplay of word and deed to convincingly portray Antony as a teacher of a philosophically viable brand of wisdom. So, in the same way that Iamblichus used anecdotes to validate the training of Pythagoras, Athanasius includes similar validating details about Antony's ascetic education. This was a particularly important literary strategy in Athanasius's text because Antony's "education" was unique for a philosopher. Whereas conventional philosophers (both Christian and pagan) had extensive literary training, Antony, we are told, "could not bear to learn letters."[51] Instead, he embarked upon his search for Christian wisdom when he heard words from scripture read aloud in church.[52] He advanced in learning not at the foot of an erudite mentor, but by watching the actions of older ascetics who dwelled on the outskirts of his town.[53] After learning all that he could from these men, Antony set out to develop his asceticism by living on his own at the farthest edge of the town.[54] Later, he moved to the desert fringes and, eventually, into the desert itself.[55]

As recounted by Athanasius, Antony's path could not have been more different from that followed by previous generations of Christian wise men. But Athanasius is clear that Antony's training was effective. When Antony emerged in public after completing his solitary ascetic training, "the Lord worked through him to heal those who suffered from physical ailments," purge demons, reconcile those hostile to one another,[56] and even make a crocodile-infested canal safe to wade across.[57] It is only then, after these proofs of Antony's wisdom are given, that Athanasius begins to lay out Antony's doc-

---

49. They are introduced briefly in *Vit. Pyth.* 7.

50. This pattern repeats itself as Iamblichus moves on to describe Pythagoras's teaching in greater detail. The next section of the work begins with an anecdote about Pythagoras's prophetic powers in which he gives the exact number of fish a group of fishermen will catch (*Vit. Pyth.* 8). This helps set the stage for the four philosophical lessons that immediately follow.

51. *Vit. Ant.* 1.

52. Ibid., 1, 2. On this apparent reference to Deuteronomy 4.9, see P. Rousseau, "Antony as a Teacher in the Greek Life," 90. To see the uniqueness of Antony's training, one only needs to compare it with Eusebius's idealized Origen. To Eusebius, Origen was the ultimate Christian philosopher—and he had the intellectual pedigree to match this title.

53. *Vit. Ant.* 3–4.

54. Ibid., 8.

55. Ibid., 12.

56. Ibid., 14. The emphasis upon reconciliation of enemies is also used to validate the teaching of Pythagoras.

57. Ibid., 15.

trines on the acquisition and practice of an ascetic wisdom that regulates the soul's intellectual part through the suppression of bodily desires and sordid thoughts.[58]

After this initial introduction to Antony's philosophy, Athanasius's account becomes a series of vignettes designed to illustrate the exceptional abilities that this new sort of wisdom had given Antony. The most memorable of these are two extended exchanges that Antony had with pagan philosophers.[59] These exchanges underpin Athanasius's identification of Antony as a philosopher with a superior sort of wisdom. In the conversations that the text presents, the philosophers were drawn to Antony because they thought that, as a simple-minded Christian, Antony would be easy to defeat in an argument. When they actually spoke with him, however, Antony outwitted them with the simplicity of his arguments.[60] Guided by divine hands, his philosophy of asceticism was shown to be superior to the teachings of non-Christian philosophers.

In the end, the educated reader of the *Life of Antony* was to take away a revolutionary message. The Christian asceticism of Antony had rendered traditional philosophy, and those teachers trained in it, irrelevant to the search for Christian knowledge. Christian intellectuals who attended pagan schools or discussed philosophical ideas were following a path that led not to wisdom but to folly. The true path to wisdom led not to the pagan schoolhouse or to the Christian teacher but to the ascetic.

Despite Athanasius's attempts to present Antony as an alternative to the traditional philosopher, it is equally clear that he wanted his readers to see that Antony was as much an exponent of philosophical ideas as other subjects of philosophical biography. Consequently, Athanasius emphasized Antony's persuasive abilities when speaking to crowds,[61] he carefully illustrated the effect his instructions had on listeners, and he drew upon academic terms to describe Antony's followers.[62] This emphasis is not surprising; the identity of Antony as an effective teacher was essential to the proper functioning of a text in which both the words and the deeds of a sage worked together to demonstrate the importance of his message. To put it simply, the literary conventions of the time would have made it difficult for Athanasius to convince educated audiences that his literary Antony was a new type of

58. This speech runs from *Vit. Ant.* 16–43. Especially interesting, in light of the text's anti-intellectual theme, is *Vit. Ant.* 20.

59. *Vit. Ant.* 72–73.

60. These discussions too are drawn from the tradition of pagan philosophical biography and are designed to show the superiority of one man's wisdom. See, for example, the extended exchanges between Thespesion and Apollonius of Tyana in *Vit. Ap.* 6.8–12.

61. E.g., *Vit. Ant.* 44.

62. On a number of occasions, Athanasius uses the term γνώριμος to describe those who affiliated themselves with Antony (e.g., *Vit. Ant.* 8, 13, 60, 91). For this vocabulary, see as well P. Rousseau, "Antony as a Teacher in the Greek Life," 93.

philosopher if the philosophical character of Antony's deeds were not convincingly explained in words.

At the same time, however, this emphasis upon Antony's efficacy as a teacher need not conflict with Athanasius's activities against intellectual Christianity, or even with his later efforts to restrict the use of the term "teacher."[63] Despite his clear teaching abilities, the Antony of the *Life* was actually called a διδάσκαλος only once and, on that occasion, Athanasius is careful to narrowly restrict the meaning of the term.[64] He describes how God preserved Antony from persecution so that "in the asceticism, which he had learned from the Scriptures, he could become a teacher to many."[65] The restricted meaning of "teacher," then, is clearly defined as one who illustrates a sort of wisdom that was both wholly derived from scripture and based upon faith instead of learning.[66] Antony, as portrayed by Athanasius, was a teacher (as this genre of text demanded), but he was not an intellectually trained teacher in the mode of Arius.[67] Instead, he was a revolutionary teacher whose biography illustrated a new type of philosophy that derived not from suspect speculation and deceptive argumentation, but from the purity of scripture and the clarity of faith.

THE ALEXANDRIAN REALITY

The revolutionary anti-intellectualism advocated by Athanasius later in his career was effectively presented and, presumably, was welcomed by some Egyptian Christians.[68] Nevertheless, the reality in Alexandria was far more complicated than Athanasius's idealized picture suggests. Alexandrian Chris-

---

63. As suggested by P. Rousseau, "Antony as a Teacher in the Greek *Life*," 100–104. It is worth noting that Athanasius's most explicit restrictions on the use of the term "teacher" are found in works composed a decade or more after the *Life of Antony*. This may reflect further development of the bishop's thought.

64. *Vit. Ant.* 46. Variations of the term διδασκαλία are used five times and, on four of the occasions, Athanasius is careful to mark this teaching as coming from Christ or the scriptures (e.g., *Vit. Ant.* 16, 78–79). The one exception is *Vit. Ant.* 82 where Arian διδασκαλία is characterized as false because it does not come from the apostles. One sees again that this is broadly consistent with Athanasius's subsequent restriction of these terms in 367.

65. The full passage reads: ὁ δὲ Κύριος ἦν αὐτὸν φυλάττων εἰς τὴν ἡμῶν καὶ τὴν ἑτέρων ὠφέλειαν, ἵνα καὶ ἐν τῇ ἀσκήσει, ἣν ἐκ τῶν Γραφῶν αὐτὸς μεμάθηκε, πολλοῖς διδάσκαλος γένηται (*Vit. Ant.* 46).

66. On this, see S. Rubenson, "Philosophy and Simplicity: The Problem of Classical Education in Early Christian Biography," in *Greek Biography and Panegyric in Late Antiquity*, ed. T. Hägg and P. Rousseau (Berkeley and Los Angeles, 2000), 118. This is also consistent with the ideas expressed in Athanasius's Festal Letter of 352.

67. This echoes the earlier assertions of S. Rubenson (*The Letters of St. Antony*, 130–32 and 143–44), against the recent ideas of P. Rousseau ("Antony as a Teacher in the Greek *Life*," 105–6).

68. The Pachomian communities, for example, would likely have been untroubled by the de-emphasis upon intellectual training among Christians. For this attitude and the way it was reflected in Pachomian biography, see, S. Rubenson, "Philosophy and Simplicity," 129–33.

tians remained interested in pagan philosophical ideas, and the teaching of Christian intellectuals, complete with philosophical, rhetorical, and argumentative influences, continued without interruption. In fact, no figure illustrates the continued relevance of intellectual training to Alexandrian Christians better than Athanasius's younger contemporary, Didymus the Blind. Didymus's life spanned much of the fourth century, and much of his time was devoted to the intellectual service of the Alexandrian church.[69] Despite his prominence during and following the episcopate of Athanasius, Didymus was a Christian intellectual with an extensive background in classical culture.[70] To these classically refined skills, Didymus added a deep understanding of the Old and New Testaments. Blending these backgrounds, Didymus "composed several treatises in exposition of the Scripture, besides three books on the Trinity, as well as commentaries on Origen's book *On Principles*."[71]

Didymus, however, was shunned by neither the clergy nor the Alexandrian Christian populace. He occupied an officially sanctioned position as a Christian teacher[72] and, perhaps just as crucially, he lent his classically refined skills to the fight against Arianism.[73] In addition to the intellectual support he gave to clergy who opposed Arianism, Didymus "was much sought after by the

---

69. Didymus was born in 309 and lived until approximately 399. On his life and teaching, see the study of R. Layton, *Didymus the Blind and his Circle in Late-Antique Alexandria: Virtue and Narrative in Biblical Scholarship* (Urbana, 2004).

70. Theodoret (*HE* 4.26) describes his training as follows: "Didymus, who from childhood had been deprived of sight, had been educated in poetry, rhetoric, arithmetic, geometry, astronomy, the logic of Aristotle, and the eloquence of Plato." This description of Didymus's education is a more concise echo of Socrates (*HE* 4.25), Sozomen (*HE* 3.15), and Palladius (*Hist. Lausiac* 4). The Tura papyri containing Didmyus's writings further reveal a teacher familiar with Stoic and Skeptic debates about epistemology and willing to chide a presumptuous student for being a "Protagorean." On these, see R. Layton, *Didymus the Blind*, 29–30.

71. Socrates, *HE* 4.25. Socrates' endorsement of his Origenistic tendencies reflects more on the historian's opinions of later anti-Origenist bishops than on his feelings about this particular element of Didymus's career. A more detailed list of his publications is found in Jerome, *de vir. illust.* 109.

72. Sozomen, *HE* 3.15. Sozomen describes the position προϊστάμενος ἐν Ἀλεξανδρείᾳ τοῦ διδασκαλείου τῶν ἱερῶν μαθημάτων. This may refer to the Catechetical School of Alexandria, but it is worth noting that Sozomen's terminology differs from that conventionally used to mark such affiliation. G. Bardy, "Pour l'histoire de l'École d'Alexandrie," *Vivre et Penser*, 2nd ser., 2 (1942): 80–109, is skeptical of Didymus's affiliation with the Catechetical school. Against this, see C. Scholten, "Die Alexandrinische Katechetenschule," 34. It is possible that Didymus, like Origen, may simply have received official sanction for the intellectual activity in which he was already engaged.

73. Among his many works were two books entitled *Against the Arians* (Jerome, *de vir. illus.* 109). Sozomen, in discussing his anti-Arian efforts, describes Didymus's abilities to "easily persuade his listeners not by violent arguments, but by sheer persuasiveness, so that each of them became able to judge for himself even the most ambiguous points" (*HE* 3.15). In essence, Didymus's skills were so developed that, instead of using blunt syllogisms, he simply taught people how to make their own judgments about the problematic elements of Arian doctrine.

Catholic church" in Egypt and, apparently, popular with those who heard him teach.[74]

In these functions, Didymus was not dramatically different from philosophically influenced Christian teachers like Origen. There was, however, one additional element of Didymus's portrait that distinguished him from these earlier teachers. Following his description of Didymus's exegetical skills, Sozomen remarks that Didymus "was praised by the orders of monks in Egypt and by the great Antony, who addressed him when he came from the desert to Alexandria to give his testimony in favor of the doctrines of Athanasius."[75] By the end of Didymus's life, asceticism, the new breed of Christian philosophy defined by the literary persona of Antony, had become an essential part of the portrait of a Christian intellectual.[76] Antony's address to Didymus, in which Antony tells Didymus that he possessed the eyes of angels "with which the Deity himself is discerned,"[77] then employs the figure of the prominent Christian ascetic philosopher to express approval of the intellectually driven Christian philosophy of Didymus.

It is unlikely that, if this meeting ever took place, Antony would have expressed his approval of Didymus in quite these terms. In fact, this moment of respectful communication between two different types of Christian philosopher is preserved only in literary traditions that derived from Didymus's own circle of students and, as such, it seems to represent the contrived sanctioning of Didymus's project by a respected pillar of Egyptian asceticism.[78] Such a sanction would have been necessary because Didymus's community differed from the desert "intellectuals" who followed the model put forth by Athanasius in the *Life of Antony*. Not only did Didymus's teaching involve intense engagement with pagan philosophical and cultural material, but he also taught within the city of Alexandria. By contrast, Athanasius's Antony (and those unlettered ascetics who imitated his lifestyle) lived in the desert and shunned pagan learning. While neither intellectualism nor an urban setting was explicitly condemned by leading desert ascetics, each was evidently seen with some suspicion by their followers.[79] The self-conscious

---

74. Sozomen, *HE* 3.15.

75. Ibid. A similar story is told in Socrates, *HE* 4.25.

76. Theodoret (*HE* 4.26) is also careful to emphasize that Didymus lived an ascetic life. By contrast, Jerome, who wrote his portrait of Didymus in 392, describes Didymus in simply intellectual terms.

77. The account is found in Socrates, *HE* 4.25; Sozomen, *HE* 3.15; Jerome, *Ep.* 68.2; and Rufinus, *HE* 11.7.

78. On this point, see the marvelous discussion of R. Layton, *Didymus the Blind,* 19–26. The meeting is not mentioned by any source devoted to Antony's life.

79. For the suspicion of overintellectual asceticism, see *Apophthegmata* (Alphabetical), Arsenius 5 and 6. On the potential acceptability of the urban setting, see *Apophthegmata* (Alphabetical) Antony 24.

identification that Didymus's community made with Antony, then, was an
assertion that asceticism and Christian intellectualism ought to be seen as
complementary and not competing types of Christian philosophy. Furthermore, Antony's recognition of Didymus's authority rendered the urban intellectual teachings of Didymus acceptable (if not particularly attractive) to
those who practiced the vibrant practical asceticism of the desert.[80]

In the generation of Alexandrian Christian intellectuals who followed
Didymus, the connections between intellectuals and ascetics increased. By
the 380s, communities of Christian intellectuals had been organized around
Alexandria (at Nitria and elsewhere).[81] These groups of intellectuals included
the influential theologian Evagrius Ponticus and the four Tall Brothers. They
lived a communal monastic life that attempted to mix ascetic practice and
intellectual speculation.[82] Their continued intellectualism resembled that
of Didymus but, unlike their predecessor, their activities took place outside
of Alexandria, in the relative seclusion of ascetic communities. This mixture
proved popular in Alexandria and, at one point, the bishop Theophilus saw
fit to force three of the Tall Brothers into ecclesiastical office.[83]

While the Tall Brothers are intriguing figures, Evagrius stands as the most
influential of this group of ascetic intellectuals. Born in Pontus, Evagrius was
a protégé of Gregory Nazianzen. By 382, Evagrius had found his way from
Constantinople to the monasteries at Nitria (about sixty kilometers outside
of Alexandria).[84] In Nitria, Evagrius authored a series of works that tried to
explain how, intellectually, the practical philosophy of ascetic discipline could
be explained and improved upon.[85] At the center of Evagrius's system was
the concept of *apatheia,* a freedom of the mind from the passions of the material world.[86] The state of *apatheia* was achieved through the elimination of

80. Layton, *Didymus the Blind,* 25–26.

81. On the communities in Nitria see, D. Chitty, *The Desert a City* (Oxford, 1966); and H. G.
Evelyn White, *The Monasteries of the Wādi'n Natrūn, pt. 2: The History of the Monasteries of Nitria*
(New York, 1932).

82. Socrates (*HE* 6.7) describes their activities as "distinguished both for the sanctity of their
lives and the extent of their erudition."

83. Socrates, *HE* 6.7. On Theophilus and his relationships with the Tall Brothers see E. Clark,
The Origenist Controversy: The Cultural Construction of an Early Christian Debate (Princeton, 1992),
37–38, 45–47; and, on a broader scale, J. H. W. G. Liebeschuetz, *Barbarians and Bishops: Army,
Church, and State in the Age of Arcadius* (Oxford, 1990), ch. 19.

84. On his path to Nitria, see E. Clark, *The Origenist Controversy,* 22. On Evagrius, note as
well R. Darling Young, "Evagrius the Iconographer: Monastic Pedagogy in the *Gnostikos,*" *Journal of Early Christian Studies* 9 (2001): 53–71.

85. Many of Evagrius's works have been lost because of his excommunication in 553. Most
significant among the surviving works are the three ascetic training manuals under his name (the
Logos Praktikos, the *Gnôstikos,* and the *Kephalia Gnôstica*), and the treatises *On Thoughts* and *On Prayer.*

86. On the concept of *apatheia* in Evagrius, see *Praktikos* 1.2 ("The kingdom of heaven is
apatheia of the soul along with true knowledge of existing things."). On this idea, see S. Rappe,

thoughts that impede prayer, many of which were in fact implanted in the mind by demons.[87] Drawing upon Stoic epistemological theory, Evagrius held that such thoughts recreate the image of objects and, through this act, incite passions in the mind that are associated with the object.[88] The task of the Christian philosopher was to distinguish between thoughts that are harmless and those that are implanted to incite passions.[89] While this process of discernment was an intellectual one, Evagrius made it clear that these intellectual processes were furthered by the physical discipline of asceticism. The *Praktikos,* for example, catalogs physical responses that a monk can take to avoid being incited to passion by the thoughts introduced by demons.[90] To Evagrius, Christianity represented "a doctrine composed from practical, physical, and contemplative elements"[91] and, in his teaching, he merged philosophically influenced speculation and ascetic practice.

Evagrius's approach was unique and eventually it proved problematic.[92] All the same, Evagrius does help to highlight some of the dramatic changes that the fourth century wrought in the intellectual life of Alexandrian Christians. Evagrius reveals that Athanasius's attempts to eliminate philosophically inclined Christian teachers did not succeed in Alexandria, but he also shows the profound impact that the identification of asceticism as a new, Christian type of philosophy had upon Alexandrian intellectuals.

Evagrius's career and the accounts of Didymus the Blind's conversation with Antony suggest that late fourth-century Christian teachers often displayed an ascetic pedigree along with a mastery of traditional philosophy and Christian scripture. The impact of asceticism on Alexandrian Christian intellectual life, however, can be seen as well in the changes it wrought upon the physical setting of Christian intellectual speculation. Had Evagrius been a contemporary of Origen (or even Arius), his teaching and theological speculations would likely have taken place within the city of Alexandria. He probably also would have had some affiliation with a pagan teacher of philoso-

"The New Math: How to Add and to Subtract Pagan Elements in Christian Education," in *Education in Greek and Roman Antiquity,* ed. Y. L. Too (Leiden, 2001), 425–26; and E. Clark, *The Origenist Controversy,* 67–69.

87. *Praktikos* 1.6–14.

88. Outlined briefly in *Praktikos* 33–34. On this idea, see E. Clark, *The Origenist Controversy,* 76. For the Stoic influences, see F. Refoulé, "Rêves et vie spirituelle d'après Evagre le Pontique," *La Vie Spirituelle* 14 (1961): 503.

89. *De diversis malignis cogitationibus* 2. See also, E. Clark, *The Origenist Controversy,* 77.

90. *Praktikos* 15–16.

91. Ibid., 1.

92. The attack on Evagrian ideas and teachers who were similar to him is outlined by E. Clark (*The Origenist Controversy,* 105–21). Origenist monks, who shared some intellectual approaches with Evagrius, were sent away from Alexandria in 400. Those who survived this exile were allowed to return in 404.

phy and some connection to Christian students of philosophy. At the turn of the fifth century, however, Evagrius and many of his like-minded peers lived in monasteries outside the city, engaged with the writings of Christian thinkers like Origen, and, presumably, had little contact with pagan philosophers, contemporary philosophical trends, or Christian students within the city of Alexandria.[93]

This general trend in Alexandrian Christianity created conditions under which contemporary philosophical ideas became less important to theological debates in Alexandria. Christian study circles led by men like Origen and Arius had served as a main conduit linking pagan and Christian teaching, but, by the 390s, they no longer performed this function.[94] What contact there was between monastic intellectualism and contemporary philosophical ideas seems to have occurred when philosophical texts found their way into the monastic environment.[95] The personal exchanges these circles had previously enabled seem to have almost vanished from our sources.

Another of the functions of the Christian study circle was also affected. In the past, these teachers brought pagan students into the church and helped to teach Christian students how to complement their Christianity with philosophical ideas. Consequently, they played a crucial role in regulating both how pagan philosophical ideas entered the Christian community and how Christian students were affected by these ideas that they were studying. Now, with the decampment of many Christian intellectual circles to monasteries, this function was not being performed. The philosophical formation of Christian students continued to be entrusted to pagan teachers, but the students were increasingly left to fend for themselves in the pagan schools. It is to this group of students and the schools they attended, then, that we will now turn our attention in order to assess how these changes affected the Alexandrian cultural environment.

---

93. It seems that Didymus, too, had little contact with students of philosophy (his students seem to have arrived with no philosophical background) and only slight contact with pagan teachers. On this, see R. Layton, *Didymus the Blind*, 33–35.

94. The recent work by I. Perczel on Pseudo-Dionysius and his popularity in Palestinian monasteries shows that some monastic intellectual engagement with Neoplatonic ideas continued well into the mid-sixth century. On this see especially I. Perczel, "Pseudo-Dionysius and Palestinian Origenism," in *The Sabaite Heritage in the Orthodox Church from the Fifth Century to the Present*, ed. J. Patrich, 261–82 (Leuven, 2001).

95. Again the Pseudo-Dionysian corpus helps one to see the degree to which monastic understanding of Neoplatonism was based upon the reading of Neoplatonic texts. Especially interesting in light of this is I. Perczel's study on the similarities in argument structure between Pseudo-Dionysius's *Divine Names* and Proclus's *Platonic Theology* ("Pseudo-Dionysius and the Platonic Theology: A Preliminary Study," in *Proclus et la Théologie Platonicienne*, ed. A. P. Segonds and C. Steel, 491–530 [Paris, 2000]). For a less specific treatment of this relationship, see C. Steel, "Proclus et Denys: De l'existence du mal," in *Denys l'Aréopagite et sa postérité en Orient et en Occident*, ed. Y. de Andia, 89–108 (Paris, 1996).

HYPATIA AND PAGAN PHILOSOPHICAL
CULTURE IN THE LATER FOURTH CENTURY

All evidence of these Christian students having been lost, perhaps the best way for one to study their experience in later fourth-century Alexandrian pagan schools is to focus upon the pagan teacher who is known to have drawn the largest number of Christian students. This teacher is the famous philosopher Hypatia. Hypatia was born to the philosopher and geometrician Theon, probably around the year 355.[96] At the time of her birth, Theon was a young man, perhaps between twenty-five and thirty years old.[97] Despite his age, it seems that he had already begun teaching philosophy in Alexandria.[98] As his career developed, Theon came to head a school of philosophy and, at some point, he himself would have taught classes in that discipline.[99] As he aged, however, he gradually shunned this sort of teaching responsibility. Some of this must have been due to a lack of interest in the minutiae of the subject (the absence of any philosophical commentaries in his name is particularly revealing in this light), but it seems that the most important reason he stopped was the intellectual development of his daughter, Hypatia. Theon had apparently begun teaching her when she was young and quickly realized her natural talents. Encouraged by what he saw, Theon kept pushing her until she "far surpassed her teacher, especially in astronomy, and taught many others the mathematical sciences."[100]

Although the modern student is often struck by the existence of such an

---

96. This is the date advocated by M. Dzielska, *Hypatia of Alexandria*, trans. F. Lyra (Cambridge, Mass., 1995), 68; an echo of the suggestion of R. Penella, *Greek Philosophers and Sophists in the Fourth Century A.D.: Studies in Eunapius of Sardis* (Leeds, 1990), 126–28. See as well Penella's earlier discussion ("When was Hypatia Born?" *Historia* 33 (1984): 126–28). In this, they are following Malalas's (14.12) classification of Hypatia as an older woman at the time of her death in 415.

97. Dzielska, *Hypatia of Alexandria*, 68.

98. Indeed, although later sources (and most modern scholars) tend to ignore his philosophical background, earlier authors like Socrates Scholasticus (*HE* 7.12) and the *Suda* (Θ 205) describe him as a philosopher, a description echoed by Malalas as well.

99. Despite this, M. Dzielska (*Hypatia of Alexandria*, 68) asserts, without any convincing evidence, that Theon did not teach philosophy. In her view, the title "philosopher" was applied to him only to indicate his wisdom. In none of the three authors mentioned above is there any indication that the term "philosopher" (φιλόσοφος) had come to mean simply "wise man." As the example of Marinus has shown, a mathematician teaching philosophy was a standard feature of schools in the fourth and fifth centuries. In addition, Synesius, in his letter to Paeonius, also explains how geometry, arithmetic, astrology, and philosophy are all necessary complements to one another. It is telling that a copy of this letter was sent along to Hypatia as well (*Ep.* 154). By this period, mathematics and geometry were abstract sciences that attracted few devoted students. Consequently, there is no reason to assume that Theon did not teach philosophy at some point.

100. Philostorgius, *Ecclesiastical History* 8.9.

erudite ancient woman, this was not an uncommon phenomenon in late antiquity.[101] Female children of intellectuals were often given quite thorough educations,[102] but, even so, one cannot know why Theon began to educate his daughter. It is probably safe to assume that he had at least considered the possibility of using her marriage to cement the succession in his school.[103] However, it seems that, when he saw Hypatia's intelligence and intellectual progress, this idea was replaced by another, more intriguing one. Her gifts were so great that Theon decided to turn some of the teaching over to her. Presumably this went quite well because eventually he decided to let Hypatia take control of the institution herself.

This was probably natural. Hypatia was his top student and probably his best assistant teacher. She was also his daughter, and dynastic considerations were one important element in the succession process in a late antique school. Another, equally important, consideration was doctrinal continuity, and this was likely of particular concern to Theon. This was because in Alexandria, as in Athens, the new adaptation of Neoplatonism created by Iamblichus was beginning to make inroads in the later fourth century, and the teachers who were responsible for this growth were often quite different from Theon and his daughter.

A number of Iamblichan Neoplatonists were active in and around Alexandria during Hypatia's lifetime, but the best known such character was a man named Antoninus.[104] Antoninus had come from good philosophical stock. His mother had been quite thoroughly educated and his father was an associate of Aedesius, one of the inner-circle students of Iamblichus himself.[105] Although Antoninus was raised in Asia Minor, he decided to settle in Canopus, a city about twenty kilometers distant from Alexandria, so that he could

101. For the education of women in antiquity, see R. Cribiore, *Gymnastics of the Mind: Greek Education in Hellenistic and Roman Egypt* (Princeton, 2001), 74–101.

102. Sosipatra, the wife of a philosopher Eustathius, was so learned that, after her husband's death, she was asked to give lectures at a school run by one of his friends (Eunapius, *Vit. Soph.* 468–69). Asclepigeneia, the daughter of Plutarch, was also knowledgeable enough to teach, although it appears that the only person she taught was Proclus (Marinus, *Vit. Proc.* 28). Slightly less accomplished were women like Aedesia, Marcella, and Eudocia.

103. The right marriage could bring an infusion of new talent or new money into the family. In Athens, the sophist Nicagoras's family arranged a marriage between a daughter and Himerius, a promising young rhetorician in the mid-fourth century (T. D. Barnes, "Himerius and the Fourth Century," *Classical Philology* 82 (1987): 222). In the same way, Plutarch's grandson Archiades wed his daughter to Theagenes when the family wealth was wiped out in a barbarian raid. Syrianus, who tried to marry his niece Aedesia to Proclus and succeeded in arranging her marriage to his student Hermeias, illustrates how these efforts also came to involve members of one's extended family.

104. Eunapius, *Vit. Soph.* 470. H. Schibli (*Hierocles of Alexandria* [Oxford, 2002], 10) is less sure about Iamblichus's influence on Antoninus.

105. *Vit. Soph.* 465.

"entirely devote himself to the worship of the gods there and to their mysteries."[106] In Canopus, Antoninus devoted himself to the teaching and practice of philosophy, but he also retained some connection with the temple of Serapis in Alexandria. When Antoninus was living in Canopus (probably from the 370s until c. 390), the Serapeum was still an important site for religious travelers and, in many cases, Eunapius writes, "These men, after they had worshipped the god, used to hurry to Antoninus . . . When they were accepted into his presence, they would put forth a logical problem and were then filled with the philosophy of Plato."[107] Eunapius continues, "But others, if they proposed something about religious rites, encountered a statue, for he would not utter a word to them."[108] Although Eunapius attributes this silence to Antoninus's piety, the philosopher probably had another reason for circumspection. At another point in his account, Eunapius says that Antoninus "displayed no tendency towards theurgy . . . because he carefully noted the imperial actions opposed to this activity."[109] In both theurgical and other religious activity, Antoninus restrained himself because he feared giving imperial officials any cause to take action against the pagan temples in and around Alexandria.

Antoninus had reason to be afraid. In the later fourth century, the Alexandrian Serapeum had become an intellectual center to which many Iamblichan Neoplatonists were attracted. The site had many features that such men would have found appealing. Not only was the temple fully functional, but the area surrounding it also provided classroom spaces for teachers and, potentially, the largest library in Alexandria.[110] Unfortunately for this community, many of the scholars who traveled there were not as circumspect as Antoninus. Damascius tells of a man named Olympus who had come to Alexandria from Cilicia.[111] When he arrived at the Serapeum, Olympus "used to gather together each of the people who associated with him and teach the rules of divine worship, the ancient traditions, and the happiness that accompanied them."[112] Unlike Antoninus, it seems that Olympus taught a full set of courses at the temple. His students seem to have been Alexandrian (although there would almost certainly have been a foreign contingent as well) and his courses seem to have been organized into both gen-

106. Ibid., 471.
107. Ibid., 472. On this, see D. Frankfurter, "The Consequences of Hellenism in Late Antique Egypt: Religious Worlds and Actors," *Archiv für Religionsgeschichte* 2 (2000): 162–94 (esp. 184–89). He sees in this travel a kind of pagan religious pilgrimage circuit that included Canopus, Menouthis, and Alexandria.
108. *Vit. Soph.* 472.
109. Ibid., 471.
110. See chapter 6.
111. *Vit. Is.* Ath. 42A; Z. fr. 91.
112. Ibid., Ath. 42F; Z. fr. 95, 97.

eral lectures and advanced seminars.[113] Olympus differed from Antoninus in what he taught as well. While fear of the imperial authorities prevented Antoninus from teaching the more controversial elements of the Iamblichan system, Olympus apparently used his classroom as a forum to encourage the practice of pagan religious rites. He taught his students new methods of pagan worship and encouraged them to revive some of the traditional methods used in the past.[114] Although no evidence exists, it is possible that Olympus also taught theurgy to the group assembled around him.[115]

Sensing the cavalier attitude of men like Olympus, Antoninus resigned himself to the fact that the group of people assembled at the Serapeum would eventually bring about the destruction of the shrine.[116] Unfortunately, Antoninus's intuition was correct. In 391, not long after Antoninus's death, a riot broke out in Alexandria when Christian workmen uncovered an old Mithraic temple.[117] They gave some of the cult images they found to the bishop, Theophilus, and he had them mockingly paraded down the streets of the city. In response to this, "the pagans of Alexandria, and especially the professors of philosophy, were unable to bear the pain."[118] They armed themselves and organized an attack on the city's Christian population. Many Christians were killed before the professors and their gang (which was probably largely made up of their students) retreated to the temple of Serapis.[119] Perched atop the highest hill in the city and surrounded by high walls, the Serapeum made an excellent base for guerilla operations. It was so secure that the professors and their students were able to wait out a Christian siege and even launch the occasional sortie. They abandoned the position only when they received an official imperial amnesty.[120]

113. This gradation is suggested by the use of the term ἑταῖροι in Vit. Is. Ath. 42H; Z. fr. 97. The use of this seems to indicate that Olympus had an inner circle of students.

114. Although it was a feature of late antique Egyptian paganism, religious antiquarianism had become particularly intriguing to Iamblichan teachers. On this particular atmosphere, see P. Athanassiadi, "The Chaldean Oracles: Theology and Theurgy," in Pagan Monotheism in Late Antiquity, ed. P. Athanassiadi and B. Frede, 20–24 (Oxford, 1999); and D. Frankfurter, "Hellenism in Late Antique Egypt," 184–92.

115. Eunapius's hearty denial that Antoninus ever practiced theurgy in Alexandria leads one to believe that at least some of the teachers assembled around the Serapeum did perform theurgic rites.

116. Eunapius tells us that Antoninus predicted the eventual destruction of the temple, not a surprising fact given the close eye he was keeping on imperial policies.

117. Socrates, HE 5.16.

118. Ibid.

119. Ibid. For an even more vivid description, see Rufinus, HE 11.22.

120. For a survey of the ancient accounts of the fall of the Serapeum and its aftermath see J. Schwartz, "La fin du Serapeum d'Alexandrie," American Studies in Papyrology, vol. 1, Essays in Honor of C. Bradford Welles, 97–111 (New Haven, 1966). For a discussion of the event's impact upon the Serapeum site, see J. S. McKenzie, S. Gibson, and A. T. Reyes, "Reconstructing the Serapeum in Alexandria from the Archeological Evidence," Journal of Roman Studies 94 (2004): 107–10.

The leader of these pagan fighters was none other than Olympus.[121] He not only organized the defenses, but also served to buttress the spirits of the defenders. Indeed, Damascius gives a brief but tantalizing hint of what the pagan teachers and students experienced during the siege. Olympus seems to have encouraged them to maintain the vigilant worship of Serapis throughout each day.[122] Finally, when the imperial amnesty was handed down and the defenders were forced to vacate the temple, Olympus led a ceremony in which Serapis abandoned the temple.[123] Following this, Olympus and the group of teachers he led vacated the temple. Christian soldiers then plundered the structure.[124]

Some of the Serapeum defenders must have been locals, but many (like Olympus) probably had originated elsewhere.[125] They had traveled to Alexandria simply to teach and worship at the great shrine. The vibrant intellectual scene they created included a number of foreign philosophers as well as teachers of grammar and, possibly, rhetoric as well.[126] Nevertheless, it seems that Theon and Hypatia had little connection with the Serapeum defenders and their new doctrines. There is no evidence that those two ever participated in theurgic rites.[127] Furthermore, when these men embarked upon their futile crusade to take up arms and defend the Serapeum, neither Theon nor Hypatia nor any of their students seem to have been involved.[128] While those affiliated with Theon's school certainly mourned the destruction of the temple, they were probably also alarmed at the uncouth group of academics whose rioting had led to its destruction.

The Serapeum defenders and their schools were newcomers to the Alexandrian intellectual scene. Theon, however, was one of the established intellectuals in the city. Indeed, he had even gained entry into the *Mou-*

---

121. Rufinus 11.22 calls him "a philosopher in name and garb only."

122. *Vit. Is.* Ath. 42G; Z. fr. 96.

123. Ibid., Ath. 42H; Z. fr. 97. The notion that a god would abandon his temple before Christians could seize him is paralleled by Athena's abandonment of the Parthenon in the *Life of Proclus* (*Vit. Proc.* 30).

124. Rufinus, *HE* 11.23. The multiple temples that Rufinus says were destroyed may well have included the Serapeum and other associated buildings within the central colonnade. The colonnade itself remained standing, evidently until the twelfth century. On this, note McKenzie, Gibson, and Reyes, "Reconstructing the Serapeum," 108.

125. M. Dzielska's suggestion (*Hypatia of Alexandria,* 80) that the Egyptian poets Palladas and Claudian were among them seems unlikely.

126. Socrates (*HE* 5.16) mentions two grammarians, Ammonius and Helladius, who had taught at the Serapeum complex and participated in its defense. His account of the siege is based in part upon oral testimony that he heard from these two teachers.

127. The interest that both Theon and Hypatia displayed in divination must be distinguished from participation in theurgy. Even in late antiquity, many types of divination existed outside of the Iamblichan system.

128. Dzielska, *Hypatia of Alexandria,* 83.

seion.[129] This *Mouseion* was a reconstituted version of the Hellenistic original but, even so, its membership was probably quite exclusive. In addition to the most accomplished intellectuals in the city, local elites were probably also included among its list of members.[130] As a member of this prestigious (and, in all likelihood, doctrinally conservative) club, Theon may have kept Iamblichan influence out of his curriculum with a certain amount of pride.[131]

Hypatia too seems to have had little interest in the teaching of Iamblichus.[132] Socrates Scholasticus suggests that she did not see Iamblichus as an intellectual ancestor.[133] Writing a century after her death, Damascius makes an even more emphatic statement to this effect. He establishes a clear contrast between the teaching of Hypatia and the Iamblichan system. First, he compares her to his own Iamblichan teacher Isidore. "Isidore and Hypatia were very different, not only as a man differs from a woman but as a philosopher differs from a mathematician."[134] Elsewhere, Damascius speaks of the great reputation she earned as a philosopher in dismissive terms. It shows, he maintains, that "even if philosophy was itself dead, its name at least was still seen as honorable."[135] Clearly, Damascius saw Hypatia's philosophical teaching as primitive and hardly worthy of the name. Although generally quite harsh towards those he saw as philosophical deviants, Damascius does not wholly exclude Iamblichan-influenced scholars from the ranks of philosophers.[136] His attempt to do this with Hypatia seems to indicate that her teaching does not measure up to even the basic standard of philosophical competence.[137]

The most compelling insight into the limited degree to which Iamblichan doctrine permeated Hypatia's teaching comes through the writings of her pupil Synesius. Based upon his evidence, it seems that Iamblichus had little real place in Hypatia's school curriculum. In his letters, Synesius makes no mention of Iamblichus. In his other works, there is again little notable

---

129. *Suda* Θ 205.

130. For this practice, see chapter 6. This makes it extremely unlikely that *Mouseion* membership was directly tied in any way to publicly funded professorships in Alexandria.

131. Dzielska, *Hypatia of Alexandria*, 83.

132. On this point, see J. M. Rist, "Hypatia," *Phoenix* 19 (1965): 214–25; and E. Évrard, "À quel titre Hypatie enseigna-t-elle la philosophie?" *Revue des Études Grecques* 90 (1977): 69–74.

133. Socrates (*HE* 7.15) says that Hypatia came to head "the school of Plato derived from Plotinus."

134. *Vit. Is.* Ath. 106A; Z. Ep. 164.

135. Ibid., Ath. 43E; Z. fr. 102.

136. Even Ammonius the son of Hermeias, for whom Damascius has the greatest contempt, is still called a philosopher.

137. Despite this, Alan Cameron and J. Long (*Barbarians and Politics at the Court of Arcadius* [Berkeley and Los Angeles, 1993], 56) maintain that Hypatia was, in fact, an Iamblichan. They dismiss the Damascian evidence as a response to Synesius's letter criticizing the school of Plutarch. This is unsupportable. There is simply no evidence that Damascius ever read Synesius's correspondence.

Iamblichan influence. In his treatise on dream divination and in his hymns, Synesius does show some awareness of the Chaldean Oracles, a crucial Iamblichan text.[138] Nevertheless, this text was familiar to Plotinus and Porphyry as well as Gnostic Christians.[139] In fact, engagement with these materials in a non-Iamblichan context was common in the late antique cultural environment. Because there are few other links between Synesius and the Iamblichan system, one can assume that Synesius probably was not introduced to the Oracles in an Iamblichan context.

Hypatia and Theon, then, were joined by doctrinal and familial links that made Hypatia an obvious candidate to succeed her father. And it seems that she was selected for this honor long before his death. This was a standard procedure when an obvious successor became apparent. As we have seen in the Athenian school, the selection was made as soon as possible in order to provide the head of the school with the opportunity to train his successor.[140] As time passed, the head of the school gradually handed more and more of his teaching and administrative responsibilities to the successor and made sure that he (or she) was introduced to the influential friends of the school.

This type of power transfer is consistent with what our sources tell us about the school of Theon and Hypatia in the 390s. By that time, Theon had almost disappeared from the historical sources. He was still active as a scholar, but his formal teaching responsibilities seem to have ended by the late 380s.[141] Again, we can tell this from Synesius. Synesius was enrolled in the school from c. 393–95. His correspondence is full of references to the institution and his time there. In all of these, he mentions Theon only once and it comes as a part of a greeting to Hypatia and her family.[142] If he ever met Theon, Synesius clearly did not know the school's titular head very well. In fact, it seems that all of his instruction came from either Hypatia or one of her assistants. This means that, by the time Synesius arrived, Hypatia had already assumed *de facto* control of the instruction given in the school.

138. On this see, most recently, Cameron and Long, *Barbarians and Politics*, 50–51.

139. For the Christian usages of these texts see M. Tardieu, "La Gnose Valentinienne et les Oracles Chaldaïques," in *The Rediscovery of Gnosticism*, vol. 1, ed. B. Layton, 194–237 (Leiden, 1980).

140. This process has been described in detail in chapter 4.

141. O. Neugebauer (*A History of Ancient Mathematical Astronomy* [New York, 1975], 873) contends that Theon's book *On the Small Astrolabe* appeared around 400 A.D. For an alternative view, see Cameron and Long, *Barbarians and Politics*, 54–55.

142. Until recently, it was thought that Synesius did not even know Theon. This has been called into question by D. Roques ("La Famille d'Hypatie: Synésios, epp. 5 et 16 G," *Revue des Études Grecques* 108 [1995]: 128–49), who equates Theon with the Theoteknos mentioned in *Ep.* 16. This argument is certainly compelling but, because the other people mentioned as family members are rhetoricians and grammarians, the greeting could just as well refer to a member of the faculty of Hypatia's school. Further confirmation is needed to make Roques's argument fully persuasive.

Recently it has been suggested that, when Hypatia assumed control of Theon's school, she also was appointed as a publicly funded professor of philosophy.[143] This argument rests upon two main supports, each of which is problematic. First, it has been suggested that, on the basis of his *Mouseion* membership, Theon was a publicly funded professor and, as his successor, Hypatia would naturally have succeeded to the public professorship as well.[144] Our knowledge about the nature of *Mouseion* membership in the fourth century is so poor that one cannot know whether any, all, or some members were public professors. This means that, while it is certainly possible that Theon was a publicly funded professor, no source suggests this and, consequently, there is no reason to accept this contention.[145] Furthermore, even if Theon were a publicly funded professor, Hypatia would have succeeded Theon only as the head of his private circle of students. As demonstrated by the case of Prohaeresius, private succession arrangements did not guarantee possession of a predecessor's public chair.[146]

The second piece of evidence seems, on the surface, to be more compelling. This is a statement by Damascius that Hypatia "explained Plato, Aristotle, and elements of other philosophers δημοσίᾳ."[147] The meaning of this passage has been frequently debated,[148] but recently, to support the notion that Hypatia was a publicly funded professor, this has been compared with another passage of Damascius that clearly uses δημοσίᾳ to describe a public professorship.[149] While seemingly compelling, this ignores a crucial difference between the two passages. In the first, we are told that Hypatia, in essence, taught δημοσίᾳ (or, roughly translated, "in public"). The second passage, however, speaks of the public professorship as τὴν δημοσίαν σίτησιν (or, roughly, "public salary or support"). This was something of a legal phrase used to describe a public salary paid to a teacher[150] and, as such, it had this specific meaning only when complete. Damascius's use of δημοσία σίτησις to describe a public professorship is deliberate and indicative of his familiarity with the term as well as its meaning. His failure to mark Hypatia as one who

143. M. Vinzent, "'Oxbridge' in der ausgehenden Spätantike oder: Ein Vergleich der Schulen von Athen und Alexandrien," *Zeitschrift für Antikes Christentum* 4 (2000): 63–69.

144. Vinzent, "'Oxbridge' in der ausgehenden Spätantike," 63.

145. As mentioned above, it strikes me as unlikely that the *Mouseion*, an institution whose membership had gotten progressively less exclusive over the previous three centuries, would suddenly become open only to the very select group of Alexandrian public professors.

146. On Prohaeresius, see chapter 3.

147. διὰ μέσου τοῦ ἄστεως ποιουμένη τὰς προόδους ἐξηγεῖτο δημοσίᾳ τοῖς ἀκροᾶσθαι βουλομένοις ἢ τὸν Πλάτωνα ἢ τὸν Ἀριστοτέλην ἢ τὰ ἄλλου ὅτου δὴ τῶν φιλοσόφων (*Vit. Is.* Ath. 43A; Z. fr. 102).

148. E.g., Évrard, "À quel titre Hypatie enseigna-t-elle la philosophie?" 69–74.

149. *Vit. Is.* Ath. 56; Z. fr. 124. This passage will be discussed in more detail in chapter 8.

150. Cf. *C. Just.* 1.11.10.

received a δημοσία σίεησις, then, if anything, argues *against* the idea that he was describing her as a publicly funded professor. Although she likely just headed a private institution, the school seems to have done well under Hypatia's stewardship. From all indications, Hypatia drew a large crowd of students (with many Christians among them).[151] Their places of origin varied. Some, like Synesius, traveled to her school from Cyrenaica. Others came from as far away as Syria and Upper Egypt.[152] While these students had an interest in philosophy, they came to her school for a cultural training and, following their departure, they became bishops,[153] government officials,[154] and, most often, estate owners with an interest in high culture.[155]

The Christian students who attended her school were given a training that suited their diverse backgrounds and interests. In Hypatia's school, philosophy was a religious mystery that revealed deep truths about God and the nature of the world.[156] The pursuit of it bound students together and allowed them to establish friendships based upon a shared journey towards enlightenment.[157] These friendships encouraged students to seek philosophical truth in a way that emphasized both intensive contemplation and personal temperance.[158] Ultimately, it was thought, this could allow the mind to ascend to the level of the divine.[159]

With its emphasis upon contemplation, Hypatia's training worked in typically Plotinian fashion. Students were taught to train their minds to approach the divine in a controlled way. Unlike Iamblichan teaching, in which theurgy was used to enhance the contemplative ascent of the mind, Hypatia's training appears to have involved no ritual elements.[160] Whether by design or not, this aspect of Hypatia's training made her philosophy accessible to Christians. In her school, Christian students did not need to worry about their convictions' conflicting with their training. Furthermore, it seems that Hy-

---

151. A thorough discussion of the students attracted to her circle is found in M. Dzielska, *Hypatia of Alexandria*, 28–43.

152. These are Olympius and Isidore.

153. This was the eventual career of Synesius himself.

154. Her student Hesychius (known from Synesius, *Ep.* 93) became the *dux* in charge of the province of Libya.

155. This was the chosen profession of Herculianus and Olympius, two of Synesius's best friends at school.

156. Synesius, *Ep.* 137.

157. Ibid., *Epp.* 137, 139.

158. Her own temperance is emphasized in Damascius, *Vit. Is.* Ath. 43A; Z. fr. 102.

159. *Ep.* 140. For more detail on this process, see M. Dzielska, *Hypatia of Alexandria*, 48–49.

160. Of this divide between Plotinian and Iamblichan Neoplatonism, Damascius remarked: "Some, such as Plotinus, Porphyry, and many others esteem philosophy but others, like Iamblichus and Syrianus and Proclus and all the theurgists (ἱερατικοὶ) esteem theurgy (ἱερατική) instead" (*Commentary on the Phaedo*, 105).

patia had little concern about the divine towards which her students worked to ascend. Both Synesius and Herculianus seem to have been Christians when they studied under Hypatia and they found her training to be a great asset to their religious experiences.[161] Indeed, it seems that the training Hypatia gave was equally appropriate for pagan and Christian students. In a city with a Christian majority, this would have made her popular indeed.

This popularity was a significant asset, but Hypatia's position at the head of the school entailed far more responsibility than simply teaching. She was also expected to develop contacts with influential people and use these relationships to protect the interests of the school. Hypatia was successful in this aspect of the job as well. Once she had firmly established herself as Theon's successor, it seems that her school became a regular stopping point for imperial officials stationed in Alexandria. Socrates remarks on the close relationships she enjoyed with both governors and the local town councilors[162] while Damascius indicates that Hypatia had such a good reputation that "the governors of the city always paid their respects to her first" when they entered the city.[163]

Hypatia had developed her public position during a relatively peaceful period in Alexandria's history. In late fourth- and early fifth-century Alexandria, the peacefulness of the city was determined by the temperament of the bishop. Much of Hypatia's administrative and political training had occurred when Theophilus was bishop (385–412) and, until his death, she operated in the political climate that he helped to create. While Theophilus could be especially provocative towards pagans, his particular targets seem to have been the motley collection of Neoplatonists who taught at the Serapeum. From all indications, Theophilus respected (or at least tolerated) Hypatia's school and the students it produced.[164] Indeed, he even encouraged two of her students to become bishops in areas under his authority.[165] Perhaps more importantly, Theophilus respected the local power structures with which Hypatia had developed relationships and did not object to the close ties that she had with prefects.

This situation changed dramatically when Theophilus died in 412. Apparently his death was something of a surprise because, while he had been training his nephew Cyril to succeed him, he did not officially mark Cyril as

161. For a thorough discussion of Synesius's religious identity and a convincing demonstration of his Christianity, see Cameron and Long, *Barbarians and Politics*, 19–39. Another demonstration is that of D. Roques, *Synésios de Cyrène et la Cyrénaïque du Bas-Empire*, Études d'antiquités africaines (Paris, 1987).

162. *HE* 7.15.

163. *Vit. Is.* Ath. 43E; Z. fr. 102.

164. Vinzent, "'Oxbridge' in der ausgehenden Spätantike," 71–72.

165. C. Haas, *Alexandria in Late Antiquity: Topography and Social Conflict* (Baltimore, 1997), 295–96.

his successor.[166] Consequently, upon his death, a violent struggle for control of the Alexandrian church began, with one party supporting Cyril and another supporting Timothy, Theophilus's archdeacon. In this fighting, each party drew support from a segment of the city but, after three days of street fighting, Cyril was able to take control of the church.[167]

Cyril then began to settle scores. As soon as he took power, he punished the Novatianists (a Christian sect that had supported Timothy) by ordering the confiscation of their church property.[168] Then, in 414, he took action against the Jews, who also may have been supporters of Timothy.[169] After a series of small but increasingly violent disputes, Cyril ordered his supporters to seize the synagogues in the city and drive the Jews from their homes. This later act incensed Orestes, the prefect of Egypt, and he sent a scathing report of the event to the emperor.[170] Events continued to spiral out of control until Orestes was nearly killed in a riot by Cyril's supporters.[171] When the monk who had incited the riot was killed during interrogation and Cyril tried to have him proclaimed a martyr, prominent Alexandrian Christians finally forced a détente upon Cyril and Orestes.[172]

While an uneasy peace had been reached, it was never destined to last. Cyril and Orestes seem to have continued their efforts to undermine each other. For Cyril, this involved turning the more excitable minds in his con-

166. Haas, *Alexandria in Late Antiquity,* 296. M. Vinzent ("'Oxbridge' in der ausgehenden Spätantike," 72–73) has recently revived the idea that Cyril was a student of Hypatia (on this, see also J. Rougé, "La politique de Cyrille d'Alexandrie et le meurtre d'Hypatie," *Cristianesimo nella storia* 11 [1990]: 496). Against this, see M. O. Boulnois, *Le paradoxe trinitaire chez Cyrille d'Alexandrie: Herméneutique, analyses philosophiques et argumentation théologique* (Paris, 1994), 394–97. Her argument that Cyril lacked the philosophical sophistication one would expect of a philosophical initiate is sound. One should also add to this debate the practical unlikelihood that, after the Athanasian campaign against philosophically trained Christian teachers, Cyril, who was being groomed to succeed his uncle as bishop, would risk alienating those members of the Alexandrian Christian community who shared Athanasius's suspicions of pagan philosophy. This is not to deny that Cyril had some philosophical training, but it would seem an intolerable political risk for an aspiring bishop to have received it in so public a fashion.

167. Socrates, *HE* 7.7.

168. Ibid.

169. For the possible involvement of the Jewish community in the succession struggle, see C. Haas, *Alexandria in Late Antiquity,* 298–301.

170. Socrates, *HE* 7.13.

171. For the anti-Jewish actions, the reaction of Orestes, and the subsequent riot see Socrates, *HE* 7.13. The reconstruction of C. Haas, *Alexandria in Late Antiquity,* 299–304, does an excellent job of placing this conflict within its Alexandrian context.

172. Socrates, *HE* 7.14, describes the riot, the death of its instigator, and the public reaction. Following the death of Ammonius, the monk who instigated the riot, Cyril tried to have him proclaimed a martyr. According to Socrates, "the more temperate people, although Christians, did not accept the urgings of Cyril about this matter. For they understood that Ammonius had been given this punishment because of his rashness and that he was not tortured to death because he refused to deny Christ." Cyril then allowed the issue to drop.

gregation against Orestes. Orestes took a more political approach and tried to organize opposition to Cyril from among the civic elite. These were politically influential individuals as well as the people most troubled by the bishop's recent conduct. They were the natural group from which one could form an effective opposition party and, to organize this group, it seems that Orestes turned to Hypatia.[173]

Hypatia was a good choice. She was well known to both the prefect and the local councilors. She was also a student of politics within the city and, through her students, she had connections to influential figures outside of the city. Most importantly, Hypatia was not a terribly controversial figure. From all we can tell, both pagans and Christians liked her. In addition, she had not been involved in any of the previous stages of this conflict. As a well-respected member of the local establishment, she was a difficult standard-bearer to attack.

Despite her reputation, it seems that Cyril (or his supporters) did begin to attack the character of Hypatia. Although all fifth-century evidence for this has perished, traces of these attacks can be found in the description of Hypatia given by the seventh-century bishop, John of Nikiu.[174] John, drawing upon Cyril's propaganda, portrayed Hypatia as a magician who put spells upon Orestes and a number of prominent Christians in the city.[175] Using her spells, she caused these Christians to assemble at Orestes' house and, John intimates, her magic then caused the attacks against the Jews that brought Cyril and Orestes into conflict.[176] This slander, an obvious reference to Hypatia's role in organizing the party opposed to Cyril, is particularly effective because it enables the bishop's supporters both to tar Hypatia as a magician and to discredit the prefect and Christians who were helping her.

John describes the effect that this rumor had on some members of the Christian population. Believing her to have cast these spells, a man named Peter assembled a mob to find Hypatia. When they did so, they brought her to the Caesareum,[177] and dragged her through the streets until she died. This crowd then burned her body at the Cinaron, a place outside of the city.[178] Fi-

---

173. See C. Haas, *Alexandria in Late Antiquity*, 312–13; and M. Dzielska, *Hypatia of Alexandria*, 88–90.

174. M. Dzielska, *Hypatia of Alexandria*, 91, rightly suggests that John of Nikiu contains elements of the popular attempt to discredit Hypatia. John's account, however, reflects both a posthumous portrait of Hypatia and the fifth-century anti-Hypatian propaganda described by Socrates Scholasticus as a διαβολή (*HE* 7.15). On this latter point, see E. Watts, "The Murder of Hypatia: Acceptable or Unacceptable Violence," in *Violence in Late Antiquity*, ed. H. A. Drake, 333–42 (Aldershot, 2005).

175. John of Nikiu, *Chronicle*, 84.87–92, trans. R. Charles (Oxford, 1916).

176. *Chron.* 84.100.

177. Ibid., 84.101.

178. Ibid., 84.102.

nally, we are told, the people of the city all glorified Cyril "as a 'new Theophilus' for he had destroyed the last remains of idolatry in the city."[179] The last statement, with its mention of Theophilus and the elimination of paganism, is clearly an allusion to the general spirit of rejoicing that swept through the Christian community following the destruction of the Serapeum in 391.

In the end, Hypatia was killed and dragged through the streets in the same way that the most vile Alexandrian criminals had been. It was a well-established custom in Alexandria to drag the bodies of particularly abhorrent criminals out of the city and dispose of them beyond the city limits.[180] In John's account, Hypatia's magical activities made her just such a criminal. Furthermore, the treatment of her body was justified as a purification of the city following the pollution she had caused.[181] To John's sources, the event may have actually seemed akin to Theophilus's destruction of the Serapeum— and it would have been met with celebration.

It seems, though, that these views were held by a distinct minority of Alexandrians. While Christian sources universally celebrate the destruction of the temple of Serapis, the murder of Hypatia is mentioned with disapproval in all sources save John of Nikiu. Socrates Scholasticus is probably typical of this feeling. Despite earlier accepting the destruction of the Serapeum as a necessary event,[182] Socrates wrote of Hypatia's murder: "This affair brought no slight opprobrium upon Cyril and the whole Alexandrian church. Indeed nothing is farther from the spirit of Christianity than murders, fights, and similar things."[183]

In this, Socrates highlights an important difference between the action taken against the Serapeum and the murder of Hypatia. The Serapeum destruction was an attack on pagan property. Hypatia, however, was simply an innocent pagan civilian. To celebrate her murder was akin to condoning indiscriminate killing on religious grounds—and no one, neither Christian nor pagan, wanted that sort of violent cycle to begin. Indeed, this distinction between destruction of pagan property and religious murder even made its way into imperial law. In a law of 408, the emperors Arcadius and Honorius command, "If any images now stand in the temples and shrines, and if they have ever received or do now receive the worship of pagans anywhere, they shall be torn down."[184] In a later law, however, it is made clear that this order does not apply to innocent persons. It reads, "We especially

179. Ibid., 84.103 (trans. Charles).
180. On this ritual, see C. Haas, *Alexandria in Late Antiquity*, 87–89.
181. For more on this, see E. Watts, "The Murder of Hypatia," 341.
182. *HE* 5.16. In his view, the riots preceding the destruction of the temple made violent response an unfortunate but necessary action.
183. *HE* 7.15.
184. *C. Th.* 16.10.19 (trans. Pharr).

command those persons who are truly Christians, or who are said to be, that they shall not abuse the authority of religion and dare to lay violent hands on Jews and pagans who are living quietly and attempting nothing disorderly or unlawful."[185]

Although it is not always the case that imperial law corresponded to public sentiment, it seems that, in this case, the killers of Hypatia had greatly offended public sensibilities in Alexandria and elsewhere. Although no evidence was ever produced directly linking Cyril to the act, he was always suspected of involvement. Indeed, even if he was not a conspirator, he was certainly the inspiration for the action. And this was not something people quickly forgot.[186]

The events immediately following Hypatia's death are not clear. Orestes and the city councilors who had been working with Hypatia were obviously shocked by the murder. Lacking the lynchpin that held their party together, their opposition seems to have fallen apart. It has been suggested by C. Haas that Orestes had himself transferred after the attack.[187] This may be right. At any rate, he is not heard from again. It seems, however, that the Alexandrian council had become alarmed enough at the bishop's conduct to send an embassy to Constantinople. This embassy apparently led to the passage of a law placing the *parabalani,* Cyril's notorious goon squad, under the control of the prefect.[188] But it was only two years before this law was overturned and Cyril regained control of their ranks.[189] By the early 420s, Cyril had come to dominate the Alexandrian council completely. And the murder of Hypatia represented the turning point that led to this victory.

Although the killing of Hypatia had eliminated any effective opposition to Cyril's regime, the brutality of the act soiled Cyril's reputation for a long time. It also had a very real effect upon the intellectual culture of the city. As we have already seen, two distinct types of philosophical teaching were competing in later fourth-century Alexandria. One, the heavily religious interpretation of Iamblichus, was popular among those who had gathered to study and teach at the Serapeum. The other, the Plotinian-influenced teaching championed by Hypatia and Theon, seems to have been the choice of the intellectual establishment in the city. Following the destruction of the Serapeum, many of the Iamblichan teachers fled Alexandria.[190] Their stu-

---

185. Ibid., 16.10.24 (trans. Pharr). Although this law dates to 423, it seems to correspond to the general public sentiment about such religious murders.

186. Writing in the mid-sixth century, John Malalas (13.39) still criticizes Cyril for giving the people of his city free rein to attack Hypatia.

187. Haas, *Alexandria in Late Antiquity,* 316–17.

188. For this law see *C. Th.* 16.2.42.

189. Haas, *Alexandria in Late Antiquity,* 314–15.

190. Two of the grammarians involved in the battle at the Serapeum turn up in Constantinople as teachers of Socrates Scholasticus.

dents who were foreign probably also left the city. Those who were Alexandrian, however, were faced with the choice of traveling to Athens to study Iamblichan Neoplatonism or staying at home to study with Hypatia.[191] One can presume that at least some of those students who might have chosen Iamblichan teaching instead elected to study under Hypatia.[192]

In contrast to the militant paganism encouraged by the Iamblichan teachers, Hypatia and her associates taught a moderate philosophy with a spiritual but non-polemical quality. In predominantly Christian Alexandria, there was a definite need for this type of philosophical teaching. It gave Christian students a valuable foundation in philosophy without provoking them to doubt their religious identities. It also limited the experience young pagans had with theurgy and other controversial doctrines.

The death of Hypatia, however, meant that no prominent teacher of this type of philosophy remained active in the city. She was gone and her school either died with her or disappeared soon afterwards (one can only imagine how such a violent death would affect student recruitment).[193] Other teachers of her brand of Platonism surely remained active in the city, but they had nothing like the stature of Hypatia.[194] The students who had a desire to study under a prominent teacher of philosophy were now driven to Athens, and our sources provide us with the names of a steady stream of Alexandrian students who traveled to the Athenian school between 415 and 470.[195]

This had a profound impact upon the Alexandrian intellectual environment. As Athenian-trained students returned to Alexandria, some of them set up their own schools in which they taught the Iamblichan-based philosophy popular in Athens. Unlike their Iamblichan predecessors who had gathered around the Serapeum, these teachers did not have to compete with more established Plotinian schools or more prominent teachers. With their Athenian pedigree, these Iamblichan teachers now became the most prestigious professors in the city.

None of this would have been a direct concern for Cyril except for the fact that Christian students, who had once attended the unthreatening school

191. This is not to say that Hypatia was the only teacher of philosophy in Alexandria who was active at that time. Nevertheless, she was likely the only one with a great enough reputation to compete with Plutarch, the Athenian scholarch.

192. Synesius's letter decrying the recruiting tactics used by Plutarch in Athens (*Ep.* 136) suggests that many students chose to make the trip even while Hypatia was alive.

193. The succession implications of her death were noticed as well by M. Vinzent ("'Oxbridge' in der ausgehenden Spätantike," 74, 77–78).

194. Indeed, these are probably the Alexandrian teachers whom Proclus found so unsatisfactory.

195. For these students and their attraction to Athens, see E. Watts, "Student Travel to Educational Centers: What Was the Attraction?" in *Travel, Communication and Geography in Late Antiquity*, ed. L. Ellis and F. Kidner, 11–21 (Aldershot, 2004).

of Hypatia, began enrolling under these Iamblichan teachers. While one may be rightly skeptical about Cyril's concern for the religious environment within the Alexandrian philosophical schools, the emergence in the Alexandrian intellectual environment of philosophical teaching hostile to Christianity did trouble Cyril. One of his projects as patriarch was to create an intellectual refutation of pagan arguments against Christianity.[196] In a number of his early festal letters, Cyril derided paganism and criticized it as unintellectual. In addition, in his festal letter of 418, Cyril began a systematic refutation of paganism in quasi-philosophical terms.[197] Later, a much-expanded anti-pagan argument was composed to contradict the criticisms of Christianity leveled by the emperor Julian. In the preface to this work, Cyril explains that this text was written because "the eloquence which the all-powerful emperor Julian possessed was used against Christ, our common savior . . . And it shakes many Christians and harms them beyond all measure. Indeed, the simple and the credulous fall easily into his way of thinking and become sweet prey for demons."[198] In essence, Cyril wrote the work to safeguard the religious faith of those Christians who might be tempted to believe Julian's arguments.[199] Consequently, it is not overstating matters to say that the patriarch was sensitive to the types of challenges intellectual paganism posed to Christians in Alexandria.

Some modern scholars have asserted that Hypatia's murder furthered both Cyril's political ambitions and his anti-pagan policies.[200] This is an overly simplistic interpretation, however. There is no denying that Hypatia's death prevented opposition to Cyril from developing among Alexandrian councilors. Nevertheless, it seems highly unlikely that this event helped his campaign to limit pagan intellectual influences in Alexandria. The negative reaction to Hypatia's murder certainly prevented the subsequent use of violence against pagan intellectuals—we know of no other violence directed against

---

196. For more detail on this project see C. Haas, *Alexandria in Late Antiquity,* 315–16.

197. Cyril, *Sixth Festal Letter,* 4.1–152.

198. Ibid., *Contra Julianum,* Preface 4.14–20.

199. A fragmentary Coptic church history (edited and translated by T. Orlandi in *Storia della Chiesa di Alessandrina,* vols. 1–2 [Milan, 1967]) provides an interesting story about Cyril's motivation for writing the *Contra Julianum.* It records a meeting between Cyril and a philosopher in which Cyril was informed that Julian's work was proving attractive to students because it was written by an emperor. Cyril then resolved to write a refutation in which, we are told, he used Julian's death in battle to attack the reliability of his ideas (vol. 2, lines 341–425). This story is known only from this source and elements of it do not agree with what is said in the *Contra Julianum* itself. At the same time, the mention of the *Contra Julianum* suggests that the text played an important role in defining one element of Cyril's career.

200. As, for example, C. Haas, *Alexandria in Late Antiquity,* 309, 316.

pagan intellectuals in Alexandria for the next seventy-two years. Further-more, Hypatia's death enabled the unchecked growth of Iamblichan Neo-platonism in Alexandria. Indeed, in a perverse way, Hypatia would have been Cyril's natural ally against the Iamblichans. While she was certainly a pagan, Hypatia (or at least her students) evidently believed that philosophical knowl-edge enhanced the religious experience of both pagans and Christians. Her aim was never to bring about the conversion of her students and, conse-quently, one can presume that her curriculum contained little explicit crit-icism of Christianity. For this reason, she was just the sort of teacher that Cyril needed to support. Instead, by killing her and destroying the only school with the reputation to compete successfully against the Iamblichan teach-ers, Cyril created an environment in which Athenian-trained (and dogmat-ically pagan) philosophers could dominate Alexandrian philosophical life.

Because of the state of Christian intellectual circles, this was a situation that would have profound consequences in the later fifth century. As we have seen, Christian intellectual circles that had once mixed philosophical ideas with Christian religious material had become scarce by the turn of the fifth century. The demise of these groups and the movement of many Christian intellectuals into monastic environments created a situation where the di-rect, personal exchange of ideas between pagan and Christian religious thinkers became less common. As a result, the many Christian students who still enrolled in philosophy courses lacked Christian teachers who could place the philosophical concepts they were learning into a Christian context.

With Hypatia's murder, these Christian students, who saw a traditionally inclusive pagan philosophical school die with Hypatia, were now led to study at the schools of those Iamblichan-trained professors who returned to Alexandria from Athens. Their faith was not respected by the teachers in these schools and it was not buttressed by Christian teachers outside of class. This was the unfortunate hand Cyril dealt to such students.

Chapter 8

Alexandrian Schools
of the Fifth Century

The immediate effects of Hypatia's murder on Alexandria's intellectual community are difficult to trace. Our sources are largely silent about Alexandrian philosophical teaching in the decade following the attack. Nevertheless, there are signs of a clear trend. The exodus of promising pagan students to Athens, which had begun around 400, seems to have accelerated in the 420s and 430s. While this student exodus surely hurt Alexandria's teachers, it did not damage the quality of intellectual life in the city. Many of the pagan students who studied in Athens returned to Alexandria and began to teach. Indeed, for most of the fifth century, these men were the most prominent Alexandrian teachers of philosophy, mathematics, and medicine. But, in the institutions they headed, the style of teaching and the religious environment differed greatly from the ones in Hypatia's school. In fact, they were similar to those found in the Athenian school at the same time.[1] As the schools of the Athenian-trained teachers grew, they attracted not only pagan students but also a contingent of Christians interested in acquiring a basic training in phi-

---

1. While there has been no disputing the fact that many of the Alexandrian teachers of the fifth century were taught by members of the Plutarchan Academy, there has been a belief that their metaphysical teaching was distinct from that of their Athenian mentors. On this, see K. Praechter ("Richtungen und Schulen im Neuplatonismus," *Genethliakon für Carl Robert* [Berlin, 1910], 105–56). Despite some reservation on his part, Praechter's thesis held sway among scholars of Alexandrian philosophy until the work of I. Hadot (*Le Problème du Néoplatonisme Alexandrin: Hiéroclès et Simplicius* [Paris, 1978]). Hadot raised questions about Praechter's interpretations of the work of Hierocles and Simplicius by demonstrating how their writings show a marked similarity to contemporary Athenian teaching. Later, K. Verrycken ("The metaphysics of Ammonius son of Hermeias," in *Aristotle Transformed*, ed. R. Sorabji [London, 1990], 199–232) raised similar points about the work of Ammonius. On the close personal ties between the two intellectual communities, see chapter 4.

losophy. The Iamblichan teaching that these instructors had imported from Athens was ill equipped to deal with the specific needs of these Christian students. It was a training shaped by an Athenian educational environment in which there was only a small Christian presence. Consequently, in Alexandria, these religious elements presented a real challenge to the beliefs of Christian students.

The character of this teaching made it inevitable that these teachers would come into conflict with Alexandria's religious authorities. In the past, independent Christian teachers would have raised challenges to such a strongly pagan curriculum, and the ideas of the Iamblichan teachers would have been attacked in Christian intellectual circles. By the mid-fifth century, however, such circles and their leaders do not seem to have existed in their traditional form.[2] Furthermore, after the negative reactions to the murder of Hypatia, the Alexandrian church had shown little interest in the teachings of Neoplatonic philosophers. Because of this, the conflict between Christianity and Iamblichan teaching was a quiet one. Only the people affiliated with the schools felt the tensions it produced. Ultimately, though, the situation did erupt in a violent confrontation that came to involve not only teachers and students but the entire Alexandrian Christian community.

THE NEW BREED

Hierocles was the first of this new breed of Athenian-trained Alexandrian teachers. While many of the details of his life are obscure, it appears that he was born sometime before the beginning of the fifth century and had died by the 470s.[3] He is known as a student of Plutarch the scholarch and as the author of two significant works, *On Providence* and *On the Pythagorean Golden Verses*. Of these two, *On Providence* is the more useful for establishing Hierocles's intellectual connections.[4] Now preserved only in the excerpts of Photius, *On Providence* was originally a work of seven books devoted "to treating Providence by bringing together the teachings of Plato and those of Aristotle."[5] In fact, the book was much more than this. Photius says: "The author wishes, in effect, to reconcile the opinions of those thinkers not only in their

2. For more on this, see chapter 7.
3. The date of his birth is based upon both his dedication of *On Providence* to Olympiodorus of Thebes in 418 and his statement that he was a student of Plutarch of Athens. Since Plutarch does not seem to have been taking regular pupils when Proclus arrived in 429, it is likely that Hierocles studied under him in the 410s or 420s. Damascius's portrait of Hierocles in the *Life of Isidore* makes it clear that the author did not know Hierocles personally, suggesting that he was dead by the time Damascius arrived in Alexandria in the 470s.
4. The second of these, *On the Golden Verses*, is fully extant. On this, see H. Schibli, *Hierocles of Alexandria* (Oxford, 2002), 14–21.
5. Photius, *Bib.* cod. 214, 171 b 33. On the text, see H. Schibli, *Hierocles*, 21–31.

views on Providence but in all things such as whether they conceive the soul to be immortal or whatever they philosophize about the heavens and earth."[6] Ultimately, Hierocles' aim seems to have been to demonstrate the existence of a general philosophical consensus that human souls existed before they entered into bodies and, by their migration into bodies, demonstrate that divine providence and human free will exist.[7]

Photius gives a brief synopsis of the contents of each book and, from these, it is clear that Hierocles was setting out a systematic synthesis of all Greek philosophical teaching on the topic of providence.[8] The first six books, which draw upon philosophy and pagan holy writings, appear to correspond to the thinking of Plutarch's Athenian school. In the seventh book, however, the connection between Hierocles and the school of Plutarch is made explicit. In summarizing this book Photius states, "The seventh book starts again by treating the doctrine professed by Ammonius [Saccas]; Plotinus and Origen and also Porphyry and Iamblichus as well as their successors, on this subject, are born of a divine stock, as far as Plutarch of Athens . . . all of these are in agreement with the philosophy of Plato in its pure state."[9]

Though clipped in Photius's epitomizing, this statement is very important for establishing Hierocles' intellectual roots. By including this list of Neoplatonic teachers in his discussion of Greek wisdom, Hierocles affirms the orthodoxy of the Athenian line of teaching. More importantly, however, this passage shows Hierocles' self-identification as a student of Plutarch and reveals his desire to use this tie to identify himself as a direct intellectual descendant of the holy race of Platonist philosophers.[10] His statement also establishes continuity between this treatise and the work of his predecessors. Not only is the influence of Athenian teaching evident in the structure of this work,[11] but it also seems that Hierocles was actually attempting to place this work within the chain of Neoplatonic texts that ran through the Athenian school.[12]

6. Photius, *Bib.* cod. 214 171 b.

7. Ibid., cod. 214 172 b 23 ff.

8. H. Schibli, *Hierocles*, 22–23.

9. Photius, *Bib.* cod. 214 171 a 5.

10. Besides Hierocles' statement about the divine stock from which Platonist philosophers came, the idea appears in Damascius's *Life of Isidore* ("The holy race led a life on its own which was pleasing to the gods, and devoted to philosophy and the worship of the gods," Ath. 73A; Z. Ep. 95). The idea of a pagan holy race is discussed at length by P. Athanassiadi, "Persecution and Response in Late Paganism," *Journal of Hellenic Studies* 113 (1993): 1–29, esp. 5–7; and G. Fowden, "The Pagan Holy Man in Late Antique Society," *Journal of Hellenic Studies* 102 (1982): 33–59.

11. I. Hadot, *Le Problème du Néoplatonisme Alexandrin*, 67–76.

12. N. Aujoulat (*Le Néo-Platonisme Alexandrin, Hiéroclès d'Alexandrie* [Leiden, 1986], 55–65) has shown that Hierocles, unlike his Athenian contemporaries, does not call attention to a single and perfect first principle from which the universe flows. H. Schibli (*Hierocles*, 44–58), however, has recently illustrated that a discussion of this point was inconsistent with the nature of Hierocles' extant works.

Hierocles' Athenian pedigree combined with his natural intellectual gifts to make him a valued member of the Alexandrian intellectual community. It seems that he was a popular teacher among both Christians and pagans because of "the breadth of his mind," "his uncommon eloquence," and "the ease with which he produced the most beautiful words and expressions."[13]

Nevertheless, Hierocles' school was younger and lower in prestige than that of Plutarch and Proclus.[14] For this reason, Alexandrian students were still spurred to study in Athens. While they were certainly motivated by the reputation of the Athenian school, an important contributing factor to their decision was the rise of Syrianus through the teaching ranks of Plutarch's school.[15] Syrianus was an Alexandrian and, while the date of his birth is not known, it is probable that he was a part of the generation of students that came to Athens following the Serapeum riot.[16] In Athens, Syrianus enrolled in the school of Plutarch, joined the school's inner circle, and, eventually, was selected to succeed Plutarch as head of the school. Despite his Athenian base, Syrianus seems to have maintained ties with some upper-class Alexandrian families. Thus, in the short period between 429 and his death in 436, at least three youths (Ulpian, Gregory, and Hermeias) traveled from Alexandria to Athens to receive their philosophical education at his school.[17]

The most interesting of these three characters is Hermeias. Damascius describes him as an exceptionally hard worker and a good (but not spectacular) student.[18] Nevertheless, Hermeias enjoyed a high status among Syrianus's pupils. In a move indicative both of his potential as a philosopher and of his natural good character, Syrianus selected Hermeias from among his pupils to marry his relative Aedesia.[19] The marriage of Hermeias, Syrianus's

---

13. Damascius, *Vit. Is.* Ath. 45A; Z Ep. 54, fr. 106. On his popularity, see H. Schibli, *Hierocles*, 11–12.

14. The speculation of M. Vinzent, ("'Oxbridge' in der ausgehenden Spätantike oder: Ein Vergleich der Schulen von Athen und Alexandrien," *Zietschrift für Antikes Christentum* 4 (2000): 74, 77) that Hierocles assumed a publicly funded chair is not supported by any ancient testimony. In fact, given Hierocles' brutal interrogation and punishment for his objectionable activities in Constantinople (described in *Vit. Is.* Ath. 45B; Z. fr. 106), it is unlikely that he would have been considered for such a public position.

15. For more on the career of Syrianus, see chapter 4.

16. Because Synesius refers to Plutarchan *sophists* in his letter criticizing Athenian student recruitment methods (*Ep.* 136), Syrianus had likely already become a prominent member of Plutarch's school by the time of Synesius's visit to Athens. This suggests that he probably arrived at Plutarch's school sometime in the 390s.

17. Although there is no way to demonstrate this conclusively, it is likely that these three were just the most accomplished of a larger group of Alexandrians who came to Athens to study under Syrianus. It is also worth noting that Proclus traveled from Alexandria to Athens at roughly this same time.

18. *Vit. Is.* Ath. 54; Z. Ep. 74, fr. 120.

19. "This was the Aedesia whom as a young girl Syrianus intended to betroth to Proclus, if some god had not prevented Proclus from entering into marriage." *Vit. Is.* Ath. 56; Z. fr. 124.

most promising pupil (save Proclus), and Aedesia was motivated by the delicate politics of scholastic succession arrangements. As an unmarried man evidently lacking children of his own, Syrianus looked at the wedding as a way to maintain the prominence of his family in philosophical teaching.[20] But, to prevent a conflict from developing with Syrianus's chosen successor Proclus, it seems that Syrianus encouraged Hermeias to leave Athens and return to a publicly funded philosophy professorship in Alexandria.[21]

For Hermeias, this marriage represented a significant opportunity, then. Besides leading to a prime teaching position in Alexandria, the marriage also produced three children. The first of these, whose name is unknown to us, was born in the mid- to late 430s and died at the age of seven.[22] The second child, Ammonius, was probably born sometime in the early 440s.[23] His brother Heliodorus followed not long after.[24] In roughly the same period, Hermeias also must have released the one book from his hand that has come down to us, his *Commentary on the Phaedrus*.[25] This work is usually seen as a summary of class notes based upon lectures by Syrianus.[26] Whether this is true or not, it seems reasonable to assume that, like the first set of commentaries from Proclus's pen,[27] the book was written with some input from his teacher. In light of this, Hermeias's positive assessment of Athenian theurgical practices is not surprising,[28] but the success of a volume that speaks in

20. In the preface to his *Commentary on Hermogenes*, Syrianus writes to ὦ φίλτατέ μοι τῶν ἐκγόνων Ἀλέξανδρε (*Comm. in Herm.* 2). It is not clear who Alexander is nor whether ἐκγόνος is to be understood in biological or philosophical terms. Alexander may be a blood relative, but one cannot be sure.

21. This is something of a controversial idea, though one that is strongly suggested by Damascius's wording. For further discussion of this point, see below.

22. Despite his death at such a young age, a series of stories about this child apparently continued to circulate among Alexandrian pagans into the 470s (e.g., *Vit. Is.* Ath. 57A; Z. fr. 76).

23. This is L. G. Westerink's rough guess on Ammonius's date of birth (*Prolégomènes à la philosophie de Platon* [Paris, 1990], xi).

24. *Vit. Is.* Ath. 57B; Z. fr. 124.

25. The most recent edition of this is that of P. Couvreur (Hermeias, *In Phaedrum*, 1901; 2nd ed. by C. Zintzen [Hildesheim, 1971]).

26. That this work came from the mind of Syrianus was first suggested by K. Praechter, "Die griechischen Aristoteleskommentatoren," *Byzantinische Zeitschrift* 18 (1909): 524. M. Dickie ("Hermeias on Plato *Phaedrus* 238D and Synesius *Dion* 14.2," *American Journal of Philology* 114 [1993]: 436–38) has suggested that the work is primarily from the pen of Hermeias.

27. The *Life of Proclus* gives us an idea of how an ambitious student wrote his first commentary. "Plutarch read Aristotle's *De Anima* with Proclus and also Plato's *Phaedo*. The great man urged Proclus to write down his lessons and, capitalizing upon the ambitious mind of the youth, he said that when these notebooks were completed there would be a commentary on the *Phaedo* written by Proclus." (*Vit. Proc.* 12).

28. For Hermeias's discussion of the importance of theurgy, see A. Sheppard, "Proclus' Attitude to Theurgy," *Classical Quarterly* 32 (1982): 214–18.

such a way about theurgy also illustrates the appeal of even the most controversial Athenian-influenced philosophical ideas in Alexandria.

The professional and personal good fortune of Hermeias's young family
came to an abrupt halt with his death in the late 440s or early 450s. This
blow robbed Aedesia and her children of the financial security they had expected and the family rapidly fell into debt.[29] Aedesia, however, made every
effort to ensure that the education of her sons did not suffer because of the
family's relative poverty. As could be expected from the matriarch of Alexandria's most prominent philosophical dynasty, she was especially concerned
that her sons received a good philosophical education.[30] When Ammonius
and Heliodorus reached the appropriate age, "they both studied philosophy under Proclus . . . And Proclus paid particular attention to them as they
were the children of Hermeias, a man who was his friend and fellow philosophical initiate."[31] Heliodorus proved to be a relatively unremarkable student.[32] Ammonius, however, showed himself to be quite intelligent. As a
young student "in geometry and astronomy he distinguished himself among
not only his contemporaries but also the more senior members of Proclus'
inner circle."[33] This early brilliance was portentous of a long and extremely
productive career.

This career began when, after leaving Athens, Ammonius took up a teaching position in Alexandria, around the year 470. The nature of his position
is unclear, but it seems to have been arranged by Ammonius's mother,
Aedesia. Aedesia "was especially concerned about the philosophical education of her sons since she desired to bestow upon them the profession[34]
of their father as their patrimonial lot. She managed to preserve for her children, when they were still young, the public salary granted to their father as
if[35] they taught philosophy."[36]

This statement, although difficult to interpret, seems to describe a situation not entirely alien to the educational environment. Aedesia was con-

29. *Vit. Is.* Ath. 56; Z. fr. 124.

30. Ibid.

31. Ibid., Ath. 57B; Z. fr.127.

32. Damascius calls him simple and superficial in both character and reasoning.

33. *Vit. Is.* Ath. 57C; Z. Ep. 79. The more senior members of Proclus's inner circle are οἱ
πρεσβύτεροι τοῦ Πρόκλου ἑταῖροι.

34. Ἐπιστήμη. For "profession" as a translation see *LSJ*⁹ I 2.

35. P. Athanassiadi (*Damascius: The Philosophical History* [Athens, 1999]); *Suidae Lexicon*, ed.
A. Adler (Leipzig, 1928–38); and all Suda manuscripts read ὡς. C. Zintzen and I. Bekker, editors of Photius, *Bibliotheke* (Berlin, 1824–25), emend this to ἕως, presumably for reasons of context. Because the manuscripts are uniform in their reading and the sentence is very deliberately constructed to work grammatically with ὡς, it seems correct to resist the temptation to
emend the manuscript reading.

36. *Vit. Is.* Ath. 56; Z. fr. 124.

cerned about the philosophical training of Ammonius and Heliodorus because she wanted them to become prominent philosophers like their father. She then made sure that the public salary granted to Hermeias as a teacher of philosophy was guaranteed for his sons when they were still young. This presumably means that the salary remained in family hands and the position once held by Hermeias was left vacant.

Although it seems to have been an uncommon thing for a parent to try to reserve a teaching position for a minor child,[37] it was not without precedent. In the early part of the fourth century, the Gallic teacher Eumenius tried to do a similar thing for his son in Autun.[38] Eumenius's grandfather was a renowned teacher of rhetoric and Eumenius himself began his career as a professor before moving into the bureaucracy. Like Eumenius's son, Ammonius was the latest member of a prominent intellectual dynasty to come ready to take a teaching position. Both his mother and his teacher were well connected to the intellectual and the civic leaders of Alexandria.[39] However, Ammonius's family had an additional advantage. The family had continued to collect the revenues from the lands marked out to pay Hermeias's teaching salary. Since this salary was in his mother's hands until the time Ammonius returned to Alexandria, it would not be difficult to place him in the associated teaching position upon his return. Indeed, Ammonius had proven himself to be an exceptionally gifted student at Proclus's school and, had there been a search, it is far from certain that the city would have found a stronger candidate to occupy the public chair.

THE RELIGIOUS ENVIRONMENT WITHIN THE SCHOOLS

In the main, Ammonius's school at this time seems to have functioned much like other Athenian-influenced Alexandrian philosophical circles.[40] In his

---

37. Damascius indicates that he knew of no parallel (*Vit. Is.* Ath. 56; Z. fr. 124).

38. In an oration dating to 298, Eumenius, who was formerly a professor of rhetoric in the city, said, "When I was trying to gain access to my old position for my son rather than for myself, [Constantius] ordered me to take up the teaching of oratory again." *Panegyrici Latini* IX.6.2. For discussion, see C. E. V. Nixon and B. S. Rodgers, *In Praise of Later Roman Emperors: The Panegyrici Latini* (Berkeley and Los Angeles, 1994). On this text, see as well R. Rees, *Layers of Loyalty in Latin Panegyric: A.D. 289–307* (Oxford, 2002), 133 ff.

39. From the *Life of Proclus* 8–9, we know that he had close relationships with city and government officials in Alexandria in the late 420s and early 430s.

40. The focus of Ammonius's teaching, even at this stage in his career, may have been different. Damascius's statement that "he was as hard-working as possible and made the greatest contribution of all commentators who ever lived; and most of all when he explained Aristotle" (*Vit. Is.* Ath. 57C; Z. Ep. 79) comes from personal experience of his teaching. It seems to suggest a greater skill at teaching Aristotle and, probably, a curriculum that subtly reflects this skill. It should not, however, be taken to mean that Ammonius did not teach a full Platonic curriculum in the 470s.

general courses, Ammonius taught a religiously mixed audience in which Christians always were a significant part.[41] Indeed, many Christian students on their way to productive careers in law or administration spent some time studying basic philosophy under Ammonius before leaving to continue their studies elsewhere. This seems to have been true of other Alexandrian pagan schools as well.[42]

Christians were concerned about the contents and implications of philosophical teaching,[43] but the atmosphere in the schools was more disconcerting to Christians than the doctrines that were taught. In the hierarchy of the school, the master stood as the most respected member of the community. He was the preeminent authority figure, the head of the school, a metaphorical father, and, usually, a pagan. There was also a hierarchy of students with the (presumably pagan) students in the philosopher's inner circle recognized as a superior subgroup of students by their peers.[44] This created a situation in which the scholastic leadership was pagan, the intellectual discourse it encouraged within the school was replete with stories illustrating the accomplishments of pagan sages, and the general environment advertised the power of paganism.[45] Thus, a young Christian could enter one of these schools and be thrust into an environment where his belief in the falsity of paganism would be challenged by the conduct of the most prominent figures he knew.

Christians with an interest in the city's schools seem to have been less than comfortable with this situation. Whereas philosophical teaching was useful to Christians, the religious messages that came from this environment could prove dangerous. Despite the religiously heterogeneous student body, a vi-

---

41. The introduction to Zacharias Scholasticus's dialog *Ammonius* suggests that such students were common. The dialog begins: "a certain student of Ammonius (a true philosopher) who was gently inclined towards paganism came to Beirut to study the law . . . I too was in Alexandria and had many dialectical debates about these things against Ammonius and Gessius the *iatrosophist*." Zacharias, *Ammonius*, Pro. 1–7.

42. This is suggested by, among other passages, Zacharias Scholasticus, *Vie de Sévère*, (ed. Kugener), *Patrologia Orientalis*, vol. 2, (Paris, 1907), 23.

43. It seems that the most pressing idea concerned the eternity of the world. On this, see below.

44. The distinction between inner-circle and average students has been discussed in chapter 3. Olympiodorus's evocative passage describing the different treatment accorded junior and senior students (Photius, *Bib.* cod. 80, 60) when they joined a school suggests that students were trained from the start of their studies to respect the distinctions created by this hierarchy.

45. Many of the miraculous stories related in texts like Eunapius's *Lives of the Philosophers*, Marinus's *Life of Proclus*, and Damascius's *Life of Isidore* come from historical gossip about famous teachers that was circulating in schools. The best example is the rumor that circulated among the students of Iamblichus that their teacher turned golden and began to levitate when he prayed (*Vit. Soph.* 458). On the role such anecdotes played in defining the common values of late antique intellectual communities, see E. Watts, "Orality and Communal Identity in Eunapius' *Lives of the Sophists and Philosophers*," *Byzantion* 75 (2005): forthcoming.

brant pagan religious culture existed among the students and their teachers. Indicative of this, one professor, Horapollon, let selected students participate in pagan sacrifices with him.[46] Paganism was also passively encouraged. Stories about the wonders performed by Neoplatonic teachers circulated among the students and furtive trips to a house-shrine of Isis in Menouthis were not uncommon and not discouraged by the professors.[47] Even more troubling to some Christians was the fact that this pagan vitality appealed to Christian students. Damascius tells of two men, Epiphanius and Euprepius, who were experts in pagan mystery religions and presided over the rites of a number of cults. "These men were not born into the traditional way of life [i.e., paganism] but they encountered and spent time with those who had been and, having benefited from their company, they became for their associates the source of many blessings."[48] Though Damascius does not say when the two men converted, he makes it clear that their conversion came about because of their social interactions with pagan intellectuals.[49]

The *Life of Severus*, a text by Zacharias Scholasticus, implies that religious experimentation and conversion like that described above often occurred among students in Alexandria and elsewhere. The text begins with a prologue that describes the work as a defense of Severus, the anti-Chalcedonian bishop of Antioch, against a slanderous pamphlet circulated by his enemies in the church. The most startling accusation in the pamphlet (or at least the only one quoted by Zacharias) was that Severus, the grandson of a bishop of Sozopolis, "at the beginning of his career, worshipped evil demons and idols."[50] Despite Zacharias's conviction that this was untrue, Severus himself gives some personal information that confirms the rumor. In a homily on St. Leontius, he discusses his scholastic career and characterizes his religious beliefs at that time. Severus says, "I know many of the young men who devoted themselves to Roman law in that turbulent city, that is Berytus, and they went off to [Tripoli] to pray and speedily left their vain erudition and way of life and purified their minds of Hellenic myths . . . so I went to the martyr's holy place and prayed. Moreover, I prayed separately because I was still a pagan."[51] Severus does not tell whether this experimentation began in Alexandria or in Beirut but, sometime during his student days,

---

46. *Vit. Sev.* 15. All translations from the *Life of Severus* are my translations of Kugener's French.

47. Ibid. 16–19. On the attraction of pagan intellectuals to this shrine, see D. Frankfurter, *Religion in Roman Egypt* (Princeton, 1998) 164–65; and "The Consequences of Hellenism in Late Antique Egypt: Religious Worlds and Actors," *Archiv für Religionsgeschichte* 2 (2000): 185–92.

48. *Vit. Is.* Ath. 41; Z. fr. 100.

49. If R. Stark (*The Rise of Christianity: A Sociologist Reconsiders History* [Princeton, 1996], 15 ff.) is correct, this same sort of model was true for early Christian conversions.

50. *Vit. Sev.* 9.

51. The homily is found in F. Trombley, *Hellenic Religion and Christianization c. 370–529*, vol. 2 (Leiden, 1993–94), 49–51; and G. Garitte, "Textes hagiographiques orientaux relatifs

this child of a prominent Christian family was persuaded to take part in pagan rites.[52] Christians apparently recognized that this environment was full of danger and chose to respond. In the third century, Christian religious teachers who were tangentially involved with the pagan schools would have directed this response. By the later fifth century, however, many Christian intellectual circles were housed in a monastic environment. Because their leaders were monks, they had little to do with pagan philosophical schools. Christian intellectuals did exist independently of the monastic environment and some seem even to have produced literature for circulation in Alexandria responding vigorously to philosophical doctrines that conflicted with Christian beliefs. Their responses, however, were not directed towards a student audience.[53] Indeed, Aeneas of Gaza, the most prominent author of such a text, populated his fictional dialog, *Theophrastus,* with middle-aged men and presented his ideas in a way that especially appealed to a mature, educated audience. Furthermore, while he was friendly with Alexandrian Neoplatonists,[54] Aeneas did not live in Alexandria and likely had little to do with students in that city.[55] Consequently, the absence of figures who could effectively bridge the divide between students and the Christian establishment meant that the Christian response to the Alexandrian scholastic climate had to take a new form.[56]

The new Christian response was, from an institutional perspective, ingenious. It came through the *philoponoi,* a confraternity of laymen whose mem-

---

à S. Leonce de Tripoli: L' homélie copte de Sévère d'Antioche," *Le Muséon* 79 (1966): 335–86. See as well the parallel points made by Severus in Homily 50.

52. R. A. Darling, "The patriarchate of Severus of Antioch, 512–518," PhD diss., University of Chicago, 1982, 21–25, makes the point that our surviving evidence does not even support Zacharias's description of Severus's Christian background.

53. Aeneas of Gaza's *Theophrastus* addresses the question of the eternity of the world, but it does so in a way designed to appeal to a non-student audience (on this, see E. Watts, "An Alexandrian Christian Response to Neoplatonic Influence," in *The Philosopher and Society in Late Antiquity,* ed. A. Smith, 215–30 [Swansea, 2005]). The *Tubingen Theosophy,* if it is of Alexandrian provenance, similarly addresses this concern in a way that would have been more convincing to older intellectuals than to students.

54. Aeneas's letters to the physician Gessius (*Epp.* 19–20), a well-known affiliate of the Alexandrian Neoplatonic schools, suggest his familiarity with members of the Alexandrian Neoplatonic social circles.

55. Aeneas did know Zacharias (*Vit. Sev.* 90 and *Vita Isaiae* 13), but this relationship seems to have developed because both men were Gazans.

56. One Christian teacher of rhetoric, a man named Aphthonius, is the only known exception. He had "many students" (*Vit. Sev.* 25), but, given the (apparently) large numbers of Christian students in the philosophical schools of Ammonius and his pagan contemporaries, one should probably question Aphthonius's real influence. It is additionally likely that he did not (and possibly could not) teach philosophy in a way that was competitive with his pagan neighbors.

bers were especially dedicated Christians. Based primarily in cities and towns throughout Egypt, the *philoponoi* seem to have been men of high social rank who likely functioned as a liaison between the bishop and his lay congregation.[57] In addition, they participated in processions for certain holy days, including the procession commemorating the death of a bishop.[58]

What made this institution especially appropriate for engaging students, however, was the close relationships that *philoponoi* had with certain monasteries. The *philoponoi* lent financial support to monasteries and served as a group of laymen who could represent the interests of monastic leaders. In return, the aged and more devout *philoponoi* could enter the affiliated monastery. Eventually, the relationships became so close that the term *philoponion*, or "meeting place of the *philoponoi*," came to refer to a monastery populated or funded by *philoponoi*.[59] Because *philoponoi* were already recognized as a link between the monasteries and the lay population, the institution to which they belonged was a natural one to use to reestablish ties between the monasteries that housed Christian intellectual circles and Alexandrian Christian students. And it seems that a group of *philoponoi* was established for this purpose.

For the *philoponoi* active in the schools of Alexandria, the affiliated monastery was almost certainly Enaton, the bastion of radical anti-Chalcedonian monks situated nine miles outside of Alexandria. In late antiquity, Enaton was actually a conglomeration of many smaller monastic groups (called *koinobia*) and an overall superior headed it. Despite the federal structure, each *koinobion* had its own church, holy men, and superior.[60] Each monastic community at Enaton also had its own individual interests. In many cases these interests were intellectual and involved the scholarly examination of theological points.[61] This was especially true of the *koinobion* headed by Apa Salomon.[62] Included among its monks were Stephen, a former teacher of

---

57. Zacharias (*Vit. Sev.* 24) indicates that other Christian groups had a similar function in other cities of the empire. For more on the functions of the *philoponoi* see C. Haas, *Alexandria in Late Antiquity: Topography and Social Conflict* (Baltimore, 1997), 238–40. See also E. Wipszycka, "Les confréries dans la vie religeuse de l'Egypte chrétienne," in *Proceedings of the Twelfth International Congress of Papyrology*, ed. R. Samuel, 511–25 (Toronto, 1970); S. Pétrides, "Spoudaei et Philopones," *Echoes d'Orient* 7 (1904): 341–48; and P. J. Sijpesteijn, "New Light on the *Philoponoi*," *Aegyptus* 69 (1989): 95–99.

58. E. Wipszycka, "Les confréries," 514.

59. Ibid., 518–20. The formal change in names starts to appear in sources of the seventh century.

60. P. van Cauwenbergh, *Étude sur les moines d'Égypte: depuis le Concile de Chalcédoine, jusqu'à l'invasion arabe* (Paris-Louvain, 1914), 64–72. See also J. Gascou, "The Enaton," *Coptic Encyclopedia* 955–56.

61. Among the scholars who worked at the Enaton were the theologians Theodorus, Archbishop Damian, Thomas Harkel, and Paul of Tella.

62. *Vit. Sev.* 15.

rhetoric, and Athanasius, an educated man he had converted.[63] While at Enaton, these figures seem to have been adept at facilitating intellectual conversations and, through them, buttressing the religious faith of Christian students.[64]

The scholastic *philoponoi* seem to have served as the link between the intellectual circles at Enaton and the Alexandrian schools. In the schools, they encouraged students to accept Christianity on intellectual grounds. Once these students did so, the *philoponoi* gave them additional religious guidance. Zacharias, who was himself a *philoponos* in the 480s, shows how this was done when he describes his initial meeting with Severus. Severus was an unbaptized catechumen studying in Alexandria at the time. Zacharias attended the same classes as Severus and began speaking to him about his intellectual interests. In the course of this conversation, Zacharias became alarmed at Severus's love for the writings of Libanius and counseled him to balance those pagan texts by reading Christian works by Basil of Caesarea and Gregory Nazianzen.[65]

In the segment of the *Life of Severus* that describes Severus's decision to learn about Christianity, Zacharias presents the *philoponoi* program in more detail. Severus's indoctrination began when he approached Zacharias and asked to speak to him about Christianity. In response, Zacharias taught Severus about scripture and gave him some texts by Basil and Gregory.[66] Zacharias then convinced Severus to join a reading group that the *philoponoi* had set up. This group was designed to help students to become aware of the rhetoric, philosophy, science, and theology of the Holy Scriptures.[67] To make this suit a student schedule, they met each Saturday afternoon and every Sunday to read and discuss these texts. In these sessions, the group read authors like Athanasius, Basil, Gregory, and Cyril. The sequence began with the anti-pagan texts written by these authors and then continued on to the *Hexameron* by Basil and the theological works of Gregory.[68]

In the academic environment of the late fifth century, the *philoponoi* program was effectively designed to prevent much of the religious experimentation that occurred among students. The student *philoponoi* provided a sup-

---

63. Ibid. 14.

64. E.g., "Stephen was very wise and quite skillful in both holy doctrines and also more broad learning. After having read many treatises from the teachers of the holy church which argued against pagans, he had received from God the gift of being able to completely defeat anyone who discussed these themes with him." *Vit. Sev.* 16.

65. Ibid., 13.

66. Ibid., 48.

67. Ibid., 52–55.

68. Ibid., 53. Apparently to broaden their appeal, they also chose only pre-Chalcedonian Christian authors. This would make their efforts accessible to both Chalcedonian and anti-Chalcedonian students.

port structure for young Christians who came to Alexandria to study. Just as Gregory Nazianzen and Basil had supported one another while both studied in Athens,[69] Zacharias and his friends reinforced the Christian values of each member of the circle. With this mutual support system in place, Christian students could feel more secure in a pagan-dominated scholastic culture. The reading groups also played a significant role in giving this group of Christian students greater self-confidence. The texts they chose were crucial in doing this. For their recommended reading, the *philoponoi* looked at the anti-pagan texts of the most stylistically accomplished Christian authors. This counteracted the notion, held by some students, that Christian literature was stylistically inferior to the works of classical authors.[70] It also gave Christian students the opportunity to read works that rationally argued against many of the pagan influences that were found in their immediate environment. In so doing, the *philoponoi* had created a subculture in the academic world that challenged the subtle religious messages sent by the hierarchy of the schools.

From the time that Athenian influenced Iamblichan Neoplatonism arrived in Alexandria, the religious situation in the pagan-run schools must have been one of increasing yet hidden tension. Pagan teachers led the best schools and they presided over young and insecure students in a permissive religious environment. Although the Alexandrian bishops took little notice of this, individual Christians recognized the danger and tried to counteract pagan influences in the schools. This ensured a rather precarious balance but, despite the religious tensions, as long as neither party did anything provocative, it seems that both were able to live with this uneasy status quo.

The spark that set off this tinderbox came in 486, not long after an Aphrodisian student by the name of Paralius arrived to study grammar with the pagan teacher Horapollon.[71] Paralius was the youngest son of a prominent pagan family. His two eldest brothers were teachers in Aphrodisias and steadfastly pagan. The third brother, Athanasius, had studied law in Beirut and then traveled to Alexandria for business. While on that trip he met Stephen, a pious Christian teacher of rhetoric, and was convinced to convert to Christianity. Soon both he and Stephen decided to join Enaton, the strongly anti-

---

69. Gregory Nazianzen, *Panegyric on S. Basil* 19 ff. This relationship is described in more detail in chapter 1.

70. For example Augustine, *Conf.* 3.5.

71. This dating is based upon a number of clues found in the text. Paralius was certainly still in Aphrodisias when Illus's revolt failed in August of 484 (*Vit. Sev.* 40–41). Furthermore, Zacharias tells us that Paralius spoke to Isidore about philosophical questions during his first year of study. It is known that Isidore was in Athens at the time of Proclus's death on April 17, 485; as the sailing season lasted from March 10 to November 10, it is likely that he had been there since the previous autumn. On the sailing season, see L. Casson, *Ships and Seamanship in the Ancient World* (Princeton, 1971).

Chalcedonian monastery that worked with the student *philoponoi*.[72] Athanasius's choice so frightened his older brothers that they feared that Paralius too would be corrupted by Christians when he went off to study. To prevent this, they sent Paralius to study under Horapollon, a teacher who was remarkably skilled as a speaker, a teacher, and a student of pagan religion.[73]

When Paralius arrived in Alexandria, Horapollon warmly welcomed him. Zacharias says, "In his dealings with Horapollon, the paganism of Paralius flourished; he was vigilant about offering sacrifices to idols with his master."[74] But Paralius's emotions eventually overcame him and, not heeding the warnings of his brothers, he went to visit his brother at Enaton. As he talked to Athanasius and his friend Stephen, the conversation turned to religion and Stephen ably sowed doubts in Paralius's mind about the power of pagan gods.[75] He then told Paralius to go and discuss his new religious concerns with the pagan teachers Horapollon, Heraiscus, Asclepiodotus, Ammonius, and Isidore (the final three of whom studied under Proclus).[76]

Because Horapollon seems to have taught in the same set of *auditoria* as those other teachers, it was not difficult for Paralius to seek them out.[77] In the course of a few days, Paralius had a number of conversations with the prominent philosophers whom he came across. He found their responses to the questions Stephen had raised to be feeble and unconvincing. Nevertheless, Paralius still held fast to his faith. His confidence was bolstered by the story of the birth of a child to the philosopher Asclepiodotus that, supposedly, had been accomplished with the aid of the goddess Isis.[78] When Stephen heard this, he told Paralius not to believe the account unless it could be proven that Asclepiodotus's wife was producing milk. Paralius returned to school, asked around, and was told that this sort of verification was impossible.

Paralius's faith was finally shaken when he visited the Isis shrine at which

---

72. *Vit. Sev.* 14.

73. Ibid., 15.

74. Ibid.

75. Ibid., 16. One wonders whether Stephen was once himself a student *philoponos*.

76. P. Athanassiadi's idea that Ammonius, Heliodorus, Asclepiades, Heraiscus, Horapollon, Isidore, and Asclepiodotus were assembled into one large school is quite interesting (*Damascius*, 20 ff.). Nevertheless, a concentration of closely affiliated intellectuals does not necessarily mean a school existed to bind them. Note, for example, the fourth-century collection of unaffiliated rhetoricians around Antioch's temple of the Muses. On this, see Libanius, *Or* 1.101–104; and R. Cribiore, *Gymnastics of the Mind: Greek Education in Hellenistic and Roman Egypt* (Princeton, 2001), 34.

77. This complex of teaching halls must have resembled that found at Kom-el Dikka. On them, see B. Tkaczow, *Topography of Ancient Alexandria: An Archeological Map* (Warsaw, 1993), 99; R. Cribiore, *Gymnastics of the Mind*, 34.

78. *Vit. Sev.* 18–19. D. Frankfurter, "The Consequences of Hellenism," 190–91, presents the miracle as an event staged in a way that reflected Christian miraculous activities.

Asclepiodotus's miracle had been performed. The shrine seems to have become well known among students as a site to which they could travel for divine guidance.[79] Paralius's experience at the shrine, however, convinced him that it gave false information.[80] Upset by this, Paralius returned to Alexandria, went back to the school, and offered harangues against the pagan gods and their shrines.[81] He mocked the prominent pagan teachers he knew and railed against the Isis shrine by comparing its priestess to a prostitute.[82]

His outbursts provoked a strong response from the pagans among his fellow students. Motivated by both loyalty to their teachers and religious anger, they waited until the following Friday, a day when most of the Christian students were not present at the school. When Horapollon was out of sight, they attacked Paralius. Paralius escaped, but the mob of pagans followed him, caught him, and began to kick him. At that point, Zacharias and two of his *philoponoi* friends came upon the scene and were only just able to spirit Paralius away from the mob. They immediately took him to their supporters at Enaton, showed the monks his wounds, and explained the incident to Salomon, the superior of the *koinobion*.[83]

Salomon rounded up a group of monks and they accompanied Paralius and the *philoponoi* to the residence of Peter Mongus, the patriarch of the city.[84] In the 480s, the relationship between Peter and the anti-Chalcedonian monks of Enaton was tense because of the patriarch's acceptance of the *Henotikon*, a document of ecclesiastical union put forth by the emperor Zeno to end factionalism in the eastern Churches.[85] With this background, it is perhaps curious that the monks from Salomon's *koinobion* would choose to approach Peter after Paralius's beating. But they had little other choice. Despite their

---

79. D. Frankfurter ("The Consequences of Hellenism," 189–92) effectively contrasts the mundane, local, religious activities of the Menouthis shrine with the more spectacular services it did for Alexandrian intellectuals and their students. The shrine was particularly attractive to these scholars because of the extraordinary efforts its priests made to accommodate the religious expectations of their visitors. On these scholars, see as well G. Bowersock, *Hellenism in Late Antiquity* (Ann Arbor, 1990), 60–61.

80. *Vit. Sev.* 20–21.

81. The *Life of Severus* does not support P. Athanassiadi's supposition (*Damascius*, 27–28) that Paralius was sent back to the school by Stephen with the express purpose of provoking the students. Compare F. Trombley, *Hellenic Religion and Christianization*, vol. 2, 11 ff.

82. *Vit. Sev.* 23.

83. Ibid., 24.

84. Ibid., 25.

85. This brought imperial recognition of Peter's previously disputed position. On the circumstances surrounding this situation, see Zacharias, *Ecclesiastical History* 6.1 in *The Syriac chronicle known as that of Zachariah of Mytilene*, trans. F. J. Hamilton and E. W. Brooks (London, 1899). C. Haas (*Alexandria in Late Antiquity*, 320–30) does a fine job of presenting Peter Mongus and the tense world in which he operated.

serious differences, Peter was still the representative of the city's Christian community and, as such, he was the man in whom all the status, authority, and political power resided.[86] At the very least, the *philoponoi* and the monks from Salomon's *koinobion* needed his assent to act against the pagans. They probably hoped to get his active support as well.

From Peter's perspective, the mission from Enaton must have been extremely welcome. The violent expression of militant paganism in the philosophical schools was something against which all of the city's feuding Christian factions could unite.[87] Furthermore, in Peter's mind, his cooperation could have brought about a degree of rapprochement with the monastery. Consequently, Peter seized this chance and sent a deputy to accompany the crowd to the court of the prefect, Entrechius.[88]

When the convoy arrived at the court of the prefect, his assessor took the reasonable step of ordering the crowd of monks and Christian students out of the courtroom.[89] He allowed only Paralius, Zacharias, and three other *philoponoi* to remain. Entrechius heard the charge and, when he learned the gravity of the situation, he told Paralius to write out an accusation. Paralius then submitted a document that described how members of the scholastic community had offered sacrifices and set upon him like brigands. Soon after this process ended, Horapollon and the other pagans named in Paralius's indictment fled. Probably wishing the whole thing would just die away, Entrechius did not worry about pursuing them.[90]

In the meantime, the entire episode had incited Alexandria's Christians. They verbally attacked Ammonius and the other pagan teachers in the churches throughout the city. Horapollon, who was seen as the cause of the whole incident, even received the sobriquet "Psychapollon" or "Soul Destroyer" for his rumored propensity to convert students.[91] The crowd was also able to satiate their need for violence when Salomon and Peter Mongus arranged a raid on the notorious Isis shrine. For Peter, this raid certainly represented a high point in his patriarchate. The entire Christian populace had unified against the soul-destroying teachers. It had even gotten to the point where a group of anti-Chalcedonian monks from Enaton and their Chalcedonian opponents from the Pachomian monastery in Canopus made

---

86. It is also possible that Salomon's *koinobion* did not agree with the factions at Enaton that did not want to hold communion with Peter. Zacharias calls Peter "a man who was very capable and of ardent piety" (*Vit. Sev.* 25), a very positive statement. The *Life of Severus,* however, was composed at a time when Peter's reputation among extreme anti-Chalcedonians had been rehabilitated.

87. Haas, *Alexandria in Late Antiquity,* 328–29.

88. *Vit. Sev.* 25.

89. Ibid. For this prudence, Zacharias attacked him as "an openly-practicing pagan."

90. Ibid., 26–27.

91. Ibid., 32.

common cause against paganism and marched together in a parade displaying the spoils from the Isis shrine.[92] For a fleeting instant Peter stood alone at the head of an undivided flock.[93]

For teachers like Horapollon and Ammonius this situation caused great concern. After nearly seventy-five years of relatively undisturbed teaching, there was again a Christian mob willing to commit acts of violence against pagan targets. These men knew the fate of Hypatia and understood that now, unlike Hypatia, they were not widely seen as innocent individuals.[94] Alexandrian Christians recognized the beating of Paralius as a provocation and, consequently, they wholeheartedly supported a violent response against the teachers and their schools. It is not at all surprising that Horapollon and the other accused men fled.[95] Given the climate in the city, it would not be shocking if Entrechius had tipped them off to avoid a genuine pogrom. Nevertheless, whatever the threat, it does not seem that Horapollon and his associates were gone for long.

What happened next is unclear. Sometime in late 487 or 488 an official named Nicomedes was sent from Constantinople to investigate the activities of these philosophers.[96] Though it cannot be proven, there is good reason to suspect that Peter Mongus was behind this. A rather cryptic passage in Damascius's *Life of Isidore* seems to support this suspicion. He calls Peter "the leader of those in charge of the state, appointed to oversee their creed" and says he was "a reckless and truly evil man."[97] Peter was well placed, powerful, and interested enough to convince the emperor Zeno to send Nicomedes to Alexandria. Peter also had an incentive to encourage an investigation like this. The year 487 had been a hard one for him. Despite the energy from the sack of the Isis shrine, the camp of dissenting anti-Chalcedonian monks

92. Ibid., 27.

93. Haas, *Alexandria in Late Antiquity*, 328–29.

94. Hypatia's death was of such significance that Damascius provides an extended account of it to show its similarities to the unjust situation in Alexandria in the 480s. On this, see E. Watts, "The Murder of Hypatia: Acceptable or Unacceptable Violence," in *Violence in Late Antiquity*, ed. H. A. Drake, 335–37 (Aldershot, 2005).

95. There is no way to know whether these additional accused included other teachers or only the students of Horapollon responsible for the beating of Paralius.

96. The opinions of J. H. W. G. Liebeschuetz (*The Decline and Fall of the Roman City* [Oxford, 2001], 260–62); C. Haas (*Alexandria in Late Antiquity*, 326); and P. Athanassiadi ("Persecution and Response in Late Paganism," 19–21) that the actions of Nicomedes took place before or at the same time as the Paralius affair are incorrect. The philosopher Heraiscus is said to have died while hiding from Nicomedes, but the *Life of Severus* mentions him as one of the philosophers to whom Paralius spoke. Both P. Chuvin (*A Chronicle of the Last Pagans*, trans. B. A. Archer [Cambridge, Mass., 1990], 111) and P. Athanassiadi's later work (*Damascius*, 29) have the order of events correct.

97. *Vit. Is.* Ath. 113I; Z. Ep. 170.

continued to grow.[98] Peter could have been forgiven for hoping that a public investigation of the teachers would again focus the attention of Alexandrian Christians on paganism and unify the various Christian factions. If he did make this appeal, the time would have been just right for it to catch the ear of the emperor Zeno. In 487, Zeno's forces were engaged in mopping up after the failed revolt of an Isaurian general, Illus, and his associate Leontius. Although it was a rather shoddily done affair, Illus's revolt is notable for the way it was organized. Illus, through the pagan poet Pamprepius, had made overtures to prominent pagans in the eastern empire. They were led to believe that, if his revolt succeeded, imperial support for paganism would be restored.[99] This inspired great hope among pagans and many sacrifices were offered on Illus's behalf.[100] Pamprepius seems to have spent much of 482 and 483 preparing the pagan population for this event, and a good deal of his effort was devoted to the philosophers of Alexandria. Damascius says that they were all put off by Pamprepius.[101] But, even if they did not like Pamprepius, Damascius and his associates seem to have agreed with the goal of his program.[102] Consequently, by the time that Illus, Leontius, and the shattered remains of their forces retreated to the castle Papirius in 484,[103] the philosophers were of suspect loyalty.

This is not to say, however, that Nicomedes was sent by Zeno to investigate the teachers of Alexandria solely because of their favorable outlook towards Illus. The pagan community of Aphrodisias was equally taken by Pamprepius's promises, but no commission was sent there.[104] Additionally, Zeno's circle of advisors knew which groups Illus had appealed to long before 487. As the September 484 deposition of Illus's supporter Claudio shows, Zeno did not hesitate to take immediate action against Illus's influential supporters.[105] After Il-

---

98. Haas, *Alexandria in Late Antiquity,* 329. Although the figure of thirty thousand angered monks given by Zacharias (*Chronicle* 6.2 and *Vit. Sev.* 101) is wildly exaggerated, there clearly was significant discontent in the city.

99. This idea is clear from *Vit. Is.* Ath. 115A; Z. Ep. 290. On pagan involvement in Illus's revolt, see H. Elton, "Illus and the Imperial Aristocracy Under Zeno," *Byzantion* 70 (2000): 403–4.

100. *Vit. Sev.* 40.

101. See for example *Vit. Is.* Ath. 113Q; Z. fr. 297, "The philosopher avoided [Pamprepius] as a man pursued by the Furies."

102. *Vit. Is.* Ath. 115; Z. Ep. 290. Detailed discussion of this passage is found in R. von Haehling, "Damascius und die heidnische Opposition im 5 Jahrhundert nach Christus," *Jahrbuch für Antike und Christentum* 23 (1980): 82–95.

103. For a description see *Vit. Is.* Ath. 114A; Z. Ep. 174. Illus and Leontius were finally and fully subdued in 488. See also J. Gottwald, "Die Kirche und das Schloss Paperon in Kililisch-Armenien," *Byzantinische Zeitschrift* 36 (1936): 86–100.

104. The interest of the Aphrodisian pagan community is shown in *Vit. Sev.* 40.

105. The fates of Claudio and his eight associates are described by W. H. C. Frend (*The Rise of the Monophysite Movement* [Cambridge, 1972], 188).

lus, however, the imperial court must have cast distrustful glances on men like Ammonius and Horapollon. Consequently, when Peter Mongus requested an investigation of these teachers, it is fair to assume that the government, which already saw these men as potential troublemakers, granted the request.

Although both the Alexandrian patriarch and the imperial government were interested in finding out about the activities of pagan Alexandrian teachers, the Church was directing things.[106] From the admittedly fragmentary evidence that Damascius has left, Nicomedes seems to have directed his attention towards determining how the schools were functioning.[107] At some point in his investigation, he ordered teaching to be suspended. Such a move would only be comprehensible if the investigation was motivated by concerns about the schools. In the course of this investigation, however, Nicomedes found out something incriminating about Ammonius and turned his attention in Ammonius's direction. Whatever it was that he found, it was serious[108] and the affair quickly came to involve the entire group of pagan teachers in the city.[109]

AMMONIUS'S AGREEMENT

It was at this point that Ammonius chose to make a deal. Damascius describes it in far from flattering terms. "Ammonius, who was sordidly greedy and saw everything in terms of profit of any kind, came to an agreement with the then overseer of the prevailing doctrine."[110] Although it is known only from this reference, Ammonius's deal bears further examination not only for what it tells about this investigation but also because it set the limits within which the city's teachers functioned for the next century. The first thing to consider is why Ammonius made a deal at this point. One reason is clear enough. Ammonius was a publicly funded teacher who was subject to closer official scrutiny than his colleagues.[111] Unlike his privately funded colleagues, Ammonius would have had a difficult time ignoring any teaching ban that was in place. Ammonius was apparently also in some financial trouble.[112] His mother Aedesia had died in the early part of the decade and left Ammonius

---

106. The fact that the investigation centered only on teachers and their schools suggests that this was not an attempt to punish Illus's supporters in the city. While the philosophers were prominent supporters of Illus, they would not have been his only, or most important, supporters in Alexandria.

107. This is consistent with P. Athanassiadi's idea (*Damascius*, 29) that Nicomedes was sent to look into the school of Horapollon.

108. This is hinted at by *Vit. Is.* Ath. 117A; Z. fr. 313.

109. *Vit. Is.* Ath. 117 B–C; Z. fr. 314–15 describes the expansion of the investigation.

110. Ibid., Ath. 118B; Z. Ep. 179, 292.

111. On this point, see R. Sorabji, "Divine Names and Sordid Deals in Ammonius' Alexandria," in *The Philosopher and Society in Late Antiquity*, ed. A. Smith, 203–14 (Swansea, 2005).

112. See P. Athanassiadi, *Damascius*, 30.

and his brother, Heliodorus, with substantial debts.[113] If he were prohibited from teaching, Ammonius would collect neither the civic salary nor the private tuition that permitted him to pay off these debts.

Peter Mongus too would have been ready to deal.[114] Peter was likely disappointed at the investigation's general failure to bring the city's various Christian communities together. A second run at the philosophical schools had not unified the Christian populace in the same way as the raid on the Isis shrine. Peter still had the vast majority of the Alexandrian populace supporting him—the investigation had not changed that—but Nicomedes' activities had done nothing to placate the Chalcedonian Christians or the anti-Chalcedonian radicals. Peter must have soon realized that continuing with the investigation would not change the mind of either party. At the same time, Peter could not let the investigation fizzle out without consequence. He needed at least a minor victory to save face. A compromise with Ammonius, if it was reached on Peter's terms, would give him such a victory. An agreement at this point then made sense for both Ammonius and Peter.

In determining what sort of agreement Ammonius made,[115] it is a good idea to look at whom it had to please. Peter Mongus is the obvious person. Behind him, however, was the group of concerned monks from Salomon's *koinobion*. One must then imagine that whatever agreement was made between Ammonius and Peter Mongus addressed some of their concerns about the atmosphere of the schools. If Zacharias can be taken as a representative of their views, it seems there were two main objections to the religious envi-

113. Although we are told that these debts came from Aedesia's excessive spending on charity (*Vit. Is.* Ath. 56; Z. fr. 124), Damascius's emphasis upon her charity as the source of the family's indebtedness is deliberate. It allows him to present Ammonius's "sordid greed" as the antithesis of his mother's pious generosity. Aedesia's lack of concern with money made her seem the most god-loving woman of all. By contrast, Ammonius's obsession with money proved a shameful vice.

114. R. Asmus (*Das Leben des Philosophen Isidoros* [Lepizig, 1911], 110, 169) tentatively identifies the bishop with whom Ammonius dealt as Peter's successor, Athanasius. There is no reason to make this identification and later scholars have refrained from doing so.

115. Scholars have come up with a long list of things that Ammonius agreed to do. H. D. Saffrey ("Le chrétien Jean Philopon et la survivance de l'École d' Alexandrie au VIe siècle," *Revue des Études Grecques* 67 [1954]: 396–410) proposed that Ammonius limited his teaching of Plato. However, Olympiodorus, who studied under Ammonius sometime between 517 and 526, states that he took a course on Plato's *Republic* that was taught by Ammonius and possibly one on the *Gorgias* as well (Olympiodorus, *Commentary on the Gorgias* 32.2). C. Haas (*Alexandria in Late Antiquity*, 229, 326) postulates that Ammonius made a hasty conversion. In light of Damascius's denunciation of Horapollon's conversion (on which see below), his complete silence about such an act argues quite strongly against this. P. Athanassiadi's interpretation (*Damascius*, 30–31), that Ammonius saved himself by telling Peter Mongus where to find his colleagues, is intriguing. While this could have been a part of the deal, it probably would have satisfied neither Nicomedes nor Peter Mongus, especially since they were in a position to extract much greater concessions from Ammonius.

ronment of the schools. The first centered upon the actual pagan elements contained in the teaching and, specifically, the claim that the world was eternal. The agreement seems to have had no effect upon this teaching.[116] But Zacharias also worked against more nebulous pagan religious influences in the schools. While these were more difficult to eradicate, it seems that Ammonius's agreement may have been intended to control them.[117] Consequently, the formal teaching of Orphic texts and, most significantly, the Chaldean Oracles ceased following the agreement. In Ammonius's works, one also sees no strong emphasis upon theurgy.[118] Furthermore, the subsequent flight of Damascius and Isidore to Athens and its relatively safe teaching environment also suggests that Ammonius's agreement changed the nature of acceptable teaching in the city. Both Damascius and Isidore were dedicated to an unreformed way of teaching[119] and, when they arrived in Athens, their teaching seems to have included the religious instruction of the inner-circle students that disappears from Alexandria after Ammonius's agreement.[120] In Athens, too, Damascius was able to compose theological treatises of a type not seen in Alexandria.[121] Ammonius's agreement in Alexandria, then, must have infringed upon this freedom in a way that Damascius found intolerable.

Ammonius's compact seems to have removed many of the overt religious elements from his philosophical teaching, but, more importantly, it allowed philosophical teaching to continue. This was a key concern even among the harshest Christian critics of the schools. Despite his obvious discomfort with the way teaching was done in Alexandria, even Zacharias never advocated the cessation of teaching or tried to present philosophy as irrelevant for Christians. In fact, in his works that argue against Ammonius, his arguments are framed in a logical, philosophical manner that presupposes philosophy's continued relevance.[122] This was because a philosophical education of some sort

---

116. Zacharias's dialog, *Ammonius,* shows both Ammonius's adherence to the doctrine of the eternity of the world and Zacharias's objection to this idea. On that text, see below.

117. This interpretation is based upon an argument from silence, but R. Sorabji's recent attempt ("Divine Names and Sordid Deals," 203–14) to link Ammonius's attitude towards divine names with this agreement finds possible confirming evidence. On this point, however, see R. M. van den Berg, "Smoothing Over the Differences: Proclus and Ammonius on Plato's *Cratylus* and Aristotle's *De Interpretatione,*" in *Philosophy, Science and Exegesis in Greek, Arabic and Latin Commentaries,* vol. 1, ed. P. Adamson, H. Baltussen and M. W. F. Store, 191–201 (London, 2004).

118. Theurgy is, however, valued by Ammonius's student Olympiodorus (e.g., *Commentary on the Phaedo,* 8.2.1–20).

119. *Vit. Is.* Ath. 31B; Z. Ep. 29, fr. 65. See also P. Athanassiadi, "Persecution and Response in Late Paganism," 22.

120. This was certainly the case with Damascius when he was the διάδοχος.

121. Sorabji, "Divine Names and Sordid Deals," 203–14.

122. On this see, E. Watts, "An Alexandrian Christian Response to Neoplatonic Influence," 215–30.

was still seen as an essential part of an upper-class Christian man's self-definition. The terms that Peter Mongus set out for Ammonius ensured that this education would continue to be available, albeit in a less religiously threatening manner.

AFTER THE AGREEMENT

Not long after Ammonius made his deal it seems that Nicomedes launched a second investigation into the activities of the teachers. This investigation was much more thorough than the first and served to scatter the extreme elements of the Alexandrian Iamblichan community.[123] It forced the philosopher Isidore to make a clumsy attempt to flee Alexandria by boat,[124] and a second, better planned, escape to Athens with Damascius.[125] The teacher Heraiscus fell ill and died while in hiding[126] and his brother, the philosopher Asclepiades, died not long after this.[127]

Although Horapollon had been tortured in the initial phase of the investigation, nothing is known about how Nicomedes' second set of questions affected him. Not long after this, however, he experienced some unpleasant things. Following the deaths of his uncle Heraiscus and his father, Asclepiades, Horapollon seems to have taken over as the head of their school.[128] He lived in Alexandria and, with his wife (who was also his cousin), he maintained possession of his ancestral estate in Phenebythis. In the early 490s, when Horapollon was in Alexandria, his wife came to the estate and, with her lover, ransacked the house.[129] Sometime after this, he converted to Christianity[130] "without any apparent compulsion," evidently a broken man.[131]

123. John Dillon's point that only two members of the Alexandrian philosophical community were actually arrested in the persecution is well taken. The investigators seem to have looked to change things in the school by sowing fear widely but punishing quite selectively.

124. *Vit. Is.* Ath. 119A–K; Z. Ep. 180–85, fr. 318–20.

125. The best account of this journey, especially its spiritual implications for Damascius, is found in P. Athanassiadi, *Damascius,* 32–38.

126. *Vit. Is.* Ath. 128; Z. fr. 335, 335a.

127. This is based upon J. Maspero, "Horapollon et la fin du paganisme Égyptien," *Bulletin de l'Institut français d'Archéologie Orientale* 11 (1914): 163–95. If the papyrus he discusses is datable to 491–93, as he claims, then Asclepiades must have died sometime before 493.

128. J. Maspero, "Horapollon et la fin du paganisme Égyptien," 166 line 15.

129. P. Athanassiadi ("Persecution and Response in Late Paganism," 21) suggests that Horapollon might have been in jail at the time. J. Maspero, "Horapollon et la fin du paganisme Égyptien," 167 line 29, seems to contradict that notion.

130. In a petition he filed against his wife between 491 and 493, Horapollon describes his father as a saint by using a subtle yet unmistakable pagan expression (ὁ ἐν τοῖς 'αγίοις μακαρι-ώτατος, line 15). This suggests that he was not yet a Christian when this legal action took place.

131. *Vit. Is.* Ath. 120B; Z. fr. 317. P. Athanassiadi's idea ("Persecution and Response in Late Paganism," 21) that this conversion may have been the result of the repeated stress of the persecution and his wife's adultery is as good an explanation as any.

After Nicomedes' inquisition, Ammonius then stood alone as the most prominent teacher of philosophy in Alexandria. Consequently, the nature of Alexandrian teaching was shaped by the terms of his agreement with Peter Mongus. Ammonius's compact removed some of the overt religious elements from his school, but it does not seem to have profoundly altered the doctrinal elements of his teaching. The standard philosophical curriculum around the turn of the sixth century began with a two- or three-year span in which a student studied the logic, ethics, physics, mathematics, and theology of Aristotle. The instructor led the student through this course of study one text at a time, spending approximately fifty days on each work.[132] When this cycle of study was done, the student then moved on to the study of Plato. Like their counterparts at the school in Athens, the Alexandrian Neoplatonists followed the Platonic curriculum laid out by Iamblichus. This had two cycles of instruction. The students began their Platonic training by studying a cycle of ten dialogs dealing with ethical, logical, physical, and theological subjects. Students who completed this first cycle then moved on to a second cycle of texts comprised of the "perfect" dialogs, the *Timaeus* and the *Parmenides*.[133] These were designed to provide discussions of physics and theology.

Ammonius seems to have followed this program even after the 480s.[134] It is certain that he wrote a commentary as well as a monograph on the *Phaedo*.[135] He also seems to have written on the *Gorgias*[136] and lectured on the *Theaetetus*.[137] However, while Platonic instruction continued, the formal presentation of Chaldean and Orphic texts seems to have stopped entirely.[138] This pattern of instruction corresponds to what one would expect from an instructor looking to present a non-theological rendering of Platonic philosophy. A student who progressed through such an Ammonian course of Platonic study would possess the cultural accoutrements that a

132. L. G. Westerink, *The Greek Commentaries on Plato's Phaedo*, vol. 1 (New York, 1976), 26.

133. This breakdown of the hierarchy of the dialogs depends a great deal on L. G. Westerink (*Prolégomènes à la philosophie de Platon*, lxvii–lxxiv).

134. It is generally assumed that the *Prolegomena* came from the Alexandrian school and took its final form under Olympiodorus, the successor to Ammonius's immediate successor.

135. See Olympiodorus, *In Phaedonem* 7.5 and 10.7 for the general commentary, 8.17 for the monograph.

136. Olympiodorus, *In Gorgiam* 39.2.

137. Asclepius, *In. Met.* 70.31. Ammonius is also known to have lectured on the *Republic* (Olympiodorus, *In Gorgiam* 32.2), a dialog that was considered too long for the curriculum but was generally taught in segments by professors. Neither he nor Olympiodorus is known to have dealt with the dialogs on the higher levels of the scale (see R. Jackson, K. Lycos, and H. Tarrant, *Olympiodorus' Commentary on Plato's Gorgias* [Leiden, 1998], 3).

138. This is not to say that Ammonius's students did not know of and use the Chaldean and Orphic texts. In fact, Olympiodorus's *Commentary on the Phaedo* echoes both the Oracles and the Orphic writings a number of times. There is just no evidence that Olympiodorus was formally taught these texts by Ammonius.

philosophical education brought, but would learn less about the religious elements of the full Iamblichan program. Despite the absence of practical religious instruction, supporters of the *philoponoi* still had significant problems with the unreformed doctrines that Ammonius was teaching. This is best illustrated by Zacharias Scholasticus's dialog, the *Ammonius*. The original version of the dialog was a reworking of the arguments published for an older, fully educated audience by Aeneas of Gaza in his dialog, the *Theophrastus*. In the *Ammonius*, which he composed after Ammonius's agreement, Zacharias reshaped these arguments and refashioned the main characters so that the discussions would appeal to students studying in the school of Ammonius.[139] The text itself is made up of a series of debates that Zacharias had with Ammonius in a scholastic setting.[140] These were ostensibly written to convince a Christian student of Ammonius to abandon certain philosophical doctrines about the eternity of the world,[141] but, in reality, the text is also a rough attack on Ammonius and the integrity of his school.

The first set piece in the dialog concerned the eternity of the world and the possibility of its eventual destruction. An eternal world, of course, could not be destroyed. However, the world's destruction was necessary for Christian resurrection to occur. This was also a particularly timely topic of discussion because Christians, even those with an education, were convinced by both chronological arguments and real-world disasters that the end of the world was nearing as the year 500 approached.[142] To the pagan friends,

139. On the specific reshaping, see E. Watts, "An Alexandrian Christian Response to Neoplatonic Influence," 215–30.

140. The discussion with Gessius (lines 371–925 in the text) is the product of a later revision of the text.

141. The dialog is found in *Patrologia Graeca*, 85.1011–1144, ed. J. P. Migne (Paris, 1864). The latest edition is by M. Colonna (Zacaria Scolastico, *Ammonio: Introduzione, testo critico, traduzione, commentario* [Naples, 1973]). Despite P. Merlan's claims to the contrary ("Ammonius Hermeiae, Zacharias Scholasticus and Boethius," *Greek, Roman and Byzantine Studies* 9 [1968]: 193–203), this dialog seems to be more a series of set pieces than an accurate historical account of exchanges between the protagonists. For more on the *Ammonius* and its relationship to Aeneas of Gaza's *Theophrastus*, see E. Watts, "An Alexandrian Christian Response to Neoplatonic Influence," 215–30. For the philosophical issues surrounding ancient debates about the world's eternity, see R. Sorabji, *Time, Creation, and the Continuum: Theories in Antiquity and the Early Middle Ages* (Ithaca, 1983), 193 ff.

142. On this fear, see Averil Cameron, "Remaking the Past," in *Late Antiquity: A Guide to the Postclassical World*, ed. G. Bowersock et al. (Cambridge, Mass., 1999), 12–13; and, more specifically, P. Magdalino, "The History of the Future and Its Uses: Prophecy, Policy, and Propaganda," in *The Making of Byzantine History: Studies Dedicated to Donald M. Nicol*, ed. R. Beaton and C. Roueché, 3–34 (Aldershot, 1993). The mentality of the time is captured quite vividly by M. Meier, *Das andere Zeitalter Justinians. Kontingenzerfahrung und Kontingenzbewältigung im 6. Jht. N. Chr.*, Hypomnemata 147 (Göttingen, 2003), 16–21. From the third century forward, a number of Christian writers had promoted the idea that the created world would last for six

classmates, and teachers of such men, these ideas must have seemed absurd, but the depth of conviction about the impending end of the cosmos apparently compelled Zacharias to demonstrate how philosophical scorn for belief in the eventual destruction of the world was misguided.

This fictionalized demonstration was set during a lecture given by Ammonius. In his talk, Ammonius had asserted that it is not good to dissolve something as perfect as the universe. When he said this, a Christian student (obviously intended to represent Zacharias) jumped in and began a systematic disproof of this point. At the end of an exchange that rebutted Neoplatonic doctrines and affirmed Christian positions with allusions to philosophers and quotations from the Bible, the class was dismissed. When the students filed out, the Christian narrator noted, "Many of those present in the class at that time . . . were placed among us and leaned towards our arguments, or more correctly, they leaned towards Christianity out of faith and love of truth."[143]

Another exchange, also between Zacharias and Ammonius, centered upon a second major point of contention—the fundamental agreement of Plato and Aristotle. This arose in the context of a lecture on Aristotle's *Ethics* and, during the lecture, Ammonius presumably made a statement to the effect that the writings of Plato and Aristotle do not contradict one another.[144] This point was a mainstay of Ammonius's teaching and Zacharias met it with the objection that Aristotle clearly does not accept Plato's theory of ideas. Eventually, the discussion came back to objections about the eternity of the cosmos before Ammonius cut it short and dismissed the class.

Zacharias's text, which was written in the 490s and revised in the 510s or 520s, seems to reveal the bitterness that the *philoponoi* felt towards Ammonius and his teaching. This becomes clear from the very beginning of the dialog. In the opening exchange, Ammonius is described as an Athenian teacher who has come to Alexandria and teaches in such a way that he brings the ideas of many teachers into harmony.[145] To this polite description, however, Zacharias adds that Ammonius is unwise, unphilosophical, and arrogant. Elsewhere he is characterized as "one who sits in a high chair in a very

---

thousand years, and had marked dates around 500 A.D. as the moment at which the world would end. Meier suggests that the political crises in the western Roman empire also lent credence to this view. On this later point, it is worth noting the remarks of John Rufus, *Plerophories*, 89.

143. *Ammonius*, lines 357–60.

144. For a discussion of how the basic agreement between Plato and Aristotle helped to shape Ammonius's work, see R. M. van den Berg, "Smoothing Over the Differences: Proclus and Ammonius on Plato's *Cratylus* and Aristotle's *De Interpretatione*," 191–201.

145. *Amm.* 19–24. The harsh nature of the description can be seen when one compares it to the polite descriptions of the fictional philosopher, Theophrastus, in Aeneas's *Theophrastus* (e.g., *Th.* 3.15 ff., *Th.* 9.4–10).

sophistical and pompous manner."[146] The pejorative power of this remark (which is, in fact, a quotation from one of Themistius's anti-sophistic orations) was as obvious to Zacharias's readers as it is to us.[147] Furthermore, as each of the exchanges reaches an end, Zacharias carefully records the silence and obvious embarrassment of Ammonius. This suggests that the text was intended both as a refutation of Ammonius's doctrines and as an attack on his personal prestige. The hope, which was probably fleeting, was that this philosophical refutation, when combined with a personal attack, would sway Christian opinion away from the problematic elements of Ammonius's teaching that Peter Mongus's arrangement had not addressed.

Ammonius's own efforts to present philosophy in a non-theological manner, however, seem to have ensured that Zacharias's concern about topics like the eternity of the world did not lead to any actions against the philosopher. These efforts are probably best seen in the later part of Ammonius's career. Ammonius died sometime after 517. Around 525, Olympiodorus, Ammonius's student and the future head of Ammonius's school, produced a commentary on Plato's *Gorgias* that seems to have been reliant upon the teachings of Ammonius. Though called a commentary, the text is actually a collection of lecture notes taken from a course Olympiodorus taught. Working primarily from the contents of this collection, H. Tarrant has put forth a novel interpretation of Olympiodorus's pedagogical interests. In his view, Olympiodorus was interested in ensuring that a proper knowledge of the Greek past was presented to his students.[148] Consequently, the commentary is filled with famous names from classical Greece and time is taken to explain the stories behind these names.[149] The goal of this seems to be the promotion of a greater awareness of Greek heritage and the figures involved in shaping it.[150] As was the case with the initial commentaries of Hermeias and Proclus, Olympiodorus's *Gorgias* commentary, datable to the earliest stages of his professional life, probably shared much in thought and approach with Ammonius's teaching on the dialog. This makes one suspect that Olympiodorus's interest in the deeds of figures of the Greek past was Ammonian in origin, a suspicion perhaps confirmed by his citation of Ammonius two times during an explanation of the correct way to understand a myth about Theseus.[151]

This suggests that Ammonius adapted to the new niche into which his

---

146. *Amm.* 99.

147. The reference is to Themistius, *Or.* 21, 243b.

148. H. Tarrant, "Olympiodorus and the Surrender of Paganism," *Byzantinische Forschungen* 24 (1997): 181–92.

149. *In Gorgiam*, 44.3–7 for Theseus; 7.3 and 33.2 for Pericles; 44.1–3 for Lycurgus; 33.2 for Themistocles.

150. Tarrant, "Olympiodorus and the Surrender of Paganism," 182–83.

151. *In Gorgiam*, 44.4, 6. See R. Jackson et al., *Olympiodorus' Commentary on Plato's Gorgias*, 282 n. 848, on this passage.

agreement with Peter Mongus had placed him by teaching in a way that communicated the cultural context of Neoplatonic philosophy to the upper-class youth, both pagan and Christian, who came to Alexandria to study. As had been the case for centuries, philosophy remained an integral part of a young man's cultural education. Ammonius apparently recognized the role his classes could play and sought to emphasize the cultural component of his lessons even more.

Despite this new emphasis, nothing seems to have deterred even the most ambitious students from studying under Ammonius.[152] Among his students were the pagans Olympiodorus, Asclepius, Eutocius, and Simplicius, as well as the Christian John Philoponus. Indeed, it is not surprising that the appeal of Ammonius's teaching extended across religious divides. His agreement with Peter Mongus had made his teaching far more religiously neutral.

The beginning of the fifth century was not a bright time for Alexandrian intellectuals. After the death of Hypatia, the quality of Alexandrian philosophical teaching declined precipitously and a number of the city's best students went to Athens to study. When high-level Alexandrian philosophical teaching finally reemerged, it had been given a different, Iamblichan, flavor by the students who had returned from the Athenian school. This ideological movement gained additional force when the Alexandrian Syrianus was scholarch in Athens. Using his connections in Alexandria, Syrianus induced a number of school-age Alexandrians to make the trip to Athens. This continued when Proclus was at the school's helm. This flow of young students meant that, by the 470s, the intellectual climate among Alexandria's philosophers quite closely resembled that of their Athenian counterparts. This produced an environment that presented paganism in a very positive light and encouraged religious experimentation by some of the Christian students.

Although the ecclesiastical hierarchy ignored this situation for much of the century, some members of the Christian community did respond to it. Working in tandem with a group of student *philoponoi*, the monks of Salomon's *koinobion* at Enaton sought to strengthen the faith of the Christian students in these schools. In this, they drew upon the older model of the Christian study circle. Using textual and oral arguments, men like Zacharias Scholasticus and Stephen the monk attacked the teaching, gossip, and religious influences that combined to make the scholastic environment so hazardous for students. They did not, however, seek to overturn the cultural foundations upon which the study of philosophy rested. Instead, they sought to

152. The limitations may, however, help explain why Simplicius left Alexandria to continue his studies under Damascius in Athens.

show how objectionable teachings were themselves inconsistent with the general tenets of the discipline.

When the volatile religious mixture in the schools exploded in the 480s, the monks of Enaton and the *philoponoi* were given a chance to bring about change. Working alongside the patriarch, they destroyed one of the major shrines still used by the intellectual pagans, harried the most dogmatic teachers into exile, and forced a compromise upon the most prominent teacher who remained. These efforts stopped the drift towards Athenian-style religious education that had occurred in the schools of the 460s and 470s. By the end of the century, the overt pagan religiosity of the schools was a thing of the past. Despite the restrictions, philosophy still represented an essential part of the cultural arsenal of the upper class. Now, however, young men could arm themselves without danger.

Chapter 9

The Coming Revolution

The later years of Ammonius's career were ones of peaceful coexistence with the Christian church and its hierarchy. With his teaching controlled by an agreement with Peter Mongus, the church left him alone. A remarkably quiet period in the Alexandrian church also helped Ammonius's position. During this time, the official Christian doctrine in the city was based upon an anti-Chalcedonian understanding of the meaning of the emperor Zeno's vague *Henotikon*. Since both Chalcedonian and anti-Chalcedonian denominations could accept the document, Alexandria remained in communion with the rest of the empire. This situation made it difficult for dissent to take root. As a result, no major doctrinal disagreement troubled the city from the death of Peter Mongus until the late 510s. This was good for everyone in the city, but especially so for pagan teachers of philosophy like Ammonius. Under less political pressure, the patriarch was less likely to be concerned with pagan teachers.

Despite the calm in the church, the campaign by the *philoponoi* to Christianize the teaching of philosophy in the city continued throughout the period, though without much success. Zacharias Scholasticus published two texts in the 510s and 520s that were directed to an audience of Christian students in Alexandria's schools. These were a revision of his dialog, *Ammonius,* and an original composition—the *Life of Severus.*[1] Both were set in the

1. The revised version of the *Ammonius* included a discussion with the pagan iatrosophist Gessius, a fellow student of Zacharias. Because of his youth at the time, he was not an important figure in the 480s and 490s. By the early sixth century, however, he was recognized as one of the most important physicians in the eastern empire (cf. Sophronius, *On the Miracles of St. Cyrus and St. John,* 30 = *Patrologia Graeca,* 87.3, 3514–20, ed. J. P. Migne [Paris, 1865]). Consequently a literary attack on Gessius makes much more sense in the 510s than it would have in the 490s.

480s and presented Zacharias and his fellow *philoponoi* to a younger audience. These texts also show that, despite the changed climate in the city's schools, the goals of the *philoponoi* had remained the same. They still aimed to attack the traditional Neoplatonic doctrine of the eternity of the world and the teachers who presented it. In its place, they looked to establish a set of teachings that affirmed the created nature of the world and Christian teachings about its eventual destruction. These goals were joined to an equally strong desire to keep students reading the more accomplished Christian authors of late antiquity. Texts like these reinforced the *philoponoi* literary program, but, in the end, the texts did not have any great impact upon intellectual debate within the city. With his agreement of the late 480s, Ammonius had created a situation in which pagan teaching could not only survive, but could do so comfortably. As long as Ammonius was at the head of his school, the agreement with Peter Mongus and his status as an experienced teacher of philosophy would allow this to continue.

PHILOSOPHICAL TEACHING AFTER AMMONIUS

The stability of the early sixth century was threatened by Ammonius's death, which occurred sometime after 517.[2] It was not a shock. Indeed, it is probable that, like the two long-lived Athenian scholarchs, Plutarch and Proclus, he had already designated his successor and turned most of his school's administrative responsibilities over to this man in the last years of his life. By doing this, the old scholarch would have made his intentions for succession quite clear and ensured that, after his death, there would be no struggle over who would succeed him. The information on this matter is scanty, but it appears that, upon Ammonius's death, control of his school passed on to a mathematician named Eutocius.[3]

On the surface, Eutocius seems a curious choice. He did not write any surviving philosophical works; only a few astronomical works from his pen

2. The *terminus post quem* is based upon Ammonius's prominence in John Philoponus's *Commentary on the Physics* (a work dated internally to 517). This prominence has been thought by many to indicate that Ammonius was still alive when the text was written. K. Verrycken ("The Development of Philoponus' thought and its chronology," in *Aristotle Transformed*, ed. R. Sorabji, 233–74 [London, 1990]) doubts that the publication of John's commentary must mean that Ammonius was still alive and teaching in 517. It is known, however, that Olympiodorus took courses in Plato with Ammonius. It is generally thought that Olympiodorus was born around 495 and, if one assumes that he progressed through the Neoplatonic curriculum at Proclan speed (no mean feat), he would still not have been prepared to study Plato under Ammonius until he was twenty-two. If we assume Olympiodorus followed a slightly less accelerated program, he likely read under Ammonius around 520.

3. L. G. Westerink, *Prolégomènes à la philosophie de Platon* (Paris, 1990), xvi. It is possible that Eutocius took over Ammonius's publicly funded chair as well, if indeed the chair was still being funded.

survive. But one of these, a commentary on a bit of Archimedes, is dedicated to Ammonius in a way that suggests Eutocius was Ammonius's student.[4] Consequently, it is probably best to understand Eutocius's succession to Ammonius's chair as something like Marinus's appointment to head Proclus's school. Both Marinus and Eutocius were known primarily as mathematicians and astronomers. Although neither mathematician specialized in pure philosophy, Marinus and Eutocius each had extensive training in the field and both men are known to have taught philosophy classes.[5]

In the end, Ammonius's careful planning for his succession had little practical effect. Eutocius died soon after taking over (possibly as early as 525) and left an unexpected vacancy at the top of the school.[6] The apparent suddenness of Eutocius's death prevented him from grooming a successor. Consequently, no established philosopher was prepared to occupy the chair and the young, inexperienced philosopher Olympiodorus succeeded Eutocius.

The sources indicating that this change took place are philosophical commentaries and, as a result, the date of this event is not entirely clear. It seems, however, that Olympiodorus took over the school sometime in the mid-520s. The best evidence for this comes from his *Commentary on the Gorgias*. There are clear traits that mark this as a work completed early in Olympiodorus's career, possibly as early as 525.[7] Most telling is the text's heavy reliance upon the teachings of Ammonius. This is consistent with the way a philosopher wrote his first commentary and stands in stark contrast to the Damascian influence seen in Olympiodorus's later Platonic commentaries.[8]

Despite its early date, the *Gorgias* commentary demonstrates Olympiodorus's personal concern with presenting a philosophical justification for the collection of school fees. This was a difficult subject for teachers of philosophy to bring up in the fifth and sixth centuries. As opposed to a teacher of rhetoric, the teacher of Platonic philosophy considered it beneath his dignity to charge a set fee for his classes.[9] Nevertheless, Olympiodorus and his contemporaries expected payment for their services. He says, "as the philoso-

4. O. Neugebauer, *A History of Ancient Mathematical Astronomy* (New York, 1975), 1042. For the commentary, see the new edition of R. Netz, *The Works of Archimedes. Translated into English, together with Eutocius' Commentary and critical edition of the diagrams*, vol. 1 (Cambridge, 2004).

5. The *Life of Proclus* suggests that Marinus read through the entire Aristotelian and Platonic curriculum and took classes in the Chaldean writings. With the exception of the Chaldean training, there is no reason to think that Eutocius's philosophical background was any different.

6. For this dating see R. Jackson, K. Lycos, and H. Tarrant, *Olympiodorus' Commentary on Plato's Gorgias* (Leiden, 1998), 3; and K. Verrycken, "The Development of Philoponus' thought," 261–63. The evidence makes no mention of Eutocius after this date. Though no source mentions his fate, it seems that Eutocius's disappearance from the sources is due to his death.

7. L. G. Westerink, *Prolégomènes à la philosophie de Platon*, xxi.

8. Ibid.

9. See here Olympiodorus, *In Alc.* 140.15–21.

pher proclaims that his task is to make good men, he hopes in this way not to be treated unfairly by them."[10] This is a gentle hint that students who had learned from a philosopher's teaching were to show their gratitude by voluntarily giving him gifts and paying sums of money.

This hint appeared in Olympiodorus's *Commentary on the First Alcibiades,* a work written in the 560s, nearly four decades after his *Gorgias* commentary. In that time, Olympiodorus had not become any less concerned with collecting student fees. He had, however, become much more subtle in his appeals for money. The *Gorgias* commentary lacks this subtlety. In it, Olympiodorus's appeals were much more frequent and less well disguised. Most of them centered upon the unique idea that Socrates accepted money for teaching.[11] The most blatant appeal, however, comes near the end of the work. In his forty-third lecture, Olympiodorus states: "Students who understand that they are being benefited do not have to hear their teachers telling them to bring fees. They rush on their own to care for their teachers and display their gratitude."[12] This great interest in the collection of fees is something that one would expect only from a man who headed a school and was forced to worry about its finances. The prominence of the theme in the *Gorgias* commentary, then, suggests that the text was published after Olympiodorus had taken over formal control of Ammonius's school.

The *Gorgias* commentary also gives the best glimpse into what the teaching in Olympiodorus's school was like. From all indications Olympiodorus's early program was designed to be religiously neutral. It has been discussed above how he seems to have mixed cultural topics into his lectures on Plato.[13] Olympiodorus was also careful not to challenge Christian religious teachings. Instead, the *Gorgias* commentary shows him making a number of deliberate efforts to stress general similarities between pagan and Christian theology.[14] So, in a discussion about the origins of the arrangement of the material world, he states: "You should not superficially understand doctrines presented in mythological terms. We ourselves also know well that God is the one initial cause [of the arrangement of the material world], for there are not many initial causes."[15] Christians, then, were not to get the impression that Olympiodorus or other pagans had a fundamental disagreement with their creation theology.

Later in the course of lectures on the *Gorgias,* Olympiodorus goes on to describe how the pagan gods like Zeus or Kronos fit into this theology. He

10. Ibid., 140.22.

11. This first appears in 40.7 and is echoed in 43.5. To my knowledge, this teaching about Socrates is not repeated by any other thinker.

12. *In Gorgiam* 43.2.

13. On this, see chapter 8.

14. L. G. Westerink, *Prolégomènes à la philosophie de Platon,* xxii–xxvi.

15. *In Gorgiam* 4.3.

says that they lie beneath the one God but above humans. It is they who are responsible for the creation of the lower world.[16] Nevertheless, Olympiodorus cautions that one ought not mock the names of these lower gods. Instead, he says, one must realize that the names of the gods indicate their creative function or otherwise represent attributes of the one God.[17] For example, he explains: "they speak of life by using the name *Zēn* (Life) as well as Zeus because it is through himself that Zeus gives life."[18] Olympiodorus then explains the pagan divine system in terms that Christians can understand while making clear that it also performs many of the same functions as the Christian God.[19]

Olympiodorus also defends pagan ideas against Christian criticism that they are ridiculous. In so doing, however, his defense merely explains the specific differences between the Christian and pagan understandings of divine powers and urges his students not to be alarmed by these distinctions.[20] He hoped to teach them to respect the system to which he adhered, but he was careful not to cause offense. This should not, however, be confused with doctrinal flexibility. On the doctrine of the eternity of the cosmos, which so concerned the scholastic *philoponoi*, Olympiodorus was firm. Like Ammonius, he unflinchingly affirmed the eternity of matter and said that there is no way the world can be destructible.[21] Olympiodorus also denied the doctrine of the eternal punishment of wrongdoers, another idea that the *philoponoi* advocated.[22] He wrote: "Indeed, we are not punished forever . . . if a soul is punished forever and never enjoys the good, it is forever in a state of vice . . . For, if a punishment brings us no benefit and does not lead us towards what is better, it is imposed in vain and neither god nor nature does anything in vain."[23] Both of these doctrines are consistent with the teachings of Olympiodorus's predecessors, and each one presented a very real challenge to Christian teaching.[24]

The accession of Olympiodorus must have seemed like an excellent time for the *philoponoi* and their monastic supporters to move to change this teaching. The new scholarch was a young man who lacked the connections of Am-

16. Ibid., 47.2.

17. G. Verbeke, "Some later Neoplatonic Views on Divine Creation and the Eternity of the World," in *Neoplatonism and Christian Thought*, ed. D. O'Meara (Albany, 1982), 46.

18. *In Gorgiam* 47.4. This is one of a number of similar statements in the passage.

19. Among other things, Olympiodorus says that the pagan divine system can give life, heal, and organize the matter of the physical world just like the Christian God (*In Gorgiam* 47.2).

20. See L. G. Westerink, *Prolégomènes à la philosophie de Platon*, xxv.

21. *In Gorgiam* 11.2. Olympiodorus's doctrines about the eternity of the world are laid out more fully in his *Meteorology* commentary, a later work.

22. E.g., Zacharias, *Ammonius* 1487–95.

23. *In Gorgiam* 50.2.

24. The first doctrine's problems for Christians have been discussed above. For the second doctrine in Christian thought see Zacharias, *Ammonius* 1487–95, and Aeneas, *Theophrastus* 61.5.

monius. Furthermore, whereas the protection of Ammonius's teaching had been defined by his agreement with Peter Mongus, the applicability of this agreement to Olympiodorus was unclear. There was a definite possibility that the young teacher could be forced to agree to even more stringent restrictions. In addition, when a relatively inexperienced man like Olympiodorus took over a prominent position like this, dissension often arose within the school. Taken together, these factors would have given the school's Christian opponents an opportunity to act.

CHRISTIAN OPPOSITION TO OLYMPIODORUS

The person who led the Christian challenge was John Philoponus, Ammonius's former editor. John was born around the year 490, probably in Alexandria.[25] Apparently raised as a Christian, he was trained in grammar and rhetoric before arriving at Ammonius's school around the year 510.[26] Not long after this, it appears that John began creating commentaries based upon the material presented at Ammonius's school. Although it has been speculated that John was doing this as some sort of an editor of Ammonius's lectures, it is more likely that, at first, this work was done on his own initiative. In fact, his commentary on Nicomachus's *Introductio Arithmetica* was not even based upon teachings he himself heard Ammonius give. Instead, John's commentary was a third-hand account of these doctrines based upon an earlier commentary written by Ammonius's student Asclepius.[27] Nevertheless, it seems that John's diligence was rewarded. He soon became the main publisher of Ammonius's teachings on various Aristotelian texts and, from 510 to 517, he recorded Ammonius's teachings in commentaries on Aristotle's *De Anima, De Generatione et Corruptione, Categories,* and *Physics.*[28]

25. H. D. Saffrey, "Le chrétien Jean Philopon et la survivance de l'École d'Alexandrie au VIe siècle," *Revue des Études Grecques* 67 (1954): 403. John lived until at least 574, so this date is about as early as one would wish to establish.

26. Saffrey, "Le chrétien Jean Philopon," 403; Verrycken, "The Development of Philoponus' thought," 238. This is despite Simplicius's statement that Philoponus was a late learner in philosophy (*in Cael.* 159.3; 159.7; *in Phys.* 1133.10). Simplicius is rarely anything but polemical in his discussions of Philoponus, and this statement fits the mold. K. Verrycken's suggestion that Simplicius is referring to Philoponus's initial training in philology discounts the fact that all philosophers of this period had philological training before beginning philosophical study. If he were twenty when he entered Ammonius's school, Philoponus would not have spent an inordinate amount of time on this training.

27. L. G. Westerink, "Deux commentaires sur Nicomaque: Asclépius et Jean Philopon," *Revue des Études Grecques* 77 (1964): 530; L. Tarán, *Asclepius of Tralles, Commentary to Nicomachus' Introduction to Arithmetic,* Transactions of the American Philosophical Society, n.s., 59 (Philadelphia, 1969), 10–13.

28. This dating is based upon R. Sorabji, "John Philoponus," in *Philoponus and the Rejection of Aristotelian Science,* ed. R. Sorabji, 1–40 (London, 1987). The conclusions of K. Verrycken

When initially completed, John's early works seem to have reflected the teachings of Ammonius. He acknowledges adding his own reflections to those of his teacher, but the philosophical system laid out in these commentaries appears consistent with Ammonian teachings; it was based upon the idea that there was a hierarchy of substances that descended from the One (a figure so pure as to be considered outside existence).[29] All the members of the system itself were eternal. That is to say, they had no beginning in time and would have no end. Atop this hierarchy rested not a personal God but a distant and unmoving figure.

While, broadly speaking, this system seems Ammonian, John's personal additions to these works are also of interest. In the *Physics* commentary, for example, John introduces arguments that challenge the teachings of Ammonius on the eternity of the world.[30] The significance of these additions is debated, as is the question of whether they represent a later revision of the commentary, but these anti-eternalist arguments do raise the possibility that John may have begun to express some dissenting views while his affiliation with the school continued.[31]

Whether or not his thinking had diverged from that of his teacher in the 510s, at some point in the 520s, John broke decisively with the school and began aggressively and programmatically attacking the eternal world doctrines that his teacher had previously espoused.[32] Like Zacharias, who was influenced by the *philoponoi*, John's attack was designed to refute the important doctrines

---

("The Development of Philoponus' thought," 244–58) are also taken into account. The only commentary from this period that has a date is his *Physics* commentary. John states that it was finished on May 10, 517 (*in Phys.* 703.16). The interpretative difficulties that this date presents are discussed below.

29. John Philoponus, *in Cat.* 49.23–51.21. This is parallel to Ammonius, *in Cat.* 35.18–36.4. See also John Philoponus, *in de Intell.* 22.21–25. This system is clearly and ably explained by K. Verrycken, "The Development of Philoponus' thought," 233–74. For John's own reflections, see *De Gen. et Cor.* 1.1–4.

30. *in Phys.* 54.8–55.26; 191.9–192.2; 428.23–430.10; 456.17–458.31; 467.1–468.4; 762.2–9.

31. Verrycken, "The Development of Philoponus' Thought," 248–49, sees these differences as indications of a later revision of the commentary and points to other passages in the *Physics* commentary that affirm the eternity of the world. A comprehensive criticism of Verrycken's argument is framed by C. Scholten, *Antike Naturphilosophie und christliche Kosmologie in der Schrift "De opificio mundi" des Johannes Philoponos* (Berlin, 1996), 118–43. Particularly important is his recognition that many of the eternity-affirming passages of the *in Phys.* are framed as discussions of Aristotle's own views. On this, see as well U. M. Lang, *John Philoponus and the Controversies over Chalcedon in the Sixth Century: A Study and Translation of the Arbiter* (Louvain, 2001), 8–10. As is discussed below, it seems difficult to deny that there was some sort of revision of the *Physics* commentary. It is less clear how this revision affected John's presentation of his views on the eternity of the world.

32. Just as his initial involvement in the school need not suggest that his faith "was superseded by Neoplatonism" (Verrycken, "The Development of Philoponus' Thought," 240), John's

that argued for the eternity of the world.[33] John, however, was much more learned than Zacharias. Zacharias was a rhetorician and the dialog that he composed (the *Ammonius*) was obviously fictitious. As such, more serious students of philosophy could have disregarded it. John, however, was well steeped in philosophy and knew the most potent philosophical arguments for the eternity of the cosmos. He was also talented enough to compose original philosophical works that refuted them. His initial efforts were published in a series of three texts. The first two of these were long, polemical refutations of the main arguments for the eternity of the cosmos. The first text (the *De aeternitate mundi contra Proclum*) was directed against a treatise written by Proclus that criticized the Christian doctrine of the creation of the world.[34] In *De aeternitate,* John promises a second text, the *Contra Aristotelem,* aimed to refute Aristotle,[35] and a third non-polemical work that apparently aimed to prove the Christian doctrines of creation, destruction of the world, and resurrection.[36] Altogether, these three works were designed to provide definitive philosophical proof of Christian cosmology. Even if John had expressed some of these ideas previously, the size and scope of this program represents a dramatic break from the scholastic tradition of Proclus and Ammonius, John's philosophical father and grandfather.[37] This clearly marks a new stage in his career.

The completion of the *De aeternitate* occurred sometime in late 529[38] and,

---

decision to turn clearly and aggressively against arguments for the eternity of the world need not represent a religious conversion.

33. In keeping with the *philoponoi* interest in the eschatological significance of the doctrine, John eventually went so far as to put forth the idea that the days of the world were symbolically numbered. On this, see W. Wolska, *La Topographie Chrétienne de Cosmas Indicopleustès* (Paris, 1962), 183 ff.

34. Proclus's original work is lost. An Arabic translation of the text by Ishaq b. Hunayn does exist. For this see A. Badawi, *Neoplatonici apud Arabes,* Islamica 19 (Cairo, 1955), 34–42. On this work see now H. S. Lang and A. D. Macro, ed. and trans., *Proclus: On the Eternity of the World (De aeternitate mundi)* (Berkeley and Los Angeles, 2001).

35. In the *De aeternitate mundi contra Proclum,* the first text in the series, John mentions a couple of times that certain Aristotelian arguments will be referred to in a later text devoted to refuting Aristotle (*De aet.* 258.22–26; 399.20–400.3).

36. This is promised in *De aet.* 259.3–5. For the order of these texts see K. Verrycken, "The Development of Philoponus' thought," 249–52.

37. It has been argued by Lang and Macro (*On the Eternity of the World,* 9–12) that the shifts in Philoponus's ideas reflect his natural philosophical development. In assessing the significance of John's literary program, it should not be ignored that early-sixth-century Alexandrian Christians had come to associate the doctrine of the eternity of the world with John's teacher, Ammonius. These texts represented John's conscious distancing of himself from Ammonius, an act perhaps made more potent by John's decision to attack the ideas of Ammonius's own teacher, Proclus, in the first of these works.

38. *De aet.* 579.14–17.

in its attack on Proclus's ideas, John's work showed both a nuanced understanding of high-level philosophy and an intellectual creativity that made its
arguments quite compelling. John made use of a number of powerful and,
to an extent, original arguments for the world's eternity.[39] In one case, he
pointed out that an eternal world would exist for an infinite number of
years.[40] This objection was problematic for advocates of the world's eternity
because philosophers, from Aristotle on, had held that there could not be
more than a finite quantity of things in the world.[41] The infinite lifetime of
the world presented them with an unsolvable paradox: how could one make
a finite time out of an infinite number of years?[42] In addition, John rejected
Aristotle's fifth element by using an argument based upon Plato.[43] He also
denied the possibility of eternal matter,[44] and asserted that the world came
into being from nothing.[45] All of these were provocative positions that attacked some of the central points supporting the argument for the eternity
of the world. This showed both John's awareness of the eternalist arguments
and his understanding of their weaknesses.

The originality of John's work is balanced by the remarkable similarity of
some of the less elevated portions of his work to the earlier composition of
Zacharias Scholasticus. The more mundane of these similarities involved
quoting the same passages of Basil's *Hexameron*, Homer's *Iliad,* and Plato's
Timaeus.[46] These passages are of little consequence in a work of this size. More
important, however, is the specific argument that God creates and destroys
the world not out of necessity (as pagans asserted) but from his inherent
goodness and of his own free will. Not only is this argument present in both
texts, but each also cites the same passage of Plato in support.[47] Although

39. The originality of his arguments is debated. A. Gudeman and W. Kroll, "Ioannes (No.
21, Ioannes Philoponus)" in *RE* 9.2, ed. G. Wissowa and W. Kroll, cols. 1764–95, deny John
any credit for their content. However, R. Sorabji ("John Philoponus," 6) has no doubt about
Philoponus's originality, despite the strong influence of thinkers such as Alexander of Aphrodisias upon his work. Nevertheless, in *de Aet.* his argument against Aristotle's fifth element bears
similarity to Xenarchus's objection to this point (see Simplicius, *in Cael.* 25.23; 42.20).

40. *De aet.* 9–11; 619.

41. Simplicius, who represented the old view, has a tentative refutation of this *in Phys.*
1179.12–26. This topic is discussed by R. Sorabji ("John Philoponus," 6, 164–79).

42. The natural response a Neoplatonist would offer to this is that the world was eternal
but time was not. The world then existed initially outside of time.

43. *De aet.* 491.12–493.5; 517.7–519.20.

44. Ibid., 458.5–7; 469.5–10.

45. Ibid., 338.21–344.26.

46. For *Hexameron* 1.3, see Zacharias, *Ammonius* 204–5; *De aet.* 158.19, 170.15. For *Iliad*
2.204–5, see *Amm.* 319–21; *De aet.* 88.19, 179.21. For *Timaeus* 31b, see *Amm.* 434; *De aet.* 18.2,
512.27.

47. The argument is emphasized in both texts as well as in Aeneas of Gaza's *Theophrastus*
and Theodoret's *Cure of Hellenic Maladies.* Each draws upon *Timaeus* 29d for support. See
Theodoret 4.33; Aeneas 44.24, 49.7; Zacharias 426–28; *De aet.* 109.2, 134.2–25, 224.25.

this was an important argument in the pagan-Christian debates about creation, John's specific use of it suggests that he was familiar with the arguments being circulated by the *philoponoi*.

The connection with the writings of the *philoponoi* becomes stronger when one also takes into account the second text in John's literary program, the *Contra Aristotelem*. Unlike the *De aeternitate*, which survives almost intact, the *Contra Aristotelem* is preserved only in fragments. The vast majority of these come from the first six books of John's work and nearly all are preserved by Simplicius. From these it is apparent that the first five books of this work were devoted to a refutation of Aristotle's teaching about ether, while the sixth was a refutation of the eternity of movement. The structure of the individual books also becomes clear. Each contained a discussion of Aristotle's doctrines and a response that demonstrated the error of his ideas about the eternity of the world.[48]

Based upon the Simplician fragments, it was thought for many years that John's work was only six books long and that his argument ended up in roughly the same place as it had in the *De aeternitate*. Simplicius, however, hints that he only summarized a part of John's work. He mentions that, later in the text, John "declares that this world changes into another world which is more divine—a proposition he elaborates in the following books."[49] Simplicius's cryptic statement about the later sections of the *Contra Aristotelem* is clarified by a reference to the contents of book eight of the work in a Syriac manuscript. The Syrian author summarized the second chapter of the eighth book with the statement "the world will not be resolved into non-being, for the words of God are not resolved into it either; for we clearly speak of new heavens and a new earth."[50] This means that John was not only dismantling a set of pagan arguments for the eternity of the cosmos in the *Contra Aristotelem*. He was also attempting to prove the Christian view of the eventual destruction and resurrection of the world, an idea that is similar to one of the ideas Zacharias tried to prove in *Ammonius*.[51]

John also structured the *Contra Aristotelem* in a manner similar to this earlier *philoponoi* text. Like the *Ammonius*, it began by refuting the doctrine of

48. A good discussion of the ideas in the *Contra Aristotle* is that of C. Wildberg, "Prolegomena to the Study of Philoponus' *Contra Aristotelem*," in *Philoponus and the Rejection of Aristotelian Science*, ed. R. Sorabji, 197–209 (London, 1987). The text itself has been translated by C. Wildberg (Philoponus, *Against Aristotle on the Eternity of the World* [Ithaca, 1987]).

49. Simplicius, *in Phys.* 1177.38–1178.5 (trans. C. Wildberg).

50. The seventh-century manuscript is in the British Museum Library and is Add. 17 214. This text is discussed in C. Wildberg, "Prolegomena to the Study of Philoponus' *Contra Aristotelem*," 198–200. The translation above is from his article.

51. Zacharias does not discuss a more divine world following the dissolution of this one, but he does discuss the resurrection of the dead and the recomposition of their bodies (*Ammonius* 1421 ff.).

the eternity of the world and then proceeded to argue in favor of the Christian doctrines of the creation and eventual dissolution of this world.[52] This structure becomes even more significant when one considers the place of the *Contra Aristotelem* in John's philosophical program. It was the middle of his three texts and, as such, marked the program's transition from a denunciation of eternalist arguments to an affirmation of Christian-influenced creationist ideas. With his polemical aims accomplished by the *De aeternitate* and books one through six of the *Contra Aristotelem*, John seems to have devoted the second half of the work and the entirety of the non-polemical work to explaining the doctrines that his program advocated. Considered in this way, it becomes clear that the overall aim of this sequence of texts was to demolish the philosophical arguments for the world's eternity, and then provide a philosophical proof for the Christian doctrines concerning the creation, destruction, and eventual remaking of the world.[53] This was an aim very much in keeping with the ideas of the scholastic *philoponoi*.

The most obvious link between John Philoponus and the *philoponoi* is, however, his sobriquet.[54] Although the significance of his nickname, Philoponus, has been debated for nearly a century, there is still no agreement about whether it proves John's affiliation with the group.[55] One cannot dispute that, while the name suggests this affiliation, it proves nothing by itself. It seems much better to add John's suggestive nickname to the similarities between his writings and those of the *philoponoi*, the goal of his philosophical program, and his knowledge of key *philoponoi* texts like Basil's *Hexameron*.[56] To this one can add the puzzling reference to a John who is described by Zacharias Scholasticus in the 520s as "one who practiced the divine philosophy with those at Enaton" and who was also an expert in profane philosophy and medicine.[57]

52. For this organizational strategy in the *Ammonius*, see E. Watts, "An Alexandrian Christian Response to Neoplatonic Influence," in *The Philosopher and Society in Late Antiquity*, ed. A. Smith, 215–30 (Swansea, 2005).

53. For this collection of texts and John's attempt to use pagan philosophical methods to affirm Christian views on the world's eternity, see C. Pearson, "Scripture as Cosmology: Natural Philosophical Debate in John Philoponus' Alexandria," PhD diss., Harvard University, 1999, 127–31.

54. For the nickname see *Suda* II 649.15 (Adler). His nickname was mocked when John was anathematized at the Council of Constantinople in 680 (see G. D. Mansi, *Sacrorum conciliorum nova et amplissima collectio*, vol. 11, col. 501 A; also H. D. Saffrey, "Le chrétien Jean Philopon," 405).

55. K. Verrycken ("The Development of Philoponus' thought," 238 n. 23) gives a long list of various scholars and where they come down on the question of whether John was a *philoponos* or not. To this add F. Trombley, *Hellenic Religion and Christianization c. 370–529*, vol. 2 (Leiden, 1993–94), 7; and C. Pearson, "Scripture as Cosmology," 7–8.

56. Not only does John show a familiarity with the *Hexameron* in the *De aeternitate*, he also wrote a commentary on it later in life.

57. *Vit. Sev.* 43. In addition to medical writings by John that are preserved in Arabic translation, two Greek medical manuscripts survive that are purportedly written by him (Mosquensis Gr. 466, fol. 157 ff., and cod. vat. Gr. 280, fol. 204 ff.). As P. Allen has shown ("Zachariah

Whether or not this *philoponoi* John is John Philoponus, when all of these factors are put together, John's identification with the *philoponoi* should not be questioned.

With the link between John's philosophical program and the *philoponoi* established, it is worthwhile to consider why someone who was previously an intellectual follower of Ammonius would write to aggressively in support of ideas associated with opponents of his teacher. The timing of John's decision holds the key to solving this puzzle. Thanks to a reference to an astrological event in the *De aeternitate*, it is known that the text was nearing completion on May 21, 529.[58] This date has caused many scholars to pause. As discussed above, 529 is the year the Athenian Neoplatonic school was closed,[59] and, consequently, it is natural to try to link John's dramatic conversion with this event.[60]

There are, however, a number of reasons to avoid this inclination. The first concerns the length of the *De aeternitate*. This work, minus its lost preface, epilogue, and a discussion of Proclus's first discourse,[61] comprises eighteen books. In Rabe's modern edition it is over 640 pages and 17,000 lines long.[62] The reference that dates the work is found on page 517. This means that John had already written at least 80 percent of the book by May of 529. The clearest discussion of the speed at which a contemporary philosopher wrote is Marinus's statement that Proclus could sometimes compose almost 700 lines in a day.[63] In the context of that particular biography, this figure must be understood to be unbelievably high, almost the upper limit of what one could believe to be possible. But, even if this is taken as representative of the rate of John's writing, and if it is assumed that fully half of his daily writing entered the published version of the *De aeternitate mundi*, he would have had to begin the text in early 529, leaving little time to both learn of the Athenian closing and plan his manuscript.

Scholasticus and the *Historia Ecclesiastica* of Evagrius Scholasticus," *Journal of Theological Studies* 31 [1980]: 471–88), Zacharias's writings are known to have been circulating in Alexandria in the 520s. This suggests that the *Life of Severus* was written in the 520s to respond to charges that were being leveled against Severus in the city. The timing further suggests that this John is John Philoponus, the new ally of Severus's *philoponoi* friends.

58. *De aet.* 579.14–17. This exact date was determined by C. Wildberg, "Prolegomena to the Study of Philoponus' *Contra Aristotelem*," 200–201, using astronomical tables.

59. On the closing of the Athenian school, see chapter 5.

60. See H. D. Saffrey, "Le chrétien Jean Philopon," 406–9; H. Chadwick, "Philoponus the Christian Theologian," in *Philoponus and the Rejection of Aristotelian Science*, ed. R. Sorabji, 41–55 (London, 1987); and K. Verrycken, "The Development of Philoponus' thought," 240–43.

61. For a discussion of this missing first discourse see J. L. Kraemer, "A lost passage from Philoponus' *Contra Aristotelem* in Arabic translation," *Journal of the American Oriental Society* 85 (1965): 319.

62. Ioannes Philoponus, *De aeternitate mundi contra Proclum*, ed. H. Rabe (Leipzig, 1899).

63. *Vit. Proc.* 22. Despite this rate of work, Proclus still took five years to compose a 240-page treatise on the Chaldean Oracles (*Vit. Proc.* 26).

The amount of time it took for John to write the *Contra Aristotelem* further suggests that this chronology is unlikely. Though the later work contains no explicit dates, it is possible to estimate how long it took John to complete it. The work is first criticized by Simplicius sometime between 534 and 536.[64] Assuming John began the text after completing the *De aeternitate*, he would have started writing around 530 and published the work, at the earliest, sometime around 533.[65] The *Contra Aristotelem* seems to have been a more carefully argued piece, but it was also about half as long as the *De aeternitate*.[66] Even if we can assume that it took less time to write the *Contra Aristotelem* than it did to compose the preceding volume, we are still left with the date of c. 525 for John to have begun work on the *De aeternitate*. The *De aeternitate*, then, must be understood not as a response to Athenian events but as John's reaction to something else.[67]

Although the exact cause cannot be known for certain, the accession of Olympiodorus probably played a large role in John's decision to begin work on this project. John was slightly older than Olympiodorus and seems to have risen to a prominent position in Ammonius's school before his younger contemporary. Furthermore, John had a complaint that many modern academics would undoubtedly echo—he had published far more than Olympiodorus and had probably done more teaching as well.[68] Nothing in the sources directly supports this idea, but it would not be surprising if John resented being passed over for the school's top position.[69] Compounding this was the possibility that John, as a Christian philosopher, would be a more appealing instructor to Christian students than his younger rival who, thrust into the position by the unexpected death of Eutocius, had not yet managed to develop a reputation as a teacher. John must have had a sense that, given the political circumstances surrounding the succession of Eutocius, there was a very real chance that he could replace Olympiodorus as the teacher un-

64. C. Wildberg, "Prolegomena to the Study of Philoponus' *Contra Aristotelem*," 201–2. The work in which this criticism is found was the first commentary Simplicius wrote after his return from Persia in 532. It certainly predates his commentary on the *Physics*, dated to 537.

65. Wildberg, "Prolegomena to the Study of Philoponus' *Contra Aristotelem*," 202.

66. For the quality of the arguments in the *De aeternitate* and the text's internal inconsistencies, see K. Verrycken, "The Development of Philoponus' thought," 266–72.

67. C. Pearson, "Scripture as Cosmology," 2–3, has argued that the apparent sudden shift in John's thinking is a product of his choice to write in a different literary genre and does not represent an intellectual transformation. Nevertheless, John did make a deliberate decision to move away from the commentary tradition and instead write a series of polemical pieces against ideas associated with his teacher. It is reasonable to conclude that this considered choice to change the nature of his writing is motivated by a significant shift.

68. For the likelihood that John did some teaching before Ammonius's death, see C. Pearson, "Scripture as Cosmology," 10.

69. For a parallel, one can note Aristotle's similar reaction to being passed over for the leadership position in the Academy.

der whom the greatest number of Alexandrian students would be inclined to study.

On a superficial level, John's action represented a return to the old Alexandrian system through which a Christian teacher was both supported by the church and involved with active, non-Christian philosophical circles. Nevertheless, while John was perhaps the best trained and most astute Alexandrian Christian teacher of traditional philosophy since Origen, the *philoponoi* were asking John to provide a type of philosophical training differing from that offered three centuries earlier by Origen. While Origen had helped students of pagan teachers integrate their philosophical learning and their Christianity by developing a teaching program that placed Biblical study at its center, John was to use his intellectual skills to present a Christian interpretation of the traditional philosophical curriculum.[70] Evidently, the goal was to combat the pagan philosophical school of Olympiodorus and provide Christian students interested in a conventional philosophical education with an alternative school that they could attend.

A common goal of attracting students (and possibly financial backers) away from Olympiodorus makes John's alliance with the *philoponoi* comprehensible, but other explanations for it have been given. Apart from Simplicius,[71] the earliest explanations for John's transformation come from Arabic scholars of the ninth and tenth centuries. Not believing the sincerity of his intellectual shift, they tried to find reasons other than a change of conviction to explain John's decision to distance himself philosophically from his teacher. In the introduction to his *Against John the Grammarian,* al-Farabi gives one set of explanations. He said of John: "One may suspect that his intention from what he does in refuting Aristotle is either to defend the opinions laid down in his own religion about the world, or to remove from himself [the suspicion] that he disagrees with the position held by the people of his religion and approved by their rulers, so as to not suffer the same fate as Socrates."[72] Other Arabic authors attributed John's *volte-face* to one of two

70. On the nature of Origen's teaching, see chapter 6.

71. Though wonderful polemics, Simplicius's explanations for John's transformation are unconvincing. He goes so far as to compare John to Herostrates, the arsonist who burned the temple of Artemis at Ephesus in order to become famous (*in Caelo,* 200.29–201.1). Although he is silent about Philoponus, one suspects that Olympiodorus may have agreed with Simplicius's characterization.

72. The translation is that of M. Mahdi, "al-Farabi against Philoponus," *Journal of Near Eastern Studies* 26 (1967): 233–60 (esp. 256–57). John himself seems to echo these thoughts in *De aet.* 331.17–332.23. He discusses Plato's hesitancy to express his true thoughts about God for fear of being forced to undergo the same fate as Socrates. See also K. Verrycken, "The Development of Philoponus' thought," 261–63. John's contemporary Simplicius seems to doubt John's motivations as well. He writes, "No one aimed in such an unserious way, because of the prevailing worthless conceptions about the demiurge of the world, only at seeming to oppose those who demonstrate the eternity of the cosmos" (Simplicius, *in Caelo* 59.13–15).

more specific causes. In the first scenario, John wrote to calm the Christian anger that was directed against him, presumably because of his Ammonian commentaries.[73] The second tradition holds that John received money from Christians in exchange for writing both the *De aeternitate* and the *Contra Aristotelem*.[74] Each of these is intriguing, but the Alexandrian political and religious context of the 520s suggests that these explanations are unlikely.

CHRISTIAN ALEXANDRIA IN THE 520s

In the 520s, the religious situation in Alexandria had become quite confused. Since Peter Mongus's acceptance of the emperor Zeno's *Henotikon* in the 480s, the see of Alexandria had been occupied by anti-Chalcedonian bishops who remained in communion with the bishop of Constantinople.[75] While Alexandria was at peace, an ecclesiastical upheaval had been taking place in the rest of the empire. After being temporarily silenced by the *Henotikon*, groups of extreme anti-Chalcedonians organized and asserted themselves during the later years of the reign of Anastasius. With the emperor's agreement, a number of Chalcedonian and Henoticist bishops in the major cities of the eastern empire were put under pressure and deposed. This trend culminated when Severus, Zacharias's friend and a former student of philosophy in Alexandria, toppled Flavian, the Henoticist patriarch of Antioch, and was appointed to oversee the city's churches in 512. For the uncompromising anti-Chalcedonians this was seen as a great victory. More importantly, with Severus's ascension, all of the major sees in the eastern empire (save those in Palestine and Egypt) were occupied by non-Henoticist anti-Chalcedonian bishops.[76]

The death of Anastasius on the night of July 8, 518, brought an end to

---

73. Abu Sulayman as-Sijistani's work *Siwan al-hikma* preserves this tradition. The idea is echoed in the *Ta'rih al-hukama* of Ibn al-Qifti (who attributes John's shift to pressure from bishops), though it seems that his account is actually describing John's eventual adherence to tritheist heresy. These texts are described in J. L. Kraemer, "A lost passage from Philoponus' *Contra Aristotelem*," 318–27; and K. Verrycken, "The Development of Philoponus' thought," 258–61.

74. as-Sijistani records this as well. He even mentions that John received the sum of twenty thousand dinars in exchange for his efforts.

75. For the doctrinal and political moderation of Alexandria's church leaders in this period see J. Maspero, *Histoire des patriarches d'Alexandrie: depuis la mort d'Empereur Anastase jusqu'à la reconciliation des églises jacobites* (Paris, 1923), 77–78. See also W. H. C. Frend, *Rise of the Monophysite Movement* (Cambridge, 1972), 173. The relative silence about Alexandria's patriarchs in Zacharias's *Chronicle* and the formulaic biographies of all the patriarchs from Peter Mongus to Timothy in the *History of the Patriarchs* indicates the doctrinal and political blandness of the Alexandrian patriarchs of the period.

76. See W. H. C. Frend, *Rise of the Monophysite Movement*, 218–20. Severus's ascension was celebrated by the anti-Chalcedonian bishop Philoxenus as the end of "ten years of resistance to Flavian" (*Letter to the Lector Maro of Anazarba*, ch. 27–32).

the success of the radical anti-Chalcedonians. Anastasius was succeeded by Justin, a general from Illyricum who reigned alongside his nephew and eventual successor Justinian. With the change of regime came a change in religious policy. The government of Justin and Justinian made it quite clear that they would not tolerate the activities of Severus and his party. A week after Anastasius's death, a crowd assembled in Constantinople and shouted their disapproval of Severus while glorifying Justin as the new Constantine.[77] This outburst, no doubt caused by agents of the emperor placed in the mob to lead the chants, led to a synod on July 20 that declared Severus deposed. This was communicated to Severus and he duly fled to Alexandria. He arrived on September 29, 518, and took up residence at Enaton.[78]

In 519 Justin expanded his action to include other anti-Chalcedonian leaders. The *Chronicle* of Zacharias states that "of the bishops of the East, and especially those in the jurisdiction of the learned Severus, some were banished and others withdrew to Alexandria."[79] In all it seems that fifty-five anti-Chalcedonian bishops were forced to leave their sees.[80] Many of them ended up in Alexandria and, like Severus, some of them seem to have been housed at Enaton.[81]

One can only imagine what Alexandria was like at this time. The patriarch Timothy had just taken office and was immediately faced with an influx of unapologetic and outspoken anti-Chalcedonian clergy. Although these exiled bishops seem to have done their best to administer their dioceses from exile, most of them were left with a good deal of free time.[82] For the well-educated among them this led to conversations about Christian doctrine and, perhaps inevitably, to doctrinal disagreement. In 519, not even one year after he had arrived in Alexandria, Severus had already fallen into a dis-

77. See A. A. Vasiliev, *Justin the First: An Introduction to the Epoch of Justinian* Dumbarton Oaks Studies I (Cambridge, Mass., 1950), 136–60; and W. H. C. Frend, *Rise of the Monophysite Movement*, 234.

78. Frend, *Rise of the Monophysite Movement*, 235. Severus's stay at Enaton is attested by Leontius of Byzantium, *De Sectis* V c. 3; *Patrologia Graeca*, 86 col. 1230, ed. J. P. Migne (Paris, 1864).

79. Zacharias, *Chronicle*, 8.5. The translation is that of F. J. Hamilton and E. W. Brooks (*The Syriac chronicle known as that of Zachariah of Mitylene* [London, 1899]). It must be noted that this section of the text was not written by Zacharias but by an unknown author.

80. The number of bishops affected by the emperor's action is disputed. On these exiles, see E. Honigmann, *Évêques et évêchés monophysites d'Asie Mineure au 6e siècle*, Corpus Scriptorum Christianorum Orientalium 127, Subs. 2 (Louvain, 1951), 145–48.

81. This was at least true of Julian of Halicarnassus. For this see P. van Cauwenbergh, *Étude sur les moines d'Égypte depuis le Concile de Chalcédoine, jusqu'à l'invasion arabe* (Paris-Louvain, 1914; rep. Milan 1973), 69.

82. Severus's letters show that he was in communication with members of the Antiochene church and responded to problems in the city. Nevertheless, Severus does also apologize for the difficulty in communicating his thoughts from exile (see E. W. Brooks, ed. and trans., *The Sixth Book of the Select Letters of Severus, Patriarach of Antioch* [London, 1902–1904], 5.15).

agreement with another exiled bishop, Julian, the prelate of Halicarnassus.[83] The disagreement between the two men quickly became a major point of contention. Both Severus and Julian wrote works against the other and each canvassed for support among the anti-Chalcedonian exiles living in Alexandria as well as the monks and clergy native to the city and surrounding area. By the early 520s, the dispute had split Egypt's anti-Chalcedonian population into two camps with each side angling to steal support away from the other.

Despite the heat of this conflict, Timothy, the new patriarch of Alexandria, chose to avoid dealing with this problem in order to retain the support of the entire anti-Chalcedonian community.[84] This unified support, however, masked the deep divides that had developed. Both Julian and Severus had drawn support from monks in and around the city (though Julian seems to have attracted a much larger group of monastic supporters).[85] Furthermore, although the majority of the higher-ranking clergy in Alexandria backed Severus, both camps also had support among the Egyptian clergy and laity.[86] The ostensibly united hierarchy of the Alexandrian church in the 520s was, in reality, quite divided and Timothy must have exercised little actual control over the conflicting parties that filled the church ranks.

JOHN PHILOPONUS AND THE CHRISTIANS

With these developments in mind, it is improbable that any church figure in this environment would have been interested in Olympiodorus's school. The relative weakness of patriarch Timothy makes it unlikely that he would be directly involved. Though both the Severans and the Julianists were still in communion with him, many people were more interested in fighting for Severus or Julian than in cooperating with the patriarch. The ancient sources' near silence about Timothy's activities seem to show that the patri-

---

83. For the rise of the Julianist heresy, see Zacharias, *Chronicle* 9.9–16 and, less accurately, *The History of the Patriarchs* (Timothy III). For modern accounts, J. Maspero, *Histoire des Patriarches d'Alexandrie*, 88–93, puts the details together well, while a less detailed account is found in W. H. C. Frend, *Rise of the Monophysite Movement*, 253–54. Note as well R. Draguet, *Julien d'Halicarnasse et sa controverse avec Sévère d'Antioche sur l'incorruptibilité du corps du Christ* (Louvain, 1924).

84. This led to a bizarre situation. The life of Timothy in the *History of the Patriarchs* is concerned almost exclusively with the argument of Severus and Julian. It mentions Timothy only so far as to say that the argument took place during his patriarchate.

85. Despite this, the story in the *History of the Patriarchs* that all the monks in the city save seven supported Julian is plain partisan nonsense.

86. The clerical support is shown by the fact that the Severan and Julianist parties were able to organize supporters to put forth rival candidates to succeed Timothy in 535. This would not have been possible had either been extremely marginalized. Relics of Severus's support among the Egyptian laity are preserved in the Coptic traditions of his life. Indeed, the *Coptic Synaxaire* contains three festal days in his honor (see *Patrologia Orientalis*, vol. 1, 313, 448; J. Maspero, *Histoire des Patriarches d'Alexandrie*, 86–88).

arch understood the limitations of his authority. As a result, Timothy undertook no major initiatives in the seventeen years of his episcopacy after the exiles arrived. This hid his weakness, but it also makes it extremely unlikely that Timothy would have put the credibility of his office on the line to try to further the career of John Philoponus or to push the *philoponoi* agenda in the schools.

The monasteries and clergy who made up the lower levels of the church political structure also would have had little time to focus upon the individual goal of one supporter and even less political capital to spend on it. Even though both parties presumably saw a benefit in establishing Christian philosophical teaching, each was too preoccupied to focus exclusively upon bringing that to pass. Although it is certainly possible that one of these groups was allied with the *philoponoi*, it is unlikely that either camp would have been of any practical use in helping John challenge Olympiodorus.

If these groups were of little help in supporting the *philoponoi* efforts to attack pagan teaching, it is extremely unlikely that they would have forced John to write his anti-eternalist works. There simply was not sufficient interest or political will for Alexandria's Christians to have done such a thing. In fact, John appears to have been eager to do his part. Contrary to the ideas of medieval Arabic-speaking scholars, it is likely that John was approached by the *philoponoi* and asked to serve as the point man for their challenge to Olympiodorus.

If he were so approached, there is little doubt that John would have agreed to participate. Throughout his life John showed a great readiness to step into intellectual fights when the subject of dispute interested him. Before the Council of Constantinople in 553 he composed an anti-Chalcedonian work of Christian theology entitled *"The Arbiter."* Sergius, a friend of John's who later became the anti-Chalcedonian patriarch of Antioch, instigated this work.[87] *The Arbiter* is an interesting work because, when it was written, John evidently did not anticipate the theological implications of his arguments. Not long after the work was published, some of the theological concessions John offered to Chalcedonian Christians provoked criticism from anti-Chalcedonians.[88] Further complicating matters, Chalcedonian Christians began to use its ostensibly anti-Chalcedonian arguments against the anti-Chalcedonian cause.[89] John then quickly followed the work with a set of strongly polemical works

---

87. For *The Arbiter* see H. Chadwick, "Philoponus the Christian Theologian," 46–48; C. Pearson, "Scripture as Cosmology," 33–35; and U. M. Lang, "Nicetas Choniates, a neglected witness to the Greek text of John Philoponus' *Arbiter,*" *Journal of Theological Studies* 48 (1997): 540–48.

88. Lang, *John Philoponus and the Controversies over Chalcedon*, 90–98. Note as well John's *First Apology for the Arbiter,* 1.63.4–8.

89. Lang, *John Philoponus and the Controversies over Chalcedon*, 98–101. Note as well John's *Second Apology,* 18.75.1–11.

against Chalcedon designed to clarify his anti-Chalcedonian arguments.[90] Although John had not fully anticipated the uses to which his writings might be put, he was still eager to respond to a request and step into the most contentious Christological fight of his lifetime.

John's better-known foray into tritheism, a complicated Christian doctrine loosely related to Aristotelian philosophy, began similarly and ended even less positively. Though the patriarch himself was perhaps unaware of this, it was also through Sergius that John became involved with tritheism.[91] In the early 560s, Sergius forwarded to John a number of the papers written by the first exponent of the doctrine.[92] They had been sent by a relative of the emperor Justinian's wife, Theodora, with the express purpose of convincing John to write a tritheist treatise. By 563, John had agreed to the request and began to write a series of treatises that supported this doctrine. This time he was clear in what he was saying, but the doctrine he advocated was soon condemned as heresy. This tritheist phase again shows John, ever the ready polemicist, eager to advocate for a set of ideas witout evidently appreciating the practical consequences.

John's propensity to insert himself into intellectual fights suggests that he willingly broke with the Ammonian school in the 520s for philosophical and personal reasons. What followed is less clear, but it is evident that, after the publication of *De aeternitate*, John continued to teach the anti-eternalist philosophy for which he had become a powerful advocate. In his commentaries on Aristotle's *Posterior Analytics* and *Meteorologica,* John argues for the creation of the cosmos and the intimate role of God in this process. This is precisely the sort of teaching that one would expect the author of *De aeternitate* to give.[93] The picture may be more complicated than this, however. In his commentary on Aristotle's *Physics*, books 1–4, John three times refers to his own previously published anti-eternalist commentary on *Physics* book 8.[94] The mention of this work suggests that the commentary on *Physics* 1–4 as we have it

---

90. These included a brief defense of the *Arbiter,* the two *Apologies* for the *Arbiter,* and the *Tmemata Against the Fourth Council.* On the first three texts, see Lang, *John Philoponus and the Controversies over Chalcedon,* 88–101. The *Tmemata Against the Fourth Council* is preserved in the *Chronicle of Michael the Syrian,* bk. 8 ch. 8 ff. It is prefaced by Michael's amusing apology for his own inability to understand John's arguments.

91. On Sergius and his various appearances in John's works, see C. Pearson, "Scripture as Cosmology," 47–49.

92. J. Maspero (*Histoire des Patriarches d'Alexandrie,* 201) suggests that Sergius was unaware of the content of the correspondence. The tritheist controversy is described by Timothy of Constantinople (*Patrologia Graeca* 86. 44, 61, 64), Leontius of Byzantium (*De sectis* 5.5), and John of Damascus (*De Haer.* 83). The genesis of the movement is described in J. Maspero, *Histoire des Patriarches d'Alexandrie,* 199–210; W. H. C. Frend, *Rise of the Monophysite Movement,* 289–90; and J. M. Schonfelder, *Die Kirchengeschichte des Johannes von Ephesus* (Munich, 1862), 267–311.

93. Verrycken, "The Development of Philoponus' Thought," 237–41.

94. The key evidence for this is three passages (*in Phys.* 458.30–31; 639.7–9; 762.7–9).

may be a revised text crafted in part to update the original to his new philo-sophical profile.[95] If so, this represents the best evidence for John's contin-ued evolution into a confident teacher of Christian philosophy. This effort shows that, far from being hesitant to teach Christianized philosophy, John genuinely wanted to serve as a Christian teacher of philosophy and proba-bly was doing so in the early 530s.[96]

JOHN PHILOPONUS THE *MATAIOPONOS*

The last months of 529 would seem to have been the best time for John's challenge to succeed. With the support of the scholastic *philoponoi* and their sponsors, he had just released a work that undermined the pagan doctrine of the eternity of the cosmos. Even better, his attack on pagan teaching would have nearly coincided with the decision to force the closure of the Athenian Neoplatonic school. With the double blessings of political support and good timing, John had reason to hope for the success of his efforts to supplant Olympiodorus as the most prominent teacher of philosophy in Alexandria. But they did not succeed.

While the exact course of events that unfolded in Alexandria in the sum-mer of 529 is hidden from us, it is clear that, in the end, Olympiodorus re-mained the head of Ammonius's school and the school remained healthy. In fact, Olympiodorus was still writing and actively teaching philosophy at the school as late as 565. Indeed, he gave a set of lectures on the *Isagoge* of Paulus of Alexandria from May to August of 564 and another on Aristotle's *Meteorology* in Alexandria in March/April 565.[97] Furthermore, the headings

95. According to K. Verrycken, "The Development of Philoponus' Thought," 245, *In Phys-ica* 8 seems also to have been a redaction of an earlier, eternalist commentary, because there are both eternalist and anti-eternalist passages found among its fragments. In the commentary on *Physics* 1–4, John makes no mention of the eternalist fragments and instead presents this work as a text that argues for the temporal creation of the cosmos. Scholten, *Antike Natur-philosophie*, 136–37, presents a reasonable explanation for the apparent doctrinal inconsisten-cies in *in Phys.* 8. Less compelling is his suggestion that the commentary on *Physics* 8 is refer-enced in *in Phys.* 1–4 because the *Physics* commentaries were not composed sequentially. While one cannot completely exclude this possibility, it seems more likely that a commentary on a large text like Aristotle's *Physics* was completed sequentially and the first part was later revised in light of John's subsequent intellectual development.

96. There is even evidence that he took on students of philosophy. Dioscorus of Aphrodito may have studied under John (see L. MacCoull, "Dioscorus of Aphrodito and John Philoponus," *Studia Patristica* 18 [1987]: 163–68). L. MacCoull's later characterization ("A New Look at the Career of John Philoponus," *Journal of Early Christian Studies* 3 [1995]: 47–60) of John as a Copto-Greek philologist "who put all his learning at the disposal of the Monophysite movement" fails to explain the amount of effort he put into composing and revising philosophical commen-taries that had little direct relevance to anti-Chalcedonianism or Christological questions.

97. O. Neugebauer, *A History of Ancient Mathematical Astronomy*, 1043–45. The later date is based upon the reference to a comet that was visible in Alexandria during those two months.

of his commentaries that survive call him a philosopher[98] and their contents are labeled: "taken from the spoken words of the great philosopher Olympiodorus."[99] It is also hard to dispute that he was still heading the school of Ammonius because, in the *Isagoge* commentary, he calls Ammonius his *progonos* or "predecessor."[100] Olympiodorus's emphasis on this link in 564 seems a certain indication that he remained the head of the school.

The works of John Philoponus, on the other hand, show no sign that he ever succeeded in establishing himself as a teacher of philosophy. The headings of his commentaries call him a *grammatikos* (a grammarian) not a *philosophos* (a philosopher).[101] His peers also only knew of him as a grammarian. Simplicius, for example, calls him "the grammarian" throughout his works.[102] To later contemporaries and Byzantine scholars, John is known as both "the grammarian" and "the *philoponos*," perhaps homage to his alliance with the scholastic *philoponoi* from the mid-520s,[103] but he is never called a philosopher. It seems, then, that John's attempt to become recognized as a teacher of philosophy failed, a failure that none could package better than the unknown man leading the acclamations at the sixth ecumenical council in 680. Although the council was discussing John's theology and not his philosophy, when it denounced him as "John the grammarian who is nicknamed the *philoponos* (the one who loves work) but is rather the *mataioponos*

98. Olympiodorus's commentaries on Plato's *Gorgias, Phaedo,* and *First Alcibiades* survive, as well as works on Aristotle's *Categories* and *Meteorology.* Fragments of Olympiodorus's commentaries on Aristotle's *De interpretatione* and Porphyry's *Isagoge* also have come down. Furthermore, Arabic bibliography indicates that a commentary on Plato's *Sophist* from his hand once existed. A complete discussion of Olympiodorus's works is found in L. G. Westerink, *The Greek Commentaries on Plato's Phaedo,* vol. 1 (New York, 1976), 21–25.

99. This is a standard introductory phrase (for its use see M. Richard, "Ἀπὸ φωνῆς" *Byzantion* 20 [1950]: 191–222), but the use of "great" shows the exceptional respect given to Olympiodorus. It is also used in an alchemical work wrongly attributed to Olympiodorus. For this work see M. Berthelot and Ch. M. Ruelle, *Collection des anciens alchimistes grecs,* 3 vols. (Paris, 1887–88; repr. London, 1963). L. G. Westerink (*The Greek Commentaries on Plato's Phaedo,* 22) denies the attribution of this work to Olympiodorus.

100. *Commentary on Paulus* (*CAG* XII, 2, 188.34–189.10). This was a standard term used to indicate intellectual descent from a professor.

101. All of his Aristotelian commentaries are attributed to "John the Alexandrian grammarian." For this see H. D. Saffrey, "Le chrétien Jean Philopon," 405.

102. Simplicius, *de Caelo* 119.7 is a good example. Although Simplicius once indicates that this was a name John chose for himself, Simplicius seems to have included this statement to attack John's credibility, possibly by highlighting his failure to establish himself as a teacher of philosophy. On this reference see, H. J. Blumenthal, "John Philoponus: Alexandrian Platonist?" *Hermes* 114 (1986): 316–17. C. Pearson's explanation that John adopted the title out of Christian humility ("Scripture as Cosmology," 11) seems unlikely.

103. The Council of Constantinople in 680 is the first example of joining the two names (*Acta Conc. Constantinopolis III Oec. VI,* Mansi, *Sacrorum conciliorum collectio,* vol. 11, col. 501A). The *Suda* also joins them. John is first called *"philoponos"* in Elias, *In Cat.* 246.14.

(the one who works in vain)," it neatly summed up the result of his efforts against Olympiodorus. In the end, his challenge had been in vain.

Upon first glance, John's challenge appears to have built upon a number of strong supports. However, closer analysis reveals the weakness of its foundation. At the very base of John's supporters were the scholastic *philoponoi*. As the preceding chapter has shown, this movement, while present in the schools, did not have particularly wide support among students. Given this, it is unlikely that they could have delivered enough students for John to sustain himself as a teacher of philosophy only. This fact probably explains why he seems to have continued providing grammatical instruction for much of the rest of his career.[104]

Perhaps equally unanticipated was the negative response that some Alexandrian Christians had to the *De Aeternitate*. John's goal in writing the text had apparently been to debut his Christian-friendly philosophical teaching by affirming the world's creation through conventional philosophical argumentation. By design, his arguments had relied upon pagan philosophical texts and not Biblical material. In the past, however, philosophically influenced Christian teachers like Origen and Didymus the Blind had made Biblical materials the centerpiece of their teaching. John's failure to do so, while potentially appealing to students looking for a conventional philosophical education, opened him up to the charges of Cosmas Indicopleustes, a member of Alexandria's small Nestorian community. To Cosmas, John's works were seen as "deceptive arguments and worldly deviousness"[105] and John himself was characterized (though not by name) as "a false Christian" for framing his arguments in such terms.[106] This criticism only reflects the views of one member of a small, marginal Christian group in Alexandria, but it is intentionally framed to appeal to a larger group of Alexandrian Christians.[107] Cosmas never explicitly identifies himself with the Nestorian Christology and focuses his criticisms on John's insufficient reliance upon Christian scripture in his anti-eternalist writings.[108] His hope, apparently, was to convince

104. The school of Horapollon (described briefly in chapter 8) is an example of a school that taught philosophy but seems to have been mainly a grammar school. Although it seems peculiar, this type of curricular diversity seems to have occurred in all but the most prestigious schools. On this, see R. Cribiore, *Gymnastics of the Mind: Greek Education in Hellenistic and Roman Egypt* (Princeton, 2001), 36–44.

105. Cosmas Indicopleustes, *Topographica Christiana*, 1.2.1–12.

106. Ibid., 1.4.1–7. Cosmas never directly refers to John, but that fact that John is the target of this attack has been convincingly argued by W. Wolska, *La Topographie Chrétienne de Cosmas Indicopleustès: Théologie et Sciences au VIe siècle* (Paris, 1962), 147–92. For a more detailed treatment of John's response, see C. Pearson, "Scripture as Cosmology."

107. Pearson, "Scripture as Cosmology," 160–62.

108. The deliberate nature of Cosmas's arguments is discussed by W. Wolska, *La Topographie Chrétienne de Cosmas Indicopleustès*, 161–67.

both Nestorian and non-Nestorian Christians that John's work was danger-ously detached from scripture. And John's response to these criticisms, which attempts to marginalize Cosmas's ideas by attacking similar teachings of the notorious Nestorian thinker, Theodore of Mopsuestia,[109] shows a real con-cern that Alexandrian Christians who were not members of the Nestorian community would be persuaded by Cosmas. This suggests that, beyond the scholastic *philoponoi,* many Alexandrian Christians apparently looked at John's project with as much apprehension as enthusiasm. He could not, then, count on broad Christian support for his efforts.

The imperial authorities also do not seem to have been much help to John. The reason was likely John's connection with the scholastic *philoponoi.* The scholastic *philoponoi* were religiously affiliated with Enaton, the monastery to which the emperor Justinian's enemy Severus had fled. The *philoponoi* also had indirect ties to Severus himself. In such a situation, the imperial officials in the city probably tried to stay as unaware of the *philoponoi* machinations as possible in order to avoid angering the emperor.

This reluctance to act on John's behalf was certainly compounded by the way Olympiodorus was comporting himself. Olympiodorus had been care-ful to make his teaching acceptable to the Christian members of his audi-ence. Although he did not compromise his doctrines, he was careful to stay away from expounding interpretations that might offend his listeners.[110] In addition, he allowed Christian teachers to occupy high positions in his school.[111] Beyond his apparent success as a teacher, there is also evidence that, at least later in his career, Olympiodorus had a strong public presence in the city.[112] Therefore, Olympiodorus was probably better positioned to beat back John's challenge than his opponents anticipated.

Olympiodorus enjoyed one more subtle yet formidable advantage—the legitimacy of his position. From the evidence available to us, the manner in which Olympiodorus assumed his teaching position and the ways he acted while holding it were consistent with what one expected of a late antique teacher of philosophy. Olympiodorus was operating as part of a system of philosophical instruction that most people, both pagans and Christians, ac-cepted. While Olympiodorus was a part of this system, John's challenge to his position attacked some of the foundations of philosophical teaching. John

---

109. This response came in *De Opificio Mundi,* a work that was probably written in the late 540s. For these tactics, see W. Wolska, *La Topographie Chrétienne de Cosmas Indicopleustès,* 162–63; and C. Pearson, "Scripture as Cosmology," 161.

110. *In Alc.* 22.14–23.1; see also L. G. Westerink, *The Greek Commentaries on Plato's Phaedo,* 25.

111. Among them were the Christian teachers Elias and David.

112. Olympiodorus's commentaries reveal very little about his public life. It is known, how-ever, that he was present when the grammarian Anatolius welcomed a governor named Hep-haestus to the city in 546 with a speech that contained a modified Homeric line. (*In Alc.* 2.80–82).

had challenged the doctrine of the eternity of the world and the presumed unity of Platonic and Aristotelian thought. For most students of philosophy, these fundamental principles were not things that one would question,[113] and, for most teachers, the challenges posed by John and the *philoponoi* were seen as particularly troubling.[114] Ultimately, John and the *philoponoi* were pushing a revolutionary agenda in a city where there was no longer much clamor for fundamental change in the schools.

The *philoponoi* challenge of the late 520s stands in stark contrast to that led by them in the 480s. In the 480s, the beating of Paralius by pagan students had infuriated the city's Christians and created a climate in which many of them were looking for vengeance. Understanding the popular mood, the patriarch of the city recognized the political possibilities of attacking paganism and gave his support. Armed with the backing of the populace, patriarch, and (in the later stages) the imperial government, this was an opportunity for the *philoponoi* to implement their agenda. Nevertheless, even in the aftermath of Paralius's beating, the popular and political support for the *philoponoi* program rested on a shallow foundation. After the initial anger of Alexandrian Christians was calmed, there was little interest in pushing for further reform. People were angered not by the system of teaching itself but by the event of Paralius's beating. So, even in those tense circumstances, there was no general push to change how teaching was done. Therefore, not long after the event, pagan teachers of philosophy resumed teaching, albeit under certain restrictions.

In the 520s the *philoponoi* and their supporters were presented with a much tougher task. Despite the opportunity that John Philoponus's opposition to the young and inexperienced Olympiodorus seemed to provide, the *philoponoi* and their supporters had difficulty in taking advantage of the situation. The Christian populace was preoccupied with the struggle between Severan and Julianist anti-Chalcedonian factions. The church hierarchy was equally divided and indecisive. Without a galvanizing issue, the *philoponoi* found it hard to attract much attention to their cause.

In the end, the *philoponoi* had taken on an impossible task. They were struggling against a moderate pagan school and hoping for popular support in an

113. Even Zacharias's fanciful classroom confrontations with Ammonius do not show any other students joining in to back up his challenge. It seems that part of the rationale of the *philoponoi* reading program was to encourage students to think about these fundamental questions in a new way. John's work certainly aimed to the do same thing.

114. Simplicius's response to the *Contra Aristotelem* shows how shocking these criticisms were to other teachers. For more on this see P. Hoffmann, "Simplicius' Polemics," in *Philoponus and the Rejection of Aristotelian Science,* ed. R. Sorabji, 57–83 (London, 1987).

environment that had constantly supported the efforts of men like Olympiodorus. Olympiodorus, like Hypatia and Ammonius before him, had adopted
a teaching posture that catered to the intellectual needs of his Christian students without threatening their religious identity. Historically, Alexandrian
Christians had rewarded such teachers with their political and financial support. With no scandal surrounding Olympiodorus and no significant outside political support, the *philoponoi* could not hope to force change upon
something so fundamental to the character of educated Alexandrians. In
the end, they were fighting not Olympiodorus but the cultural environment
created in the fourth century B.C., sustained by Hellenistic and Roman institutions, and supported by people throughout late antiquity. It was a fight
the *philoponoi* could not possibly hope to win.

Conclusion

Olympiodorus survived not only the events of 529 but also Justinian's subsequent anti-pagan campaigns of 546 and 562.[1] He kept his position through the 560s and kept teaching the doctrines that the *philoponoi* found objectionable. He seems to have been followed in this by Elias, presumably a Christian.[2] While Elias adopted some of the points laid out by John Philoponus,[3] he remained true to Olympiodorus's school of thought on the crucial question of the eternity of the world.[4] David, Elias's apparent successor, also seems to hold this Olympiodorean doctrine.[5] Stephanus, in turn, followed David.

It is with Stephanus, the last in this line of Alexandrian teachers, that this study will conclude. Stephanus taught in Alexandria from the later decades of the sixth century until around 610 when he was called by the emperor Heraclius to take a public teaching post in Constantinople.[6] In his commentaries, Stephanus unconditionally accepted Christian teaching and the

1. See Alan Cameron, "The Last Days of the Academy at Athens," *Proceedings of the Cambridge Philological Society* 195 (1969): 9.
2. The link between Olympiodorus and Elias is apparent from the similarities in their writings. For these see L. G. Westerink, *Prolégomènes à la philosophie de Platon* (Paris, 1990), xxxii–xxxv. Elias's Christianity has recently been questioned by C. Wildberg, "Three Neoplatonic Introductions to Philosophy: Ammonius, David, and Elias," *Hermathena* 149 (1990): 33–51.
3. Like John, he does admit the possibility of miracles that come directly from divine providence (see L. G. Westerink, *Prolégomènes à la philosophie de Platon*, xiv n. 21 and xxxvi).
4. Westerink, *Prolégomènes à la philosophie de Platon*, xxxvi (see Elias, *In Categorem* 120.16–17; 187.6–7).
5. David too seems to affirm the eternity of matter (Ps. Elias, 42.20) and the divinity of celestial bodies (34.27). Nevertheless, he also seems inclined to see God actively involved in the creative process. For his views see L. G. Westerink, *Prolégomènes à la philosophie de Platon*, xxxviii.
6. Ibid., xl.

authority of the Bible.[7] At the same time, he also affirmed the Aristotelian idea of the eternity of the world,[8] the existence of Aristotle's fifth element,[9] and other key doctrines that lay beneath the teachings of the traditional, Neoplatonic philosophical system. Westerink observed that the best way to bring together Stephanus's Christianity and his affirmation of these doctrines is to understand that, unlike John Philoponus, Stephanus was a part of the system of classical philosophical thought. As the "official representative" of classical philosophy Stephanus was unable to criticize it.[10] While this may have been true, there is a more comforting way to see his position. In Stephanus, one sees the convergence of pagan doctrine and *philoponoi* ambition. He is a Christian scholarch who, nonetheless, teaches philosophy in the traditional way. This was possible because Stephanus's overt Christianity rendered his advocacy of the eternity of the world unthreatening to Christians.[11] It must be remembered that the *philoponoi* opposition to this idea sought to prevent Christian students from converting to paganism. When this doctrine was taught by a scholarch who publicly declared his Christianity in his writings, this would not have been a serious concern. For the philosophical purists (and the pagans who remained), Stephanus's adherence to traditional interpretations was equally reassuring. It showed that his public advocacy of Christianity in no way prevented him from teaching classic philosophical doctrines. In the end, this pagan-Christian conflict that had involved so many men, caused so many texts to be written, and ruined so many careers had simply melted away. In his unique way, Stephanus had peacefully Christianized philosophical teaching.

Ultimately the careers of Olympiodorus, Elias, David, and Stephanus reveal a fundamental truth about how education was viewed by citizens of the later Roman empire. On one level, the families of late antiquity felt that the traditional system of philosophical education worked well. At the same time, there was a concern about how a religiously based system of instruction would adapt to an evolving religious environment. The unease of the Christians who frequented Alexandria's schools arose out of a desire to be reassured about the religious message that was attached to teaching. This did not, however, change their hope that the school's teaching would remain true to the traditional curriculum. Olympiodorus and his successors were successful be-

---

7. Ps. Philoponus = Stephan, *De anima* 527.29–32; 547.11–14.

8. *De anima* 540.27.

9. Ibid., 448.6–7.

10. Westerink, *Prolégomènes à la philosophie de Platon*, xl.

11. Stephanus's teachings on this are particularly notable in light of the renewed apocalyptic fears that seized Christians around the turn of the seventh century. On these fears see Theophylact Simocatta, *Historia*, 5.15.3–4 and P. Magdalino, "The History of the Future and Its Uses: Prophecy, Policy, and Propaganda," in *The Making of Byzantine History: Studies Dedicated to Donald M. Nicol*, ed. R. Beaton and C. Roueché, 3–34 (Aldershot, 1993), 18–19.

cause they allayed this fear without changing the traditional foundation of their teaching. In the classrooms of each professor, there was a tacit assurance that his religious belief, be it Christian or pagan, would not interfere with or fundamentally alter the philosophy he taught.

Athenian teachers like Proclus, Hegias, and Damascius gave their students no such assurances. They were pagan, their teaching emphasized this paganism, and the atmosphere in their schools did nothing to downplay this fact. On a practical level, Athenian teachers too recognized that their schools provided a cultural training, but they were unwilling to provide any assurance to Christians that their teaching would not be religious in character.[12] It was not their aim nor was it their concern to adapt their teaching to the needs of a changing cultural world. This attitude was their eventual downfall.

Athens had long been a haven for unrepentantly religious pagan philosophers and rhetoricians. Its anachronistic religious and political culture enabled well-connected professors to teach the doctrines they wanted in the manner they felt was most appropriate. Into the last decades of the fifth century, pagan philosophers could rely upon pagan patrons to protect their interests in the city. This situation permitted Athenian teachers to develop their teaching as they saw fit, but it also conditioned them to consider only the philosophical import of their doctrines. When an overwhelmingly Christian power structure came to exercise authority over the city in the sixth century, the Athenian teachers chose not to adapt to this new reality. Instead, the last two heads of the Athenian school doggedly refused to recognize the need to change their teaching or their religious activities. Inevitably, they became the losing side in a struggle against local Christian authorities.

Pagan philosophy in late antiquity lived and died based upon the abilities of its teachers to adapt to the religious climate of the city around them. In Athens, philosophers enjoyed a religious climate that was generally hospitable to their activities. The Athenian Christian church was a weak institution and its influence over education could be counteracted by the collective efforts of pagans in the city. Athenian teachers were never forced to work with the Christian establishment and, consequently, each group saw the other only as an adversary. This adversarial relationship meant that, when the power of the church finally eclipsed that of the Athenian pagan aristocracy, Christians in the city had little affection for pagan philosophical schools and no history of compromise with them. Although Athens had long been an educational center, the city's Christian population had never benefited from close relationships with the schools. Consequently, it had little concern for their continued existence.

---

12. The teaching of rhetoric by Syrianus and the collection of rhetoricians affiliated with the Proclan circle each show an awareness of the need to provide training for students besides those who wanted to become full Neoplatonic initiates.

Pagan teaching in Alexandria had an entirely different character. Almost from its inception, the Alexandrian Christian community had been intimately connected to pagan intellectual circles. This social and intellectual interaction spawned a diverse Christian teaching culture that drew upon pagan philosophy for theological inspiration. At the center of this was the Christian study circle, an informal institution that helped Christians harmonize their learning and their religious beliefs. As their community grew into the largest religious group in the city, Christians struggled to redefine their relationship to pagan teachers and pagan culture. The Christian study circles, with their history as a breeding ground for heresy, were attacked. By the end of the fourth century, they existed primarily in monasteries, far away from the pagan schoolhouse. Indeed, for much of the fourth century, some leaders of the Alexandrian church looked to distance Christians from pagan intellectual culture altogether.

Throughout this process, a steady stream of Christian students flowed into pagan philosophical and rhetorical schools to pursue their educations. It was the persistence of these students that forced the Alexandrian Christian establishment to become directly involved again in the pagan schools. While the church and Christian intellectuals had turned their attention away, the religious content of Alexandrian pagan teaching had been increasingly emphasized. Christians responded by creating the scholastic *philoponoi*, a group devoted to reestablishing the institutional links between the pagan philosophical school and Christian intellectual culture. Efforts were also made to reform the philosophical curriculum so that it would be friendlier to the needs of Christians. Despite the animosity that this process engendered, Alexandrian pagan teachers understood that large numbers of Christian students attended their classes. The more sensible among them recognized that this reality would not change and that they were best served by adapting to it. At the same time, ordinary Christians, with their long history of interaction with pagan teachers, were willing to accept reformed pagan teaching in the city. Consequently, there was little popular demand for the closure of pagan schools.

One can certainly say that the Alexandrian school of Olympiodorus succeeded and the Athenian school of Damascius failed because Olympiodorus was more willing to adapt to the environment around him. However, such an assertion misses a crucial part of the picture. While their personal choices had a great deal to do with the fate of their schools, the historical relationship between city and school was an equally strong factor in the eventual fate of pagan teaching in Athens and Alexandria. Olympiodorus was able to succeed in part because historical circumstances had bound Alexandrian pagan professors to Christian students for centuries. This created a solid and enduring link between pagan philosophical teaching and the city's Christian community. As a result, a pagan professor who was sensitive to the needs of his Christian students had the ability to survive in relative comfort. Damascius and his school failed because there had never been close ties between pagan teachers and Christians in Athens. In Athens, pagan teachers and Christians had a largely adversarial relationship. Indeed, the only thing that bound them was a common physical space. Some exceptional individual could conceivably have overturned this history and saved the Athenian Neoplatonic school through a creative compromise with Christian authorities, but, for all his brilliance, Damascius was not interested in that task.

Despite the dramatic changes that rocked the Roman world in late antiquity, the Roman empire was still a society in which traditional culture was prized—as long as it did not actively oppose local Christian norms. The teachers who realized this and made their activities unthreatening to the Christians in their city thrived. The pagans and Christians who attacked the moderation of these men suffered. In a situation where compromise was more highly valued than confrontation, it is fitting that we turn our final thought towards Stephanus. As a teacher who was able to successfully understand the needs of his city and peacefully realize both pagan and Christian hopes for philosophical teaching, his career illustrates the guiding principles of this study. At the same time, Stephanus leads us into an age when the tensions animating this narrative were no longer relevant. By the seventh century, local conflicts about the role of pagan teachers had largely passed. There were few such teachers left and even fewer who taught Christian students. This slow fade into irrelevance represents pagan intellectual culture's sad final moment.

ἐν οἷς ἡ παροῦσα θεωρία σὺν θεῷ πληροῦται.

And here, with God's help, let the present discussion end.[13]

13. Stephanus of Alexandria, *In Aristotelis librum de interpretatione Commentarius* 2.9–11.

BIBLIOGRAPHY

The following is a list of the secondary sources cited in the text. Unless otherwise mentioned, the ancient sources cited are all derived from the standard editions. Editions worth special note are listed below.

Alexandre, O. "Κέκροπος 7–9." *Archaiologikon Deltion* 24 (1969): 50–53.

Allen, P. "Zachariah Scholasticus and the *Historia Ecclesiastica* of Evagrius Scholasticus." *Journal of Theological Studies* 31 (1980): 471–88.

Ameling, W. *Herodes Atticus.* 2 vols. Hildseheim, 1983.

Anderson, G. *The Second Sophistic: A Cultural Phenomenon in the Roman Empire.* London, 1993.

Asmus, R. *Das Leben des Philosophen Isidoros.* Lepizig, 1911.

Athanassiadi, P. "Dreams, Theurgy and Freelance Divination: The Testimony of Iamblichus." *Journal of Roman Studies* 83 (1993): 115–30.

———. "Persecution and Response in Late Paganism: The Evidence of Damascius." *Journal of Hellenic Studies* 113 (1993): 1–29.

———. "The Oecumenism of Iamblichus: Latent Knowledge and its Awakening." *Journal of Roman Studies* 85 (1995): 244–50.

———. "The Chaldean Oracles: Theology and Theurgy." In *Pagan Monotheism in Late Antiquity,* edited by P. Athanassiadi and B. Frede, 149–83. Oxford, 1999.

———. ed. and trans. *Damascius: The Philosophical History.* Athens, 1999.

———. "Philosophy and Power: The Creation of Orthodoxy in Neoplatonism." In *Philosophy and Power in the Graeco-Roman World,* edited by G. Clark and T. Rajak, 271–91. Oxford, 2002.

Aujoulat, N. *Le Néo-Platonisme Alexandrin, Hiéroclès d'Alexandrie.* Leiden, 1986.

Avotins, I. "The Holders of the Chairs of Rhetoric at Athens." *Harvard Studies in Classical Philology* 79 (1975): 313–24.

Bagnall, R. S. "Landholding in Late Roman Egypt: The Distribution of Wealth." *Journal of Roman Studies* 82 (1992): 128–49.

Baldwin, C. *Medieval Rhetoric and Poetic (to 1400) Interpreted from Representative Works.* Gloucester, Mass., 1959.

Banchich, T. "The Date of Eunapius' *Vitae Sophistarum.*" *Greek, Roman, and Byzantine Studies* 25 (1984): 183–92.

———. "On Goulet's Chronology of Eunapius' Life and Works." *Journal of Hellenic Studies* 107 (1987): 164–67.

———. "Julian's School Laws: *Cod. Theod.* 13.3.5 and *Ep.* 42." *The Ancient World* 24 (1993): 5–14.

———. "Eunapius in Athens." *Phoenix* 50 (1996): 304–11.

Bardy, G. "Pour l'histoire de l'École d'Alexandrie." *Vivre et Penser,* 2nd ser., 2 (1942): 80–109.

Barnes, T. D. "Porphyry *Against the Christians:* Date and Attribution of Fragments." *Journal of Theological Studies* 24 (1973): 424–42.

———. "Angel of Light or Mystic Initiate? The problem of the *Life of Antony.*" *Journal of Theological Studies* 37 (1986): 353–68.

———. "Himerius and the Fourth Century." *Classical Philology* 82 (1987): 206–25.

———. Review of *The Letters of St. Antony,* by S. Rubenson. *Journal of Theological Studies* 42 (1991): 723–32.

———. *Athanasius and Constantius: Theology and Politics in the Constantinian Empire.* Cambridge, Mass., 1993.

Barry, W. D. "Aristocrats, Orators, and the 'Mob': Dio Chrysostom and the World of the Alexandrians." *Historia* 42.1 (1993): 82–103.

Beard, M. et al. *Literacy in the Roman World.* Ann Arbor, 1991.

Beaucamp, J. "Le philosophe et le joueur: La date de la fermeture de l'école d'Athènes." *Mélanges Gilbert Dagron.* Travaux et Mémoires 14 (2002): 21–35.

Berthelot, M., and Ch. Ruelle. *Collection des anciens alchimistes grecs.* 3 vols. Paris, 1887–88. Reprinted London, 1963. (Page references are to the 1963 edition.)

Bidez, J., ed. and trans. *L'Empereur Julien: Oeuvres Complètes.* 2 vols. Paris, 1972.

Blockley, R. C. *The Fragmentary Classicising Historians of the Later Roman Empire: Eunapius, Olympiodorus, Priscus, and Malchus.* 2 vols. Liverpool, 1981–83.

Bloomer, M. "Schooling in Persona: Imagination and Subordination in Roman Education." *Classical Antiquity* 16.1 (1997): 57–78.

Blumenthal, H. J. "529 and its Sequel: What Happened to the Academy?" *Byzantion* 48 (1978): 369–85.

———. "*Marinus' Life of Proclus:* Neoplatonist Biography." *Byzantion* 54 (1984): 471–93.

———. "John Philoponus: Alexandrian Platonist?" *Hermes* 114 (1986): 314–35.

Bonner, S. F. *Education in Ancient Rome.* Berkeley and Los Angeles, 1977.

Booth, A. D. "Elementary and Secondary Education in the Roman Empire." *Florilegium* 1 (1979): 1–14.

Boulnois, M. O. *Le paradoxe trinitaire chez Cyrille d'Alexandrie: Herméneutique, analyses philosophiques et argumentation théologique.* Paris, 1994.

Bowersock, G. *Greek Sophists in the Roman Empire.* Oxford, 1969.

———. *Julian the Apostate.* Cambridge, Mass., 1978.

———. *Hellenism in Late Antiquity.* Ann Arbor, 1990.

Bowman, A. K. "Landholding in the Hermopolite Nome in the 4th century A.D." *Journal of Roman Studies* 75 (1985): 137–63.

Boyancé, P. *Le culte des muses chez les philosophes grecs: Études d'histoire et de psychologie religieuses.* Paris, 1937.

Bradbury, S. "A Sophistic Prefect: Anatolius of Berytus in the Letters of Libanius." *Classical Philology* 95 (2000): 172–86.

Brakke, D. "Canon Formation and Social Conflict in Fourth Century Egypt." *Harvard Theological Review* 87 (1994): 395–419.

———. *Athanasius and the Politics of Asceticism.* 2nd ed. Baltimore, 1998.

Brandt, S. *Eumenius von Augustodunum und die ihm zugeschriebenen Reden.* Freiburg, 1882.

Breccia, E. *Catalogue générale des antiquités du Musée d'Alexandrie (nos. 1–568): Iscrizioni greche e latine.* Cairo, 1911.

Brooks, E. W., ed. and trans. *The Sixth Book of the Select Letters of Severus, Patriarach of Antioch.* 4 vols. London, 1902–1904.

Brown, P. *Power and Persuasion in Late Antiquity: Towards a Christian Empire.* Madison, Wisc., 1992.

Browne, G. M., ed. *Sortes Astrampsychi.* Vol. 1. Leipzig, 1983.

Browning, R. *The Emperor Julian.* Berkeley and Los Angeles, 1976.

Brunt, P. A. "The Bubble of the Second Sophistic." *Bulletin of the Institute of Classical Studies* 39 (1994): 25–52.

Burman, J. "The Athenian Empress Eudocia." In *Post-Herulian Athens: Aspects of Life and Culture in Athens, A.D. 267–529,* edited by P. Castrén, 63–87. Helsinki, 1994.

Bury, J. B. "The Nika Riot." *Journal of Hellenic Studies* 17 (1897): 92–119.

Butler, A. J. *The Arab Conquest of Egypt.* 2nd ed., edited by P. M. Fraser. Oxford, 1978.

Cameron, Alan. "Iamblichus at Athens." *Athenaeum* 45 (1967): 143–53.

———. "The Last Days of the Academy at Athens." *Proceedings of the Cambridge Philological Society* 195 (1969): 7–29.

———. "Isidore of Miletus and Hypatia: On the Editing of Mathematical Texts." *Greek, Roman and Byzantine Studies* 31 (1990): 103–27.

Cameron, Alan and J. Long. *Barbarians and Politics at the Court of Arcadius.* Berkeley and Los Angeles, 1993.

Cameron, Averil. *Agathias.* Oxford, 1970.

———. *Christianity and the Rhetoric of Empire: The Development of Christian Discourse.* Berkeley and Los Angeles, 1991.

———. "Remaking the Past." In *Late Antiquity: A Guide to the Postclassical World,* edited by G. Bowersock, P. Brown, and O. Grabar, 1–20. Cambridge, Mass., 1999.

———. "Form and Meaning: The *Vita Constantini* and the *Vita Antonii.*" In *Greek Biography and Panegyric in Late Antiquity,* edited by T. Hägg and P. Rousseau, 72–88. Berkeley and Los Angeles, 2000.

Canfora, L. *The Vanished Library: A Wonder of the Ancient World.* Translated by M. Ryle. Berkeley and Los Angeles, 1990.

Casson, L. *Ships and Seamanship in the Ancient World.* Princeton, 1971.

Castrén, P. "General Aspects of Life in Post-Herulian Athens." In *Post Herulian Athens: Aspects of Life and Culture in Athens, A.D. 267–529,* edited by P. Castrén, 1–14. Helsinki, 1994.

Chadwick, H. *Early Christian Thought and the Classical Tradition: Studies in Justin, Clement, and Origen.* Oxford, 1966.

————. "Philoponus the Christian Theologian." In *Philoponus and the Rejection of Aristotelian Science*, edited by R. Sorabji, 41–56. London, 1987.

Chauvot, A. "Curiales et paysans en orient à la fin du Ve et au debut du VIe siècle: Note sur l'institution du *vindex*." In *Sociétés urbaines, sociétés rurales dans l'Asie Mineure et la Syrie hellénistique et romaine*, edited by E. Frézouls, 271–87. Strasbourg, 1987.

Chitty, D. *The Desert a City: An Introduction to the Study of Egyptian and Palestinian Monasticism under the Christian Empire*. Oxford, 1966.

————, trans. *The Letters of St. Antony the Great*. Oxford, 1975.

Chuvin, P. *A Chronicle of the Last Pagans*. Translated by B. A. Archer. Cambridge, Mass., 1990.

Clark, E. *The Origenist Controversy: The Cultural Construction of an Early Christian Debate*. Princeton, 1992.

Clark, G., trans. *Iamblichus On the Pythagorean Life*. Liverpool, 1989.

Combès, J. and L. G. Westerink, eds.and trans. *Damascius, Traité des premiers principes*. Paris, 1986–91.

Cox, P. *Biography in Late Antiquity: The Quest for the Holy Man*. Berkeley and Los Angeles, 1983.

Cribiore, R. *Gymnastics of the Mind: Greek Education in Hellenistic and Roman Egypt*. Princeton, 2001.

Croke, B. "Malalas, The Man, and his Work." In *Studies in John Malalas*, edited by E. Jeffreys et al., 1–25. Sydney, 1990.

————. "The development of a critical text." In *Studies in John Malalas*, edited by E. Jeffreys et al., 311–24. Sydney, 1990.

Crouzel, H. "L'École d'Origène à Césarée." *Bulletin de littérature ecclésiastique* 71 (1970): 15–27.

Darling, R. A. "The patriarchate of Severus of Antioch, 512–518." PhD diss., University of Chicago, 1982.

———— (Darling Young). "Evagrius the Iconographer: Monastic Pedagogy in the *Gnostikos*." *Journal of Early Christian Studies* 9 (2001): 53–71.

Day, J. *An Economic History of Athens Under Roman Domination*. New York, 1942.

Delia, D. "From Romance to Rhetoric: The Alexandrian Library in Classical and Islamic Traditions." *American Historical Review* 97 (1992): 1449–67.

Delvoye, C. *L'art byzantin*. Grenoble, 1967.

DePalma Digeser, E. "Lactantius, Porphyry, and the Debate over Religious Toleration." *Journal of Roman Studies* 88 (1998): 129–46.

Dickie, M. "Hermeias on Plato *Phaedrus* 238D and Synesius *Dion* 14.2." *American Journal of Philology* 114 (1993): 421–40.

Dillon, J. *Iamblichi Chalcidensis in Platonis dialogos commentariorum fragmenta*. Leiden, 1973.

————. "Iamblichus of Chalcis." *Aufstieg und Niedergang der Römischen Welt* 2.36.2 (1987): 862–909.

————. *The Middle Platonists 80 B.C. to A.D. 220*. 2nd ed. Ithaca, 1996.

————. *The Heirs of Plato: A Study of the Old Academy*. Oxford, 2003.

Dindorf, L., ed. *Ioannis Malalae Chronographia*. Bonn, 1831.

Dionisotti, A. C. "From Ausonius' Schooldays? A Schoolbook and its Relatives." *Journal of Roman Studies* 72 (1982): 83–125.

Dodds, E. R. *The Greeks and the Irrational*. Berkeley and Los Angeles, 1973.

Dold, A. "Die Orakelsprüche im St. Galler Palimpsestcodex 908 (die sogenannten 'Sortes Sangallenses')." *Österreichische Akademie der Wissenschaften* 225.4. Vienna, 1948.

Dombrowski, D. A. "Asceticism as Athletic Training in Plotinus." *Aufstieg und Niedergang der Römischen Welt* 2.36.1 (1987): 701–12.

Dörrie, H. "Ammonios, der Lehrer Plotins." *Hermes* 83 (1955): 439–77.

———. *Platonica Minora*. Munich, 1976.

Draguet, R. *Julien d'Halicarnasse et sa controverse avec Sévère d'Antioche sur l'incorruptibilité du corps du Christ*. Louvain, 1924.

———. "Une letter de Sérapion de Thmuis aux disciples d'Antoine (A.D. 356) en version syriaque et arménienne." *Le Muséon* 64 (1951): 1–25.

Drecoll, C. *Die Liturgien im römischen Kaiserreich des 3. und 4. Jh. n. Chr.* Stuttgart, 1997.

Dzielska, M. *Hypatia of Alexandria*. Translated by F. Lyra. Cambridge, Mass., 1995.

Edwards, M. "Ammonius, Teacher of Origen." *Journal of Ecclesiastical History* 44 (1993): 169–81.

———. "Birth, Death and Divinity in Porphyry's *On the Life of Plotinus*." In *Greek Biography and Panegyric in Late Antiquity*, edited by T. Hägg and P. Rousseau, 52–71. Berkeley and Los Angeles, 2000.

———, trans. *Neoplatonic Saints: The Lives of Plotinus and Proclus by their Students*. Liverpool, 2000.

Elm, S. "Hellenism and Historiography: Gregory of Nazianzus and Julian in Dialog." *Journal of Medieval and Early Modern Studies* 33.3 (2003): 493–515.

Elton, H. "Illus and the Imperial Aristocracy Under Zeno" *Byzantion* 70 (2000): 393–407.

Enea di Gaza. *Epistole*. Edited and translated by L. Positano. Naples, 1962.

Erskine, A. "Culture and Power in Ptolemaic Egypt: The Museum and Library of Alexandria." *Greece and Rome* 42 (1995): 38–48.

Etienne A., and D. O'Meara. *La philosophie épicurienne sur pierre: Les fragments de Diogène d'Oenoanda*. Paris, 1996.

Evelyn White, H. G. *The Monasteries of the Wādi'n Natrūn, pt. 2: The History of the Monasteries of Nitria*. New York, 1932.

Évrard, É. "Les convictions religieuses de Jean Philpon et la date de son Commentaire aux Météorologiques." *Bulletin de L'Académie royale de Belgique, Classe des lettres, sciences morales et politiques*, 5th ser., 39 (1953): 299–357.

———. "Le maître de Plutarque d'Athènes et les origines du Néoplatonisme Athénien." *L'Antiquité Classique* 29 (1960): 108–33.

———. "À quel titre Hypatie enseigna-t-elle la philosophie?" *Revue des Études Grecques* 90 (1977): 69–74.

Fernández, G. "Justinano y la clausura de la escuela de Atenas." *Erytheia* 2.2 (1983): 24–30.

Fischel, H. A. "Studies in Cynicism and the Ancient Near East." In *Religions in Antiquity: Essays in Memory of Erwin Ramsdell Goodenough*, edited by J. Neusner, Numen Supplement 14, 372–411. Leiden, 1968.

Fitzgerald, A., trans. *The Letters of Synesius of Cyrene*. Oxford, 1926.

Fögen, M. T. "Balsamon on Magic." In *Byzantine Magic*, edited by H. Maguire, 99–115. Dumbarton Oaks, 1995.

Follet, S. *Athènes au IIe et au IIIe Siècle*. Paris, 1976.

Fornara, C. "Eunapius' *Epidemia* in Athens." *Classical Quarterly* 39 (1989): 517–23.
Fowden, G. "The Platonist Philosopher and His Circle in Late Antiquity." *Φιλοσοφία* 7 (1977): 359–83.

———. "The Pagan Holy Man in Late Antique Society." *Journal of Hellenic Studies* 102 (1982): 33–59.

———. "Nicagoras of Athens and the Lateran Obelisk." *Journal of Hellenic Studies* 107 (1987): 51–57.

———. "City and Mountain in Late Roman Attica." *Journal of Hellenic Studies* 108 (1988): 48–59.

———. "The Athenian Agora and the Progress of Christianity." *Journal of Roman Archeology* 3 (1990): 494–500.

Frankfurter, D. *Religion in Roman Egypt: Assimilation and Resistance.* Princeton, 1998.

———. "The Consequences of Hellenism in Late Antique Egypt: Religious Worlds and Actors." *Archiv für Religionsgeschichte* 2 (2000): 162–94.

Frantz, A. "From Paganism to Christianity in the Temples of Athens." *Dumbarton Oaks Papers* 19 (1965): 185–205.

———. "Honors to a Librarian." *Hesperia* 35 (1966): 377–80.

———. "Pagan Philosophers in Christian Athens." *Proceedings of the American Philosophical Society* 119 (1975): 29–38.

———. "Did Julian the Apostate Rebuild the Parthenon?" *American Journal of Archaeology* 83 (1979): 395–401.

———. *The Athenian Agora XXIV: Late Antiquity; 267–700.* Princeton, 1988.

Fraser, P. *Ptolemaic Alexandria.* Oxford, 1972.

Frend, W. H. C. *The Rise of the Monophysite Movement.* Cambridge, 1972.

Friedländer, P., ed. *Spätantiker Gemäldezyklus in Gaza: Des Prokopios von Gaza Ekphrasis eikonos.* Vatican City, 1939.

Frier, B. W. "Natural Fertility and Family Limitation in Roman Marriage." *Classical Philology* 89 (1994): 318–33.

Galvão-Sobrinho, C. R. "The Rise of the Christian Bishop; Doctrine and Power in the Later Roman Empire, A.D. 318–80." PhD diss., Yale Unversity, 1999.

Garitte, G. "Textes hagiographiques orientaux relatifs à S. Leonce de Tripoli: L' homélie copte de Sevère d'Antioche." *Le Muséon* 79 (1966): 335–86.

Garnsey, P., and R. Saller. *The Roman Empire: Economy, Society, and Culture.* Berkeley and Los Angeles, 1987.

Geagan, D. *The Athenian Constitution After Sulla.* Hesperia Supplement 12. Princeton, 1967.

———. "Roman Athens: Some Aspects of Life and Culture I. 86 B.C.–A.D. 267." *Aufstieg und Niedergang der Römischen Welt* 2.7.1 (1979): 371–437.

Geiger, J. "Notes on the Second Sophistic in Palestine." *Illinois Classical Studies* 19 (1994): 221–30.

Gerostergios, A. *Justinian the Great, the Emperor and Saint.* Belmont, Mass., 1982.

Gleason, M. *Making Men: Sophists and Self-Presentation in Ancient Rome.* Princeton, 1995.

Glucker, J. *Antiochus and the Late Academy.* Göttingen, 1978.

Goldhill, S. *Being Greek under Rome: Cultural Identity, the Second Sophistic, and the Development of Empire.* Cambridge, 2001.

Goodenough, E. *The Politics of Philo Judaeus: Practice and Theory.* New Haven, 1938.

Gottschalk, H. B. "Notes on the Wills of Peripatetic Scholarchs." *Hermes* 100 (1972): 314–42.

Gottwald, J. "Die Kirche und das Schloss Paperon in Kililisch-Armenien." *Byzantinische Zeitschrift* 36 (1936): 86–100.

Goulet, R. "Sur la chronologie de la vie et des oeuvres d'Eunape de Sardes." *Journal of Hellenic Studies* 100 (1980): 60–72.

———. "Prohérésius le païen et quelques remarques sur la chronologie d'Eunape de Sardes." *Antiquité Tardive* 8 (2000): 209–22.

Grabbe L., and R. F. Hock, trans. "Nicolaus of Myra, *Progymnasmata.*" In *The Chreia in Ancient Rhetoric*. Vol. 1, *The Progymnasmata*, edited by R. F. Hock and E. N. O'Neil, 235–70. Atlanta, 1986.

Graindor, P. *Chronologie des archontes athéniens sous l'empire*. Brussels, 1922.

———. *Un Milliardaire antique, Hérode Attique et sa famille*. Cairo, 1930.

———. *Athènes sous Hadrien*. Cairo, 1934.

Grant, R. M. "Eusebius and His Lives of Origen." In *Forma Futuri: Studi in onore del Cardinale Michele Pellegrino*, 635–49. Turin, 1975.

Gregg, R. Review of *Arius: Heresy and Tradition*, by R. Williams. *Journal of Theological Studies* 40 (1989): 247–54.

Gregg, R., and D. Groh. *Early Arianism—A View of Salvation*. Philadelphia, 1981.

Gutas, D. "Plato's Symposium in the Arabic Tradition." *Oriens* 31 (1988): 36–60.

———. *Greek Thought, Arabic Culture*. New York, 1998.

Haas, C. *Alexandria in Late Antiquity: Topography and Social Conflict*. Baltimore, 1997.

Hadot, I. *Le Problème du Nèoplatonisme Alexandrin: Hiéroclès et Simplicius*. Paris, 1978.

———. "Les Introductions aux commentaires exégétiques chez les auteurs néoplatoniciens et les auteurs chrétiens." In *Les Règles de l'Interprétation*, edited by M. Tardieu, 99–123. Paris, 1987.

———, ed. *Simplicius: Commentaire sur le Manuel d'Épictète*. Leiden, 1996.

Hadot, P. *Marius Victorinus: Recherches sur sa vie et ses oeuvres*. Paris, 1971.

Hällström, G. "The Closing of the Neoplatonic School in A.D. 529: An Additional Aspect." In *Post-Herulian Athens: Aspects of Life and Culture in Athens, A.D. 267–529*, edited by P. Castrén, 141–60. Helsinki, 1994.

Hamilton, F. J., and E. W. Brooks, eds. and trans. *The Syriac chronicle known as that of Zachariah of Mitylene*. London, 1899.

Hanson, A. "Galen: Author and Critic." In *Editing Texts*, edited by G. Most, 22–53. Göttingen, 1998.

Harries, J. "The Background to the Code." In *The Theodosian Code*, edited by J. Harries and I. Wood, 1–16. Ithaca, 1993.

Harris, W. V. *Ancient Literacy*. Cambridge, Mass., 1989.

———. *Restraining Rage: The Ideology of Anger Control in Classical Antiquity*. Cambridge, Mass., 2001.

Hartmann, U. "Geist im Exil: Römische Philosophen am Hof den Sasaniden." In *Grenzüberschreitungen: Formen des Kontakts zwischen Orient und Okzident im Altertum*, edited by M. Schuol, U. Hartmann, and A. Luther, 123–60. Stuttgart, 2002.

Heath, M. "The Family of Minucianus?" *Zietschrift für Papyrologie und Epigraphik* 113 (1996): 66–70.

Heather, P., and D. Moncur, trans. *Politics, Philosophy, and Empire in the Fourth Century: Select Orations of Themistius*. Liverpool, 2001.

Heitsch, E. *Die griechischen Dichterfragmente der römischen Kaiserzeit.* Göttingen, 1961–64.

Hoffmann, P. "Simplicius' Polemics." In *Philoponus and the Rejection of Aristotelian Science*, edited by R. Sorabji, 57–83. London, 1987.

Holum, K. G. *Theodosian Empresses: Women and Imperial Dominion in Late Antiquity.* Berkeley and Los Angeles, 1982.

Honigmann, E. *Évêques et évêchés monophysites d'Asie Mineure au 6e siècle.* Corpus Scriptorum Christianorum Orientalium 127, subs. 2. Louvain, 1951.

Hult, K. "Marinus the Samaritan: A Study of *Vit. Isid.* Fr. 141." *Classica et Mediaevalia* 43 (1993): 163–75.

Husson, P., and P. Nautin, trans. *Origène: Homélies sur Jérémie 1–11.* Sources Chrétiennes 232. Paris, 1976.

Igal, J. "The Gnostics and 'The Ancient Philosophy' in Plotinus." In *Neoplatonism and Early Christian Thought*, edited by H. J. Blumenthal and R. A. Markus, 138–49. London, 1981.

Jackson, R., K. Lycos, and H. Tarrant, trans. *Olympiodorus' Commentary on Plato's Gorgias.* Leiden, 1998.

Jenkins, R. J. H. "The Bronze Athena at Byzantium." *Journal of Hellenic Studies* 67 (1947): 31–33.

John of Nikiu. The *Chronicle of John, Bishop of Nikiu.* Translated by R. Charles. Oxford, 1916.

Jones, A. "The Horoscope of Proclus." *Classical Philology* 94 (1999): 81–88.

Jones, A. H. M. *The Later Roman Empire, 284–602.* Norman, 1964.

Jones, C. P. "A Friend of Galen." *Classical Quarterly* 17 (1967): 311–12.

———. "The Date of Dio of Prusa's Alexandrian Oration." *Historia* 22 (1973): 302–309.

———. "The Reliability of Philostratus." In *Approaches to the Second Sophistic*, edited by G. Bowersock, 11–16. University Park, Penn., 1974.

———. *The Roman World of Dio Chrysostom.* Cambridge, Mass., 1978.

Kapetanopoulos, E. "The Reform of the Athenian Constitution under Hadrian." *Horos* 10–12 (1992/98): 215–37.

Karivieri, A. "The So-called 'Library of Hadrian' and the Tetraconch Church in Athens." In *Post-Herulian Athens: Aspects of Life and Culture in Athens, A.D. 267–529*, edited by P. Castrén, 89–113. Helsinki, 1994.

———. "The House of Proclus on the Southern Slope of the Acropolis: A Contribution." In *Post-Herulian Athens: Aspects of Life and Culture in Athens, A.D. 267–529*, edited by P. Castrén, 115–39. Helsinki, 1994.

Kaster, R. A. "The Salaries of Libanius." *Chiron* 13 (1983): 37–59.

———. *Guardians of Language: The Grammarian and Society in Late Antiquity.* Berkeley and Los Angeles, 1988.

Kennedy, G., trans. *Progymnasmata : Greek textbooks of prose composition and rhetoric.* Leiden, 2003.

Kim, C. H. *Form and Structure of the Familiar Greek Letter of Recommendation.* Missoula, Mont., 1972.

Klingshirn, W. "Defining the *Sortes Sanctorum:* Gibbon, Du Cange, and Early Christian Lot Divination." *Journal of Early Christian Studies* 10 (2002): 77–130.

Klotz, A. "Studien zu den Panegyrici Latini." *Rheinisches Museum* 66 (1911): 513–72.

Konstan, D. "How to Praise a Friend: Gregory Nazianzus's Funeral Oration for St.

Basil the Great." In *Greek Biography and Panegyric in Late Antiquity,* edited by T. Hägg and P. Rousseau, 160–79. Berkeley and Los Angeles, 2000.

Kraemer, E. *Le Jeu d'Amour: Jeu d'aventure du moyen âge.* Commentationes Humanarum Litterarum 54. Helsinki, 1975.

Kraemer, J. L. "A lost passage from Philoponus' *Contra Aristotelem* in Arabic Translation." *Journal of the American Oriental Society* 85 (1965): 318–27.

Lamberton, R. *Homer the Theologian: Neoplatonist Allegorical Reading and the Growth of the Epic Tradition.* Berkeley and Los Angeles, 1986.

————. "The Schools of Platonic Philosophy of the Roman Empire: The Evidence of the Biographies." In *Education in Greek and Roman Antiquity,* edited by Y. L. Too, 433–58. Leiden, 2001.

Lameer, J. "From Alexandria to Baghdad: Reflections on the Genesis of a Problematical Tradition." In *The Ancient Tradition in Christian and Islamic Hellenism,* edited by G. Endress and R. Kruk, 181–91. Leiden, 1997.

Lane Fox, R. *Pagans and Christians.* New York, 1986.

Lang, H. S. and A. D. Macro, ed. and trans. *Proclus: On the Eternity of the World (De aeternitate mundi).* Berkeley and Los Angeles, 2001.

Lang, U. M. "Nicetas Choniates, a neglected witness to the Greek text of John Philoponus' *Arbiter.*" *Journal of Theological Studies* 48 (1997): 540–48.

————. *John Philoponus and the Controversies over Chalcedon in the Sixth Century: A Study and Translation of the Arbiter.* Louvain, 2001.

Laniado, A. *Recherches sur les notables municipaux dans l'empire protobyzantin.* Travaux et Mémoires: Monographies 13. Paris, 2002.

Layton, B. *The Gnostic Scriptures.* New York, 1987.

————. "The Significance of Basilides in Ancient Christian Thought." *Representations* 28 (1989): 133–51.

Layton, R. *Didymus the Blind and His Circle in Late-Antique Alexandria: Virtue and Narrative in Biblical Scholarship.* Urbana, 2004.

Le Boulluec, A. "L'École d'Alexandrie: De quelques aventures d'un concept historiographique." In Ἀλεξανδρινά. *Hellénisme, judaïsme et christianisme à Alexandrie, Mélanges offerts à C. Mondésert,* 403–17. Paris, 1987.

Lepelley, C. *Les cités de l'Afrique romaine au Bas-Empire.* 2 vols. Paris, 1979–81.

Lewis, N. "The Non-Scholar Members of the Alexandrian Museum." *Mnemosyne* 16 (1963): 257–61.

————. "*Literati* in the service of Roman Emperors: Politics before culture." In *Coins, Culture and History in the Ancient World: Numismatic and Other Studies in Honor of Bluma L. Trell,* edited by L. Casson and M. Price, 149–66. Detroit, 1981.

Lewy, Y. *Chaldean Oracles and Theurgy.* 2nd ed., edited by M. Tardieu. Paris, 1978.

Liebeschuetz, J. H. W. G. *Antioch: City and Imperial Administration in the Later Roman Empire.* Oxford, 1972.

————. *Barbarians and Bishops: Army, Church, and State in the Age of Arcadius.* Oxford, 1990.

————. *The Decline and Fall of the Roman City.* Oxford, 2001.

Lilla, S. *Clement of Alexandria: A study in Christian Platonism and Gnosticism.* Oxford, 1971.

Lorenz, R. "Die Christusseele im arianischen Streit." *Zeitschrift für Kirchengeschichte* 94 (1983): 1–51.

Louth, A. "St. Athanasius and the Greek Life of Antony." *Journal of Theological Studies* 39 (1988): 504–509.

Luna, C. Review of *Simplikios und das Ende der neuplatonischen Schule in Athen*, by R. Thiel. *Mnemosyne* 54 (2001): 482–504.

Lyman, R. "Hellenism and Heresy." *Journal of Early Christian Studies* 11.2 (2003): 209–22.

Lynch, J. P. *Aristotle's School: A Study of a Greek Educational Institution*. Berkeley and Los Angeles, 1972.

MacCoull, L. "Dioscorus of Aphrodito and John Philoponus." *Studia Patristica* 18 (1987): 163–68.

———. "A New Look at the Career of John Philoponus." *Journal of Early Christian Studies* 3 (1995): 47–60.

Magdalino, P. "The History of the Future and Its Uses: Prophecy, Policy, and Propaganda." In *The Making of Byzantine History: Studies Dedicated to Donald M. Nicol*, edited by R. Beaton and C. Roueché, 3–34. Aldershot, 1993.

Mahdi, M. "al-Farabi against Philoponus." *Journal of Near Eastern Studies* 26 (1967): 233–60.

Majercik, R. *The Chaldean Oracles: Text, Translation, and Commentary*. Leiden, 1989.

Mansfeld, J. "Alexander and the History of Neoplatonism." In *An Alexandrian Platonist Against Dualism: Alexander of Lycopolis' Treatise "Critique of the Doctrines of Manichaeus*," translated with an introduction by P. W. van der Horst and J. Mansfeld, 6–48. Leiden, 1974.

———. *Studies in Later Greek Philosophy and Gnosticism*. London, 1989.

———. *Prolegomena: Questions to Be Settled before the Study of an Author or Text*. Leiden, 1994.

———. *Prolegomena Mathematica: From Apollonius of Perga to Late Neoplatonism*. Leiden, 1998.

Mansi, G. D. *Sacrorum conciliorum nova et amplissima collectio*. 54 vols. Paris, 1901–27.

Marcus, W. *Der Subordinatianismus als historiologisches Phänomen*. Munich, 1963.

Marrou, H. I. *ΜΟΥΣΙΚΟΣ ΑΝΗΡ·* Étude sur les scènes de la vie intellectuelle figurant sur les monuments funéraires romains. Grenoble, 1937.

———. *Saint Augustin et la Fin de la Culture Antique*. Paris, 1938.

———. *Histoire de l'Éducation dans l'Antiquité*. Paris, 1956.

———, ed. *Le pédagogue [par] Clément d'Alexandrie*. 3 vols. Paris, 1960.

Maspero, J. "Horapollon et la fin du paganisme égyptien." *Bulletin de l'Institut français d'Archéologie Orientale* 11 (1914): 163–95.

———. *Histoire des Patriarches d'Alexandrie: depuis la mort d' Empereur Anastase jusqu' à la reconciliation des églises jacobites*. Paris, 1923.

Masson, O. "Θεότεκνος <Fils de Dieu>." *Revue des Études Grecques* 110 (1997): 618–19.

Matthews, J. *The Roman Empire of Ammianus*. London, 1989.

———. "The Making of the Text." In *The Theodosian Code*, edited by J. Harries and I. Wood, 19–44. Ithaca, 1993.

———. *Laying Down the Law: A Study of the Theodosian Code*. New Haven, 2000.

Mattingly, D. J. "First Fruit? The Olive in the Roman World." In *Human Landscapes in Classical Antiquity: Environment and Culture*, edited by G. Shipley and J. Salmon, 213–53. London, 1996.

McKenzie, J. S., S. Gibson, and A. T. Reyes. "Reconstructing the Serapeum in Alexandria from the Archeological Evidence." *Journal of Roman Studies* 94 (2004): 73–121.

McLynn, N. "The Fourth Century 'Taurobolium.'" *Phoenix* 50 (1996): 312–30.

Meier, M. *Das andere Zeitalter Justinians. Kontingenzerfahrung und Kontingenzbewältigung im 6. Jht. N. Chr.* Hypomnemata 147. Göttingen, 2003.

Meijering, E. P., ed. and trans. *Athanasius: Contra Gentes.* Leiden, 1984.

Merlan, P. "Ammonius Hermiae, Zacharias Scholasticus and Boethius." *Greek, Roman and Byzantine Studies* 9 (1968): 193–203.

Millar, F. "P. Herennius Dexippus: The Greek World and the Third Century Invasions." *Journal of Roman Studies* 59 (1969): 12–29.

———. *The Emperor in the Roman World.* Ithaca, 1977.

Miller, S. "A Roman Monument in the Athenian Agora." *Hesperia* 41 (1972): 50–95.

Mitchell, S. "Maximinus and the Christians in A.D. 312: A New Latin Inscription." *Journal of Roman Studies* 78 (1988): 105–24.

Mitsos, M. Ἀπὸ τοὺς καταλόγους Ἀθηναίων Ἐφήβων κλπ. (III), Archaiologikē Ephēmeris, 56–65. Athens, 1971.

Moles, J. L. "The Career and Conversion of Dio Chrysostom." *Journal of Hellenic Studies* 98 (1978): 79–100.

Momigliano, A. *The Development of Greek Biography.* Cambridge, Mass., 1971.

Morgan, T. *Literate Education in the Hellenistic and Roman Worlds.* Cambridge, 1998.

Musurillo, H., ed. *Acts of the Pagan Martyrs.* Oxford, 1954.

Naour, C. *Tyriaion en Cabalide: Épigraphie et géographie historique.* Zutphen, 1980.

Nautin, P. *Origène: Sa vie et son œuvre.* Paris, 1977.

Neugebauer, O. *A History of Ancient Mathematical Astronomy.* New York, 1975.

Nixon, C. E. V., and B. S. Rodgers. *In Praise of Later Roman Emperors: The Panegyrici Latini.* Berkeley and Los Angeles, 1994.

Norman, A. F. *Libanius: Autobiography and Selected Letters.* 2 vols. Cambridge, 1990.

Nutton, V. "Two Notes on Immunities: Digest 27.1.6.10 and 11." *Journal of Roman Studies* 61 (1971): 52–63.

O'Brien, D. "Plotinus and the Secrets of Ammonius." *Hermathena* 157 (1994): 117–53.

Oliver, J. H. *Marcus Aurelius: Aspects of Civic and Cultural Policy in the East.* Hesperia Supplement 13. Princeton, 1970.

O'Meara, D. *Pythagoras Revived: Mathematics and Philosophy in Late Antiquity.* Oxford, 1989.

Parsons, P. J. "Petitions and a letter: The Grammarian's Complaint." In *Collectanea Papyrologica, Texts Published in Honor of H. C. Youtie,* edited by A. Hanson, 409–46. Bonn, 1976.

Patillon, M., ed. and French trans. *Aelius Theon: Progymnasmata.* Paris, 1997.

Pearson, C. "Scripture as Cosmology: Natural Philosophical Debate in John Philoponus' Alexandria." PhD diss., Harvard University, 1999.

Peek, W. "Zwei Gedichte auf den Neuplatoniker Plutarch." *Zeitschrift für Papyrologie und Epigraphik* 13 (1974): 201–204.

Penella, R. "When was Hypatia Born?" *Historia* 33 (1984): 126–28.

———. *Greek Philosophers and Sophists in the Fourth Century A.D.: Studies in Eunapius of Sardis.* Leeds, 1990.

Pépin, J. *Théologie cosmique et théologie chrétienne.* Paris, 1964.

Perczel, I. "Pseudo-Dionysius and the Platonic Theology: A Preliminary Study." In

Proclus et la Théologie Platonicienne, edited by A. P. Segonds and C. Steel, 491–530. Paris, 2000.

———. "Pseudo-Dionysius and Palestinian Origenism." In *The Sabaite Heritage in the Orthodox Church from the Fifth Century to the Present,* edited by J. Patrich, 261–82. Leuven, 2001.

Petit, P. *Les Étudiants de Libanius.* Paris, 1957.

Pétrides, S. "Spoudaei et Philopones." *Echoes d'Orient* 7 (1904): 341–48.

Philoponus. *Against Aristotle on the Eternity of the World.* Translated by C. Wildberg. Ithaca, 1987.

Pleket, H. W. "Urban Elites and the Economy of the Greek Cities of the Roman Empire." *Münsterische Beiträge z. antiken Handelsgesichte* 3 (1984): 3–36.

Pouilloux, J. "Une famille de sophistes thessaliens à Delphes au deuxième siècle ap. J.C." *Revue des Études Grecques* 80 (1967): 379–84.

Praechter, K. "Die griechischen Aristoteleskommentatoren." *Byzantinische Zeitschrift* 18 (1909): 516–38.

———. "Richtungen und Schulen im Neuplatonismus." *Genethliakon für Carl Robert,* 105–56. Berlin, 1910.

Quass, F. "Zum Problem der Kultivierung brachliegenden Gemeindelandes kaiserzeitlicher Städte Griechenlands." *Tekmeria* 2 (1996): 82–117.

Rappe, S. "The New Math: How to Add and to Subtract Pagan Elements in Christian Education." In *Education in Greek and Roman Antiquity,* edited by Y. L. Too, 405–32. Leiden, 2001.

Raubitschek, A. E. "Iamblichos at Athens." *Hesperia* 33 (1964): 63–68.

Rees, R. *Layers of Loyalty in Latin Panegyric: A.D. 289–307.* Oxford, 2002.

Refoulé, F. "Rêves et vie spirituelle d'après Evagre le Pontique." *La Vie Spirituelle* 14 (1961): 470–516.

Richard, M. " Ἀπὸ φωνῆς." *Byzantion* 20 (1950): 191–222.

Ridley, R. T., trans. *Zosimus: New History.* Canberra, 1982.

Rist, J. M. "Hypatia." *Phoenix* 19 (1965): 214–25.

———. "The Importance of Stoic Logic in the *Contra Celsum.*" In *Neoplatonism and Early Christian Thought,* edited by H. J. Blumenthal and R. A. Markus, 64–78. London, 1981.

Robert, L. *Épigrammes du Bas Empire (Hellenica IV).* Paris, 1948.

Roberts, L. "Origen and Stoic Logic." *Transactions of the American Philological Association* 101 (1970): 433–44.

Rodziewicz, M. "A Review of the Archeological Evidence Concerning the Cultural Institutions in Ancient Alexandria." *Graeco-Arabica* 6 (1995): 317–32.

Roques, D. *Synésios de Cyrène et la Cyrénaïque du Bas-Empire.* Études d'antiquités africaines. Paris, 1987.

———. *Études sur la Correspondance de Synésios de Cyrène.* Brussels, 1989.

———. "La Famille d'Hypatie (Synésios, epp. 5 et 16 G)." *Revue des Études Grecques* 108 (1995): 128–49.

———. "Θεότεκνος <Fils de Dieu>." *Revue des Études Grecques* 111 (1998): 735–56.

Rothaus, R. *Corinth: The First City of Greece.* Leiden, 2000.

Roueché, C. *Aphrodisias in Late Antiquity: The Late Roman and Byzantine Inscriptions.* London, 1989.

―――. "The Functions of the Governor in Late Antiquity: Some Observations." *Antiquité Tardive* 6 (1998): 31–36 and 83–89.

Rougé, J. "La politique de Cyrille d'Alexandrie et le meurtre d'Hypatie." *Cristianesimo nella storia* 11 (1990): 485–504.

Rousseau, P. "Antony as a Teacher in the Greek Life." In *Greek Biography and Panegyric in Late Antiquity*, edited by T. Hägg and P. Rousseau, 89–109. Berkeley and Los Angeles, 2000.

Rubenson, S. *The Letters of St. Antony: Origenist Theology, Monastic Tradition and the Making of a Saint.* Lund, 1990.

―――. "Philosophy and Simplicity: The Problem of Classical Education in Early Christian Biography." In *Greek Biography and Panegyric in Late Antiquity*, edited by T. Hägg and P. Rousseau, 110–39. Berkeley and Los Angeles, 2000.

Ruffini, G. "Late Antique Pagan Networks from Athens to the Thebaid." In *Ancient Alexandria between Egypt and Greece*, W. V. Harris and G. Ruffini, eds., 241–57. Leiden, 2004.

Saffrey, H. D. "Le chrétien Jean Philopon et la survivance de l'École d' Alexandrie au VIe siècle." *Revue des Études Grecques* 67 (1954): 396–410.

―――. "Neoplatonist spirituality II: From Iamblichus to Proclus and Damascius." In *Classical Mediterranean Spirituality: Egyptian, Greek, Roman*, edited by A. H. Armstrong, 250–65. New York, 1986.

―――. "Accorder entre elles les traditions théologiques: une caractéristique du Néoplatonisme Athénien." In *On Proclus and his Influence in Medieval Philosophy*, edited by E. P. Bos and P. A. Meijer, 35–50. Leiden, 1992.

Saffrey, H. D., and L. G. Westerink, eds. and trans. *Proclus: Théologie Platonicienne.* 6 vols. Paris, 1968–1997.

Schibli, H. *Hierocles of Alexandria.* Oxford, 2002.

Schissel, O. "Die Familie des Minukianos." *Klio* 21 (1926/7): 361–73.

Schneemelcher, W. "Zur Chronologie des arianischen Streites." *Theologische Literaturzeitung* 79.7–8 (1954): 393–99.

Scholten, C. "Die alexandrinische Katechetenschule." *Jahrbuch für Antike und Christentum* 38 (1995): 16–37.

―――. *Antike Naturphilosophie und christliche Kosmologie in der Schrift "De opificio mundi" des Johannes Philoponos.* Berlin, 1996.

Schroeder, F. M. "Ammonius Saccas." *Aufstieg und Niedergang der Römischen Welt* 2.36.1 (1987): 493–526.

Schubert, P. "Philostrate et les sophistes d'Alexandrie." *Mnemosyne* 48.2 (1995): 178–88.

Schwartz, J. "La fin du Serapeum d'Alexandrie." *American Studies in Papyrology.* Vol. 1, *Essays in Honor of C. Bradford Welles*, 97–111. New Haven, 1966.

Schwyzer, H. R. *Ammonios Sakkas, der Lehrer Plotins.* Opladen, 1983.

Scott, R. "Malalas and Justinian's Codification." In *Byzantine Papers*, edited by E. Jeffreys et al., 12–31. Canberra, 1981.

―――. "Malalas, *The Secret History*, and Justinian's Propaganda." *Dumbarton Oaks Papers* 39 (1985): 99–109.

Seeck, O. *Die Briefe des Libanius.* Berlin, 1906.

Shaw, G. "Theurgy: Rituals of Unification in the Neoplatonism of Iamblichus." *Traditio* 41 (1985): 1–28.

Shear, T. L. "The Athenian Agora: Excavations of 1970." *Hesperia* 40 (1971): 241–79.
———. "The Athenian Agora: Excavations of 1971." *Hesperia* 42 (1973): 121–79.
———. "Athens: From City-State to Provincial Town." *Hesperia* 50 (1981): 356–77.
Sheppard, A. "Proclus' Attitude to Theurgy." *Classical Quarterly* 32 (1982): 212–24.
Sijpesteijn, P. J. "New Light on the *Philoponoi*." *Aegyptus* 69 (1989): 95–99.
Siorvanes, L. *Proclus: Neo-Platonic Philosophy and Science*. New Haven, 1996.
Sironen, E. "An Honorary Epigram for Empress Eudocia in the Athenian Agora." *Hesperia* 59 (1990): 371–74.
———. "Life and Administration in Late Roman Attica." In *Post-Herulian Athens: Aspects of Life and Culture in Athens, A.D. 267–529*, edited by P. Castrén, 15–62. Helsinki, 1994.
———. *The Late Roman and Early Byzantine Inscriptions of Athens and Attica*. Helsinki, 1997.
Smith, A. *Porphyry's Place in the Neoplatonic Tradition: A Study in Post-Plotinian Neoplatonism*. The Hague, 1974.
Smith, M. F. *The Philosophical Inscription of Diogenes of Oinoanda*. Vienna, 1996.
———. *Supplement to Diogenes of Oinoanda The Epicurean Inscription*. Istituto Italiano per gli Studi Filosofici. La Scuola di Epicuro. Naples, 2003.
Sodini, J. P. "L'habitat urbain en Grèce à la veille des invasions." In *Villes et peuplement dans l'Illyricum protobyzantin: Actes du colloque organisé par l'École française de Rome 78*, 341–97. Paris, 1984.
Sorabji, R. *Time, Creation, and the Continuum: Theories in Antiquity and the Early Middle Ages*. Ithaca, 1983.
———. "John Philoponus." In *Philoponus and the Rejection of Aristotelian Science*, edited by R. Sorabji, 1–40. London, 1987.
———. "Divine Names and Sordid Deals in Ammonius' Alexandria." In *The Philosopher and Society in Late Antiquity*, edited by A. Smith, 203–14. Swansea, 2005.
Spatharē, E. and M. Chatziotē. "Λεωφίας Βασ. Σοφίας και Ηρώδου του Αττικού 2." *Archaiologikon Deltion* 38 (1983): 23–25.
Stark, R. *The Rise of Christianity: A Sociologist Reconsiders History*. Princeton, 1996.
Stead, G. C. "In search of Valentinus." In *The Rediscovery of Gnosticism*, vol. 1, edited by B. Layton, 75–102. Leiden, 1980.
———. "Arius in Modern Research." *Journal of Theological Studies* 45 (1994): 24–36.
———. "Was Arius a Neoplatonist?" *Studia Patristica* 32 (1997): 39–51.
Steel, C. "Proclus et Denys: De l'existence du mal." In *Denys l'Aréopagite et sa postérité en Orient et en Occident*, edited by Y. de Andia, 89–108. Paris, 1997.
Stuart, D. R. *Epochs of Greek and Roman Biography*. Berkeley, 1928.
Swain, S. "The Reliability of Philostratus' *Lives of the Sophists*." *Classical Antiquity* 10.1 (1991): 148–63.
Taormina, D. *Plutarco di Atene: l'uno, l'anima, le forme*. Rome, 1989.
Tarán, L., ed. *Asclepius of Tralles: Commentary to Nicomachus' Introduction to Arithmetic*. Transactions of the American Philosophical Society, n.s., 59. Philadelphia, 1969.
Tardieu, M. "La Gnose Valentinienne et les Oracles Chaldaïques." In *The Rediscovery of Gnosticism*, vol. 1, edited by B. Layton, 194–237. Leiden, 1980.
———. "Ṣābiens Coraniques et 'Ṣābiens' de Harrān." *Journal Asiatique* 274 (1986): 1–44.

————. *Les Paysages reliques. Routes et haltes syriennes d'Isidore à Simplicius.* Louvain-Paris, 1990.

Tarrant, H. "Olympiodorus and the Surrender of Paganism." *Byzantinische Forschungen* 24 (1997): 181–92.

Telfer, W. "St. Peter of Alexandria and Arius." *Analecta Bollandiana* 67 (1949): 117–30.

Thompson, H. "Athenian Twilight: A.D. 267–600." *Journal of Roman Studies* 49 (1959): 61–72.

Thurn, I., ed. *Ioannis Malalae Chronographia.* New York, 2000.

Tkaczow, M., *Topography of Ancient Alexandria: An Archeological Map.* Warsaw, 1993.

Tobin, J. *Herodes Attikos and the City of Athens: Patronage and Conflict under the Antonines.* Amsterdam, 1997.

Too, Y. L. "Introduction: Writing the History of Ancient Education." In *Education in Greek and Roman Antiquity,* edited by Y. L. Too, 1–21. Leiden, 2001.

Trabattoni, F. "Per un biografia di Damascio." *Rivista di storia della filosofia* 40 (1985): 179–201.

Trigg, J. W. "God's Marvelous *Oikonomia:* Reflections of Origen's Understanding of Divine and Human Pedagogy in the *Address* Ascribed to Gregory Thaumaturgus." *Journal of Early Christian Studies* 9 (2001): 27–52.

Trombley, F. *Hellenic Religion and Christianization c.* 370–529. 2 vols. Leiden, 1993–94.

Tuilier, A. "Les evangelistes et les docteurs de la primitive église et les origines de l'École (didaskaleion) d'Alexandrie." *Studia Patristica* 17.2 (1982): 738–49.

van Cauwenbergh, P. *Étude sur les moines d'Égypte: depuis le Concile de Chalcédoine, jusqu'à l'invasion arabe.* Paris-Louvain, 1914; reprinted Milan, 1973.

Van Dam, R. *Kingdom of Snow: Roman Rule and Greek Culture in Cappadocia.* Philadelphia, 2002.

————. *Families and Friends in Late Roman Cappadocia.* Philadelphia, 2003.

van den Berg, R. M. "Smoothing Over the Differences: Proclus and Ammonius on Plato's *Cratylus* and Aristotle's *De Interpretatione.*" In *Philosophy, Science and Exegesis in Greek, Arabic and Latin Commentaries,* vol. 1, edited by P. Adamson, H. Baltussen and M. W. F. Store, 191–201. London, 2004.

van den Broek, R. "The Christian 'School' of Alexandria in the Second and Third Centuries." In *Centres of Learning: Learning and Location in Pre-Modern Europe and the Near East,* edited by J. W. Drijvers and A. M. MacDonald, 39–47. Leiden, 1995.

van den Hoek, A. "The 'Catechetical' School of Early Christian Alexandria and its Philonic Heritage." *Harvard Theological Review* 90 (1997): 59–87.

van Unnik, W. C. *Tarsus or Jerusalem?* Translated by G. Ogg. London, 1962.

van Uytfanghe, M. "L'Hagiographie: un genre chrétien ou antique tardif?" *Analecta Bollandiana* 111 (1993): 135–88.

Vasiliev, A. A. *Justin the First: An Introduction to the Epoch of Justinian.* Cambridge, Mass., 1950.

Verbeke, G. "Some later Neoplatonic Views on Divine Creation and the Eternity of the World." In *Neoplatonism and Christian Thought,* edited by D. O'Meara, 45–53. Albany, 1982.

Verrycken, K. "The metaphysics of Ammonius son of Hermeias." In *Aristotle Transformed,* edited by R. Sorabji, 199–232. London, 1990.

————. "The Development of Philoponus' thought and its chronology." In *Aristotle Transformed,* edited by R. Sorabji, 233–74. London, 1990.

Vessey, M. "The Origins of the *Collectio Sirmondiana:* A New Look at the Evidence." In *The Theodosian Code,* edited by J. Harries and I. Wood, 178–99. Ithaca, 1993.

Vinzent, M. "'Oxbridge' in der ausgehenden Spätantike oder: Ein Vergleich der Schulen von Athen und Alexandrien." *Zeitschrift für Antikes Christentum* 4 (2000): 49–82.

von Haehling, R. "Damascius und die heidnische Opposition im 5 Jahrhundert nach Christus." *Jahrbuch für Antike und Christentum* 23 (1980): 82–95.

von Harnack, A. *Porphyrius "Gegen de Christen."* Berlin, 1916.

Walden, J. W. H. *The Universities of Ancient Greece.* New York, 1909.

Walker, J. "The Limits of Late Antiquity: Philosophy between Rome and Iran." *Ancient World* 33 (2002): 45–69.

Watts, E. "The Late Antique Student's Perspective on Education Life." *New England Classical Journal* 27.2 (2000): 73–78.

———. "Student Travel to Intellectual Centers: What Was the Attraction?" In *Travel, Communication, and Geography in Late Antiquity,* edited by L. Ellis and F. Kidner, 11–21. Aldershot, 2004.

———. "Justinian, Malalas, and the End of Athenian Philosophical Teaching in A.D. 529." *Journal of Roman Studies* 94 (2004): 168–82.

———. "An Alexandrian Christian Response to Neoplatonic Influence." In *The Philosopher and Society in Late Antiquity,* edited by A. Smith, 215–30. Swansea, 2005.

———. "The Murder of Hypatia: Acceptable or Unacceptable Violence." In *Violence in Late Antiquity,* edited by H. A. Drake, 333–42. Aldershot, 2005.

———. "Orality and Communal Identity in Eunapius' *Lives of the Sophists and Philosophers.*" *Byzantion* 75 (2005): forthcoming.

Webb, R. "The Progymnasmata as Practice." In *Education in Greek and Roman Antiquity,* edited by Y. L. Too, 289–316. Leiden, 2001.

Westerink, L. G. "Deux commentaires sur Nicomaque: Asclépius et Jean Philopon." *Revue des Études Grecques* 77 (1964): 526–35.

———, ed. and trans. *The Greek Commentaries on Plato's Phaedo.* 2 vols. New York, 1976–77.

———, ed. and trans. *Prolégomènes à la philosophie de Platon.* Paris, 1990.

Whittow, M. "Ruling the Late Roman and Early Byzantine City: A Continuous History." *Past and Present* 129 (Nov., 1990): 3–29.

Wildberg, C. "Prolegomena to the Study of Philoponus' *Contra Aristotelem.*" In *Philoponus and the Rejection of Aristotelian Science,* edited by R. Sorabji, 197–209. London, 1987.

———. "Three Neoplatonic Introductions to Philosophy: Ammonius, David, and Elias." *Hermathena* 149 (1990): 33–51.

Williams, M. A. "The *Life of Antony* and the Domestication of Charismatic Wisdom." In *Charisma and Sacred Biography,* edited by M. A. Williams, JAAR Thematic Studies 48, 23–45. Chambersburg, Pa., 1982.

———. *Rethinking "Gnosticism": An Argument for Dismantling a Dubious Category.* Princeton, 1996.

Williams, R. "The Logic of Arianism." *Journal of Theological Studies* 34 (1983): 56–81.

———. *Arius: Heresy and Tradition.* London, 1987. *[Arius¹]*

———. *Arius: Heresy and Tradition.* 2nd ed. Grand Rapids, 2002. *[Arius²]*

Williamson, R. *Jews in the Hellenistic World: Philo.* Cambridge, 1989.

Wilson, N. G., ed. *Saint Basil on the Value of Greek Literature.* London, 1975.

Winter, B. *Philo and Paul Among the Sophists: Alexandrian and Corinthian Responses to a Julio-Claudian Movement.* 2nd ed. Cambridge, 2002.

Wipszycka, E. "Les confréries dans la vie religeuse de l'Egypte chrétienne." In *Proceedings of the Twelfth International Congress of Papyrology,* edited by R. Samuel, 511–25. Toronto, 1970.

Wolf, P. *Vom Schulwesen der Spätantike: Studien zu Libanius.* Baden, 1952.

Wolska, W. *La Topographie Chrétienne de Cosmas Indicopleustès: Théologie et Sciences au VIe siècle.* Paris, 1962.

———— (Wolska-Conus). "Stéphanos d'Athènes et Stéphanos d'Alexandrie: Essai d'identification et de biographie." *Revue des Études Byzantines* 47 (1989): 5–89.

Youtie, H. C. "*ΑΓΡΑΜΜΑΤΟΣ*: An Aspect of Greek Society in Egypt." *Harvard Studies in Classical Philology* 75 (1971): 161–76.

————. "βραδέως γράφων: Between Literacy and Illiteracy." *Greek, Roman, and Byzantine Studies* 12 (1971): 239–61.

Zacaria Scolastico. *Ammonio: Introduzione, testo critico, traduzione, commentario.* Edited by M. Colonna. Naples, 1973.

Zacharias of Mytilene. *Vie de Sévère.* Translated by M. A. Kugener. Patrologia Orientalis, vol. 2. Paris, 1907.

Zeller, E. *Philosophie der Griechen.* Leipzig, 1876–89.

Zintzen, C., ed. *Vitae Isidori Reliquiae.* Hildesheim, 1967.

INDEX

Achaea, 36, 37, 128, 131; Christians in, 84–87, 128, 131, 140; Heruls in, 38; magistrates of, 42, 45, 60, 125, 136, 137

Aedesia, 101, 207–10; death of, 222; education of sons, 209

Aedesius, 50n6, 188

Aeneas of Gaza, 213, 227; letters of, 16; *Theophrastus*, 213

Agathias, 139

agneuontas, 145

akroatēs, 31, 32, 34, 35, 43, 68, 147, 160

Alcinous, 4

Alexander, bishop of Alexandria, 174–75

Alexander of Lycopolis, 167; Plotinian influences, 172n16

Alexandria, 128, 143–55; "Catechetical School" of, 162n107, 163–64; Caesareum of, 144, 149, 198; center of Theon's teaching, 187; Christian community, 153, 166–68, 169, 171–86, 196–98, 211–16, 219–20, 246–49; Christian intellectual centers outside of, 184–86; *collegia* of, 152–53; Didymus the Blind in, 183; Dio Chrysostom in, 143; diversity of, 151; Gazan students in, 9; Iamblichan Neoplatonism in, 188–92; Jewish community, 151–53, 197, 198; Library, 146, 148–51; *Mouseion*, 146–

48; physical setting, 143–44; Proclus's studies in, 92; temples of, 144–45; urban violence in, 151–52

al-Farabi, 245–46

Amelius, student of Plotinus, 52

Ammianus Marcellinus, 20

Ammonius, 16, 227–29, 232, 239; and John Philoponus, 240, 241; relationship to *Theophrastus* of Aeneas of Gaza, 227. *See also* Zacharias Scholasticus

Ammonius Saccas, 91, 155–61, 164, 166–67, 206; division of students within school, 156–57; Christian Origen's study under, 159–61

Ammonius, son of Hermeias, 208–11, 217, 219, 220, 222–34, 237, 239, 244, 252, 256; Aristotelian commentator, 210n40; Christian students of, 210–11; and John Philoponus, 238; and Nicomedes' investigation, 222, 226; Platonic teaching, 226; political influence, 18; views on eternity of the world, 228

Anastasius, 129–30, 246

Andromachus, 41

anger, 7n33, 18

anti-pagan violence, 84, 190–91, 198–201, 219–20

Antoninus, 188–90

Antoninus Pius, 69

Compositor: Integrated Composition Systems
Text: 10/12 Baskerville
Display: Baskerville
Printer and binder: Friesens Corporation